The Collected Courses of the Academy of European Law

Series Editors: Professor Philip Alston, *New York University School of Law*; Professor Gráinne de Búrca, *European University Institute, Florence*; and Professor Bruno de Witte, *European University Institute, Florence*

VOLUME XIII/2

Europe's Area of Freedom, Security and Justice

The Collected Courses of the Academy of European Law
Edited by Professor Philip Alston, Professor Gráinne de Búrca, and Professor Bruno de Witte

This series brings together the Collected Courses of the Academy of European Law in Florence. The Academy's mission is to produce scholarly analyses which are at the cutting edge of the two fields in which it works: European Union law and human rights law. A 'general course' is given each year in each field, by a distinguished scholar and/or practitioner, who either examines the field as a whole through a particular thematic, conceptual or philosophical lens, or who looks at a particular theme in the context of the overall body of law in the field. The Academy also publishes each year a volume of collected essays with a specific theme in each of the two fields.

Europe's Area of Freedom, Security and Justice

Edited by

NEIL WALKER

Academy of European Law
European University Institute

OXFORD
UNIVERSITY PRESS

OXFORD
UNIVERSITY PRESS

Great Clarendon Street, Oxford OX2 6DP

Oxford University Press is a department of the University of Oxford.
It furthers the University's objective of excellence in research, scholarship,
and education by publishing worldwide in

Oxford New York

Auckland Bangkok Buenos Aires Cape Town Chennai
Dar es Salaam Delhi Hong Kong Istanbul Karachi Kolkata
Kuala Lumpur Madrid Melbourne Mexico City Mumbai Nairobi
São Paulo Shanghai Singapore Taipei Tokyo Toronto

Oxford is a registered trade mark of Oxford University Press
in the UK and in certain other countries

Published in the United States
by Oxford University Press Inc., New York

First published 2004

ISBN 0–19–927464–9 (hbk)
ISBN 0–19–927465–7 (pbk)

Typeset by Kolam Information Services Pvt. Ltd, Pondicherry, India
Printed by Biddles Ltd., King's Lynn

Preface

So rapidly has the European Union's capacity in migration and internal security matters developed in the last fifteen years or so, and so many and varied have been the institutional adaptations and policy initiatives during that period, that there can never be a perfect time to sit back and take stock of the overall state of the law. A freeze-frame analysis will always risk failure to capture emerging trends and unexpected departures. With the drafting of a new Constitutional Treaty in the Summer of 2003, at a point when the flow of legal and policy initiatives from the new Area of Freedom, Security and Justice introduced under the Treaty of Amsterdam threatened to become a torrent, that risk is, if anything, greater now than it has ever been. Yet it is precisely because so much of importance is happening simultaneously—at the policy, institutional, and, now, the constitutional levels—that it is vital to try to capture, however imperfectly, the major current themes and dynamics in the field. That is what this volume sets out to do.

As with the others in the Series, this volume started out as a course of lectures at the Academy of European Law in Fiesole. The lectures were given in the Summer of 2002, and updated for publication in the last months of 2002 and the early months of 2003. For the subject matter of most of the chapters the draft Constitutional Treaty—whose fate remained in the balance in the early months of 2004 after the failure of the IGC to adopt its text in December 2003—is of central relevance, but the timing of its publication made it impossible for all the authors to do full justice to its contents. In recognition of this, the opening chapter attempts to provide an overview of constitutional developments, and the various substantive chapters that follow should be read in the light of this.

This volume could not, of course, have been brought to publication without the co-operation and support of all of the Directors and staff of the Academy of European Law. A special word of thanks, however, is due to Barbara Ciomei, without whose constant organizational presence and excellent editorial assistance the project would never have been completed, and to Mike Wilkinson, whose attention to detail was invaluable in the preparation of the final text.

NEIL WALKER

Contents

Tables of Cases

COURT OF JUSTICE OF THE EUROPEAN COMMUNITIES

EUROPEAN COURT OF HUMAN RIGHTS

NATIONAL COURTS

Germany

United Kingdom

Tables of Treaties, Legislation, and other Relevant Instruments

EU LEGISLATION AND OTHER OFFICIAL DOCUMENTS

INTERNATIONAL TREATIES, CONVENTIONS AND OTHER RELEVANT INSTRUMENTS

NATIONAL LEGISLATION

Notes on Contributors

Cyrille Fijnaut is Ordinary Professor of (Comparative and International) Criminal Law at the University of Tilburg, the Netherlands, and Extraordinary Professor of Criminology and Criminal Law at the KU Leuven, Belgium. His current main research topics relate to organized crime problems in a transatlantic perspective, international police and judicial co-operation in Europe, and the political history of policing in the Low Countries. His more recent publications include: (together with F. Bovenkerk, G. Bruinsma and H. van de Bunt) *Organized Crime in The Netherlands* (The Hague: Kluwer Law International, 1998); (together with L. Huberts) *Corruption, Integrity and Law Enforcement* (The Hague: Kluwer Law International, 2002) and (together with H.-J. Albrecht) *The Containment of Transnational Organized Crime; Comments on the UN Convention of December 2000* (Freiburg B.: Max Planck Institute for Foreign and International Criminal Law, 2002). He is co-editor of the *European Journal of Crime, Criminal Law and Criminal Justice* and of *The International Encyclopaedia of Criminal Law.*

Kay Hailbronner has held a chair in public law, international law, and European law at the University of Konstanz, Germany since 1979, and is Director of the Center for International and European Law on Immigration and Asylum which was established in 1994. Professor Hailbronner has also been Chairman of the ILA (International Law Association) Committee on Refugee Procedures. Since 1999 he has been a member of the German Advisory Council on Science (*Wissenschaftsrat*), and since 2000 a member of the Advisory Board of the German Federal Office for the Recognition of Refugees. Between 2000 and 2001 he was a member of the Governmental Commission on Immigration Issues. Additionally, he is co-editor of the leading journal on the law of aliens in Germany. Among his principal publications are his monograph *Immigration and Asylum Law and Policy of the European Union* (The Hague: Kluwer Law International, 2000), his commentary on the law of aliens (*Kommentar Ausländerrecht*) and his commentary on citizenship (*Kommentar zum Staatsangehörigkeitsrecht*, together with G. Renner).

Ferruccio Pastore obtained a PhD from the European University Institute in 1996. He is currently co-ordinator of research work on 'International Migration/New Security Issues' and Deputy Director of the Centro Studi di Politica Internazionale (CeSPI), an independent think-tank based in Rome. Alongside his research activity, he has worked as an adviser for the Italian Parliament (Schengen–Europol Commission) (1997–1999) and for the

Presidency of the Council of Ministers (2000). His most recent publications include: 'Lo spazio di libertà, sicurezza e giustizia tra allargamento e costituzionalizzazione', in G. Vacca (ed.), *Il dilemma euroatlantico. Rapporto 2004 della Fondazione Istituto Gramsci sull'integrazione europea* (Bari: Dedalo, 2004), 'Immigration and European Immigration Policies: Myths and Realities' (with G. Sciortino), in J. Apap (ed.), *Justice and Home Affairs in the EU: Liberty and Security Issues after Enlargement* (Cheltenham: Edward Elgar, 2004) and the monograph *Dobbiamo temere la migrazioni?* (Roma-Bari: Laterza, 2004).

Steve Peers is Professor of Law at the Human Rights Centre at the University of Essex. He is the author of *EU Justice and Home Affairs Law* (Harlow: Longman, 2000, 2nd edition forthcoming) and the co-editor with Angela Ward of *The EU Charter of Rights: Context and Possibilities* (Oxford: Hart) and, with Nicola Rogers, of *EU Immigration and Asylum Law: Text and Commentary* (Leiden: Martinus Nijhoff, forthcoming). He has written extensively on issues of justice and home affairs, external relations, and human rights in EU law.

Christine Van den Wyngaert teaches criminal law and criminal procedure at the University of Antwerp and is currently serving as a judge at the ICTY in the Hague. She has published widely in the fields of international and comparative criminal law, including *The Political Offence Exception to Extradition* (Deventer: Kluwer, 1981), *Criminal Procedure Systems in the European Community* (London: Butterworths, 1993) and various articles in law reviews. She was *rapporteur* for the International Law Association (Buenos Aires, 1996, Taipei, 1998—extradition and human rights) and general reporter for the Association Internationale de Droit Pénal (Budapest—international criminal co-operation for organized crime). In 2001, she became a doctor *honoris causa* of the University of Uppsala, Sweden. She was a judge *ad hoc* at the International Court of Justice in the *Yerodia* case (2000–2002) and was elected by the UN General Assembly as a judge *ad litem* in the International Criminal Tribunal for the former Yugoslavia (2001).

Neil Walker has been Professor of European Law at the European University Institute, Florence, since 2000. He has published extensively on general questions of constitutional theory, and also on questions of policing and internal security in both domestic and transnational contexts. His recent publications include a monograph, *Policing in a Changing Constitutional Order* (London: Sweet and Maxwell, 2000) and an edited collection, *Sovereignty in Transition* (Oxford: Hart, 2003). He is a member of the editorial boards of the *European Law Journal* and the *Edinburgh Law Review*, and is currently Dean of Studies of the European University Institute.

Part One

Constitutional Overview

1

In Search of the Area of Freedom, Security and Justice: A Constitutional Odyssey

NEIL WALKER

1. INTRODUCTION: DESIGNING THE VOLUME

Anyone seeking to assemble a collection on the emerging body of law and policy under the EU's Area of Freedom, Security and Justice faces some basic design problems. While the notion of an Area of Freedom, Security and Justice may be a relatively novel legal brand, launched as recently as the 1997 Treaty of Amsterdam,[1] it is a brand under whose name a significant volume of law—'hard' and 'soft'—has already accumulated. Much of that law is new, the result of the new competences and institutional possibilities put in place at Amsterdam. However, much of it is also the product of the formidable legacy of the pre-Amsterdam years. The pre-Amsterdam *acquis* is located in large part within the original 'third pillar' introduced into the European supranational treaty framework as part of the 1992 Maastricht Treaty, which in turn drew much of its initial momentum from informal arrangements in the domain of justice and home affairs negotiated in the shadow of the earlier treaty framework, including European political co-operation, the Working Group on Immigration, the Trevi Group, the Working Group on Judicial Co-operation, the Customs Mutual Assistance Group, and, from 1989, the Group of Co-ordinators on free movement of persons.[2] Yet the pre-Amsterdam corpus has still other and more diverse sources in a range of instruments which began their life in quite separate legal frameworks, notably

[1] The legal literature on AFSJ is voluminous. Valuable general sources include S. Peers, *EU Justice and Home Affairs Law* (Harlow: Pearson, 2000) ch.3 *et seq.*; E. Denza, *The Intergovernmental Pillars of the European Union* (Oxford: OUP, 2002) on the Third Pillar dimension; E. Guild and C. Harlow (eds), *Implementing Amsterdam: Immigration and Asylum Rights in EC Law* (Oxford: Hart, 2001) on the Title IV EC dimension.

[2] See, for example, S. Peers, *supra* note 1, ch.2; E. Denza, *supra* note 1, ch.3; M. Anderson, M. Den Boer, P. Cullen, W. Gilmore, C. Raab and N. Walker, *Policing the European Union* (Oxford: OUP, 1995) ch.3.

the Schengen accords of 1985 and 1990[3] and a variety of Council of Europe instruments in the area of mutual legal assistance.[4]

So the first problem faced by the editor of a collection on AFSJ is the sheer weight and volume of legal material eligible for inclusion. In principle, one solution to that problem would be an encyclopaedic approach—a commitment to exhaustive coverage of the terrain. Yet even if such an approach were taken, this would not address a second initial editorial difficulty, namely the coherence of the overall enterprise. And given that the present volume has neither the space nor the ambition to be exhaustive, the question of overall coherence takes on a more immediate significance, since this must provide the basis for selection of the areas covered by the essays and inform the questions which are addressed in these essays.

What, then, do we mean by coherence, and in what sense is the present volume shaped by an idea of coherence? Clearly, the search for coherence is also—to recall the title of this introductory essay—a search for some defining feature or features of the Area of Freedom, Security and Justice itself. There are two different means by which such a search could be conducted. In the first place, and most obviously, we may look for *internal* coherence. In this sense, the overall coherence of any linked set of commentaries on the AFSJ depends upon some idea of coherence which is intrinsic to, or can be imputed to, or—in a more normative register—may be aspired to within the subject-matter of AFSJ itself. In the second place, we may look for *external* coherence. From this perspective, coherence attaches not to the positive features of the object of study itself—to the legal doctrines and constitutional fundamentals that it espouses or the political objectives that it harbours—but to the distinctiveness of the external factors and forces which bear upon that object of study. External coherence, in other words, is concerned with our ability to make sense of and explain the object of study in terms of various defining characteristics of its social and political context.

Both types of coherence—internal and external—are equally important, equally relevant to an understanding of the common themes of the present volume. It is also the case, as we shall illustrate in due course, that the factors and forces that we identify with a view to explanatory or external coherence are as likely to confound as to support internal coherence. Let us begin, then, by discussing the ideas of internal and external coherence, and, on that basis,

[3] The literature on Schengen is also legion. On its origins see, for example, D. O'Keefe, 'The Schengen Convention: A Suitable Model for European Integration?', 11 *YEL* (1991) 185; J. Schutte 'Schengen: Its Meaning for the Free Movement of Persons in Europe', 28 *CMLRev* (1998) 549.

[4] On the development of the Council of Europe *corpus*, see, for example, J. Schutte 'Judicial Co-operation under the Union Treaty', in J. Monar and R. Morgan (eds), *The Third Pillar of the European Union* (Brussels: European Interuniversity Press, 1994) 181. See also Anderson *et al*, *supra* note 2, ch.7.

seek to explain how the various contributions to this volume may be treated as a whole. In turn, since questions of internal and external coherence alike bear closely upon our understanding of the constitutional dimension of AFSJ, this will provide a natural bridge to the second half of the essay, in which the current constitutional debate around AFSJ is directly addressed.

2. INTERNAL COHERENCE: AFSJ AS A DISTINCTIVE LEGAL FIELD

For all that internal coherence is the more obvious type of coherence for a legal study to pursue, it is not, in fact, immediately apparent, beyond the bare label of the Area of Freedom, Security and Justice, what the various issues collected under that label *do* have in common. A number of candidate forms of coherence suggest themselves, but some do not withstand close inquiry.

To begin with, we might speak of a basic *thematic* coherence in the area of FSJ—a fundamental unity of subject matter. Yet unlike many of the major domains of European law, whether core domains such as the internal market, competition, agriculture or fisheries, or flanking domains such as employment or the environment or social policy, the subject matters assembled under AFSJ do not form a 'natural' unity in terms of a clearly defined overall project. Although analogies have often been drawn between the '1992' Single Market project and the AFSJ, the two are not comparable in terms of precision and internal consistency. The '1992' project concerned a well-defined set of objectives directed towards a particular *finalité*,[5] even if this continues to require substantial adjustment and refinement in light of changing economic circumstances and the demands of other and competing objectives. In contrast, the AFSJ, even if part of its initial Maastricht inspiration was the attempt to supply a menu of compensatory measures concerning the control of movements across the EU's external borders and the development of new capacities for the internal monitoring of populations in light of the supposed 'security deficit' attendant upon the completion of an internal market in which goods, persons, services, and capital should in principle move freely, has no *finalité* other than continuing adherence to a highly abstract triumvirate of values. And, as we shall see in due course, the very presence of a plurality of values in the headline theme invites major problems of balance and reconciliation and militates against internal consistency.

But if there is no clearly defined overall project implicit in the very idea of AFSJ, perhaps there is a kind of *historical* coherence in terms of a

[5] On the importance of the idea of *finalité politique* in the development of the EU see, for example, N. Walker, 'The Idea of a European Constitution and the *Finalité* of Integration', in B. de Witte (ed), *The Emergence of the European Constitution* (Oxford: OUP, forthcoming).

tried-and-tested pattern of common treatment—of common coverage within a single policy community. Here, too, however, only a weak argument can be made. The Treaties tell us that AFSJ is concerned on the one hand, under Title IV EC, with 'Visas, Asylum, Immigration and Other Policies Related to Free Movement of Persons',[6] including judicial co-operation in civil law or private law matters having cross-border implication, and on the other hand, under Title VI TEU, with 'Provisions on Police and Judicial Cooperation in Criminal Matters'.[7] Yet we need only look at the variety of government departments under which these policies are traditionally organized in various European states to conclude that history lends no obvious coherence to the enterprise. We find the AFSJ competences liberally and variably distributed over departments of the Interior (or Home Affairs), Justice and Defence, to name only their most prominent homes. Indeed, even in the initial name given to their new internal security domain under the Maastricht Third Pillar—Justice *and* Home Affairs—we have a clear indication that its character is aggregative rather than integrative.

Another type of coherence, then, might be *institutional* coherence. Is the AFSJ characterized by a distinctive institutional methodology? Evidently, the answer must again be no. Ironically, this answer is clearer now than it was under Maastricht. In the initial Maastricht settlement, there was an institutional coherence of sorts, with the vast majority[8] of matters presently found under AFSJ loosely organized under the same regime of 'soft' law and executive and operational co-operation, albeit the very open-endedness of the legal framework made for much diversity in the subsequent institutional development of the various sub-areas. Under Amsterdam, however, there is a clear divide between the communitarized Title IV EC and the more state-centred rump Third Pillar under Title VI EU, even if Title IV EC remains only partly and incrementally communitarized and Title VI EU allows a greater role for EC institutions and instruments than its Maastricht predecessor.[9] And to the general division in institutional methodologies between the two major pillars we must of course add the particular asymmetries and institutional variations required by the reception of the Schengen *acquis*, with its complex allocation across Pillars and its intricate series of opt-ins and opt-outs for states located both inside and outside the EU.[10]

[6] Arts. 61–80 EC. [7] Arts. 29–42 TEU.

[8] But not all. See, in particular, Art.110c EC, as amended by the Maastricht Treaty, by which some aspects of a common visa policy were from the outset distinguished from the new Third Pillar competences and made part of 'First Pillar' or Community competence.

[9] See, for example, Peers, *supra* note 1, ch.3.

[10] See the relevant Protocols added by the Treaty of Amsterdam and annexed to the Treaty on European Union and to the Treaty Establishing the European Community, namely: Protocol Integrating the Schengen Acquis into the Framework of the European Union;

Strikingly, however, institutional diversification has developed hand-in-hand with a new impetus towards *policy* coherence, and this provides a first basis on which we can justify and explain the selection and the common and interconnected concerns of the essays in this volume. The new internal security domain may lack any precise and singular objective, may lack a common national pedigree of distinctive and coherent treatment, and may be institutionally diversified, yet the post-Amsterdam era is clearly marked by an attempt to *construct* a new kind of policy whole out of diverse parts.[11] To begin with, the very coining of the concept of an Area of Freedom, Security and Justice in the Treaty of Amsterdam is a statement of intent to consider the matters under Title IV EU and Title VI EC as a common policy domain, their new institutional separation notwithstanding. Secondly, the Amsterdam system goes some way to providing the institutional wherewithal for a common policy commitment, by providing the Commission with increased powers of initiative in all parts of AFSJ—even if these powers are not uniform, and by allowing the preservation of a common Justice and Home Affairs Council across the domain. Thirdly, and perhaps most notably, the special Tampere European Council late in 1999[12] drew upon the new rhetoric and institutional capability in order to launch an explicit and ambitious programme of action to develop a common policy field within and across four general headings—A Common EU Asylum and Migration Policy; A Genuine European Area of Justice; A Unionwide Fight Against Crime and Stronger External Action—complete with timetable and milestones. Finally, with Tampere as a significant catalyst and the European reaction to the Twin Towers attack on September 11 as a powerful reinforcement, there is increasing evidence of systematic policy connections being made from various specific starting points within AFSJ.[13] Whether we are dealing with asylum policy (Kay Hailbronner), the general entry control framework (Ferruccio Pastore), family reunion policy (Steve Peers), the gradual insinuation of the *corpus juris* philosophy into the emerging framework of European criminal justice (Christine Van den Wyngaert) or the development of a system of

Protocol on the Application of Certain Aspects of Article 14 of the Treaty Establishing the European Community to the United Kingdom and to Ireland; Protocol on the Position of the United Kingdom and Ireland; Protocol on the Position of Denmark; OJ 1997 C340/92.

[11] See, for example, M. Anderson and J. Apap, *Striking a Balance Between Freedom, Security and Justice* (Brussels: Centre for European Policy Studies, 2002).

[12] Tampere Special European Council, October 1999; http://europa.eu.int/council/off/conclu/oct99.

[13] See, for example, W. Gilmore, 'The Twin Towers and the Three Pillars' (European University Institute Law Department Working Paper: Fiesole, 2003); M. Den Boer and J. Monar, '11 September and the Challenge of Global Terrorism to the EU as a Security Actor', 40 (Annual Review) *JCMS* (2002) 118; N. Walker, 'The Pattern of Transnational Policing', in T. Newburn (ed.), *Handbook of Policing* (Uffculme: Willan, 2003) 111.

police co-operation within and around Europol (Cyrille Fijnaut)—to introduce the matters which are the subject of the five substantive chapters to follow in this volume—we can observe an increasing readiness within the various policy communities not only to develop a more rounded and integrated approach within their various fields but to begin to imagine the various parts of the FSJ jigsaw as a single tableau.[14]

The beginnings of this more systematic approach are equally apparent in the two main pillars—first and third, migration control and police and judicial co-operation in criminal matters—that the AFSJ straddles, and on the basis of which the book is organized. So in Part Two, which deals with the first pillar, Kay Hailbronner demonstrates that the field of asylum law is unfolding against the emerging outline of a European migration policy, and it is with the various other overlapping contours of that general outline—in particular the relationship between visa and border controls and general immigration policy—that Ferruccio Pastore's chapter is concerned. For his part, in tracing the broad institutional and policy ramifications of the apparently more easily demarcated issue of family reunion, Steve Peers demonstrates that in fact significant questions of coherence arise between the Council of Europe human rights framework and the EC framework, and, within the EC framework, between rules for EC nationals, rules for third country nationals and rules for the hybrid category of those covered by the plethora of EC Association Agreements. In Part Three of the book, dealing with the third pillar, a similar concern with the systematic connection between the parts is developed. Christine Van den Wyngaert is concerned with how Eurojust, (the proposed) European Public Prosecutor and, if to a lesser extent, Europol articulate with one another and also with the idea of a common European judicial space in the administration and enforcement of criminal justice. Cyrille Fijnaut, too, poses an important series of systemic questions, asking both how the central agency Europol connects with the broader framework of 'bottom-up' police co-operation—of which the Schengen system is the most pronounced instance—and how police co-operation

[14] The emphasis upon policy coherence is a first reason why the one main aspect of AFSJ that is excluded from consideration in the present volume is judicial co-operation in civil matters, as specified in Art. 65 EC. There are some continuities between this and other aspects of AFSJ, particularly as regards the principle of 'mutual recognition' between national authorities of legal decisions and judgments, now enshrined in Art. III–158 of the Draft Treaty Establishing a Constitution for Europe. For the most part, however, judicial co-operation in civil matters is treated as a separate matter by a quite distinct legal policy (and academic) community whose domain of expertise is the conflict of (private) laws and of jurisdiction. Furthermore, the other elements of coherence which we are concerned to develop in the text below, in particular constitutional coherence and coherence in terms of the distinctiveness of external pressures and tensions, also argue against inclusion of judicial co-operation in civil matters, where the constitutional questions and the broader macro-political environment are for the most part of a different order.

in its many manifestations may be co-ordinated across the first, second, and third pillars.

Of course, the fact that the contributors point to new systematic tendencies or properties within their various fields does not mean either that they believe these systematic properties to be sufficiently well developed or that they endorse the particular institutional balance or substantive priorities which a more (but perhaps still insufficiently) systematic approach has led to. Indeed, all the commentators remain more or less critical of the developments within their respective fields. This in turn points us to a second type of internal coherence with which each of the contributions is concerned and which supplies common ground between them, namely *constitutional* coherence.

With the drafting of a Constitutional Treaty by Valéry Giscard d'Estaing's Convention on the Future of Europe in July 2003,[15] and the subsequent deliberations of the Intergovernmental Council on the question of that treaty's content and signature, now is a decidedly significant constitutional moment for the European Union, about which more in due course. However, that a documentary Constitution may at last be on the horizon, notwithstanding the initial refusal of the Intergovernmental Council to endorse the draft Constitutional Treaty at Brussels in December 2003, should not blind us to the fact that the EU already has a small-c 'constitutional' tradition. This takes the form of an institutional structure which has been developed and rationalized with at least some measure of self-conscious concern for the legitimacy of the overall legal shape of a new and distinctive non-state or post-state polity, together with a critical and constructive debate in political and academic circles about the adequacy of that emergent constitutional *acquis*.[16] That is to say, over the first half century of the European supranational project, in both positive and critical jurisprudence, increasingly explicit attention has been directed to the following sorts of questions—questions which are familiar to public lawyers from constitutional development and debate at the traditional state level but which are given a distinctive hue by the particular circumstances of the EU. Do the range and priority of fundamental values to which the EU officially subscribes capture and promote the best vision of the kind of polity the EU is and may become, bearing in mind its historical mission, its current substantive objectives and its relationship to other polities including national polities? Are the institutional design and framework of individual and group empowerment and protection adequate to the articulation of that set of fundamental value priorities? Relatedly, and at a more detailed level, does the framework afford sufficient protection against an undue emphasis upon some of these values and against the relative

[15] The Convention presented its final draft on 10 July. See OJ 2003 C169/1.

[16] There is an enormous literature on this emergent constitutional tradition. See in particular, J.H.H. Weiler, *The Constitution of Europe* (Cambridge: CUP, 1999).

neglect of others, bearing in mind particularly the peculiarity of the EU's multi-level governmental framework and the way in which that governmental framework both impacts upon individual citizens and renders complex the idea of collective representation?

As we shall see, these have always been especially urgent questions in the context of the AFSJ in view of the particular difficulty of adapting a juridical framework developed for market regulation to the very different needs of internal security, the sheer speed with which this adaptation has taken place, the resilience of questions of national sovereignty in this field, and the particular vulnerability of citizens, and indeed non-citizen 'subjects', in an area where they often have very limited voice and public sympathy and where executive action is particularly apt to strike at their most fundamental rights and interests.[17] Each of the authors in the present collection is keenly aware of the importance of a distinctively constitutional perspective, and each addresses at least some aspects of the questions posed above in their contribution. Each author also puts forward certain normative proposals for improving the constitutional *acquis*—whether within the frame of the present Convention and IGC constitutional window, or more generally.

Unavoidably, and indeed not unhealthily, since constitutionalism is a form of framework practical reasoning whose normative implications are and should remain contestable, although all the authors are clearly committed to the importance of the constitutional perspective in general, not all of their particular criticisms and suggestions run in the same direction. Rather than provide an overview of these criticisms and proposals, however, a more useful introductory step is to situate them in a deeper explanatory context—to try to identify their progeny. That is to say, the evolution and prospects of the fundamental constitutional framework and the difficult choices to be made within that framework can only be understood by introducing the external perspective—by looking at the social forces and political factors which have defined the very conditions of possible development of AFSJ.

3. THE AFSJ IN SOCIAL AND POLITICAL CONTEXT: RESILIENT TENSIONS AND CONSTITUTIONAL DILEMMAS

The 'search' for the AFSJ, therefore, now moves on from these forms of coherence which can be found or read into the regulatory field as a whole—whether thematic, historical, institutional, policy-orientated, or positive constitutional coherence—to a consideration of some of the distinctive contextual features of the regulatory field which help to make sense of the

[17] See, for example, I. Loader, 'Governing European Policing: Some Problems and Prospects', 12 *Policing and Society* (2002) 291.

ongoing difficulties, perhaps even *in*coherences, which attend attempts at constitutional evaluation and engineering. This broader explanatory dimension and its relationship to pervasive questions of constitutional design may be usefully illuminated by outlining a number of oppositions, or at least tensions, between different tendencies that have characterized the development of FSJ to date—including each of the topics covered by the five substantive contributions—and which remain manifest in the issues addressed in the current constitutional debate.[18] While they are introduced separately, it should become clear that the oppositions or tensions in question are in fact closely related, and that the broadest tension—between policy effectiveness and efficiency on the one hand and accountability on the other—is in some respects a cumulation of all the others.[19]

A. Reactive or Proactive?

One striking characteristic of the development of JHA has been the extent to which it has taken the form of a *reaction* to current events or to secular trends, *or at least has been presented in these terms*. If we look at the fragmented history of developments in police and criminal justice co-operation and in co-operation in immigration and related matters before the Treaty of Maastricht, we see a series of developments that respond to or purport to respond to external threats or dangers. To name but a few of the more prominent strands, from 1976 onwards the Trevi policing network was justified as a response to developments in international terrorism and, later, in transnational organized crime in drugs and elsewhere; from 1986 onwards the Working Group on Immigration was justified as a response to migration trends from a politically destabilizing East and an economically impoverished South; and from 1989 onwards a Co-ordinator's Group of civil servants began to prepare an integrated package of JHA 'compensatory measures' in response to the more immediate 'threat' posed by the dismantling of border restrictions under the 1992 Single Market Programme.[20] One can see a similar pattern of threat and response in the major institutional developments of the 1990s—the establishment of a Third Pillar bringing JHA matters under the official embrace of the European Treaty structure in 1992; the important initiative in 'communitarizing' aspects of the Third Pillar at

[18] For a similar approach, but less focused on the specifically constitutional dimension, see J. Monar, 'The Problem of Balance in EU Justice and Home Affairs and the Impact of 11 September', in M. Anderson and J. Apap (eds), *Police and Justice Co-operation and the New European Borders* (The Hague: Kluwer, 2002) 165.

[19] This section of the essay draws in some measure on N. Walker, 'Freedom, Security and Justice', in B. de Witte (ed.), *Ten Reflections on the Constitutional Treaty for Europe* (Fiesole: European University Institute, 2003) 163.

[20] See, for example, Denza, *supra* note 1, ch.3.

Amsterdam in 1997; the launching of the ambitious Tampere policy programme in the Area of Freedom, Security and Justice in 1999; even the more modest institutional changes of Nice in 2001. In each case, the development of institutional strength and policy capacity in FSJ was preceded, accompanied, and endorsed by a policy attitude and language that sought to address or contain new or extended threats to the security of the European Union in the form of new types or intensities of transnational crime and new 'push' and 'pull' factors in the sphere of immigration and asylum. The latest and largest security threat to mobilize development in FSJ is of course, the destruction of the Twin Towers at the World Trade Center, New York on 11 September 2001, but the policy response to this must be seen as only the most vivid and recent example of a trend rather than as a radical departure.[21]

Of course, the language of threat and response to some extent has an objectively valid basis in FSJ. The very idea of internal security as a public good implies the containment within acceptable limits of risks and threats generated in the wider social environment.[22] Its concern with the wider social environment and the diverse range of dangers which may emerge from that environment means that security policy is bound to deal with matters which are in significant respects (although by no means entirely) beyond the control and prediction of the policy-maker—much more so, indeed, than in any other areas of EU policy with the exception of defence (which, of course, is also concerned with security, in this case from *external* rather than *internal* threats). Security policy, then, must be sensitive to 'events', and no sensible security policy can be blind to gradual or sudden environmental changes.

Yet reaction is not the whole story. Just as it would be naïve to dismiss events and the threats they dramatize as simple scaremongering—as mere rhetorical constructions with no grounding in social reality—we should by the same token not take the reactive postures of European internal security politics entirely at face value. It is important to note that security policy is never *compelled* by external events, even if the representation of certain events through a security framework often conveys a powerful message otherwise. For the security metaphor can have a deep ideological resonance. It can supply a conveniently reductive method of viewing diverse and multi-faceted policy issues as aspects of one single problem—a point which should not be

[21] On the earlier development of an internal security ideology in the European Union see, for example, D. Bigo, 'The European Internal Security Field: Stakes and Rivalries in the Newly Developing Area of Police Intervention', in M. Anderson and M. den Boer (eds), *Policing Across National Boundaries* (London: Pinter, 1994) 161.

[22] On the idea of internal security as a public good see I. Loader and N. Walker, 'Policing as a Public Good: Reconstituting the Connections between Policing and the State', 5 *Theoretical Criminology* (2001) 9; see also N. Walker, 'The Problem of Trust in an Enlarged Area of Freedom, Security and Justice: A Conceptual Analysis', in Anderson and Apap (eds), *Police and Justice Co-operation*, *supra* note 18, at 19.

lost when we consider just how the post-Amsterdam idea of a single and coherent policy programme and community has managed to evolve. And by framing diverse events in security terms, not only can this subordinate other policy alternatives and value considerations to the 'self-evident' security response, it can also help to convey a sense that these events pose such a fundamental and urgent challenge to the existing social and political fabric that they must be responded to immediately and decisively—by 'extraordinary means'[23] if necessary—and preferably through the decisions of 'security experts'.[24]

In other words—and this a theme to which we will return—the reactive, security-centred approach may have an in-built tendency to marginalize familiar constitutional constraints, such as the proper balancing of fundamental values, the primacy of democratic decision, due process in individual cases, and a robust system of separation and diversification of powers and of institutional checks and balances. Moreover, in acknowledging that a reactive posture tends to mask the active choices that are being made, we should also be alert to the factors that *do* inform these choices. These include, quite apart from genuine if often controversial value considerations concerning the proper definition and priority of 'security', 'freedom', and 'justice', a number of other indirect factors. Prominent amongst these are national and transnational professional and bureaucratic interests,[25] the opportunism of national politicians in playing on popular fears and priorities, and, perhaps of greatest prominence, the broader polity-building agenda and debate within the EU.

These indirect factors, therefore, are often as important as direct sectoral policy considerations as *proactive* influences upon the direction of AFSJ policy-making. Indeed, with regard to the broader polity-building agenda, the policy and institutional agenda associated with internal security may be mobilized in quite novel ways in consequence of and as part of that broader agenda. For example, Chancellor Kohl's strong sponsorship of the Europol idea prior to the Maastricht Treaty was not unconnected to the desire of one of the most Europhile Member States to develop an audaciously 'state-like' conception of the EU at the pre-Maastricht highpoint of integrationist self-confidence.[26] To take a larger example, we cannot understand the extensive scale and ambitious claims of the Tampere initiative apart from an

[23] O. Waever, 'European Security Identities', 34 *JCMS* (1996) 103, at 106.

[24] See Bigo, *supra* note 21, and also his *Police en Réseaux; l'experience européene* (Paris: Presses de Science Po., 1996).

[25] See ibid.; A. Turnbull and W. Sandholtz, 'Policing and Immigration: The Creation of New Policy Spaces', in A. Stone Sweet, W. Sandholtz and N. Fligstein (eds), *The Institutionalization of Europe* (Oxford: OUP, 2001) 194.

[26] See P. Cullen, *The German Police and European Co-operation* (Edinburgh: European Police Co-operation Working Paper No.2, 1992).

appreciation of the growing desire in many EU policy circles to find a new 'big idea' to mobilize support for the European Union at a point when the founding ideals of the Union—peace and prosperity—had lost some of their earlier freshness (if not their relevance) and public opinion was becoming increasingly ambivalent about the legitimacy of increasing integration.[27] Equally, as we shall pursue in due course, the relatively (compared to other policy fields) significant developments in AFSJ competence proposed by the Convention on the Future of Europe are by no means unrelated to the broader cut and thrust of debate over the future course of the EU as a whole.

B. Dynamic or Blocked?

Both the pressure to react to events and the way in which FSJ has been invoked within proactive initiatives help to account for the highly dynamic nature of the development of AFSJ since its origins at Maastricht. The cement embedding the Maastricht Third Pillar had barely solidified when the foundations were dug up again at Amsterdam and migration policy was resituated in the first pillar, leaving only police and criminal justice co-operation in a streamlined third pillar. The Treaty of Nice, too, saw significant changes only months after Amsterdam had entered into force, notably in providing constitutional permission for Eurojust and, as we shall see, this restless institutional dynamic shows no signs of abating in the present constitutional debate.

Beneath the institutional dynamic we may observe an equally urgent policy dynamic, an 'abundant incrementalism',[28] which by the late 1990s meant that Justice and Home Affairs had become one of the busiest areas of policy initiative, even before the new impetus provided at Tampere. For example, as early as 1997 and before the new Amsterdam capacities had been put in place, Justice and Home Affairs had become easily the largest single area for which the Council Secretariat serviced meetings, amounting to a third of the meetings convened and over 40 per cent of the papers circulated,[29] and the figures for legislative or quasi-legislative initiatives and for institutional modification and proliferation have been just as remarkable. Again, as the depiction of recent policy developments in each of the contributions to this volume graphically illustrates, far from ebbing or levelling out, this policy agenda has become even more intensive in the first years of the new century.

[27] See, for example, N. Walker, *Policing in a Changing Constitutional Order* (London: Sweet and Maxwell, 2000) ch.8.

[28] See M. Den Boer, 'Police and Judicial Cooperation in Criminal Matters: A Dynamic Policy Area Adrift?', in M. P. van der Hoek (ed.), *Handbook of Public Administration and Policy in the EU* (The Hague: Kluwer, 2003).

[29] M. Den Boer and W. Wallace, 'Justice and Home Affairs', in H. Wallace and W. Wallace, *Policy-Making in the European Union* (Oxford: OUP, 2000) 493, at 503.

One important feature of this dynamism is that since the outset Justice and Home Affairs has been marked by a close interlinking of the policy and the institutional—the instrumental and the structural—with a tendency for broader constitutional questions concerning optimal design and citizen protection to be driven by, and sometimes even obscured by, vigorous and impatient policy agendas. As noted above, this may in some part be attributable to the power of the security metaphor. More prosaically, however, it is also a simple function of the relatively late start made in a domain as expansive, complex, and functionally interconnected with the core mandate of market regulation as the FSJ domain. More pronouncedly than in other areas, in the still relatively new AFSJ the EU remains a polity-in-progress rather than a mature structure, and it is unavoidable that much of the building of the constitutional ship should take place while it is sailing in fast-flowing policy waters. Indeed, the very fact that the Convention on the Future of Europe selected FSJ as one of only four (alongside defence, economic governance, and social Europe) Working Groups[30] focusing upon a policy area rather than a general legal or institutional question (as with the other seven Working Groups) suggests its awareness of the 'constitutional deficit' in this area. Yet here, too, as we shall see, the politically specific threatened to eclipse the constitutionally general. For all that its Final Report and the subsequent draft Treaty do take questions of constitutional controls seriously, much of the debate within and around the Working Group, and indeed the tone of many of its conclusions, suggest that for many the Convention was more important as a new and large opportunity to adapt the institutional framework to the burgeoning needs of the policy agenda than as an occasion to reflect on what a lasting constitutional structure for FSJ might look like.

However, for all its institutional restlessness and abundant incrementalism, it would be inaccurate to see the history of FSJ as one of remorseless integration. Alongside the record of expansion, there have been many examples of frustration and blocked ambition. Each institutional initiative has left some parties disappointed with its modesty, each new initiative (as in Amsterdam) has been preceded by a critique of the ineffectiveness of the old, and each *résumé* of progress (as in the Tampere mid-term report by the Belgian presidency in 2001)[31] has produced an indictment of the conditions impeding progress. Why has this been the case?

[30] For the final report of this Working Group see Working Group X on Freedom, Security and Justice, Final Report, Brussels, 2 December 2002, CONV, 426/02.

[31] European Council, 6 December 2001, Council Doc. 14926/01. Discussed in J. Monar, 'Justice and Home Affairs', 40 *JCMS* (2002) 121.

C. Supranational or Intergovernmental?

As all the contributors recognize, the history, and indeed pre-history, of recognition of FSJ within the treaty structure has been marked by an ideological faultline between intergovernmental and supranational positions. In the most basic terms, adherents to an intergovernmental approach have stressed the continuing priority of national authority within the FSJ structure, while adherents to a supranational approach have stressed the importance of transferring a significant measure of authority to the European supranational framework itself. The basic reason for this division is straightforward. The longstanding macro-political distinction between those who are more or less reluctant to cede authority to the European level tends to be reinforced and highlighted in a policy area—internal security—which is a traditional preserve of the state, and, indeed, which many would see as part of what Cyrille Fijnaut calls the 'hard core'[32]—the indispensable *raison d'être*—of state sovereignty.

Of course, the reality is much more complicated than that simple opposition would suggest. First, some of the more Eurosceptic states, such as the United Kingdom, have been amongst the most enthusiastic sponsors of at least certain areas of JHA co-operation—even if such enthusiasm tends to be couched in terms of an enlightened conception of the *defence* of national sovereignty in an increasingly interconnected and porous world rather than the *pooling* of sovereignty within a new post-state institutional complex—and have been prepared to countenance a fairly extensive measure of institutional integration on that basis.

Secondly, what counts as 'intergovernmental' rather than 'supranational' in institutional terms cannot be reduced to a single metric. Rather, it is a multi-faceted affair, and we must look to a number of different indices or measures to gain an overall picture of the degree of integration of any particular policy sector. These indices cover the whole range of incidents of the exercise of legal authority, including right of initiative (national or Commission); procedure for adoption (with or without significant input from the more 'European' institutions of Commission or Parliament; with or without the unanimous consent of national executive representatives; with or without the influence of national Parliaments); location of competence (extent of European law-making and executive jurisdiction, and whether exclusive or shared), intensity of measures adopted (whether compulsory or advisory, facilitative or prescriptive, directly or indirectly effective in national law); mode of implementation (whether through national or supranational administrative channels)

[32] More precisely, Fijnaut is referring to the area of 'public order and security' and, thus, to the third pillar, rather than to AFSJ more generally. On the distinction between first and third pillar AFSJ matters from a sovereigntist perspective see text below.

justiciability (whether or not and to what extent susceptible to adjudication by the ECJ) and forms of *post factum* oversight (monitoring, evaluation or even quasi-adjudication by national or supranational bodies—such as the European Parliament and the European Ombudsman). Given this multi-faceted picture, there is much scope for an uneven institutional pattern, more or less intergovernmental or supranational depending upon the index in question.

Thirdly, and reflecting both the complexities of national bargaining positions and the broad scope for variation within and between different indices, the fairly sharp distinction between the 'intergovernmentalism' of Justice and Home Affairs and the 'supranationalism' of the core European capacities did not in any event survive the reform of the Maastricht Treaty at Amsterdam. And even if this initial permission for Justice and Home Affairs to join the supranational core was purchased at the cost of a new *internal* distinction within the renamed Area of Freedom, Security and Justice between those matters promoted to Title IV of the first pillar and those remaining in a residual third pillar, we should be careful not to overstate the significance of the new distinction. Regardless of their 'pillar' domicile, *all* aspects of FSJ moved in a more or less 'communitarized' direction at Amsterdam, and just as newly supranational elements in the area of initiative, intensity of measures, and—to a limited extent—justiciability and oversight were invested in the residual third pillar, so too some significant 'intergovernmental' elements, especially as regards the key issue of unanimity in adoption, were retained in Title IV. As we shall see, moreover, this untidy and incomplete trend towards communitarization across the board is likely to be reinforced in the current constitutional process, so much so indeed that the effective dismantling of the new internal distinction introduced at Amsterdam appears a foregone conclusion.

Fourthly, not only is the intergovernmental/supranational division a much more complex and uneven code for making sense of institutional development in AFSJ than is often appreciated, it is also one which does not fully take into account some existing and emerging dimensions of the European architecture and the tensions and conflicts of representation which these reflect. For instance, to take but one particularly topical example of institutional innovation, national Parliaments can expect a much closer involvement in a more formally constitutionalized AFSJ than they are presently allowed.[33] In one sense, this may be understood as a blow struck in favour of intergovernmentalism—as a credit to be added to the account of *national* interest. But in a deeper sense, it speaks to an attempt at a new form of institutional design that cuts across the categories of intergovernmental and supranational and responds to other political concerns. For national

[33] See Section 4 below.

Parliaments are as easily viewed as checks on national executives as on supranational institutions, and, indeed, in national constitutional theory and doctrine this is one of their most familiar and significant functions. In turn, this alerts us that what is often presented as a generic and undifferentiated intergovernmental/supranational divide is in fact often a set of interconnected tensions between national *executive* authority, other forms of national representation, and the claims of new supranational institutions (which, of course, may themselves be viewed as traditionally representing different constituencies).[34] On that view, the addition of new ingredients such as national Parliaments to the institutional mix indicates a more complex scenario than can be evoked by the traditional binary opposition.

Yet the basic intergovernmental/supranational tension *does* remain a defining character trait of AFSJ institutional politics, even if it should be viewed in more limited terms than are sometimes conveyed, and even if it is now better understood in terms of variable points on a multi-dimensional spectrum with all points experiencing a secular shift to the supranational pole, rather than as a simple and settled dichotomy. The intergovernmental 'purity' of the original Maastricht settlement with its firm alignment of predominantly national initiative, restricted supranational competence, soft(er) law, state-centred implementation, absence of justiciability, and paucity of European oversight may be long gone, but the fault-line, however unstable, blurred and jagged, is still discernible. This is so because the reasons and prejudices which have long underpinned state sovereigntist positions have not simply evaporated, even if many of the counter-arguments in favour of collective action are nowadays more readily countenanced (though still less so in rhetoric than in practice).

In line with the basic Amsterdam division (even if it appears consigned to a limited shelf-life), this sovereigntist logic remains in some respects more pronounced in third pillar matters. Police and criminal justice powers and institutions, with their decisive function in the coercive self-assertion of the state, their nationally particular and culturally autochthonous negotiation of the acceptable limits of legislative and executive encroachment on private and public freedoms, and even their symbolic links to the affective foundations of national identity, remain significantly resistant to forms of integration which subsume national units of authority rather than facilitate co-operation between them.[35] Migration policy, on the other hand, may be less directly linked to the traditional coercive monopoly of the state and, as Ferruccio Pastore points out, is certainly more obviously continuous with the logic of

[34] For a sophisticated reading of the EU as a 'mixed polity' whose institutional design represents a complex array of interests see G. Majone, 'Delegation of Regulatory Powers in a Mixed Polity', 8 *ELJ* (2002) 319.

[35] See Loader and Walker, *supra* note 22; see also N. Walker, 'Policing and the Supranational', 12 *Policing and Society* (2002) 307.

the single market. The free movement of persons was from the outset 'cast as part of the Single Market programme',[36] and immigration could easily 'be assimilated to ... a well-developed set of institutions and policy frames' in which the common regulation of a single external border was key. Again, however, as all three chapters in Part Two of the volume make clear, sovereigntist considerations are not so easily displaced. The logic of a comprehensive shift of migration policy to the external border requires a 'state-blind' control system in which migrant populations are subject to the same procedural controls on entry and expulsion, the same conditions of entry and movement, and the same legal incidents of temporary or permanent residence. Yet any such project quickly comes up against the desire of individual states to retain control of the size, source and purpose of primary immigration flows, their concern not to be disproportionately burdened even with exceptional flows such as those related to asylum and other forms of special protection, and their limited trust in the good faith and competence of their similarly preoccupied neighbours to act in a way that guarantees respect for these fundamental native concerns.[37] What this suggests, therefore, is that while monopolistic coercive authority—the focal point of the rump third pillar—may traditionally have been the distinctive *modality* of state power, the ordered assignation of a particular population to a particular territory—the focal point of the first pillar dimension of AFSJ—can for its part lay claim to be a defining *condition* of statehood, and in the final analysis just as indispensable to the retention of a 'hard core' of state sovereignty.

Of course, the way in which this indispensability manifests itself in legal-constitutional terms differs between the two sectors. In police and criminal justice matters, precisely because the coercive authority or modality itself is key, this accounts for the severity of the constitutional objection to the alienation of the legal means necessary to exercise and enforce that coercive authority, whether in the form of a federal police, prosecution, or court system. It is the tenacity of that same idea of national constitutional purity, moreover, which in the early history of the third pillar has encouraged both naïve and cynical voices to deny, in the name of the protection of national sovereignty, sufficient supranational controls over even those not insubstantial police and criminal justice capacities in matters of information exchange and practical co-operation which *have* nevertheless escaped the constitutional confines of the state. In the area of migration, on the other hand, it is the macro-political objective—population control—that appears sacrosanct, and

[36] Turnbull and Sandholtz, *supra* note 25, at 219.

[37] For a recent penetrating analysis of the problems of burden-sharing in the field of asylum law in particular see S. Barbou des Places, *Burden Sharing in the Field of Asylum: Legal Motivations and Implications of a Regional Approach* (Florence, Robert Schuman Centre Working Papers 2002/66, 2003).

thus it is easier to countenance a more expansive collective constitutional means or capacity in this area provided that this macro-political objective is not subverted. We should not be surprised, therefore, at the more advanced level of integration in migration as opposed to police and criminal justice co-operation, but, equally, we should not mistake this relative lack of constitutional impediment for the successful transcendence of sovereigntist concerns. Rather, as the difficulties encountered in the implementation of the Tampere programme indicate, the sovereigntist legacy in immigration translates itself into a policy-making environment in which national jealousies and priorities are never far from the surface. Kay Hailbronner may be right to say, invoking the case of asylum law, that the existence of longstanding international standards guards against a 'lowest common denominator' approach and makes the 'Fortress Europe' label unduly pejorative. Yet there is no denying that the logic of collective action in an area where state interests remain so fundamental tends towards successful solutions only where it is possible for concurrent national interests within the collective framework to be mobilized against external threats to those interests, rather than in the reconciliation or transcendence of national interests within the collective framework where these national interests remain distinctive and diverse.[38]

However variable in its causes and regulatory implications, therefore, an intergovernmental brake has long operated within the machinery of FSJ. This accounts in significant measure for the uneven development of FSJ and for the conviction of some participants and commentators that, notwithstanding the remarkable early vigour of this policy domain, the development of a properly rounded supranational legal capacity and policy community has been repeatedly blocked. As we shall see, that this tension remains palpable may be seen in some of the compromises and disagreements emerging from the present constitutional process. The more immediate point, however, is to stress the resilience of the tension between competing visions of the role of the states and the European centre in the development of FSJ as a factor conditioning its constitutionalization.

D. Legislative or Executive?

Like any polity, the European Union requires and possesses both legislative and executive capacity, even if its division of powers is more complex than

[38] Ferruccio Pastore develops this point at length in his contribution, and also indicates that the logic of collective action in the migration field becomes yet more complex and precarious in the context of the present enlargement, when yesterday's 'outsiders' and security threats are in the process of being transformed into today's 'insiders' or security subjects. On the general problems of trust in AFSJ in the context of enlargement, see Walker, *supra* note 22, and Anderson and Apap, 'Promoting Trust in an Enlarged European Union', in Anderson and Apap (eds), *supra* note 18, at 241.

most national polities—a feature exacerbated by the fact that in the overall European system of 'multi-level governance'[39] legislative and executive dimensions of the one policy process often take place at different sites and levels of governance. It remains the case, however, that, as is typically true of national systems, the way in which the overall constitutional order of the EU is conceived—by insiders and outsiders alike, and, indeed, built into the reflexive constitutional logic of the system itself—remains *legislation-centred*. The key measure of Union competence, for example, is legislative. The key basis for the demarcation and discussion of the relationship between EU 'supremacy' and national 'sovereignty' is legislative power. The key trigger for identifying and elaborating different legal frameworks to channel and regulate the various stages of the policy cycle (both policy-making and policy accountability) in different policy sectors—and, so it follows, the key axis around which the ideological debate between intergovernmental and supranational positions is played out—has tended to be the *legislative* act. Indeed, and of most immediate relevance, this is mirrored in the organizing premiss of the pillar structure itself, with its distinction between a central edifice in which the various legal incidents of *legislation* are more maturely communitarized than in the two outside columns.

The diagnosis of the EU legal order as legislation-centred is not meant as a general criticism. It is difficult, if not impossible, to imagine how a constitutional logic firmly embedded in the idea of the rule of *law* could operate otherwise—could adopt an alternative juridical template. However, it does mean that to the extent that a particular area of policy departs from the legislation-centred norm, there is a danger that the constitutional treatment of that area may not be fully appreciative of its distinctive texture.

While there are many areas of FSJ in which legislation is at the centre of the policy agenda, particularly in Title IV of the EC Treaty,[40] in police and criminal justice co-operation this is far less evidently the case. Clearly, the provisions for approximation of substantive criminal law and compatibility of procedural measures are legislation-centred, but just as, if not more, significant a thrust in the residual third pillar is towards executive action, whether co-operation between existing national executive and operational[41]

[39] G. Marks, L. Hooghe and K. Blank, 'European Integration since the 1980s: State-Centric Versus Multi-Level Governance', 34 *JCMS* (1996) 341.

[40] Which, therefore, fits well in constitutional terms with the legislation-centred logic of the First Pillar EC Treaty. Indeed, the structural similarity to other EC matters of policy-making in this area is one additional reason why its incorporation did not meet strong resistance at the time of the Treaty of Amsterdam.

[41] For present purposes (i.e. distinction from legislation) 'executive' and 'operational' do not themselves require to be distinguished, both referring to the post-legislative (or in some cases non-legislation-based) phase of policy application and implementation. In fact, it is difficult to develop any meaningful distinction between 'executive' and 'operational', and

agencies or the development of new Europe-wide agencies such as Europol and Eurojust. The reasons for this distinctive policy texture are complex. They have to do with the way in which state sovereigntist sensibilities have been most jealous of the more familiar and more symbolically loaded legislation-centred indices of national authority and so have been more permissive and less vigilant of other aspects of policy co-operation (provided of course that it does not interfere with that other powerful shibboleth of constitutional nationalism, the retention of the ultimate coercive foundations of executive authority).[42] They also have to do with the fact that, by their very nature, those dimensions of internal security policy which are concerned with primary law enforcement—namely police and prosecution—involve tasks of an intrinsically executive or operational character.

What this entails is that notwithstanding state sovereigntist concerns about the Europeanization of internal security, we are arguably witnessing a degree of executive (as opposed to legislative) penetration of national systems and challenge to statist prerogatives, through new agencies and other systems and instruments of co-operation which have persuasive or compulsory consequences for both the national governments involved and the individual citizens affected, that is unmatched in any other area of integration. In constitutional terms, the danger arises that a legislation-centred perspective will fail fully to appreciate this development, and its various implications for the individual (to affected citizens) and collective (to democratically accountable bodies) accountability of such new agencies and mechanisms.

In this regard, the emphasis in the Convention Working Group Report on the importance of a separation between 'legislative' and 'operational' tasks, with each requiring its own distinctive constitutional treatment, shows a welcome general awareness of the constitutional distinctiveness of the AFSJ. However, it remains the case that there is a legacy of relative neglect here which is not easily overcome and that, in their novel peculiarity, the constitutional questions which arise in controlling an emerging transnational security executive that is not closely confined by legislative instruments are

theuse of this terminology often obscures rather than illuminates. On the one hand, 'executive' is often used to characterize the phase of 'high' governmental activity, and 'operational' to characterize the phase of 'low' bureaucratic or policy-professional activity. On the other hand, 'executive' may be used to denote the availability of coercive legal instruments, as in the idea that the 'executive powers' of the police are those of search, seizure, detention, and arrest, and this clearly refers not to high political activity, but to the final point of application of 'operational' powers. In this regard, it is somewhat unfortunate that the Convention Working Group on Freedom, Security and Justice chose as one of its 'golden rules' the distinction between 'legislative' and 'operational' tasks without close definition of what was meant by 'operational', although, as noted in the main text, the general thinking behind this distinction is constitutionally helpful.

[42] See section 3C above.

in any event particularly difficult to answer. In their respective contributions, both Cyrille Fijnaut and, at greater length, Christine Van den Wyngaert also acknowledge the urgency of this accountability deficit, and are ready to explore various solutions. What they point to is the need to generate a framework of what one author has dubbed 'complex accountability',[43] in which 'multiple forms of accountability of powerful... actors and organisations can compensate for the imperfections of single lines of accountability', and, in particular, the need to develop a framework in which external forms of accountability to legal and democratic institutions operate in symbiosis with internal forms of accountability within and between particular third pillar agencies. Even with the requisite political will, there are no easy answers here, but the kind of creative and detailed institutional projections that we find in these contributions nevertheless provides a welcome antidote to a constitutional inertia born of neglect or fatalism.

E. Accountability or Effectiveness?

These preliminary thoughts on accountability form a natural bridge to the final tension to be examined. For everyone, it seems, is agreed that *the* major constitutional challenge facing the AFSJ, and the one in whose terms the other more particular challenges may be reframed, is the achievement of the right balance between an effective and efficient policy capacity and output on the one hand, and an appropriate system of individual and collective accountability on the other (which accountability measures may be aptly conceptualized in terms of security's flanking values of 'freedom' and 'justice').[44]

In one sense this is a negative consensus. It has long been a mantra of discussion of FSJ in higher policy circles that the latest institutional structure remains obstinately deficient both in terms of the efficiency and effectiveness of decision-making procedures and products and in terms of their accountability. These complaints were voiced before the Treaty of Amsterdam, again before the Treaty of Nice, and were commonplace in and around the Convention on the Future of Europe. Yet there are also positive features to this consensus. A first is that there is consensus at all, albeit pitched at an extremely high level of abstraction, and often honoured more in the word than in the deed. Yet even the rhetorical recognition of the need for balance imposes certain constraints on the policy debate, and in that sense, as it post-dates the reception of Justice and Home Affairs into the Treaty structure since

[43] M. Saward, 'A Critique of Held', in B. Holden (ed.), *Global Democracy: Key Debates* (London and New York: Routledge, 2000) 32, at 41–2.

[44] For a recent restatement see H. Grabbe, 'Justice and Home Affairs: Faster Decisions, Secure Rights', Centre for European Reform Policy Brief, October 2002.

Maastricht, is arguably one beneficial consequence of the shift from the informal, low-profile, and professionally dominated co-operative culture of the pre-Maastricht years to the more formal, higher-profile, and more explicitly politicized atmosphere of the post-Maastricht years. A second positive feature is that the consensus indicates that the relationship between efficiency and accountability is not zero-sum, but is in at least some measure mutually supportive and so cumulative. So in general terms it may be asserted with some confidence that one characteristic of a less complex, diverse, and cumbersome, and therefore more efficient, institutional structure should necessarily be greater transparency and comprehensibility, and for that reason such a structure may also be more amenable to collective and individual accountability. Conversely, it is persuasive that a structure emphasizing protection of individual rights and facilitation of collective voice and monitoring should increase public support for or tolerance of FSJ measures, so making their efficient and effective implementation more likely.

Yet virtue is not so easily achieved. Against this general consensus, there remains a great deal of disagreement and uncertainty as to how the (potentially) positive-sum relationship between efficiency and accountability should be articulated. There are a number of different dimensions to this. To begin with, even before we can address the question of optimal balance directly, there are significant problems of normative justification, political feasibility, and policy implementation concerning how we should specify our conceptions of efficiency and effectiveness on the one hand and accountability on the other.

With regard to the issue of normative justification, the bland neutrality of the terms 'effectiveness' and 'efficiency' tends to mask quite significant substantive choices concerning the baseline against which these standards should be measured. These substantive choices or aspirations necessarily engage with a multiplicity of possible values and policy priorities, many of which may be non-cumulative or even in direct conflict. Steve Peers, for example, looks critically at EU family reunion policy in terms of its tendency towards racism, class bias, sex discrimination, homophobia, disregard for children's rights, an unduly narrow conception of the family, and a disregard for the individual life-chances of migrants beyond the narrowly defined family context. And as Kay Hailbronner's and Ferruccio Pastore's contributions show, these are but several manifestations of a more general conflict between a cluster of values and policy priorities which puts the interests of the host states in the close substantive delimitation and procedural policing of migration to the fore, and a cluster of values and policy priorities which seek to equiparate the respect and concern due to migrant populations with those of indigenous nationals. Similarly broad value choices attend the specification of priorities in the third pillar. In asking how we can possibly operationalize the highly indeterminate objective of providing citizens with 'a high level of safety within an area of freedom, security and justice' under Article 29 TEU, Cyrille Fijnaut indicates the scale of the problem. 'Safety' is a multi-dimensional concept, referring not only to the aspiration to live in an environment secure from the threats of criminality and public disorder, but also, and often just as importantly—and for certain minorities even more urgently—the desire to live in security from undue interference from law enforcement bodies themselves.[45] Relatedly, safety is rarely a public good which can be evenly distributed amongst the population, and one important aspect of the question of the optimal distribution of safety between groups tends to echo the tension identified in the migration field between the priority to be accorded to settled, indigenous populations and that to be accorded to groups in transit or with more precarious residence claims.

If we turn to accountability, here, too, deep philosophical choices require to be made. We may be tempted to declare that, all else being equal and with no other values and priorities to be taken on board and weighed in the balance (which is not of course the case), 'more' rather than 'less' accountability to constituencies and groups for the making and implementation of the policies by which they are affected is the only normative guideline we need attend to. But it is not as simple as that. Conceptions of optimal accountability—including the balance between internal and external accountability, or between expert and lay accountability, or between individual rights-based and collective political accountability, or between accountability for rule-compliance and for optimal performance, or between proactive or directive accountability and reactive or explanatory accountability—turn upon underlying choices about the proper nature of the political sphere, including the relative merits of technocracy and democracy, representative and participatory democracy, rights fundamentalism and majoritarianism, and so on.[46]

These fundamental value dilemmas are compounded by problems of political feasibility and implementation. With regard to political feasibility, as is particularly clear from Christine Van den Wyngaert's discussion of the *corpus juris* project and Ferruccio Pastore's analysis of the tentative evolution of an EU entry control system, the question of the proper balance between mutual recognition and harmonization is central to any appreciation of what effectiveness and efficiency can realistically mean. This question, which unsurprisingly also preoccupied the Convention Working Group on AFSJ, poses certain sharp, and probably irresoluble conundrums. On the one hand, a system that favours mutual recognition regardless of underlying

[45] See, for example, Walker, *supra* note 27, ch.1, and *supra* note 33. See also Loader, *supra* note 17, J. Waldron, 'Security and Liberty: The Image of Balance', 11 *Journal of Political Philosophy* (2003) 191.

[46] See, for example, Walker, *supra* note 27, ch.1.

harmonization involves less centralizing interference in areas of national law, whether procedural or substantive. On the other hand, a robust system of mutual recognition in the absence of harmonization requires states to place the support of their systems of coercive public authority behind decisions and practices emanating from other national contexts which these same states may not themselves endorse—so asking much of the qualities of trust in and tolerance of other national frameworks and solutions the very scarcity of which underpins the difficulty of harmonization.[47] The question of accountability likewise raises certain conundrums of the politically possible. At least part of the ambivalence associated with more robust forms of democratic accountability has to do with an absence of trust in the representative quality and capacity for effective oversight of institutions other than the traditional national ones. But as with the proverbial chicken and egg, it is difficult to see how supranational institutions can generate the levels of committed and effective engagement with accountability tasks necessary to win such trust unless and until they are first trusted with the requisite powers and resources.

As for implementation, in our discussion of the reactive dimension in FSJ policy- and decision-making, the point was made that much of what must be addressed in the policy agenda emerges from and takes place in social environments beyond the easy prediction and control of policy-makers. This point is as pertinent to detailed questions of policy application as it is to the broad sweep of agenda-setting. The activities that police officers, magistrates, prosecutors, criminal courts, border guards, immigration officers, and the various other agencies involved in FSJ are concerned to address, tend to take place in regions of low visibility, to have multiple and diverse sources, to be subject to discreet and unpredictable pressures, and to resist easily quantifiable measures of operational success. In turn, this can confound the best efforts to develop methodologies for testing and improving performance. Just as pertinently, as an alternative to engaging with these hard questions and admitting the precariousness of best practice, the implementation gap can lead to an emphasis upon form rather than substance, out*puts* rather than out*comes*, the ceremony of institutional capacity rather than concrete results. Cyrille Fijnaut makes this point trenchantly in his critique of the poverty of existing understandings of the nature and understanding of organized crime and of the specific 'added value' of policing as a way of combating organized crime, and of the complacency or obduracy of official attitudes in the presence of this knowledge deficit. Yet the case he makes could be multiplied over various sectors of FSJ.

A very similar point can be made about the operational effectiveness and efficiency of accountability techniques. Rather like the FSJ institutions they are set up to monitor, systems of accountability in the area of FSJ are

[47] On this, see in particular Ferruccio Pastore's and Christine Van den Wyngaert's chapters.

concerned in significant measure with the prevention or sanctioning of rule infraction. Accordingly, again rather like the institutions they monitor, it is difficult to develop output measurements and evaluations which are an accurate and sensitive index of effective performance in the task of holding to account rather than simply reflections of changes in independent environmental variables or, indeed, indications of the higher visibility of mistakes and malpractice which might have gone unnoticed and unremarked in the absence of these very accountability mechanisms. In other words, just as with questions of policy effectiveness and efficiency, whether and to what extent this or that accountability technique is effective in achieving its underlying objectives is as likely to be a matter of faith or prejudice as of systematic analysis of reliable evidence. This knowledge gap, moreover, speaks not only to the limits of our *general* understanding of the practical worth of accountability systems for security institutions. It is exacerbated by the previously remarked fact that many of the problems and challenges of transnational executive accountability in the particular sphere of FSJ are quite novel in nature, and so our sense of what constitutes an effective monitoring regime lacks any reliable historical benchmark.

The point of this deconstruction of the ideas of policy effectiveness and efficiency and of accountability is not to suggest that the question of balance between these two is chimerical or beyond meaningful evaluation, but merely to indicate that any such meaningful evaluation demands, and in point of fact will already assume, answers to other and equally hard questions concerning fundamental values, political feasibility, and operational performance. So, for instance, if in the realm of collective accountability we are trying to find a balance between, on the one hand, the value to police or other security experts of the capacity to engage in operational activities free from the frustrations, delays, and confidentiality risks that may attend external monitoring or direction by non-experts and, on the other, the dividend of close public accountability in terms of protection against corruption, neglect, inefficiency, or oppressive behaviour, and in terms of the enhancement of public understanding and confidence and the canvassing of a broader range of policy opinions, we must acknowledge that any such calculation is complicated by the other factors mentioned above. The same is true of individual accountability to courts and other monitoring agencies and tribunals, and the fundamental rights they are deemed to protect. Whether we are dealing with the particular tensions and trade-offs between police information-gathering and data protection and its attendant rights of privacy, between efficient co-operation between criminal justice agencies and the rights of suspects and accused to be protected by rigorous (or at least nationally familiar) procedural and evidential standards, between efficient immigration controls and the rights of asylum-seekers to due consideration of their case, or, more generally, between free movement and reasonable standards of anticipatory and reactive security, the other questions of value judgment, political feasibility, and implementation loom large on either side of the equation.

4. IN SEARCH OF A CONSTITUTIONAL SETTLEMENT

A. The Changing Constitutional Landscape

It appears, then, that the master tension which frames any meaningful constitutional debate in AFSJ is in effect not simply one major question of balance but a compound, complex, and controversial series of dilemmas and trade-offs. If that is the case, how do the various features of the constitutional landscape revealed in our discussion of the other background tensions affect the way in which this debate tends to be addressed?

To begin with, as we have seen, the sheer ideological potency of security talk and the weight and urgency which this lends to security interests are such that there has been a longstanding tendency for positions stressing an efficient capacity to achieve 'security' objectives and respond to 'security' threats without undue interference with 'security' expertise or unwarranted delay in mobilizing policy-making or operational capacity to prevail. Particularly in the heightened atmosphere of 'security reaction' which an event like September 11 brings in its wake, the danger arises that this may lead to a narrow definition of the security community to be protected, a glossing over of the deep-rooted problems of political feasibility and implementation to which a coherent security policy must attend, and, more generally, to the relegation of accountability to the status of an afterthought rather than an equiprimordial consideration. Other factors may exacerbate the tendency to downgrade accountability concerns, including the truncated time-frame within which a new internal security capacity has sought to catch up with the more mature competences of the EU polity, the consequent temptation to treat opportunities for institution-building as occasions for extending capacity rather than holding existing capacities to fuller account, and the danger of judging constitutional probity in terms of an inappropriately legislation-centred template with insufficient attention to the executive-centred character of at least some aspects of FSJ.

Some additional factors we have considered, however, point to a more nuanced picture. In particular, the resilience of the intergovernmental/supranational fault-line has interestingly diverse constitutional ramifications. In many respects it has tended to cut across and further obscure candid consideration of the optimal balance between effectiveness and accountability. In other respects, however, it connects the FSJ sector to larger debates in a manner which can provide useful illumination and may precipitate effective consideration of the constitutional issues at stake in the specific sector in question. On the downside, as we have seen, preoccupation with national sovereignty—

either with its retention or with its transcendence—can lead to opposite but equal forms of constitutional myopia. The myopia of the sovereigntist can lead to the refusal of mature European-level techniques for holding European-level institutions and capacities to account, *just because* these techniques are supranationally situated and might be seen as giving succour to the integrationist project. From the opposite perspective, federalist fervour can encourage empire-building and competence expansion for its own sake, or at least with very little critical scrutiny of its merits, and so may provide a broader macro-political alibi for a strongly security-centred expansionism.

More positively, however, the broader macro-political considerations are as capable of opening up the constitutional debate in a way which allows a fuller engagement with the complex and controversial balance between accountability and policy effectiveness as they are of closing it down into an implacable opposition between rival camps. On the side of those who are cautious about further Europeanization, this is often more than a cynical or myopic refusal to countenance integration on any grounds, but may speak to a genuine concern that Europeanization of FSJ capacities and controls is likely to entail a loss of nationally valued protections and an attenuation of the links between people and polity that are crucial to viable forms of accountability, and even a dilution and diminution of effective decision-making. To take the first of these, Christine Van den Wyngaert is of course correct to point out in response to criticisms of the idea of a European Public Prosecutor that 'the proposition that the rights of the defendants are better protected under national law is not necessarily correct, and may flow from a certain degree of chauvinism that states have about their own criminal justice systems'. Yet, as her formulation implies, the proposition in question is not *necessarily* wrong either, and so conservative assumptions may at least have the merit of forcing a fuller consideration of the issues at hand. Similar considerations apply to arguments about the cohesiveness and democratic effectiveness of supranational structures.

As for those who are on the side broadly committed to integration, the significance of their approach in encouraging a fuller debate of the balance between accountability and effectiveness is less direct but potentially more wide-ranging. The present drive towards a documentary Constitution has diverse origins, but one key factor undoubtedly lies in the recognition of those committed to a deep supranational trajectory that there exists a significant legitimacy deficit that an explicit constitution-making project might hope to fill. As we have seen, the history of European integration generally, and not just of the AFSJ latecomer, has often been policy or 'functionally'[48] driven, with institutional design and control pragmatically tailored

[48] On the significance of functionalism and neo-functionalism in the politics of European Integration see, for example, the classic work of L.N. Lindberg, *The Political Dynamics of European Integration* (Stanford, Calif.: Stanford University Press, 1963).

to ever-expanding policy aspirations rather than articulating a sense of the best constitutional settlement for a mature polity. The new constitution-making project involves recognition that the plausibility and success of further integration, in the face of a post-Maastricht decade in which popular disengagement from the European project has become more manifest and political scepticism towards it more organized, may require that imbalance to be redressed, or at least be seen to be redressed.[49] In turn this has opened up a political space in which it has become easier—indeed, for the committed supranationalist, obligatory—to make an explicit argument that with particular regard to the AFSJ, just as in other policy sectors, the new European scale of internal security politics implies both that a co-ordinated and effective policy capacity must be uniformly European and that suitably tailored accountability mechanisms be pitched at the same level. Under the sign of the new constitutionalism, one part of the package cannot prosper without the other, and so even for those whose main priority may be the expansion of competence and to whom the establishment of a framework of constitutional constraints presents itself as a price as much as an opportunity, it is a price whose payment can no longer be avoided.

Of course, the macro-political opposition in question remains palpable, and even if the present grand debate has inevitably led to a new quality of engagement we should not be too hasty to see in the more explicit confrontation of competing visions the prospect of a more reasoned reconciliation and constitutionally satisfactory resolution. Differences in overall vision are likely to remain quite entrenched in some quarters, as are the assumptions of political feasibility which tend both to flow from and reinforce these visions, and which themselves, as we noted earlier, represent one of the deep imponderables complicating the search for an optimal balance between accountability and policy effectiveness.[50] Nevertheless, following the above analysis, the very framing of the current debate in terms of the explicit constitution-building project set in motion at Laeken in December 2000, continued in the

[49] On the broader politics of the present constitution-making process see, for example, Walker, *supra* note 5; see also J. Shaw, 'Process, Responsibility and Inclusion in EU Constitutionalism', 9 *European Law Journal* (2003) 43, and Weiler, *supra* note 16.

[50] For example, it seemed to be a working assumption of the *Joint Submissions by The Standing Committee of Experts on International, Immigration, Refugee and Criminal Law; The Immigration Law Practitioners Association, Statewatch and the European Council of Refugees and Exiles To Working Group X* (D. Curtin and S. Peers (eds), Utrecht and London, 14 November 2002) (http://www.statewatch.org/) that as much Europeanization of policy tools and accountability mechanisms as possible is a good thing. This document is full of good arguments and useful suggestions for increased accountability, but there is insufficient investigation of the political viability and effective social foundations of the premiss of increasing 'communitarization' on which much of the framework depends (including a European Public Prosecutor, European Police Force and European Criminal Court, as well as robust accountability institutions of both an individual and a collective nature). It seems simply to be assumed—and hoped—that these political and social objections can and should be overcome.

draft Constitutional Treaty, and, perhaps, set to be signed and sealed in the current IGC and in the subsequent national notification process, has undoubtedly on balance favoured a more supranational approach, and has done so in a manner which ties increases in competence and capacity to new constitutional checks and constraints. A brief and necessarily selective overview of the relevant provisions of the draft Constitutional Treaty will illustrate this,[51] while also demonstrating the tenacious legacy of the national sovereigntist perspective.

B. The Draft Constitutional Treaty

A significant mark of both increased capacity and, if to a lesser extent, enhanced accountability was the design choice, made very early in the proceedings of the Convention, to eliminate the basic distinction between the pillars, and to subsume FSJ in general within a single institutional framework.[52] This is part and parcel of the general drive to unity within the Constitutional Treaty—a single treaty with a single organizational template for an entity with a single legal personality.[53] With regard to capacity, a number of linked developments flow from the establishment of the unity principle; the general adoption of qualified majority voting (QMV) across FSJ, involving both an overturning of the conventional wisdom that had previously insisted on unanimity and national veto for general policy decisions in Title VI of the third pillar and a completion of the move towards QMV already initiated in Title IV of the first pillar; a general enhancement of the legislative power of the Parliament through the adoption of the 'ordinary legislative procedure' (previously co-decision procedure); and the replacement of 'soft' legislative measures by 'hard' measures through adoption of 'European laws' (previously regulations) and 'European framework laws' (previously directives) as the law-making norm.[54] With regard to

[51] The detailed provisions on AFSJ are found in Part III, Title III, Chapter IV (Arts III–158 to III–178) of the Draft Treaty Establishing a Constitution for Europe (hereinafter DCT). See also Art. 1–41, which supplies general principles of action under AFSJ.

[52] Indeed, the adoption of a 'common general legal framework' was the other 'golden rule' endorsed by Working Group X (alongside the legislative/operational distinction (see *supra* note 40)), albeit qualified by the proviso that the common framework should 'recognize the peculiarities of this area'.

[53] Art. I–6, DCT.

[54] These linked developments are achieved by establishing laws and framework laws as the legislative norm in AFSJ under Art. I–41(1) DCT, which species of law are in the usual case to be proposed by the Commission and jointly adopted by the European Parliament and a qualified majority of the Council of Ministers under the new ordinary legislative procedure (Arts. I–32–33 and III–302 DCT). As regards those matters for which unanimity in the Council is retained, in some cases (i.e. Arts. III–175(1), 171(2)(d), and 172(1) DCT) the consent of the European Parliament is required, whereas for others (i.e. Arts. III–176(2) and

accountability, the major implications of the new unitary structure are the general extension of the jurisdiction of the ECJ to all aspects of FSJ,[55] together with the decision to make the previously merely 'declaratory' Charter of Fundamental Rights legally enforceable against Community institutions.[56]

Nevertheless, the shadow of sovereigntist concerns continues to hang over this brave new unitary structure, affecting both capacity and accountability. Unanimous voting in the Council is retained for certain especially sensitive areas of police and criminal justice co-operation, in particular the setting up of the European Public Prosecutor,[57] operational co-operation between national law enforcement authorities,[58] the cross-border competence of national law enforcement and judicial authorities,[59] and the extension of the areas of procedural[60] and substantive[61] criminal law which may be subject to approximation at the European level beyond those already specified in the constitutional text. Similarly, the most intense and only directly effective form of legislative action—the new European law—is not available even in those relatively limited areas of procedural[62] and substantive[63] criminal law which are explicitly set out in the constitutional text as eligible for approximation. As to new legislative procedure more generally, the Member States, provided at least one quarter of them are in agreement, retain a residual right of legislative initiative alongside the Commission in the area of the old third pillar,[64] while the Parliaments of the Member States may also take advantage of a new general power to object to a proposed new legislative measure on the

178 DCT) only consultation of the Parliament is required (see, further, text and associated notes 57–61 below). Consultation of the European Parliament is also the norm in those cases where the Council of Ministers is specifically empowered to adopt 'regulations'—another and in some respects, lesser species of law provided under the draft Constitutional Treaty (Art. I–32(1)). See, in particular, Art. III–164 DCT (administrative co-operation between government departments) and Art. III–167(3) DCT (emergency measures of asylum and temporary protection policy).

[55] See in particular Art. I–28(1), Art. I–28(3), Art. III–265 to III–267, Art. III–270, Art. III–272, Art. III–274.

[56] Art. I–7 and Part II DCT. It would be wrong, however, to view the Charter as set out in Part II of the DCT exclusively as a check on AFSJ action in the name of individual rights. As Art. II–5 makes explicit, 'security of [the] person' is also a right, and to that extent affords an example of the Charter legitimating as opposed to constraining legislative and executive action under the AFSJ.

[57] Art. III–175(1) DCT.

[58] Art. III–176(3) DCT.

[59] Art. III–178 DCT.

[60] Art. III–171(2)(d) DCT.

[61] Art. III–172(1) DCT.

[62] Art. III–171(2) DCT.

[63] Art. III–172(1) DCT.

[64] Art. III–165(b) DCT.

grounds that it breaches the principle of subsidiarity.[65] A broader, if less direct, qualification of the Commission's right of initiative is found in the right of the European Council—representing the heads of state of the EU and so the most explicitly intergovernmental institution within the Union—to define the strategic guidelines for legislative and operational planning within the AFSJ.[66] As regards the Court of Justice, too, some form of exceptionalism persists in the area of policing. The old embargo on central judicial review of the validity or proportionality of law enforcement operations or the exercise of member state responsibilities with regard to law and order and internal security is substantially retained,[67] the contrary recommendation of the Convention Working Group notwithstanding,[68] and despite the fact that many 'European' policing initiatives and operations remain state-centred at the point of delivery and apt to interfere with individual freedoms.

Policy capacity is of course not just a matter of institutional wherewithal, but also one of jurisdictional competence. Here, too, there is some expansion, but again this is balanced by the reinforcement of certain 'no-go' areas. This tension is prefigured in Part I of the Constitutional Treaty, and perhaps this is unsurprising since, as well as containing the basic principles and structural outline of the new settlement, Part I, as the most visible part of the new Treaty and the part most vigorously debated in and beyond the Convention, is also host to some large symbolic acknowledgements of the deep and sometimes conflicting motivations of the Constitutional Treaty's authors. On the one hand, therefore, we find immediately after the basic endorsement of Union competence in AFSJ, a 'solidarity' clause that empowers the Union to mobilize all the resources (including military resources) at its disposal in the event of a terrorist attack or other disaster of a similar magnitude.[69] If that provision speaks eloquently to the importance of an event on one continent—the attacks on the American mainland on 11 September 2001—as a legitimating catalyst for the expansion of collective security competence in another continent, earlier in Part I we find, on the other hand, an equally ringing endorsement of the importance of maintaining existing national

[65] Art. III–160(1) DCT. According to the Draft Protocol on the Application of the Principles of Subsidiarity and Proportionality, para. 6, the threshold for requiring the Commission to review 'third pillar' proposals on grounds of subsidiarity (at the request of one quarter of national Parliamentary bodies) is lower than the threshold for requiring review (i.e. one third) as regards other areas of European law.

[66] Art. III–159 DCT.

[67] Art. III–283 DCT. Note, however, that the exception with regard to state responsibilities in the maintenance of law and order and the safeguarding of internal security is *not* retained for the limited part of the first pillar dimension of the AFSJ to which it previously applied, namely measures calculated to ensure an absence of controls on persons crossing internal borders under Art. 62(1)EC; see Art. 68(2) EC.

[68] Report of Working Group X, Section CV.

[69] Arts. I–42 and III–231 DCT.

prerogatives in the security field. Article I–5 sets out the duty of the Union to respect 'essential state functions', of which the maintenance of law and order and the safeguarding of internal security is specified as a prominent example.[70]

A similar pattern is apparent in the more detailed elaboration of competences in Part III. The already wide-ranging capacities in the area of migration and entry control are largely retained and rationalized,[71] with some notable developments in the form of the introduction of an integrated system for the management of external borders[72] and of an explicit principle of solidarity between Member States and fair sharing of responsibility, including financial burden-sharing.[73] However, to these developments must be counterpoised a late amendment which removes any shadow of doubt that primary immigration policy is still beyond the pale, 'volumes of admission of third country nationals'[74] remaining within the exclusive remit of the Member States. In police and criminal justice co-operation, there is some fleshing out of the framework of co-operation between criminal justice agencies, the approximation of substantive and procedural criminal law, and the jurisdiction and operational scope of police co-operation.[75] There is also, for the first time, the enshrinement of the basic principle of mutual recognition of decisions,[76] and, although attended by much controversy, the constitutional capacity to establish a European Public Prosecutor.[77] On the other side, an explicit fence is built around the traditional monopoly of legitimate violence by the state, 'the application of coercive measures' continuing to 'be the exclusive responsibility of the competent national authorities'.[78]

In the crucial area of executive and operational activity, there are also important developments on both sides of the equation, and in these developments again the tension between intergovernmental and supranational approaches and the intricate demands of balancing remain discernible. As regards strengthening the effectiveness of Union capacity, apart from the general consolidation of existing agencies such as Europol[79] and Eurojust[80] and the new constitutional prospect of a European Public Prosecutor, in line

[70] Art. I–5(1) DCT. [71] Arts. III–166 to III–169 DCT.

[72] Art. III–166(1)(c) and (2)(d) DCT.

[73] Art. III–169. For a fuller discussion of the borders and immigration provisions in the DCT see section 3(c) of Ferruccio Pastore's chapter in this volume.

[74] Art. III–168(5). Contemporary news reports indicated that the German governmental representatives to the Convention insisted on this addition to the text.

[75] Arts. III–171 to III–178 DCT.

[76] Art. III–158(3). As argued in section 3(e), however, this is not necessarily to be read in categorically pro-integrationist terms.

[77] Art. III–175 DCT.

[78] Art. III–177(3) DCT.

[79] Art. III–174 DCT.

[80] Art. III–177 DCT.

with the Working Group's emphasis upon a clearer distinction between legislative policy and operational/executive co-ordination and implementation, there is now a more explicit and stronger operational co-ordination role for a Standing Committee of the Council of Ministers[81] than is to be found in the present Treaty 'executive'—the so-called Article 36 Committee. Another key innovation, and one which, by contrast, empowers the Commission (albeit in collaboration with member state governments), involves the extension of the system of mutual evaluation of the activities of national implementing authorities which it co-ordinates to all AFSJ activities.[82] Finally, as regards the 'harder' sanction of judicially-backed administrative enforcement in the case of national failure to fulfil an EU obligation—a traditional area of Commission prerogative—the strategy of extending traditional EC powers to AFSJ is again utilized further to empower the Commission.[83]

As regards accountability, some modest improvements are provided both in national and supranational controls. National Parliaments are entitled to participate in the Commission's mutual evaluation procedures[84] and the European Parliament to be informed of the content and results of such evaluation,[85] while both national Parliaments and the European Parliament are entitled to participate in the political monitoring of Europol[86] and in the evaluation of Eurojust's activities.[87] These rights, however, remain couched in vague and abstract terms, their value entirely dependent upon the way in which they are specified in subsequent European laws. Elsewhere, even the abstract rights are more modest. As regards the Council's new Standing Committee on operational co-ordination—the major driving forces of practical collaboration—the right of national and European Parliaments is restricted to one of information.[88] If we return to individual accountability, as we have seen, there are some improvements in the capacity of the ECJ to hold the FSJ institutions to account. However, the explicit refusal of jurisdiction over operational policing and over matters deemed to fall within national responsibility, together with the continuation of the general cross-pillar restriction on individual standing before the ECJ to review the legality of acts of EU institutions,[89] curtail the value of these rights in the executive domain.

[81] Art. III–162 DCT.
[82] Art. III–161 DCT.
[83] Arts. III–265 to III–267 DCT.
[84] Art. III–160 DCT.
[85] Art. III–161 DCT.
[86] Art. III–174(2) DCT.
[87] Art. III–177(2) DCT.
[88] Art. III–162 DCT.
[89] Art. III–270 (4) DCT.

5. CONCLUSION

By way of conclusion, a cautionary note should be entered. For all that the current constitutional debate has tended to dominate the recent political landscape of AFSJ, and for all that it promises a more serious treatment than hitherto of the accountability side of the equation, we should be careful not to invest too much in its final product—if and when it is finally delivered. There are a number of reasons for this reservation.

First, and most obviously, it bears repetition that, particularly in the light of September 11, there is an abiding danger that, even in an explicitly constitutionalized setting, concerns with the 'effectiveness' of security policy will continue to outstrip available accountability mechanisms, the latter destined to play an unending game of 'catch-up' with the former. Secondly, it also bears repetition that the mindset which conceives of a fundamental divide between 'intergovernmental' and 'supranational' can still hinder attempts to constitutionalize protection at the appropriate level—witness the continuing limitations on the jurisdiction of the ECJ. Thirdly, the problem of implementation discussed earlier does not resolve itself through the formal authority of a solemn constitutional settlement. As regards accountability mechanisms, there is many a slip between ringing constitutional declaration and concrete implementation. In its somewhat abstract declaration of the rights of democratic involvement of both national and European Parliaments, and in its reliance on future legislation for the proper articulation of these schemes, the constitutional settlement does little to address that gap. Fourthly, we should in any case recall that many of the controversies surrounding AFSJ are not easily, if at all, treated by constitutional means. The labels of effectiveness and optimal security mask the hard policy choices which have to be made in this area, and those who are concerned that migration policy or criminal justice policy is too dismissive of the claims of incomers and marginal communities, or, indeed, too receptive to these claims, will not find any easy answers or solid comfort in a constitutional settlement.

This alerts us, however, to a final reason why we should not take the present constitutional phase too seriously, but one that may offer a more positive message. If the underlying tensions which I have outlined, and which the contributors to this volume elaborate in greater detail, tend to qualify the value of any freeze-frame constitutional settlement, they also ensure that the post-IGC text will not be the last word. These tensions, like many similar tensions in other areas of the EU polity, will continue to play out at the political level, and if a sense of the susceptibility of these tensions to broad constitutional treatment and deliberation remains reasonably prominent within public consciousness, then any particular constitutional text, however infused with a sense of *finalité*, should not be allowed to rest in peace. In other words, the possibility of the AFSJ benefiting from the kind of sustained vigilance towards and constructive long-term engagement with the unresolved (and never definitively resoluble) tensions in its foundations that seem indispensable for this policy domain to have any prospect of generating and consolidating a broader and deeper social legitimacy, depends upon widespread acknowledgement that the current constitutional debate offers no once-and-for-all solution—provided, of course, that complacency is not simply replaced by a disappointed fatalism, and that further constitutional debate is not thereby dismissed as redundant. If, however, the sense of constitutionalism as an event rather than a process does prevail, and if the constitutional moment *is* treated as having passed with the successful completion of the IGC, and a climate of reactive and strategic policy-making proceeds to reassert itself fully after the interlude of more reflexive and balanced polity-building, then, given the nature of the quotidian influences in the AFSJ domain documented in the present chapter, it is difficult to see what will prevent the resurgence of an unduly narrow and skewed security agenda. Having achieved a moment of prominence, therefore, it is vital that the constitutional outlook now be privileged as the master frame—adjustable in detail but resilient in its principled search for the optimal reconciliation of diverse fundamental values—for the ongoing evaluation and development of the AFSJ project.[90]

[90] On the limitations of the idea of the Constitutional Treaty as a 'constitutional moment' see N. Walker, 'After the Constitutional Moment', in I. Pernice (ed.), *The Draft Constitutional Treaty* (Baden-Baden: Nomos, 2003).

Part Two

Border Controls, Asylum, and Immigration

2

Asylum Law in the Context of a European Migration Policy

KAY HAILBRONNER

1. INTRODUCTION

A. Facts and Statistics

While legal immigration of migrant workers from third countries into the EU Member States has been increasingly restricted, asylum applications, though subject to special regimes, have increased. A peak was reached in 1992/1993, when 438,000 persons asked for asylum in Germany, approximately 70 per cent of all asylum seekers within the European Union. The number of asylum requests in the European Union declined from its peak in 1992/1993, but rose again from mid-1996.[1] In spite of smaller numbers since 2000, asylum law has continued to provide a backdoor for illegal immigration into the European Union. A substantial number of asylum seekers, who do not satisfy the criteria for international protection under the Geneva Convention or other international or national instruments, will nevertheless enter and remain in one of the EU Member States. The fight against illegal immigration, policies of voluntary and involuntary return, conclusion of readmission agreements, and measures against trafficking in human beings have become prominent on the European agenda.

The fact is that only a relatively small percentage of applicants have been recognized under the Geneva Convention.[2] This does not necessarily imply an abuse of asylum claims. The typical demand for humanitarian protection in the 1990s is based on flight from armed conflicts and situations of

[1] COM(2000)755 final—towards a common asylum procedure and a uniform status, valid throughout the Union, for persons granted asylum.

[2] In total, 89,576 persons have been recognized between 1997 and 1999, of which 39% are in Germany, 16% in the United Kingdom, 15% in France and 11% in the Netherlands: see COM(2000)755 final, figure 3.

insecurity and human rights violations that do not easily fit within the criteria of the Geneva Convention. Nevertheless, they must be considered as persons in need of protection, partly based upon international legal instruments, such as the European Convention on Human Rights ('international protection'), and partly based on national admission schemes providing for temporary shelter for victims of war, civil war, or human rights violations. The growing numbers of asylum seekers generally have followed the immigration trends in the EU Member States. Although the EU Member States have unanimously denied that they are countries of immigration, by and large all have eventually become *de facto* immigration countries. The flow of asylum applicants has become a major source of *de facto* immigration.

The European Union has become one of the most important destinations for migration movements, resulting in a serious debate among Member States on migration control.

Nevertheless, as Tables One and Two indicate, migration patterns differ widely among Member States. Reasons for this are the history of colonialism, recruitment of migration workers policies, national differences in the recognition of asylum seekers, and geographical facts. In the year 2001, more than 1.1 million persons immigrated to the European Union. Net migration was highest in Germany, followed by Spain and Italy. The highest quota of foreigners is in Luxembourg (34%), while Austria and Germany (9%) share second place. The quota is lowest in Spain, Greece, and Finland (1.5%).

Although the number of asylum applications recently decreased slightly, there is no decline in immigration. This is, *inter alia*, due to a considerable rise in family reunification and demand-oriented immigration of workers. In some Member States the reception of family members accounts for more than 50 per cent of total immigration. According to Table Three, about 366,000 asylum applications were made in the EU in 2001. Once again, Germany ranks first in 2001 in the number of applications after being replaced by the United Kingdom in the year 2000.

As Table Four indicates, a comparison of the number of applications and the size of the domestic population shows that small European countries in particular admitted a large number of asylum seekers in relation to their population. In the year 2000, applications per 1,000 inhabitants were highest in Slovenia, followed by Belgium, Ireland, the Netherlands, and Switzerland.

More than 50 per cent of all asylum seekers arrive from ten countries. As is illustrated in Tables Five and Six, since 2000, the Federal Republic of Yugoslavia, which was the single greatest source of asylum seekers throughout the 1990s, has been deposed as the top country of origin. In 2001, most asylum seekers came from Iraq and Afghanistan, followed by Turkey and, only then, Yugoslavia.

Table One. *Population development in 2001*

Country/ Region	Population 1.1.2001	Natural Increase	Net Migration	Population 1.1.2002[3]
		× 1000		
Belgium	10 263,4	11,3	32,6	10 307,3
Denmark	5 349,2	7,0	12,2	5 368,4
Germany	82 259,5	−91,0	262,5	82 431,0
Greece	10 564,7	−1,4	35,0	10 598,3
Spain	40 121,7	56,0	231,7	40 409,3
France	59 037,2	246,8	60,0	59 344,0
Ireland	3 826,2	28,1	30,0	3 884,2
Italy	57 844,0	3,9	170,0	58 017,9
Luxembourg	441,3	1,7	3,3	446,4
Netherlands	15 987,1	62,9	50,3	16 100,3
Austria	8 121,3	0,7	18,0	8 140,0
Portugal	10 262,9	7,7	65,0	10 355,6
Finland	5 181,1	7,6	6,1	5 194,9
Sweden	8 882,8	−2,3	28,6	8 909,1
United Kingdom	59 894,2	64,7	155,0	60 113,9
EU total	**378 036,6**	**403,7**	**1 160,3**	**379 600,7**
Bulgaria	8 149,5	−44,2	−175,8	7 929,5
Czech Republic	10 295,3	−17,0	−8,6	10 269,7
Hungary	10 200,0	−35,0	14,0	10 179,0
Poland	38 644,2	5,0	−16,7	38 632,5
Romania	22 430,5	−39,2	−4,9	22 386,3
Slovakia	5 378,8	−0,8	1,0	5 379,0
Slovenia	1 990,1	−0,8	4,7	1 994,0

Source: Eurostat

B. Legal Basis for a European Harmonization of Asylum Law

A long-term European asylum policy was made a matter of non-binding intergovernmental co-operation as a result of the 'third pillar' of the Maastricht Treaty. Subsequently, the Amsterdam Treaty assigned the most important areas of alien and asylum law to the competence of the European Community. Articles 62 and 63 ECT provide the Community with extensive competencies and enable it to enact standards within a period of five years relating to the following areas:

—conditions of entry and residence of third-country nationals,
—measures against illegal immigration and illegal residence including repatriation of illegal residents,

[3] Most figures are provisional national estimates or Eurostat estimates.

Table Two. *Population growth in the EU in 2001*

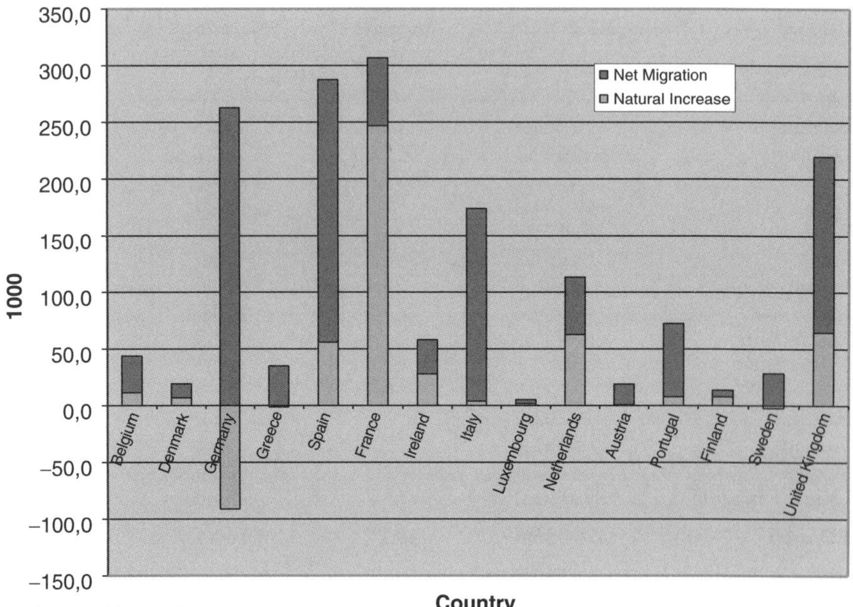

Source: Eurostat

—minimum standards on asylum procedures,
—minimum standards on the reception of asylum seekers,
—minimum standards with respect to the qualification of third-country nationals as refugees,
—criteria and mechanisms for determining which Member State is responsible for considering an application for asylum,
—minimum standards for giving temporary protection to displaced persons,
—burden-sharing concerning the reception of refugees and displaced persons.

However, enacting standards requires unanimity, at least for a period of five years. It remains to be seen whether the Council will pass a decision in five years time providing that substantial parts of the measures covered in Title IV EC are to be governed by the co-decision procedure referred to in Article 251 EC. Further, it has to be considered that only minimum standards shall be enacted and, according to the principle of subsidiarity of Article 5 EC, the Community shall only take action if the objectives of the measures cannot be achieved sufficiently by the Member State and, therefore, by reasons of the scale or effects, can be achieved better by the Community.

Table Three. *Asylum applications in Europe between 1999 and March 2002*

	Asylum Applications in Europe						
State	**1999**		**2000**		**2001**		**01.03.02**
Austria	20.100	4,3%	18.280	4,0%	30.140(2)	6,7%	8.270
Belgium	35.780	7,6%	42.690	9,4%	24.550	5,5%	4.690
Bulgaria	1.330	0,3%	1.760	0,4%	2.430	0,5%	1.090
Czech Rep.	7.290	1,5%	8.770	1,9%	18.040	4%	2.730
Denmark	6.470	1,4%	12.200	2,7%	12.400	2,8%	1.880
Finland	3.110	0,7%	3.170	0,7%	1.650	0,4%	390
France	30.910	6,6%	38.590	8,5%	47.260	10,5%	12.630
Germany	95.110	20,2%	78.760	17,4%	88.360	19,7%	19.230
Greece	1.530	0,3%	3.000	0,7%	5.500	1,2%	–(1)
Hungary	11.500	2,4%	7.800	1,7%	9.550	2,1%	1.680
Ireland	7.720	1,6%	10.920	2,4%	10.320	2,3%	2.530
Italy	33.360	7,1%	15.560	3,4%	9.760	2,2%	–(1)
Liechtenstein	520	0,1%	10	0,0%	110	0%	20
Luxembourg	2.910	0,6%	590	0,1%	690	0,2%	160
Netherlands	39.300	8,3%	43.890	9,7%	32.580	7,3%	6.300
Norway	10.160	2,2%	10.840	2,4%	14.780	3,3%	4.330
Poland	2.960	0,6%	4.400	1,0%	4.530	1%	870
Portugal	310	0,1%	200	0,0%	190	0%	50
Romania	1.670	0,4%	1.360	0,3%	2.380	0,5%	290
Slovakia	1.310	0,3%	1.550	0,3%	8.150	1,8%	1.950
Slovenia	870	0,2%	9.240	2%	1.510	0,3%	140
Spain	8.410	1,8%	7.040	1,6%	9.220	2,1%	2.530
Sweden	11.230	2,4%	16.300	3,6%	23.510	5,2%	7.250
Switzerland	46.070	9,8%	17.660	3,9%	20.770	4,6%	5.610
United Kingdom	91.080	19,3%	98.900(4)	21,8%	70.140(3)	15,6%	–(1)
Total	**471.010**	**100%**	**453.480**	**100%**	**448.520**	**100%**	**84.630**
EU	**387.330**	**82,2%**	**390.090**	**86%**	**366.250**	**81.7%**	**65.910**

The figures for 2001 and 03/2002 are provisional.

(1) No figures available.

(2) Figures for 2001 include 5.622 persons (with 95% of them coming from Afghanistan), who sought asylum in Austrian embassies. Only a few of them will be able to enter Austria. Corresponding figures for the years 1999/2000 are not available.

(3) Cases.

(4) Includes family members.

Source: UNHCR

Table Four. *Asylum applications lodged and total population in Europe in 1999/2000*

Asylum country	No. of applications		National population estimate		Applications per 1,000 inhabitants			
					Total		Ranking	
	1999	2000	× 1000	Share (%)	1999	2000	1999	2000
Austria	20.100	18.280	8 210,5	1,7	2,45	2,23	6	7
Belgium	35.780	42.690	10 161,2	2,1	3,52	4,20	4	2
Bulgaria	1.330	1.760	8 225,0	1,7	0,16	0,21	21	21
Czech Rep.	7.290	8.770	10 244,2	2,1	0,71	0,86	14	13
Denmark	6.470	12.200	5 293,2	1,1	1,22	1,90	11	8
Finland	3.110	3.170	5 175,7	1,1	0,60	0,64	15	16
France	30.910	38.590	59 079,7	12,2	0,52	0,65	17	15
Germany	95.110	78.760	82 220,5	17,0	1,16	0,96	12	12
Greece	1.530	3.000	10 644,7	2,2	0,14	0,28	22	20
Hungary	11.500	7.800	10 035,6	2,1	1,15	0,78	13	14
Ireland	7.720	10.920	3 730,2	0,8	2,07	2,93	8	3
Italy	33.360	15.560	57 298,4	11,8	0,58	0,31	16	17
Liechtenstein	520	10	32,0	0,0	16,25	0,31	1	18
Luxembourg	2.910	590	430,6	0,1	6,76	1,37	2	11
Netherlands	39.300	43.890	15 785,7	3,3	2,49	2,78	5	4
Norway	10.160	10.840	4 464,7	0,9	2,28	2,31	7	6
Poland	2.960	4.400	38 765,1	8,0	0,08	0,11	23	23
Portugal	310	200	9 874,9	2,0	0,03	0,02	25	25
Romania	1.670	1.360	22 326,5	4,6	0,07	0,06	24	24
Slovakia	1.310	1.550	5 387,2	1,1	0,24	0,29	19	19
Slovenia	870	9.240	1 985,6	0,4	0,44	4,65	18	1
Spain	8.410	7.040	39 629,8	8,2	0,21	0,18	20	22
Sweden	11.230	16.300	8 910,2	1,8	1,26	1,84	10	9
Switzerland	46.070	17.660	7 385,7	1,5	6,24	2,39	3	5
United Kingdom	91.080	98.900(4)	58 830,2	12,2	1,55	1,66	9	10
Europe	**471.010**	**452.350**	**484 127,1**	**100,0**	**0,97**	**0,93**		
EU	**387.330**	**389.590**	**375 275,5**	**77,5**	**1,03**	**1,04**		

Source: UNHCR

Table Five. *Asylum applications submitted in the European Union: Top 10 countries of origin 1992–2001*[4]

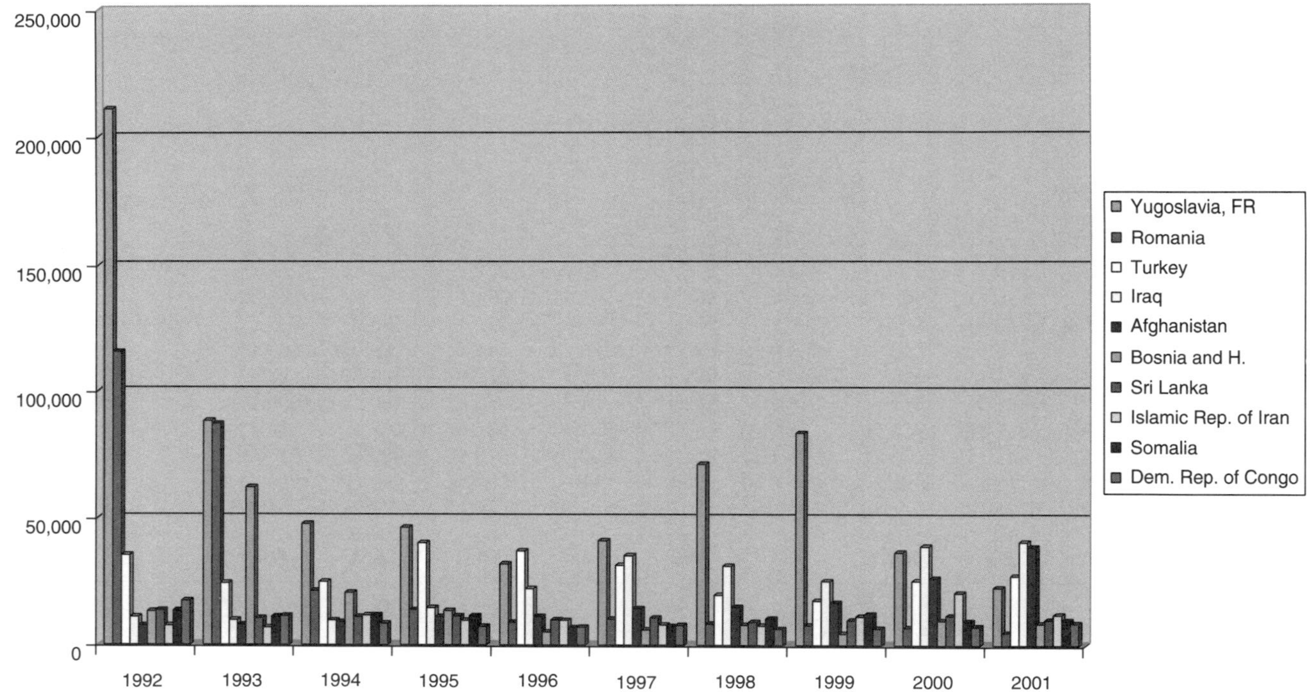

[4] Figures refer generally to first-instance applications. Figures for 2001 are provisional and subject to change. The countries included are Austria, Belgium, Denmark, Finland, Germany, Greece, Ireland, Italy, Luxembourg, the Netherlands, Portugal, Spain, Sweden, and the UK. Denmark: data includes applications lodged at embassies abroad. In the case of Germany, the 1995–1997 figures include reopened applications.

Table Five. *(continued)*

Origin	1992	1993	1994	1995	1996	1997	1998	1999	2000	2001	Total
Yugoslavia, FR	210.907	88.228	47.683	46.105	32.001	40.994	71.185	83.444	36.564	22.816	679.927
Romania	115.556	87.145	21.422	13.943	8.964	10.300	8.450	7.811	6.954	4.907	285.452
Turkey	35.240	24.388	25.019	40.055	36.918	31.466	19.797	17.629	25.472	27.294	283.278
Iraq	11.085	9.892	9.789	14.806	22.295	35.173	31.216	25.328	38.852	40.577	239.013
Afghanistan	7.660	7.920	9.185	11.166	11.344	14.515	15.117	16.778	26.474	38.620	158.779
Bosnia and H.	13.231	62.000	20.717	13.524	5.126	6.059	7.959	4.577	9.655	8.486	151.334
Sri Lanka	13.667	10.632	11.198	11.537	10.060	10.694	9.072	9.858	11.615	10.010	108.343
Islamic Rep. of Iran	7.608	6.883	11.755	9.746	9.794	7.993	7.658	11.315	20.730	12.054	105.536
Somalia	13.551	11.155	11.782	11.498	6.892	7.397	10.425	12.285	9.401	9.871	104.203
Dem. Rep. of Congo	17.373	11.435	8.526	7.412	7.111	7.845	6.383	6.637	7.407	8.614	88.743

Source: UNHCR

Table Six. *Asylum applications lodged in Europe, countries of origin, Jan.–Jun. 2002 (Covering all 20 European countries which reported data for all six months)*

Origin	Jan–Mar	Apr–Jun	Total	Change (%)
Afghanistan	5.700	4.018	9.718	−30%
Albania	605	628	1.233	4%
Algeria	2.433	2.164	4.597	−11%
Angola	1.922	1.697	3.619	−12%
Armenia	2.147	1.892	4.039	−12%
Azerbaijan	869	955	1.824	10%
Bangladesh	798	780	1.578	−2%
Belarus	693	729	1.422	5%
Bosnia and Herzegovina	2.125	1.638	3.763	− 23%
Bulgaria	617	512	1.129	−17%
Cameroon	783	791	1.574	1%
China	1.707	1.747	3.454	2%
Colombia	683	374	1.057	−45%
Congo	940	706	1.646	−25%
Cuba	1.119	74	1.193	−93%
Dem. Rep. of the Congo	2.411	2.574	4.985	7%
FYR of Macedonia	1.168	1.076	2.244	−8%
Georgia	1.968	2.020	3.988	3%
Guinea	892	767	1.659	−14%
Haiti	789	488	1.277	−38%
India	1.571	1.669	3.240	6%
Iran (Islamic Rep. of)	1.899	1.473	3.372	−22%
Iraq	8.123	6.267	14.390	−23%
Mali	777	692	1.469	−11%
Mauritania	900	960	1.860	7%
Nigeria	2.346	2.642	4.988	13%
Pakistan	784	760	1.544	−3%
Rep. of Moldova	1.092	1.161	2.253	6%
Romania	644	1.507	2.151	134%
Russian Federation	3.535	3.901	7.436	10%
Sierra Leone	1.501	1.052	2.554	−30%
Slovakia	893	926	1.819	4%
Somalia	993	998	1.991	1%
Sri Lanka	1.031	913	1.944	−11%
Syrian Arab Rep.	833	867	1.700	4%
Togo	720	648	1.368	−10%
Turkey	6.278	6.128	12.406	−2%
Ukraine	1.793	1.639	3.432	−9%
Vietnam	1.140	899	2.039	−21%
Yugoslavia, FR	5.924	6.336	12.260	7%
Other	9.465	9.285	18.750	−2%
Total	**82.611**	**76.353**	**158.964**	**−8%**

Source: UNHCR

There is a broad consensus that the principle of unanimity prevailing in immigration and asylum law must be considered as a major reason for the rather slow and frequently unsatisfactory legislative process. Proposals of the Commission are discussed by Member States primarily from the perspective of maintaining traditional national legal concepts without regard for their efficiency and suitability for a common European asylum law. With the enlargement of the European Union in 2004 the unanimity rule may easily lead to a total block of the legislative development unless the legislative framework of a European asylum law has been adopted by then. The Treaty of Nice has produced only a small step forward for a more efficient and democratic legislative procedure. The Council under the amended Article 67 EC shall adopt, in accordance with the procedure of Article 251 (qualified majority rule; co-decision of the European Parliament):

—measures on asylum provided for in Art. 63 para. 1 and
—measures on refugees and displaced persons in the area of minimum standards for giving temporary protection to displaced persons from third countries.

The new procedure, however, is subject to the requirement 'that the Council has previously adopted Community legislation determining the common rules and basic principles governing these issues'. Moreover, measures promoting a balance of effort between Member States in receiving and bearing the consequences of receiving refugees and displaced persons have explicitly been excluded from the possibility of accelerated transfer to the co-decision procedure. It follows that majority decisions will only be possible to clarify and implement unanimously adopted rules and principles, primarily on minimum standards of procedures, on reception of asylum seekers, on rules with respect to the qualification as refugees and on criteria for determining which Member State is responsible.

By the end of 2002 only a few legal instruments on asylum had been adopted, in particular in the field of temporary protection and the responsibility of examining asylum applications (Dublin Convention):

—Council Directive 2001/55/EC of 20 July 2001 on minimum standards for giving temporary protection in the event of a mass influx of displaced persons and measures promoting a balance of efforts between Member States in receiving such persons and bearing the consequences thereof.[5]
—Council Decision of 28 September 2000 establishing a European Refugee Fund.[6]

[5] OJ 2001 L212/12. [6] OJ 2000 L252/12.

—Council Regulation No. 2725/2000 of 11 December 2000 concerning the establishment of EURODAC for the comparison of fingerprints for the effective application of the Dublin Convention.[7]
—Council Regulation No. 407/2002 of 28 February 2002 laying down certain rules to implement regulation No. 2725/2000 concerning the establishment of EURODAC for the comparison of fingerprints for the effective application of the Dublin Convention.[8]

The European Commission has also submitted a number of communications and proposals on asylum policy:

—Communication from the Commission to the Council and the European Parliament towards a common asylum procedure and a uniform status valid throughout the European Union, for persons granted asylum, COM(2000)755 of 22 November 2000;
—Communication on the common asylum policy, introducing the open method of co-ordination, COM(2001)710 final of 28 November 2001;
—Amended proposal for a Council Directive on minimum standards on procedures in Member States for granting and withdrawing refugee status, COM(2002)326 final of 28 June 2002;
—Proposal for a Council Directive on minimum standards on procedures in Member States for granting and withdrawing refugee status, COM(2000)578 final of 20 September 2000;
—Proposal for a Council Directive laying down minimum standards on the reception of applicants for asylum in Member States, COM(2002)181 final of 3 April 2001;
—Proposal for a Council Directive on minimum standards for the qualification and status of third-country nationals and stateless persons as refugees or as persons who otherwise need international protection, COM(2001)510 final of 12 September 2001;
—Proposals for a Council Regulation establishing the criteria and mechanisms for determining the Member State responsible for examining an asylum application lodged in one of the Member States by a third-country national, COM(2002)447 final of 26 July 2001.

By the end of February 2003, two proposals had been adopted by the Council: the Council Directive laying down minimum standards for the reception of asylum seekers[9] and a Council Regulation establishing the criteria and mechanisms for determining the Member State responsible

[7] OJ 2000 L316/1. [8] OJ 2002 L62/1.
[9] Council Directive 2003/9/EC of 27 January 2003, OJ 2003 L31/18.

for examining an asylum application lodged in one of the Member States by a third-country national.[10]

In spite of the EU Member States' different legal traditions, concepts, and political views about the ways and means of controlling illegal immigration and adequate procedures for examining applicants for protection, there are common values and principles that may be considered as fundamental to a European asylum law. All EU Member States are parties to the Geneva Convention relating to the status of refugees of 28 July 1951 and the Additional Protocol of 31 January 1967. The Geneva Convention prohibits in Article 33 the expulsion or return (*refoulement*) of a refugee in any manner whatsoever to the frontiers of territories where his life or freedom would be threatened on account of his race, religion, nationality, membership of a particular social group, or political opinion. All EU Member States are also bound by the European Convention on Human Rights (ECHR), which under Article 3 prohibits torture and inhuman and degrading treatment or punishment. The European Court of Human Rights has derived from Article 3 ECHR a prohibition on expulsion or return to countries in which a refugee would be in danger of torture or inhuman or degrading treatment regardless of the responsibility of the state (for instance a lack of sufficient medical treatment for persons suffering from serious diseases). Both Conventions provide a source of principle for the draft directives on qualification as a refugee and asylum procedure. In addition, Article 18 of the Charter of Fundamental Rights of the European Union of 18 December 2000[11] provides:

Art. 18:
The right to asylum shall be guaranteed with due respect for the rules of the Geneva Convention of 28 July 1951 and the Protocol of 31 January 1967, relating to the status of refugees and in accordance with the Treaty establishing the European Community.

In addition, Article 19 provides:

1. Collective expulsions are prohibited.
2. No one may be removed, expelled or extradited to a state where there is serious risk that he or she would be subjected to the death penalty, torture or other inhuman or degrading treatment or punishment.

Although the Charter as yet is not a binding legal instrument, it will probably be adopted as such in the course of the present constitutional reform process.

[10] Council Regulation (EC) No. 343/2003, OJ 2003 L50/1.

[11] OJ 2000 L364/1.

C. Aims and Problems of a Common European Asylum Policy

The aims of a common EU asylum and migration policy have frequently been described in policy guidelines of the Council and the European Commission. The Tampere Presidency Conclusions of October 1999 identified a number of aims, including the necessity of partnerships with countries of origin and the development of a common European asylum system. This system, according to the conclusions, should include:

> A clear and workable determination of the state responsible for the examination of an asylum application, common standards for a fair and efficient asylum procedure, common minimum conditions of reception of asylum seekers, and the approximation of rules on the recognition and content of the refugee status. It should also be completed with measures on subsidiary forms of protection offering an appropriate status to any person in need of such protection.

The conclusions also envisage that, in the longer term, community rules should lead to a common asylum procedure and a uniform status for those who are granted asylum that is valid throughout the Union.

Article 63 of the EC Treaty rests on the assumption that the abolition of international border controls require a harmonization of alien and asylum law. As third-country nationals may move within the European Union without border controls, more or less restrictive national rules on entry and admission will affect all EU Member States. It is not surprising, therefore, that the most significant progress has been achieved in the field of common rules of external border controls (Schengen Agreement) and measures against illegal immigration. Yet, even in the field of rules on entry and admission to the Schengen area there are substantial gaps. In spite of a uniform visa regime within the European Union there are different practices on the issue of visas to third-country nationals which may influence illegal immigration into other EU Member States.

In addition, different rules on, e.g. the reception of refugees, access to social benefits and the labour market, length of asylum procedure, may considerably affect migratory movements within the European Union. Hence, the concept of a European 'area of freedom, security and justice' calls for a harmonization of basic conditions under which applicants for protection are admitted, examined, and returned, should their application turn out to be unfounded. A common European asylum system according to the European Commission must satisfy the following criteria:[12]

- —clear principles offering guarantees to those who are legitimately seeking protection in the European Union

[12] Communication towards a common asylum procedure, COM(2000)755 final of 22 November 2000.

—application of the Geneva Convention in full and inclusively
—fair, effective, and rapid high-quality decision-making to identify those who genuinely need protection
—development of a procedure and a status within the context of a common migration policy that covers all aspects (partnership with countries of origin, fair treatment for third-country nationals, management of migration flows)
—the specificity of humanitarian admissions as distinct from other grounds of admission to be preserved, with respect for the particular demands of humanitarian admission to be balanced against the legitimate objectives of preventing and combating illegal immigration.

The Commission believes that the Member States would be better placed to combat what is presented as a real abuse of the asylum system if they had a wide range of open and transparent immigration management policies taking better account of the economic and demographic situations of the Member States. The Commission further notes that secondary movements influenced solely by the diversity of applicable rules are to be limited. Therefore, divergent asylum policies in the different Member States must disappear and an effort must be made to harmonize conditions in order to avoid negative effects upon the Member States' interests.

To achieve these goals, the Commission proposes a two-stage procedure,[13] in which in the short term some minimum standards are established in all Member States but with the possibility, to a certain extent, of Member States retaining their national procedures and interpretations of certain concepts. In the long term, however, the definition of a common procedure should imply a restriction of the discretion offered to the Member States at the first stage, thus arriving at common standards on appeal, admission procedures, and time limits, as well as on certain concepts such as the 'safe countries of origin' or 'safe third countries'. A 'scoreboard to review progress on the creation of an area of freedom, security and justice in the European Union' was established at Tampere to keep track of legislative developments and to measure them against the aims set in the Treaty or such political documents as the Tampere Conclusions of the Presidency. To reinforce this aim, the Commission in its Communication has already envisaged a so-called 'open co-ordination method' to monitor legislative development in asylum matters. This method is explained in more detail in a Communication of the Commission issued a year later in 2001,[14] which

[13] Ibid. at II, p. 8.

[14] Communication from the Commission to the Council and the European Parliament on the common asylum policy, introducing an open co-ordination method. First Report by the

also constitutes the first report on the implementation of the 2000 Communication.

In a nutshell, the approach implies drawing up strategic guidelines, benchmarking, target-setting, and monitoring mechanisms to evaluate progress. More specifically,[15] it will be up to the Commission, quite apart from establishing the legislative framework by submitting proposals in the asylum area and monitoring enforcement and compliance with legislative acts already in force, to draw up proposals for European guidelines and for the content of national action plans as well as to co-ordinate national policies, while constantly monitoring and evaluating the impact of Community policies. These multi-annual guidelines have to be approved by the Council, together with a short-, medium-, and long-term timetable to meet these aims. The instruments for implementing these guidelines are national action plans which will have to be re-examined and adjusted annually, by reviewing action in earlier years and proposing measures for further years at the national, regional, and local level, again framed by a timetable. Moreover, the European institutions will be involved in the development of asylum policy by regularly being updated and consulted on progress in this area, as will the UNHCR and 'civil society', who will be invited to participate actively in framing the future asylum policy.

Finally, the Commission recommends that the Council set deadlines for adopting instruments for the first stage of harmonization in asylum matters.[16]

D. Fortress Europe?

Developments at the Community level have constantly been monitored and commented on by international bodies such as UNHCR, the Council of Europe, and by NGOs such as the European Council on Refugees and Exiles (ECRE).[17] There have been wide criticisms, especially from those bodies which as a policy voice the concerns of refugees and other persons in need of protection or which are concerned with human rights law.

Commission on the application of Communication COM(2000)755 final of 22 November 2000, 28 November 2001, COM(2001)710 final, available at http://europa.eu.int/eur-lex/en/com/cnc/2001/com2001_0710en01.pdf.

[15] Ibid. at V, pp. 16–22.

[16] Ibid. at VI, pp. 21–22.

[17] See ECRE, 'Taking stock of the harmonization process at the end of the Danish presidency: the European Union must make decisions to preserve the integrity of its asylum policies', 19 December 2002, available at http://www.ecre.org/eu_developments/presidencies/assessment.doc.

On various occasions, UNHCR has expressed its concern about the 'dichotomy' of European asylum policy:[18] Member States have made many efforts to stop illegal immigration by imposing 'external' controls such as visa policies and documentation checks, 'externalized' controls such as carrier sanctions and readmission agreements, and 'internal' controls including employer sanctions and the invocation of notions such as 'safe third country' or 'safe country of origin' together with special, accelerated procedures in cases of 'manifestly unfounded asylum claims'.[19] While UNHCR does not deny the need for the European Member States effectively to combat illegal immigration, it is concerned that those migration control measures fail to distinguish between refugees and non-refugee migrants and thus undermine the foundations of the refugee protection regime.[20] Academic writers[21] have also voiced concerns that such restrictive measures, however legitimate they may be from the perspective of public international law, may result in a violation of the principle of non-*refoulement* if they are not properly reconciled with the individual's right to asylum. Furthermore, UNHCR is concerned about the example the European Member States have thus set for the (mostly) economically weaker rest of the world: it is agreed that the application of the 'safe third country' rule can hardly be reconciled with the notion of fair burden sharing within Europe, at least *vis-à-vis* applicant countries in

[18] E.g. in its paper 'Managing Migration in The Wider Europe: A Refugee Protection Perspective', Geneva, November 1998; for a comprehensive assessment see UNHCR, *Towards a Common European Asylum System*, Geneva, December 2002.

[19] Amnesty International in a 1999 Report provided some additional examples of hindering asylum seekers from effectively arriving at their destination, such as immediate controls at the aeroplane door in Switzerland and France to prevent asylum seekers who do not possess all the documents considered necessary for processing their asylum claim inside the country, as well as the English example of detention centres at isolated places to prevent asylum seekers from gaining access to community groups and lawyers which are specialized in this area.

The Council of Europe, Committee on Migration, Refugees and Demography in its paper of 15 November 1999, AS/Mig (1999) 32 rev., expressly voices its concerns regarding such measures, at II.3.: 'visa requirements may prevent legal departure from the country of origin. On the other hand, if the asylum seeker obtains a visa, the fact that he or she departed legally may undermine the validity of the asylum claim on arrival.... Where asylum seekers are forced to flee persecution without the requisite documentation, it is virtually impossible for them to travel by air since airlines are required to check that documentation is valid before allowing passengers to board.... Travel through different countries may also result in access to asylum procedures in the country of destination being denied because of the application of the "safe third country" or similar restrictive principles...'; see also Amnesty International, *Missing: A Common Asylum Policy that is Ambitious, Coherent and Protection-centred*, Brussels, November 2002.

[20] UNHCR, *supra* note 18, III., p. 4.

[21] Such as J. van der Klaauw, 'Refugee Protection in Western Europe: A UNHCR Perspective', in J.-Y. Carlier and D. Vanheule (eds), *Europe and Refugees: A Challenge?* (The Hague: Kluwer, 1997), at 232.

Central and Eastern Europe, which have to bear the main consequences of the abovementioned European policy.[22]

Finally, some organizations have voiced concerns on the conclusion of readmission agreements between the EU and other countries in which asylum seekers originate or through which they transit.[23] They fear that these agreements in certain cases prevent the asylum seeker gaining access to the refugee determination procedure in the country to which he is returned, because in some cases 'chain deportations' are organized and the asylum seeker straight away finds himself back in the country of origin from which he fled a short time previously and where his protection is not guaranteed.[24]

By and large, these concerns are unjustified. Although it may be too early to evaluate the effects of a common European asylum policy in the absence of a sufficient number of binding legal instruments, it is clear that measures that have been undertaken in the field of common visa requirements, readmission agreements, prevention against trafficking in human beings, and the like have not created an insurmountable barrier for third-country nationals seeking protection in the European Union. The number of asylum applications in the EU has risen again since mid-1996. There is no evidence supporting the assumption that visa requirements and carrier sanctions have produced a 'fortress Europe'. The first binding legal instrument, the Directive on Temporary Protection, although falling short of satisfying the need for a comprehensive legal instrument for the management of mass refugee movements, for the first time has created a framework for co-ordinated action by the EU Member States in the event of mass refugee movements.

The political agreements reached by the end of 2002 on substantial principles of the draft directives on reception of asylum seekers, qualification of refugees, and the responsibility for processing asylum claims do not support the theory of 'a lowest common denominator' harmonization. As comparative surveys indicate, the prospect of a common European asylum system already has produced harmonization effects in the national legislation. For the first time, all EU Member States have agreed on common minimum

[22] See also Council of Europe, *supra* note 19, at II. 5., p. 5; European Parliament, *Report on the Commission Working Document entitled 'Towards common standards on asylum procedures'*, SEC(1999)271, Committee on Citizens' Freedoms and Rights, Justice and Home Affairs, Rapporteur: Ingo Schmitt; FINAL A5-0123/2000, at III, pp. 12–13.

[23] Council of Europe, *supra* note 19, at II. 7, p. 6; ECRE, 'Comments by the European Council on Refugees and Exiles on the Working Document by the Committee on Citizens' Freedoms and Rights, Justice and Home Affairs'.

[24] For these reasons, it is UNHCR's position that the return of asylum seekers should only take place after the sending state has established that the receiving state will admit the asylum seeker to its territory, will observe the principle of non-*refoulement*, and will consider the claim and eventually allow the asylum seeker to remain as a refugee: see Council of Europe, *supra* note 19, at II. 7, p. 6.

standards on the treatment of asylum seekers with respect to social benefits. In the area of definition of refugees, agreement could be reached on basic principles to identify persons in need of protection which will enable more clarity and transparency in the asylum procedure.

In summary, there are no indications as yet that the common European asylum system will result in a reduction of the chances for genuine asylum seekers to seek protection within the European Union. As the Commission has rightly observed, the decline in admissions to refugee status as a proportion of total admission in the European Union cannot be explained by a more and more restrictive interpretation of the Geneva Convention in such situations. For one thing, requests originating from easily identifiable *Verfolgerstaaten* continue to correspond to high admission rates. For another, trends in decision-making suggest that new situations are being brought within the Geneva Convention.[25] In addition, there are new forms of subsidiary protection in order to give applicants temporary or provisional protection even if their demands do not fit within the criteria of the Geneva Convention.

2. SUBSTANTIVE ASYLUM LAW

A. Identifying Persons in Need of Protection

The substantive content of the Commission's Proposal on recognition of refugees builds upon the Joint Position of 4 March 1996 promulgated under Article K.3 of the Maastricht Treaty on the harmonized application of the definition of the term 'refugee' in Article 1 of the Geneva Convention ('the Joint Position'). Despite the adoption of the Joint Position large differences remain in the way Member States interpret provisions of the Geneva Convention and their ambit, for example, in the area of non-state agents of persecution and the area of gender-based persecution. The Commission's Proposal seeks to eradicate divergent concepts and practices. The Explanatory Memorandum to the Proposal indicates that the Handbook on Procedures and Criteria for Determining Refugee Status of the Office of the UNHCR and the Conclusions of the Executive Committee of the UNHCR were also used in shaping the substantive principles of asylum law contained in the Proposal.

The Proposal deals with both protection in the form of recognition as a refugee within the meaning of the Geneva Convention and forms of subsidiary protection. The Proposal uses the term 'international protection' to refer

[25] See for instance the decision of the German Constitutional Court concerning political persecution in Afghanistan by quasi-state authorities: see Judgment of 18.10.2000, *Informationsbrief Ausländerrecht* 2000, 521.

jointly to the two types of protection,[26] although strictly speaking the term 'international protection' is not correct since international protection, as distinct from protection by states, is the sole responsibility of the UNHCR.[27] The Proposal further assumes that a person who applies for protection by a Member State is in fact applying for international protection more generally, that is, unless the person explicitly indicates otherwise, the application relates to both refugee status and subsidiary protection. As noted by some commentators, this presumption follows as a matter of course from considerations of procedural fairness.[28]

The Proposal has been criticized for applying only to third-country nationals and stateless persons and not to citizens of Member States. This limitation is reflected in the definition of 'refugee' in Article 2(c) as well as the provisions governing subsidiary protection. UNHCR has noted that, while it is extremely unlikely that nationals of EU Member States would have any valid claim to asylum or subsidiary protection, this would present no basis for excluding EU nationals from the definition.[29]

B. Definition of 'Refugee' according to the Geneva Convention

The Proposal addresses many of the issues in substantive asylum law which have given rise to divergence in state practice, both within the EU and within the wider international community. It is with regard to the concept of persecution that the principles stipulated by the Proposal are most significant.

The Proposal adopts the established grounds for persecution that are set out in the definition of refugee under the Geneva Convention.[30] In Article 12 it elaborates on the content of each of those grounds in a non-exhaustive fashion, and in a way which reflects a broad understanding of the notion of persecution. The UNHCR has indicated its general agreement with the clarification of the grounds given in Article 12.[31] It is perhaps worth commenting on two of the grounds in particular. A particular social group includes a group defined either by relation to certain fundamental characteristics (e.g. age, gender, sexual orientation) or by the sharing of a common

[26] Art. 2(g) of the Proposal for a Council Directive on minimum standards for the qualification and status of third country nationals and stateless persons as refugees or as persons who otherwise need international protection, COM (2001) 510 final.

[27] UNHCR's Observations on the European Commission's proposal for a Council Directive on minimum standards for the qualification and status of third-country nationals and stateless persons as refugees or as persons who otherwise need international protection, Geneva, November 2001, p. 4.

[28] H. Storey, Seminar Outline Paper on behalf of the IARLJ, *Complementary Protection: Should There be a Common Approach to Providing Protection to Persons who are not Covered by the 1951 Geneva Convention?*, p. 15.

[29] *Supra* note 27, at 4.

[30] Art. 5(1) of the Proposal, COM (2001) 510.

[31] *Supra* note 27, at 10.

characteristic or background that is so fundamental to identity or conscience that it should not need to be renounced in order to avoid persecution.[32] The Explanatory Memorandum indicates that the application of the former category will depend on the particular circumstances in the country of origin and the characteristics of the actors involved. The latter category is designed to encompass situations in which a group of people suffer persecution from non-state actors because they enjoy inferior protection by the law, or because the state uses the law in a discriminatory manner. This aspect of the definition of particular social group overlaps with the nature of persecution as defined in Article 11(1)(b). Political opinion is defined in Article 12(5) to include imputed political opinion or action, and again this is a specific example of the general principle concerning the nature of persecution set out in Article 11(2)(b).

Possible forms that persecution can take, such that the persecution will be considered to be objectively well founded, are listed in Article 11 of the Proposal. Article 11 is intended to be flexible and sufficiently open so that new forms of persecution will fall within it.[33] Broadly speaking Article 11 distinguishes between three forms of persecution: intentional and sustained or systematic acts; legal, administrative, or judicial policies that are discriminatory on their face or are discriminatorily implemented; and criminal prosecutions or punishments which are discriminatory or impede the exercise of a fundamental international human right. Article 11 contains a special provision for refusal to perform military service in situations of war or conflict. Article 7(4) of the Proposal is also relevant to a consideration of forms of persecution because it recognizes that they can be gender specific.

In addition to the general forms of persecution, Article 11 sets out three general principles regarding persecution, not all of which are currently applied by Member States. First, the Proposal recognizes that persecution may stem from non-state actors where the state is unable or unwilling to provide effective protection, or from parties and organizations controlling the state. Secondly, persecution may take place on a ground that is imputed to the victim by the agent and, lastly, persecution may take place even though *all* persons in a particular country face generalized oppression. The Explanatory Memorandum makes clear that the last principle is designed to assist in the recognition as refugees of people who have fled situations of large-scale oppression and violence.

The first of the general principles outlined above is itself the subject of an earlier Article in the Proposal, and applies to the assessment of the need for subsidiary protection as well. Article 9(1)(c) and (2) of the Proposal deals in particular with the issue of persecution by non-state actors and the circumstances in which the protection provided by a state against such persecution

[32] Art. 12(4) of the Proposal.

[33] Explanatory Memorandum, comment to Art. 11, COM (2001) 510.

may be considered effective. The Explanatory Memorandum to the Proposal contains an extensive list of factors which should be taken into account in determining whether effective protection within the meaning of Article 9(2) exists. Article 9(3) represents, according to the Explanatory Memorandum, a logical extension of Article 9(2), in that it foresees that in limited circumstances non-state actors may potentially offer protection against persecution. This provision has been criticized by the UNHCR as being inappropriate because the control exercised by non-state actors is often more temporary and less extensive than the sovereignty exercised by a state.[34]

With respect to *sur place* claims, the Proposal recognizes in Article 8 that grounds for recognition as a refugee or the grant of subsidiary protection may arise after people leave their country of origin. Article 8(2) deals with those situations in which the grounds for protection arise as a result of an individual's activities since leaving the country of origin, and makes an exception for activities which are engaged in for the sole purpose of creating a need for protection. This exception is designed to deal with the abuse in *sur place* cases, although in the view of some commentators it would have been preferable to deal with the issue of abuse through the making of appropriate credibility assessments and consideration of burden of proof issues in individual cases.[35]

The Proposal in Article 7 explicitly refers to the matters which must be taken into account when assessing whether the persecution or the need for subsidiary protection is objectively well founded. This aspect of the Proposal would appear to be unique as it is the first time that such matters would be included in a legislative document; hitherto in most Member States they have been developed in judicial decisions on asylum. The Explanatory Memorandum indicates that in drafting Article 7 regard was had to the text of the Geneva Convention, the Joint Position and the UNHCR Handbook. Article 7(2) defines the well-foundedness of a fear of persecution or serious and unjustified harm (the criterion for subsidiary protection) in terms of a *reasonable possibility* that the applicant will be persecuted or subjected to harm if he or she returns to the country of origin. The Explanatory Memorandum clarifies that this definition does not require that there be a clear probability of persecution or harm, although a mere chance or remote possibility is not sufficient.

Article 7(4) requires a holistic approach to the assessment of the well-foundedness of the fear, in light of the particular circumstances of the case and bearing in mind the specific forms in which persecution of women and children in particular may be manifested. The provision expressly indicates that persecution within the Geneva Convention may be effected through sexual violence or other gender-specific means. Article 7(5) requires consideration of any credible evidence that the law in force and applied in the country

[34] *Supra* note 27, at 9. [35] Ibid., at 8.

of origin authorizes or condones the persecution or infliction of harm. UNHCR has expressed concern that this consideration may mislead because persecution often results from an arbitrary or discriminatory application of the law.[36]

With regard to the cessation and exclusion of refugee status the Proposal substantially adopts in Articles 13 and 14 the provisions of Articles 1C and 1F of the Geneva Convention respectively.[37] The Proposal stipulates the fault requirement of 'personal knowing conduct' for crimes, on the basis of which a person is to be excluded. In this regard the Proposal draws upon well-accepted principles of public international law.

C. Subsidiary Protection

The topic of subsidiary protection has attracted increasing attention within Europe and the wider international community. Subsidiary protection is generally understood to include complementary forms of human rights and humanitarian protection that a state may grant when a person does not satisfy the requirements for refugee status under the Geneva Convention. Although public international law is not completely silent on the topic, it does not provide a comprehensive legislative framework for subsidiary protection.[38] As a result, a wide divergence in state practice—in the forms of, and the circumstances in which, subsidiary protection is granted—has emerged both at the international and at the regional level. Within Europe the need for harmonization of forms of subsidiary protection has long been recognized. In 1988 the Parliamentary Assembly of the Council of Europe recommended that the Committee of Ministers 'examine the possibility of preparing a European Convention, including the establishment of a consultative body, dealing with people falling outside the scope of the Geneva Convention, but requiring protection and on whose fate the Council of Europe, under the term "de-facto refugees" has been proposing concrete measures for many years'.[39]

The provisions in the Proposal concerning subsidiary protection represent the first concrete European initiative to protect those who fall outside the

[36] Ibid., at 7.

[37] The UNHCR has pointed to a minor discrepancy between Art. 14 and Art. 1F of the Convention, in that the Proposal does not require the Member State to have acceded to or to have ratified the international instrument defining the crime which is considered to be committed: *supra* note 27, at 10.

[38] K. Hailbronner, 'Principles of International Law Regarding the Concept of Subsidiary Protection', in D. Bouteillet-Paquet (ed.), *Subsidiary Protection of Refugees in the European Union: Complementing The Geneva Convention?* (Brussels: Bruylant, 2002), p. 1 *et seq.*

[39] Recommendation 1088 of the Parliamentary Assembly, cited in European Council on Refugees and Exiles 'On the need for a Complementary Protection Mechanism'.

refugee definition.[40] There are different explanations for the emergence of subsidiary protection as a legal institution and the suitability of the concept. On one view subsidiary protection has arisen as an issue because of the increasingly narrow interpretation that Member States give to the definition of refugee. There is no factual evidence supporting this theory. Nevertheless, states may consider subsidiary protection a more suitable mechanism for matching their public interests with the humanitarian interests of refugees.[41] Another view would attribute the rise of subsidiary protection to the emergence of new protection needs which cannot be encompassed even by a liberal and purposive interpretation of the Geneva Convention.

Whatever the actual reasons for the increasing use of the institution of subsidiary protection may be, there are fundamentally two ways in which the institution may be approached. One alternative is to regard it as an expansion of refugee status. According to this approach the scope of subsidiary protection is governed by an expanded definition of refugee and is consequently rather broad. The other approach is to regard it as an expression of human rights obligations incumbent on Member States under public international law, primarily Article 3 ECHR and/or Article 3 of the Convention against Torture. The scope of subsidiary protection with this second approach is less open-ended and is able to be more easily determined through political initiative and discretion.[42] A perusal of the provisions of the Proposal dealing with subsidiary protection shows that it clearly has the former approach in mind, which is also favoured by some commentators.[43]

Pursuant to Article 5(1) of the European Commission's Proposal, a person is entitled to subsidiary protection where he or she does not qualify for recognition as a refugee (or has not sought such recognition) yet nonetheless has a well-founded fear of suffering serious and unjustified harm. Article 15 then specifies three possible forms the serious and unjustified harm may take. The Explanatory Memorandum states by way of background that the forms of harm, which are informed by the obligations arising from the ECHR and the jurisprudence of the European Court of Human Rights, represent a clarification and codification of existing practice. Each form will be examined in turn.

The first form of harm mentioned in Article 15(a), torture or inhuman or degrading treatment or punishment, reflects the content of Article 3 of the ECHR. The Explanatory Memorandum indicates that in determining whether this criterion is satisfied Member States should not apply a more

[40] ECRE, 'On the need for a Complementary Protection Mechanism', European Council on Refugees and Exiles.

[41] Hailbronner, *supra* note 38, at 1.

[42] Ibid., at 5.

[43] ECRE and the UNHCR favour the first approach.

exacting standard than is required by the ECHR. The judgments of the European Court of Human Rights reveal, however, considerable confusion surrounding the application of Article 3 ECHR, in particular concerning whether the effective denial of adequate medical treatment through deportation constitutes inhuman or degrading treatment.[44] It is desirable that Article 15(a) of the Proposal provide more precise guidelines on the nature of inhuman and degrading treatment generally. In so far as the Proposal foresees admission to Member States as a result of a need for protection against this type of harm, it represents an extension of current international law principles. The European Court of Human Rights has in relation to Article 3 ECHR, for instance, recognized only a right to prevent expulsion, rather than to compel admission.[45]

Article 15(b) addresses serious or unjustified harm resulting from a violation of a human right which is sufficiently severe to engage a Member State's international obligations. This formulation begs the question which international obligations could be relevant in this context. On the one hand there is general recognition by Member States, in relation to certain fundamental human rights at least, of a duty not to expose a person to a concrete and imminent violation of those rights. So far this recognition has clearly extended—outside the scope of the Geneva Convention—only to torture or inhuman or degrading treatment as covered by Article 3 ECHR. On the other hand, state practice also demonstrates that a general violation of human rights is not in itself sufficient to give rise to a duty of protection.

The last form of harm to be covered by Article 15(c) is a threat to life, safety, or freedom as a result of indiscriminate violence arising in situations of armed conflict, or as a result of systematic or generalized violations of human rights. The Explanatory Memorandum explains that this provision is taken from Article 2(c) of the Council Directive on minimum standards for giving temporary protection in the event of a mass influx of displaced persons. Temporary protection is, however, to be distinguished from subsidiary protection. It represents an exceptional, stop-gap, emergency measure in which it is not possible to determine protection needs on an individual basis;[46] whereas subsidiary protection is potentially a long-term measure which depends on an individual assessment of protection needs—in the context of Article 15(c), a determination in each particular case of a well-founded fear for life, safety or freedom.

In this respect Article 15(c) does not recognize a general duty to protect victims of civil war or systematic violence or human rights violations, so as to give rise to an individual right to such protection. Indeed, were the Proposal

[44] Hailbronner, *supra* note 38, at 6. [45] Ibid., at 7.

[46] UNHCR, *The International Protection of Refugees: Complementary Forms of Protection*, at 6.

to go this far, it would greatly exceed the current ambit of public international law. Such general humanitarian protection is rightly regarded as a prerogative of the state.[47] The requirement in Article 15(c) of a well-founded fear for life, safety, or freedom narrows the scope of subsidiary protection so that it is consistent with that of the particular circumstances in which subsidiary protection is currently recognized, for example, inhuman or degrading treatment or an imminent and concrete danger of gross human rights violations. This would suggest that Article 15(c) overlaps to a large extent with Article 15(a) and (b).

On 26 November 2002 a political agreement was reached on a proposal for a Council directive which contains several substantial changes to the Commission's Proposal.[48] The conditions to qualify for subsidiary protection have been substantially tightened by including a provision whereby serious harm consists of:

—death penalty or execution; or
—torture or inhuman or degrading treatment or punishment of an applicant in his or her country of origin, or in the case of a stateless person, in his or her country of former habitual residence; or
—serious and individual threat to a civilian's life or person by reason of indiscriminate violence in situations of international or internal armed conflict.

The amended Proposal, if adopted, would eliminate some of the concerns previously mentioned. In particular, the somewhat vague reference to a violation of human rights has been replaced by the more concrete and generally recognized cases of death penalty and torture or inhuman or degrading treatment.

The Commission's Proposal in Article 17 excludes persons from subsidiary protection status on substantially the same terms that are set out in the Geneva Convention. Article 17(5) makes the provision subject to obligations which Member States may have under international law and is designed to allow the Proposal to give effect to absolute and unlimited protection obligations, for example, that arising under Article 3 ECHR. The exclusion provision as amended by the Council has deleted this reference. Under Article 17 (1)(d) a third-country national is excluded from being a person eligible for subsidiary protection, where there are serious reasons for considering that he/she constitutes a danger to the community or to the security of the country in which he/she is. This provision, obviously intended to cover dangers of terrorism, strangely refers only to the country of residence. One would expect that, in a European context, exclusion clauses refer not only to the country of

[47] Hailbronner, *supra* note 38, at 11 and 12.
[48] Council DOC 14643/1/02 of 26 November 2002.

residence, but to the whole European Union. A similarly strange restriction can be found in Article 14(b) of the amended Council Proposal on revocation, termination, or refusal to renew the refugee status of a third-country national. Article 14(b)(4) authorizes Member States to revoke refugee status when there are reasonable grounds for regarding the person in question as a danger to the security of the EU Member State in which he or she is situated. Does that really mean that German authorities may not revoke the refugee status of a person presenting a concrete danger to the security of the neighbouring EU Member States?

D. Content of International Protection

An important aspect of substantive asylum law is the nature and extent of the practical and legal protection which is afforded to a person who has been recognized as a beneficiary. The content of the two protection statuses recognized by the Proposal is defined in Chapter 3, which is expressed to be without prejudice to rights contained in the Geneva Convention. In addition to the basic protection against *refoulement*, the Protocol provides that beneficiaries of international protection shall be granted residence permits, travel documents, access to employment, education, integration facilities, and social welfare and health services. Although these benefits would appear to meet the standards adopted by the UNHCR,[49] they are not required by customary international law.[50] Nor is there any public international law principle requiring these benefits to be extended to the accompanying family members of beneficiaries of subsidiary protection, as laid down Article 18(2).[51]

The Commission's Proposal envisages further that beneficiaries of subsidiary protection will enjoy substantially the same rights as refugees. To this general position the Proposal contains three exceptions. First, residence permits for subsidiary protection status must only be valid for a year and thereafter renewable yearly, provided that the need for protection still exists; whereas residence permits for refugee status must be valid for five years and renewable automatically.[52] This distinction is to some extent ameliorated by the obligation in Article 22 to grant beneficiaries of subsidiary protection long-term residence status on the terms applicable to refugees. The other two exceptions to the equality of the protection statuses relate to access to the labour market, which is to follow immediately upon recognition of refugee

49 UNHCR, *supra* note 46, at 5.
50 Hailbronner, *supra* note 38, at 7.
51 Ibid., at 9.
52 Art. 21.

status but is to be delayed by six months for those of subsidiary protection status,[53] and access to integration programmes, which is also to be delayed—in this case for one year—for beneficiaries of subsidiary protection.[54] The content of subsidiary protection status has been substantially changed during Council debates. One provision concerns the family unit. The Proposal as discussed by Council suggests in Article 21(a) that 'Member States shall ensure that family members of the same nationality as the beneficiary' of refugee or subsidiary protection status are entitled to a status which enables them to stay with the beneficiary. The Member State with the largest number of persons admitted on subsidiary protection has suggested, however, that family reunion be restricted to those family members who have lodged their application for international protection before or at the same time as the refugee or without any delay after entering the territory of the Member State, and if a marriage or a stable relationship with an unmarried partner already existed in the country of origin of the refugee or his/her spouse or unmarried partner. In addition, children born on the territory should receive the same status.

Another controversial issue is access to employment of persons enjoying subsidiary protection status. As noted, the Proposal as discussed by the Council in November 2002 provides for access of persons enjoying subsidiary protection status under the same conditions as nationals no later than six months after such status is granted. There are, however, reservations. Some Member States do want to avoid any link between duration of stay and access to work. Other Member States want a longer time limit. Equally, the last word has not yet been said on the proposed Article 26 on social welfare, whereby Member States shall ensure that persons enjoying international protection receive, under the same conditions as nationals of the Member State that has granted the protection, the necessary assistance in terms of social welfare and means of subsistence. Generally, clauses on equal treatment with nationals concerning social welfare, health, and psychological care, and other social benefits do highlight serious issues concerning those Member States which practise different treatment of persons recognized as Convention refugees and those receiving only temporary protection on the basis of a subsidiary protection status.

The differences in the protection standard result from the view, held by a majority of Member States, that subsidiary protection is temporary.[55] Yet as UNHCR points out, in reality the duration of subsidiary protection is often just as lengthy as protection under the Geneva Convention.[56] Article 22 of the Commission's Proposal is based on the consideration that the needs and

53 Art. 24(1) and (3). 54 Art. 31.

55 Explanatory Memorandum, comment to Art. 21, COM (2001) 510.

56 *Supra* note 27, at 11.

circumstances of beneficiaries of subsidiary protection are much the same as those of refugees, and that after five years have elapsed their need for protection can no longer be considered temporary.[57] The latter argument, that beneficiaries of subsidiary protection are in a comparable situation to refugees, is also advanced by commentators who urge that there should be no distinction in the protection afforded by each status.

On the other hand, there is clearly a need to limit residence rights according to actual protection needs. For that reason Member States have a legitimate right to prevent *de facto* immigration when only provisional protection is needed. This should, however, apply to the Geneva Convention refugees as well as persons in need of subsidiary protection. This would require a deviation from the traditional concept of Convention refugees enjoying permanent residence in contrast to other refugees enjoying only temporary protection.

3. ASYLUM PROCEDURE

A. Temporary Protection Directive

Directive 2001/55/EC[58] is the first legal instrument in asylum law to be passed in the legislative programme since Tampere. Its content was influenced by the experience of the reception of displaced persons from Yugoslavia in the last decade, many of whom received temporary protection on the basis of different national admission programmes. The Directive is intended as an effective instrument of temporary protection for displaced persons in the context of mass refugee movements and at the same time as a framework for (voluntary) burden sharing.

In view of the specific character of a mass influx of displaced persons, protection is of limited duration. It is limited to one year, but may be extended automatically by six months or by one year on the basis of a Council decision.[59] Maximum duration is one year, but a Council decision adopted by a qualified majority can terminate protection,[60] provided that the situation in the country of origin permits a safe and enduring return with due respect for human rights and fundamental freedoms.[61]

[57] Explanatory Memorandum, comment to Art. 22, COM (2001) 510.

[58] Council Directive 2001/55/EC of 20 July 2001 on minimum standards for giving temporary protection in the event of a mass influx of displaced persons on measures promoting a balance of efforts between Member States in receiving such persons and bearing the consequences thereof: OJ 2001 L212/12.

[59] Art. 4 of the Directive.

[60] Art. 6(1)(b) of the Directive.

[61] Art. 6(2) of the Directive.

In order to secure Europe-wide agreement on the necessity of the admission of displaced persons, the existence of the situation of a mass influx shall be established by a Council decision adopted by a qualified majority on a proposal from the Commission, which is binding upon all Member States. The decision has to describe the specific group of persons to whom admission is granted, establish when protection should commence and include information from the Member States on their reception capacity.

Although the Council decision is binding upon all Member States, there is no obligation to admit a specific number of persons within the scope of application of the Directive. The decision to admit rests on the information of Member States on their reception capacity. Particulars of the procedure are laid down in Chapter VI on solidarity. Member States admit persons being in need of temporary protection in a spirit of 'Community Solidarity'. They indicate—in figures or in general terms—their reception capacity. This information shall be set out in the Council decision. Once this decision has been adopted, Member States may indicate additional reception capacity by notifying the Council and the Commission. Thus, only persons listed in the information of the Member States qualify for admission. If the number of those who are eligible for temporary protection exceeds the reception capacity according to the Council decision, following a sudden and massive influx, the Council shall, as a matter of urgency, examine the situation and take appropriate action, including the recommendation of additional support for Member States affected.

This procedure means a step towards a European system of burden sharing in the event of a mass influx. It is, however, far from Community solidarity. In particular, there is no mechanism within the Directive to enable a distribution of financial burdens resulting from the admission of refugees to the Member States.

In addition to residence rights Member States have to grant displaced persons access to employment. For reasons of labour market policies, they may give priority to EU citizens, citizens of states parties to the Agreement on the European Economic Area, and to legally resident third-country nationals who receive unemployment benefit.[62] Family reunification comes into consideration only in cases where family units already existed in the country of origin. Provided this is the case, it does not affect eligibility that family members are presently based in different Member States or that they are not yet in a Member State.[63]

The Directive governs the relationship between temporary protection and asylum procedure. An asylum application is also admissible within the scope of temporary sojourn in the EU.[64] The criteria and mechanisms of the

[62] Art. 12 of the Directive.
[63] Art. 15 of the Directive.
[64] Art. 17 of the Directive.

Dublin Convention are applicable. The Member State responsible for examining an asylum application shall be the Member State that has accepted transfer of the displaced person onto its territory.[65]

As protection is temporary, principles and measures for the return to the country of origin are envisaged. Voluntary return in full knowledge of the facts is preferable.[66] If voluntary return cannot be arranged, enforced return is provided for.[67] The European Refugee Fund provides for financial means to support measures according to the Directive.[68] The Directive required implementation by national legislation by the end of 2002.

B. Harmonization of Asylum Procedures

The harmonization of asylum procedures is of paramount importance for a common asylum system, first, because common or at least similar procedures help to prevent secondary movements, secondly as a matter of non-discrimination on a European level because asylum seekers upon entry into force of the Dublin Convention are no longer able freely to choose their country of application, and thirdly to enable in the long run a follow-up EC legislative act to the Dublin Convention which defines the Member State responsible for examining an asylum application according to the country in which the asylum seeker has applied for protection. Such a system can work only in a balanced manner, without imposing very different burdens on Member States, if there are no incentives for asylum seekers to choose one country rather than another because of better protection guarantees, shorter asylum procedures, or the incentive to be able to stay in a country due to lax enforcement of expulsion decisions even after a claim has been rejected.

In September 2000, the Commission put forward a Proposal for a directive on minimum standards for asylum procedures[69] in which several procedural aspects suitable for harmonization are addressed. First, the Proposal deals with certain guarantees, some of which seem self-explanatory,[70] while others are more controversial, such as the right to remain at the border or in the

[65] Art. 18 of the Directive.

[66] Art. 21 of the Directive.

[67] Art. 22 of the Directive. But Member States shall prove whether any compelling humanitarian reasons are opposed to return, Art. 22(2), or whether the respective persons cannot, in view of their state of health, reasonably be expected to travel, Art. 23(1). Moreover, the Member States may adjourn the return of families whose children are minors until the children concerned complete a current school period, Art. 23(2).

[68] Art. 24 of the Directive.

[69] Proposal for a Council Directive on minimum standards on procedures in Member States for granting and withdrawing refugee status of 20 September 2000, COM(2000)578 final, available at http://europa.eu.int/eur-lex/en/com/pdf/2000/en_500PC0578.pdf.

[70] Such as Art. 7 including the right to an interpreter or Art. 6 on individual, objective, and impartial decisions on applications for asylum.

territory of the Member State in which the asylum application is examined until a final decision,[71] the exclusion of time limits for filing asylum applications,[72] or the right to be notified in writing of decisions on applications for asylum.[73]

In particular, the proposals for a three-stage procedure consisting of a 'determining authority', a 'reviewing body', and an 'appellate court'[74] have provoked heavy resistance from some Member States. The declaration of the Laeken European Council has requested the Commission to bring forward a modified proposal.[75] The 2002 modified proposal subsequently made a number of important changes taking account of the objections of some Member States. The Draft Directive is divided into three major parts. Chapters I and II in the first part contain rules on scope and definitions as well as basic principles and guarantees. A second part (Chapter III) deals with procedures at first instance regulating different types of procedure (accelerated procedure, application of the concept of first country of asylum, application of the safe third-country concept, subsequent applications, border procedures). A third part (chapter IV) determines appeal procedures, in particular the right to a remedy before a court of law.

Most guarantees in the first part have been modified following suggestions of Member States and the European Parliament. Article 5 guarantees access to the procedure. An application cannot be rejected on the sole ground that it has not been made as soon as possible. This does not exclude time limits as such, but only in so far as they may be used to circumvent an appropriate examination of an application.[76] Article 6 provides for a right to stay pending the examination of the application by the determining authority. By a new provision, however, Member States have been allowed to establish a special procedure for subsequent applications. By a preliminary examination Member States will be allowed to examine whether or not there is reasonable cause to reopen the asylum procedure. From the moment it is decided not to do so, Member States will be free to remove applicants from their territory. Several provisions deal with the guarantees for asylum applicants (right to a personal interview, legal assistance, guarantees for unaccompanied minors). The right to be granted legal assistance free of charge has been restricted by the right of Member States to make available legal assistance only to those who lack sufficient resources and in so far as such assistance is necessary to ensure their effective access to justice. In addition, free legal

[71] Art. 5 of the Proposal.

[72] Art. 4(1) of the Proposal and the Commission's comments on that Art. at 11.

[73] Art. 7(d), (e) and (f) of the Proposal.

[74] See Chapter V and Art. 2(d), (e) and (f) of the Proposal.

[75] Amended Proposal for a Council Directive of 18 June 2002, COM (2002) 326 final.

[76] See Explanatory Memorandum of the amended Proposal, comment to Art. 5, COM (2002) 326 final.

assistance may be restricted to legal advisers specifically designated by national law.[77] In some contrast to the practice of certain Member States Article 16 introduces the concept of the 'benefit of the doubt', if the following conditions are met:

—the applicant has made a genuine effort to substantiate his claim;
—all available evidence has been obtained and, where possible, checked; and
—the examiner is satisfied that the applicant's statements are coherent and plausible and do not run counter to generally known facts relevant to his/her case.

The issue of detention pending a decision by the determining authority has been resolved by the principle that Member States shall not hold an applicant in detention for the sole reason that his application for asylum needs to be examined before a decision is taken by the determining authorities. Member States are allowed to hold an applicant for asylum in detention during the examination of the application where such detention is 'objectively necessary for an efficient examination of the application' or where there is 'a strong likelihood of his absconding'.[78] In addition, Member States may hold an applicant in detention if there are grounds for believing that the restriction on his freedom of movement is necessary for a quick decision to be made (up to two weeks).

Concerning the procedure at first instance the modified proposal largely follows Council conclusions providing for the possibility of introducing accelerated and regular procedures. Instead of a separate admissibility procedure (rejection of an asylum application primarily in the application of the first country of asylum concept), such applications may be processed in accelerated procedures. In addition, applications considered to be manifestly unfounded may be processed in accelerated procedures. Special standards on two new types of accelerated procedures have been introduced: a procedure to examine applications lodged at the border or at the entry to the territory and a procedure in which the need to initiate a new procedure for subsequent application is assessed. If there is evidence of misconduct by the applicant or abuse of the procedure, applications may also be processed in accelerated procedures.

The application of the 'safe third country concept' is optional for the Member States. There are, however, certain limits even for those countries which have introduced legislation allowing for the designation by law of safe third countries. A country may only be considered as a safe third country for a particular applicant, if:

[77] See Art. 13 of the Directive.

[78] See Art. 17(1).

—the applicant has either a connection or close links with the country
—or has had an opportunity to avail himself/herself of the protection of the authorities of that country
—and there are grounds for considering that this particular applicant will be admitted or readmitted
—and there are no grounds for considering that the country is not a safe third country in his/her particular circumstances.[79]

The relationship of this provision to the provision in Article 27 whereby Member States may retain legislation that allows for the designation by law of safe third countries, provided that such laws are compatible with the requirements of Article 28, is not very clear. It seems that the Article 28 measures providing for an individual examination of safety must be applied even if there is a legal designation of a country as a safe third country by law—and, therefore, regardless of any such designation.

On the initiative of Germany Article 33 deals with subsequent applications. Specific procedures involving a preliminary examination are allowed. If the conditions for a re-examination of the asylum claim are not fulfilled (e.g. change of circumstances, new evidence), the right of asylum seekers to remain may be terminated.

Specific procedures may also apply in the case of applicants for asylum arriving at the border, at airports, or at port transit zones. A decision to refuse entry must be taken within two weeks. Non-compliance with the time limit will result in the applicant for asylum being granted entry to the territory.

The most substantial changes in relation to the first proposal of the Commission can be found in Part 3 on the appeals procedures. The original obligation to introduce a two-level appeal system, in which a court of law would have to be competent at least once to review a decision, has been replaced by the right of every applicant for asylum to have an effective remedy before a court of law against the decision of his application, leaving the institutional arrangements for review or appeal to national discretion. In addition, obligations to set a reasonable time limit for taking a decision under the regular procedure, to consider non-compliance with this time limit as a negative decision against which an applicant can lodge an appeal, as well as obligations for appeal bodies to take decisions within a reasonable time limit, have all been discarded as impracticable.

Special rules will apply concerning review and appeal proceedings in accelerated procedures. First, Member States may make provision for circumstances in which applicants for asylum are not to be allowed to remain on the territory of the Member State, pending the outcome of the proceedings. In this case, however, a court has to be given the right to make

[79] See Art. 28(1).

an order to allow the applicant to remain on the territory. Until such a decision is made, the application for appeal has suspensive effect. There are, however, certain exceptions in the case of inadmissibility of asylum applications, subsequent asylum applications, and on grounds of national security and public policy.[80] The deadline for adopting the common standards for the Asylum Procedures Directive has been set as the end of 2003.[81]

C. Determination of the Member State responsible for Examining an Asylum Application (Dublin II)

The Dublin Convention of 1990 to which all Member States of the EU are party, is based upon the idea that an asylum seeker should have access to an asylum procedure in one of the EU Member States only once on the basis of the certain criteria of responsibility. 'Asylum shopping' thus should be avoided by returning an applicant to a country which is primarily responsible for proceeding with his/her asylum claim. The criteria of responsibility are the issue of a residence permit or a visa, or illegal entry or admission in the absence of an entry or residence permit. In practice, the Dublin Convention has worked less satisfactorily than might have been expected. The reasons are basically the same as in the case of the application of safe third-country concepts. Frequently, asylum applicants will hide their travel route or a previous residence or transit through another EU Member State. In the absence of evidence on the identity and travel route of an asylum seeker it will frequently be difficult to convince other Member States that a particular applicant has previously entered another Member State irregularly by land, sea, or air, having come from a third state, thereby making the transit state primarily responsible. The Dublin system, therefore, depends heavily upon the effective operation of the Council regulation of December 2000 concerning the establishment of 'EURODAC' (Européen/Dactyloskopie) for the comparison of fingerprints.[82] EURODAC, which entered into force as of 15 January 2003, obliges all Member States to establish a system whereby, for the purpose of identifying the responsibility under the Dublin system, asylum seekers or persons illegally resident can be identified by comparison of fingerprints.

According to Article 63(1)(a) EC, the Community has been given legislative power to adopt a system for determining responsibility for considering applications. Following a proposal of the Commission for a Council

[80] See Art. 40(3).

[81] Council DOC 10525/3/02 of 20 November 2002, Road Map for the Follow-up to the Conclusions of the European Council in Seville—Asylum, Immigration and Border Control.

[82] Council Regulation EC No. 2725/2000 of 11 November 2000, OJ 2000 L316/1.

Regulation of July 2001,[83] a regulation was passed by the Council in November 2002 replacing the Dublin Convention.[84] The text agreed upon by the ministers is based upon the Commission proposal. The changes mainly concern the time limits relevant to identifying the Member State responsible for examining the asylum application in case of illegal entry. Where it is established that an asylum seeker has irregularly crossed the border into a Member State, that Member State shall be responsible for examining the asylum claim for up to twelve months after the date of the border crossing. After this period expires, the responsibility for examining the claim will be incumbent upon the Member State in which the asylum seeker was previously living for at least five months. The Regulation aims primarily at closing the loopholes and correcting some of the inaccuracies detected in the Dublin Convention. These concern, primarily, excessively rigid time limits for the procedure and some unnecessarily bureaucratic requirements concerning the proof of another Member State's responsibility.

Originally, in its Explanatory Memorandum the Commission had suggested that a credible alternative to the existing system would be a scenario in which responsibility for examining an asylum application would solely depend on the Member State where an application has been lodged. According to the Commission this could be a clear and certain system which would prevent refugees in orbit. The Member States, however, have rightly decided to stick with the Dublin concept of criteria of responsibility since reliance upon the country of application would introduce a system of 'free choice', which may provide an unwanted incentive for illegal entry into the European Union.

Dublin II, as well as the Dublin Convention, rests upon a hierarchy of criteria for allocating responsibility. The Council Regulation maintains the foundation of general principles of the first Dublin Convention. Member States shall examine the application of any third-country national who applies at the border or in their territory according to criteria set out in the Regulation. Any Member State shall, however, maintain the right, pursuant to its national laws, to send an asylum seeker to a third state, in compliance with the Geneva Convention. This implies a right to apply a safe third-country clause with respect to an asylum seeker who has previously been in a safe third country. Each Member State may also examine an application even if it is not responsible for the examination of an application according to Dublin II.

[83] Proposal for a Council Resolution establishing the criteria and mechanisms for determining the Member State responsible for examining an asylum application lodged in one of the Member States by a third-country national of 26 July 2001, COM(2001)447 final, available at http://www.europa.eu.int.eur-lex/en/com/pdf/2001/en_501PC0441.pdf.

[84] Council DOC 14651/02 of 25 November 2002; with the exception of Denmark, which is not participating in the legislative process under Art. 63(1)(a).

Articles 6–8 and 15 reflect the principle of family unity and the responsibility of a Member State for examining the application of an unaccompanied minor in cases where a member of his/her family is legally present. The same applies if the family unit was already formed in the country of origin and a family member has been allowed to reside as a refugee in a Member State.[85] If the asylum seeker has a family member in a Member State whose application has not yet been the subject of a first decision, that Member State shall also be responsible for examining the new application for asylum, provided that the person concerned so desires. Other criteria are possession of a valid residence document, and the fact that an asylum seeker has irregularly crossed the border into a Member State by land, sea, or air, having come from a third state. As already noted, when a Member State can no longer be held responsible under this provision, and where it is established that the asylum seeker, having illegally crossed the border at the time of lodging the application, was previously living for a continuous period of at least five months in another Member State, that Member State shall be responsible for examining the application for asylum.[86] Finally, where a Member State can be designated on the basis of the criteria listed in the Regulation, the first Member State in which the application for asylum was lodged shall be responsible. There is also a humanitarian clause providing that any Member State may reunite family members on humanitarian grounds. Article 15, which provides for this, is not drafted as an individual right but rather as a procedure between the Member States concerned.

A number of provisions deal with taking charge of an asylum seeker and taking back asylum seekers in case of responsibility. Learning from the difficulties with the Dublin Convention, the Regulation sets shorter time limits for the request made to another Member State considered as responsible to take charge of the applicant, and longer time limits for carrying out the transfer due to practical problems which have occurred in the implementation of the Dublin Convention time limits for such transfers. The Regulation also tries to take account of the difficulties concerning proof of responsibility. In addition to formal proof, circumstantial evidence has been considered sufficient—including indicative elements.

Article 19 provides for notification to the applicant if a requested state accepts that it should take charge of an applicant. The decision may be subject to an appeal or a review without, however, suspensive effect pending the final decision, unless the courts or competent bodies so decide on a case-by-case basis according to national law. The transfer of the applicant is carried out in accordance with national law. Refugee organizations have criticized

[85] Art. 7. [86] Art. 10(2).

this provision, arguing that a transfer to another Member State may amount to refoulement.[87]

Another possible deficiency of the framework is the scope of the provisions, which are expressly only applicable to *asylum* applications, being defined as applications which can be understood as requests for international protection from a Member State, under the Geneva Convention. Article 2(c), however, adds that any application for international protection is presumed to be an application for asylum, unless a third-country national explicitly requests another kind of protection that can be applied for separately. The Dublin system, thus, could be circumvented by explicitly asking for other forms of protection that are not subject to the Dublin system. The exclusion from the application of other forms of protection also may lead to inconsistencies. There may be problems in the case of applicants withdrawing their application for refugee status once the transfer to another Member State has been decided. This difficulty is not sufficiently addressed in Article 4(5), which provides that an asylum seeker who is present in another Member State, and there lodges an application for asylum after earlier withdrawing an application during the process of determining the state responsible, shall be taken back by the Member State with which that initial application for asylum was lodged, with a view to completing the process of determining the state responsible for examining the application for asylum.

In addition, the Regulation may raise difficulties concerning the criterion of legal residence. Illegal residence may turn out to be a very unclear and unsatisfactory criterion in so far as it solely depends on the actions of the asylum seeker. In addition, it is unclear how proof of the toleration of an unlawful stay shall be demonstrated in practical terms. Refugee organizations frequently have arrived at the conclusion that the Dublin system as such is not very effective, since it may often turn out to be a lengthy and unsuccessful procedure to try to identify a Member State's responsibility for illegal entry. The resources spent therefore should rather be used for the fair and efficient examination of asylum requests.[88] It has been further argued that the criteria proposed by the Commission are fair neither to the Member States nor to the asylum seekers. With regard to Member States, linking responsibility for asylum applications with responsibility for entry controls may have the result of shifting greater responsibility to those states with extended land and sea borders, and particularly newly acceding states in Eastern Europe, which will generally have the least developed asylum infrastructures in Europe. As

[87] ECRE, 'Comments from the European Council on Refugees and Exiles on the Proposal for a Council Regulation establishing the criteria and mechanisms for determining the Member State responsible for examining an asylum application lodged in one of the Member States by a third-country national', December 2001, at 12, available at http://www.ecre.org/eu_developments/responsibility/dubcomms.doc.

[88] Ibid., at 3.

regards asylum seekers, it is argued, Member States have been encouraged illegally to *refoule* asylum seekers at their land and sea borders through such measures as sending immigration officers overseas to enforce border controls extraterritorially or through further privatizing enforcement such as by carrier sanctions.

Nevertheless, the concept of Dublin is preferable from a long-term perspective. The alternative proposal to base responsibility on the criteria of family unity and the place where an asylum application is lodged meets with serious disadvantages mentioned by the Commission in its Explanatory Memorandum, particularly with the problem of returning to a system of free choice of asylum country. The Dublin system, however, has to be linked with the system of financial compensation and assistance for building up an administrative asylum structure for Member States receiving high numbers of asylum seekers. From a long-term perspective the institution of a proper common asylum system will reduce the incentive to apply in a country with 'better economic and administrative conditions'. There is, therefore, no satisfactory alternative to Dublin in combination with EURODAC.

D. Reception Conditions

There is general agreement that different reception conditions in the EU Member States may be a substantial factor for migratory movements of refugees within the European Union. In addition to the purpose of eliminating unwanted push-factors for irregular movements, the very idea of a common judicial space and considerations of equal justice argue strongly in favour of comparable reception conditions in the EU Member States, following the logic of the Dublin Convention, whereby asylum seekers have only one chance of filing an asylum application within the European Union without being able to choose freely the country of application. In 2001, the Commission put forward a proposal for a directive on minimum standards for the reception of asylum seekers[89] which are deemed sufficient to ensure that asylum seekers have a dignified standard of living in all EU Member States. The directive covers all third-country nationals and stateless persons who make an application for asylum at the border or in the territory of a Member State as long as they are allowed to remain in the territory, as well as certain family members. In January 2003, the Council passed the Directive laying down minimum standards for the reception of asylum seekers.[90]

[89] Proposal for a Council Directive laying down minimum standards on the reception of applicants for asylum in Member States of 3 April 2001, COM(2001)181 final, available at http://www.europa.eu.int.

[90] OJ 2003 L31/18; cf. also Council DOC 14658/02 on a proposal for a Council Directive laying down minimum standards for the reception of asylum seekers in Member States, 22 November 2002.

The Directive contains specific provisions for residence and freedom of movement, family unity, schooling, and the education of minors. On the most controversial issue, the access of asylum seekers to employment, political agreement has been reached whereby Member States shall decide the conditions for granting access to the labour market for the applicant.

According to provisions of the respective Amsterdam protocols on the position of the United Kingdom and Ireland as well as of Denmark, the United Kingdom has notified its intention to participate in the adoption of this proposal, whereas Ireland and Denmark have not done so, and consequently are not bound by the Directive's provisions and application.

The Preamble to the Directive makes clear that it is in the very nature of minimum standards that Member States have the power to introduce or maintain more favourable provisions for third-country nationals. This, however, would mean that Member States would possibly create unwanted pull-factors for asylum seekers seeking better international protection in a particular Member State. The Directive only applies to asylum seekers. Member States are, however, invited to apply the provisions of the Directive in connection with procedures for deciding on applications for forms of protection other than protection emanating from the Geneva Convention.[91]

The Directive, however, does not apply where the provisions of Council Directive of 20 July 2001 on minimum standards for giving temporary protection in the event of a mass influx of displaced persons are applied.[92]

Chapter 2 contains various general provisions on reception conditions, including matters such as information, documentation, residence and freedom of movement, medical screening, schooling, and the controversial matter of employment, as well as material reception conditions and health care.

Freedom of movement is generally accorded to asylum seekers within the territory of the host state 'or within an area assigned to them by that Member State'.[93] The assigned area shall not affect the inalienable right to private life and shall allow sufficient scope for guaranteeing access to all benefits under the Directive. Taking into account the more restrictive regulations of some EU Member States, the Directive contains a variety of possibilities to restrict freedom of movement. Under Article 7(3) Member States may confine an applicant to a particular place in accordance with their national law, 'when it proves necessary for example for legal reasons or reasons of public order'. These exceptions must be made on an individual basis, under the conditions laid down in the Directive. Refugee organizations have

[91] It ought to be noted, however, that according to Art. 2b any application for international protection is presumed to be an application for asylum.

[92] Art. 3(3)—referring to the Draft as amended by the Council on 22 November 2002.

[93] Art. 7(1).

criticized these provisions as unduly wide and ineffective. It has been argued that confining an applicant to a particular place is not in accordance with human rights provisions on freedom of movement and in any case is ineffective in ensuring the availability of applicants. It cannot be denied, however, that according to the practice of most EU Member States, measures restricting freedom of movement are considered essential to ensure a speedy asylum procedure as well as preventing applicants absconding.

The most heavily disputed provision concerns access to employment. The redrafted Article 11 now provides that Member States shall determine a period of time during which an applicant shall not have access to the labour market. If a decision at first instance has not been taken within one year of the presentation of an application for asylum and this delay cannot be attributed to the applicant, Member States, however, shall specify the conditions for granting access to the labour market for the applicant. Access to the labour market shall not be withdrawn during appeal procedures—the appeal against a negative decision in a regular procedure having suspensive effect until such time as the final negative decision is notified. The provision must be interpreted against the background of reservations of some Member States concerning an individual right of asylum seekers to be granted access to the labour market if a decision at first instance has not been taken within one year. On the other hand, refugee organizations claim that the right of Member States to prohibit access to the labour market for a period of up to one year and even longer (since the priority of EU citizens may always be enforced), does not fulfil the requirements for a minimum harmonization, as Member States can in practice provide for quite different conditions concerning access to the labour market. In addition, they claim, depriving asylum seekers of access to employment may prevent the integration of asylum applicants into society and forces them into a ghetto-like situation with all its well-known social disadvantages. Nevertheless, access to the labour market (although access to the black market may be even more important) must be considered as a considerable pull-factor in attracting applicants for predominantly economic reasons.

A problem of a lack of harmonization rather than minimum standards arises in connection with the rules on material reception conditions and health care. It is fairly obvious that harmonization raises substantial difficulties considering the different social standards and living conditions within the EU. The Directive obliges Member States to make provisions on material reception conditions 'to ensure a standard of living adequate for the health of applicants and capable of ensuring their subsistence'.[94] Material reception conditions, in addition, may be provided in kind, or in the form of financial allowances or vouchers or in a combination of these provisions. The provision

[94] Art. 13(2).

leaves a wide margin of discretion to the Member States. There had been a number of proposals to include in the Directive more objective criteria like the level of social assistance or minimum welfare assistance in parity with nationals.[95] Equivalent treatment may appear the logical solution if one argues from a human rights point of view, connecting human dignity with access to social benefits. A majority of EU Member States, however, have clearly declined to draw this conclusion, instead maintaining a different level of social benefits for asylum seekers or the exclusion of asylum seekers from regular welfare assistance. Two considerations argue in favour of differentiated treatment: first the essentially functional nature of an asylum seeker's requirements, limited to a fair and speedy asylum procedure, rather than facilitating integration into the society of the receiving state; secondly, the pull-factor of material reception conditions (although difficult to verify accurately), which at least in connection with other factors (e.g. access to the labour black market; prospect of legalization; joining a network) may be in tension with the generally recognized aim to control legal immigration.

Articles 14 and 15 contain a number of provisions on the modalities for material reception conditions and health care. Health care may be limited to emergency care and essential treatment of illness. As to accommodation, Member States have a large amount of discretion whether they use specific premises during the examination of an application for asylum lodged at the border or accommodation centres or private houses. In addition, exceptionally, Member States may set different material reception conditions for a reasonable period, if material reception conditions as provided for in the Article are not available, or if the asylum seeker is in detention or confined to border posts. Again, this leaves the Member States a wide amount of discretion, which was precisely the aim of the amended text.

Reception conditions may be restricted or withdrawn in a number of cases, including the case where an asylum seeker abandons the place of residence or does not comply with reporting duties, or where an applicant has concealed financial resources and has therefore unduly benefited from material reception conditions. At the request of some Member States, to this list has been added the case where an asylum seeker has failed to demonstrate that the asylum claim has been made as soon as reasonably practicable after arrival in that Member State. Member States may also determine sanctions applicable to serious breaches of the rules of the accommodation centres as well as to seriously violent behaviour. Generally speaking, the provisions on restriction

[95] ECRE Briefing: 'Summary of ECRE's position on right to social assistance for asylum seekers, with reference to the Proposal for a Council Directive laying down minimum standards on the reception of applicants for asylum in Member State', February 2002, at 1, available at http://www.ecre.org/statements/assist.shtml.

or withdrawal are a useful addition to the text of the Directive, since they take account of the abuse of the reception system.

4. EU RETURN POLICY

Return policy is an integral part of any European migration policy. The regulations for examining a request for asylum or a humanitarian residence permit become redundant if following a negative decision the effective termination of residence is not accomplished and immigrants remain in the country either illegally or on the basis of toleration. Also, it would be an illusion to rely exclusively on the concept of a voluntary return based upon incentives and psychological and financial assistance. No large return programme has worked efficiently without a corresponding mechanism to enforce return. Obviously any programme of voluntary return must be accompanied by rules on involuntary return in the case of termination of a residence permit.

Thus, a clear and transparent return policy in an EU context is essential 'to ensure that admission policy is not undermined and to enforce the rule of law, which is a constituent element of an area of freedom, security and justice'.[96]

A. EU Competence for Return and Repatriation Policy

The EC Treaty does not contain a general competence to enact measures on return. Under Article 63(3)(b) EC the Council shall adopt measures on immigration policy within the area of 'illegal immigration and illegal residence, including repatriation of illegal residence'. The scope of application of this provision and its inherent limitations are not altogether clear. The European Parliament in a report on the draft directive on mutual recognition of decisions on the expulsion of third-country nationals[97] has argued that according to the wording, context, and purpose, Article 63 EC authorizes the Council to determine the substantial conditions under which entry and stay must be considered as illegal and therefore subject to expulsion or deportation. The mutual recognition of national decisions, however—according to the report—is not covered by this provision. This view cannot be endorsed. Immigration policy cannot be limited to a harmonization of rules relating to the conditions under which the entry and stay of a third-country national is

[96] Green Paper on a Community Return Policy on Illegal Residents, COM(2002)175 final of 10 April 2002, available at: http://europa.eu.int/eur-lex/en/com/gpr/2002/com2002_0175en01.pdf.

[97] OJ 2001 L149/34.

legal or illegal. This may be the final stage in a successful process of convergence. In the meantime, however, an immigration policy must take into account that termination of residence is still based upon national measures. Therefore, mutual recognition is an inevitable interim measure in order to achieve a further harmonization on illegal immigration and illegal residence. In addition, Article 63(3)(b) EC establishes a comprehensive competence to regulate termination of residence as far as return and repatriation of illegal immigrants are concerned. The term illegal 'residence' should not be interpreted in a restrictive sense. It is intended to cover all persons without a valid residence permit. Community competence with respect to termination of residence, however, is not exclusive. Article 63 EC also provides that measures adopted by the Council shall not 'prevent any Member States from maintaining or introducing in the area concerned national provisions which are compatible with this treaty and with international agreements'. Hence, Member States and the Community share a responsibility for both adoption and implementation of immigration policy, including illegal immigration and illegal residence and repatriation. Finally, measures on return and repatriation affecting particularly sensitive areas of national sovereignty must meet the test of subsidiarity. It is not to be expected that Member States will easily opt for giving up their national rights in favour of a comprehensive EU return and repatriation policy. It is, therefore, essential to examine closely to what extent Member States consider a common European return policy necessary to further their separate national goals of a more efficient return and repatriation policy.

B. Impediments to Expulsion and Deportation

A clear and transparent return policy requires, first, an examination of the legal and factual impediments to return. In a large number of cases, return fails due to impediments attributable to the person ordered to leave or to his home country. Major impediments to return of persons ordered to leave are:

—destroying or concealing identification or travel documents,

—concealing true identity or nationality by various false names or identities,

—in particular, claiming to be a national of a state to which no deportations are possible for legal or factual reasons,

—'disappearing' into illegality,

—lack of co-operation in verifying identity/nationality and travel documents,

—refusing to sign an application for travel documents or other official documents, or to appear at the embassy or consulate for the purpose of clearing nationality,

—resistance to enforcement measures, often immediately before deportation at the airport; for example, by claiming factual impediments to deportation such as illness during the deportation process.

Frequently factual or legal impediments also result from a lack of co-operation of home countries in the process of clearing identity and issuing travel documents. The following problems are most commonly noted:

—Bureaucratic and time-consuming procedures for issuing travel documents;
—Extremely high requirements for proving the nationality of the home country in spite of clear indications of the person's true nationality;
—Making return dependent upon an explicit declaration of the person that he wishes to return voluntarily to the state of which he is a national;
—Issue of travel documents made dependent upon a time period during which the person in question is able to work.

In addition, deportations are frequently made impossible by violent resistance immediately before a deportation or during a flight. Since there are no clear legal rules concerning assisted forced return, problems may arise due to the lack of co-operation of authorities of a transit state during a transit stop. Therefore, one essential element of a common EU return and repatriation policy must be the development of a mechanism to cope with these difficulties. National efforts cannot solve the impediments efficiently, particularly the difficulties arising in relation to home countries. Co-operation with these countries and its authorities is an indispensable requirement for a successful return policy. In this regard, the traditional connection of some EU Member States with home countries could and should be used to establish a more efficient return procedure. Therefore, the establishment of specialized institutions for organizing the return of particular categories of persons ordered to leave the country should be sought. Certainly, such an effort can only be undertaken at this stage on a voluntary inter-state level.

Furthermore, in the case of countries fulfilling their readmission obligations unwillingly, readmission agreements should be negotiated. There is a wide consensus that such agreements should be negotiated at the EU level. A number of issues relating to the lack of co-operation can only be solved by combining the EU's economic and political weight. The agreements should set out the practical procedures and modes of transportation.[98] Also the insertion of readmission standard clauses in association or co-operation agreements obligating the contracting parties to readmit their own nationals and third-country nationals can address impediments to return, and this policy will be continued by the Commission.[99] Since the readmission

[98] See Commission Green Paper, *supra* note 96, sub 2.5 at 11.
[99] See ibid., sub 4.1.2 at 24.

standard clauses have in some cases not led to the expected improvements in co-operation, the proposal has been made to incorporate more binding regulations, which are comparable to those in a readmission agreement.[100]

On the level of legal barriers to deportation it seems important to achieve a uniform interpretation of such safeguards arising from the concept of inhuman or degrading treatment or punishment under Article 3 of the European Convention on Human Rights. The jurisprudence of the European Court of Human Rights has created a substantial amount of uncertainty concerning the concept of inhuman treatment with relation to the general conditions in a deportee's home country. In addition, the relationship of Article 3 ECHR to the exclusion clauses under Article 1 F of the Geneva Convention is unclear. It is insufficient to refer in draft directives and communications to the existing public international law obligations of Member States with regard to the non-*refoulement* principle arising from the Geneva Convention and Article 3 ECHR. In recognition of divergent practice there should be an effort to harmonize the interpretation of these concepts.

C. Common Standards for Expulsion and Deportation

The Commission has in its communication on a common policy on illegal immigration[101] already indicated that it will bring forward proposals for a harmonization of standards on expulsion. A harmonization of these standards is the logical consequence of common standards on immigration. Obviously, the harmonization of conditions under which third-country nationals are to be granted a residence permit in one of the Member States must result in harmonized rules on the termination of such residence rights and the execution of such decisions. In its Green Paper on a Community return policy, the Commission presents concrete proposals for harmonization as a basis for discussion and formulation of a proposal for a Council Directive on Minimum Standards for Return Procedures.[102] Among other ideas, the Commission mentions common standards concerning the ending of legal residence, such as the expiry of visa or residence permit and expulsion orders.[103] Specific statutory grounds for an expulsion decision could be

[100] See e.g. Comment of Germany, Federal Ministry of the Interior, on the Commission Green Paper on a Community Return Policy, at p. 4 available at http://europa.eu.int/comm/justice_home/unit/doc_asile_immigrat/hearing_160702/contributions/germany_de.pdf.

[101] Communication from the Commission to the Council and the European Parliament on a Common Policy on Illegal Immigration, COM(2001)672 final of 15 November 2001, sub 4.8 at 24–25, available at http://www.europa.eu.int/eur-lex/en/com/pdf/2001/com2001_0672en01.pdf.

[102] See Commission Green Paper, *supra* note 96, Part II at 11 *et seq.*

[103] See ibid., sub 3.1.2, at 12–14.

developed. Certain groups, privileged third-country nationals, refugees, as well as people under other forms of international protection, may only be removed for grave reasons of public security and public order. Measures terminating illegal residence have to be applicable throughout the whole EU to avoid secondary movements. However, in the context of expulsion for reasons of public order and security a comprehensive regulation should be avoided to leave scope to embrace different national conceptions of public order. Further, the Commission considers that an appeal against a subsequent removal order could have a suspensive effect. In their first reactions, some Member States and regional authorities reject this suggestion because of its essential interference with effective readmission practice and also because it contradicts national regulations.[104] Certainly, people who are affected should have the opportunity to apply for preliminary legal protection. Regarding detention, the Commission proposes to set minimum standards at the EU level for detention orders defining the competence of responsible authorities and the preconditions for detention. Detention orders should be issued or confirmed without delay within statutory limits by a judicial authority. Moreover minimum rules on the conditions of detention and possible time limits should be developed.[105]

As regards the removal of illegal residents the creation of minimum standards in four areas is mentioned:[106] first a final safeguard for non-*refoulement* requirements according to obligations under international law; secondly basic requirements to ensure the physical state and mental capacity of the people concerned prior to departure; thirdly enforcement and security standards for the removal itself; finally a mechanism whereby the Member States could streamline their present return practice in relation to specific countries of origin, where the actual situation makes removals questionable due to compelling humanitarian reasons.

The Green Paper also addresses the mutual recognition of return decisions.[107] Basic substantive rules and common minimum standards on procedure are necessary to achieve a more effective system and enforcement of return decisions. The Council directive of 28 May 2001[108] is only applicable

[104] See e.g. comment of Austria on the Green Paper, at 3, available at http://europa.eu.int/comm/justice_home/unit/doc_asile_immigrat/hearing_160702/contributions/austria_de.pdf and the comment of Ministry of the Interior Baden-Württemberg, at 3 and 4, available at http://europa.eu.int/comm/justice_home/unit/doc_asile_immigrat/hearing_160702/contributions/baden_en.pdf.

[105] See Commission Green Paper, *supra* note 96, sub 3.1.3, at 14.

[106] See ibid., sub 3.1.4, at 15.

[107] See ibid., sub 3.1.5, at 16.

[108] Council Directive 2001/40/EC on the mutual recognition of decisions on the expulsion of third-country nationals of 28 May 2001, OJ 2001 L149/34, available at: http://europa.eu.int/eur-lex/pri/en/oj/dat/2001/l_149/l_14920010602en00340036.pdf.

to expulsion decisions issued by a competent administrative authority of an issuing Member State, and only obligatory under specific conditions of a serious and present threat to public order or national security and safety by a third-country national. Besides, the Directive does not specify a binding framework for the mutual recognition of these decisions. Therefore a more binding and comprehensive system should be established to avoid returnees moving between Member States.

D. Readmission and Transit Rules among Member States

If the Dublin Convention and the procedures for the determination of the responsibility for asylum claims and Article 11 of the Council Directive on temporary protection[109] are not applicable, readmission among Member States only takes place within the scope of bilateral readmission agreements or informal co-operation. Therefore, the Commission Green Paper, on the basis of a Finnish initiative,[110] proposes the establishment of a clear legal framework for readmission in the Member State going beyond the determination of responsibility for asylum claims according to the Dublin Convention and its successor Council regulation.[111]

Furthermore, a common framework should be established in relation to transit, including the use and competence of escorts in transit and regulations on failure to secure return. Especially in cases of voluntary return, if the returnee has to cross internal borders of Member States and is in need of a visa for it, a secure standard travel document issued by the Member State returning the person should be provided to ensure a non-bureaucratic mode of return.[112]

E. Administrative Co-operation between Member States

The Green Paper proposal demands the complete and detailed sharing of information by all Member States on the basis of common definitions. The Commission is set to bring forward a plan to introduce a public annual report on asylum and migration, including a section on return. In addition, suitable identification measures during administrative procedures should be carried out, or Member States should introduce appropriate identification measures during visa application procedures.[113] Finally, there should be a broad exchange of best practices concerning methods of enforcing return and of information on concrete return operations.

[109] See *supra* note 58. [110] See OJ 1999 C535/6. [111] See *supra* note 84.
[112] See Commission Green Paper, *supra* note 96, sub 3.3, at 18.
[113] See ibid., sub 3.4.2, at 19.

F. Conclusions

First reactions to the Commission's Green Paper indicate that there is consent on certain points. However, Member States and particularly regional authorities do have reservations concerning comprehensive regulations in certain areas. Further reactions remain to be seen. Above all, a clear and consistent return policy is needed, which must be embraced as the guiding principle in every relevant directive or decision on immigration, asylum, and the integration of persons so as to avoid contradictory signals in different areas of Community policy. There must be lucid and transparent rules and procedures under which third-country nationals will be returned if they do not possess a valid residence permit.

3

Visas, Borders, Immigration: Formation, Structure, and Current Evolution of the EU Entry Control System

FERRUCCIO PASTORE*

> In this world, shipmates, sin that pays its way can travel freely, and without a passport; whereas virtue, if a pauper, is stopped at all frontiers.
>
> (Herman Melville, *Moby Dick*)

1. INTRODUCTION: A SYSTEMIC APPROACH TO MIGRATION CONTROL

At the time Melville wrote these bitter and prophetic words, the political role of external borders was undergoing radical changes, particularly in Europe. For centuries after the birth of nation-states, the populations of states were generally seen by their ruling elites as a key resource in terms of size, to be consolidated within their own borders in order to support economic and military expansion. As a result, border controls were designed principally as a check on exit from the national territory targeting primarily those born within its confines. It was only from the nineteenth century onwards that the capacity to delimit 'negatively' the boundaries of the national community became a specific attribute of national sovereignty, enforced by a wide range of tools. Indeed, it was during this period that nationality laws were codified, current administrative techniques for identification of individuals (passports, birth, marriage, and death registers) were developed, and the practice of frontier controls on entry spread, even in peacetime.[1]

* I would like to convey my heartfelt thanks to Adelina Adinolfi for her valuable comments on a previous draft of this text.

[1] J. Torpey, *The Invention of the Passport. Surveillance, Citizenship and the State* (Cambridge: Cambridge University Press, 2000); K. Bade, *L'Europa in movimento. Le migrazioni dal Settecento a oggi* (Rome: Laterza, 2001).

The *jus includendi et excludendi* therefore emerged only relatively recently as a central tenet of contemporary sovereignty. Nevertheless, from the second half of the nineteenth century onwards, the consolidation of this prerogative for sovereignty in practice and in international law was relatively swift, and today a number of corollaries to this general principle have become set in stone in the international sphere, making them very difficult to contest in customary international law. During the twentieth century—and especially in post-war Europe—certain important legal limits to the *jus includendi et excludendi* were established: the principle of *non-refoulement* and the banning of collective deportation, the right to appeal against bureaucratic decisions and the rights of the family unit, *inter alia*. In spite of this, the power to select entrants and to turn away unwanted foreigners has remained a fundamental and essentially unchallenged part of state sovereignty.[2]

From a sociological point of view, the migration controls which exist today are a relatively recent phenomenon. It was during the inter-war period that the majority of European states adopted tools for entry control (visas) and subsequent authorization (residency permits and the like) to stay and work, as well as rules and standard procedures for deportation. But it was only after the general adoption between 1972 and 1975 by almost all European states of measures to block new entries for economic reasons that the idea of systematic and widespread border controls to block illegal entry became implanted amongst European elites.[3]

It has only been in the last thirty years, then, that complex systems of migration control have developed in Western Europe, functioning as a regulatory tool for legal entry and residence, on the one hand, and as a repressive tool against illegal entry and residence on the other. Both these basic functions are currently carried out in European countries through various bureaucratic processes, which can be broken down into three levels: (1) the selection of parties allowed to enter and the prevention/prohibition on non-authorized expatriations by means of activities performed in the country of origin and/or of transit; (2) the selection of parties allowed to enter and the rejection of those who are not by means of checks and surveillance at borders; (3) the selection of parties allowed residence and the deportation of those who are not by means of activities performed within the country of destination.

From the second half of the 1970s until today, the structural complexity of the European migration control system has only increased, particularly as a result of the generalization of compulsory visas even for short

[2] R. Plender (ed.), *Basic Documents on International Migration Law* (The Hague: Kluwer, 1997).

[3] G. Brochmann and T. Hammar (eds), *Mechanisms of Immigration Control* (New York: New York University Press, 1999); G. Sciortino, *L'ambizione della frontiera. Le politiche di controllo migratorio in Europa* (Milan: F. Angeli, 2000).

stays,[4] and of a tendency to externalize migration controls by transferring responsibility to private parties (carriers' liability) and to the governments of sending countries, which are submitted to intense international political pressure to introduce (or in some cases, as with formerly socialist Eastern bloc countries, *re*introduce) the dubious notion of a crime of unauthorized exit and clandestine emigration into their national laws.

It is important to note that the complexity of migration controls in Europe and their peculiar structure, based on concentric circles of defence, are not only key to sociological understandings, but are also increasingly a feature of the explicit political, strategic, and operational models contained in policy[5] and legal documents.[6] One of the most recent and detailed versions of this model of migration control is illustrated in the *EU Schengen Catalogue*, drafted by the Working Party on Schengen Evaluation and presented by the Spanish Presidency at the meeting of the Justice and Home Affairs Council (JHA) on 28 February 2002. This document, whose legal status is somewhat vague, sets out an 'integrated border security model', designed as a 'mechanism of different tiers/filters' on four levels:

(1) Activities in third countries, especially in countries of origin and transit, including the collection of information by liaison officers as well as the key role of the consular post abroad in the process of issuing visas.
(2) International border co-operation.
(3) Measures at external borders: border management (border checks and border surveillance).
(4) Further activities inside the territory of the Schengen states and between Schengen states.[7]

[4] The requirement of compulsory visas for stays shorter than three months, which represented an exception in the international regime of movement of people applied in the West after the Second World War, has gradually become the rule. This is particularly evident in the case of EU Member States: on the basis of Council Regulation 539/2001 (OJ 2001 L81/1), there are 135 (Ecuador was added in March 2003 by Regulation 453/2003, OJ L69/10) countries whose citizens—who make up an overwhelming majority of the world's population—need to obtain a visa to visit the EU, whereas only 45 countries have this requirement waived.

[5] See, for example, the strategy paper presented by the Austrian Presidency of the EU in the second term of 1998.

[6] In the Schengen context, the concentric circles model which has inspired many aspects of its *acquis* was formalized with particular clarity in a 1998 document—Working group 1 'Police and security', note to the Central Group, *Protection of external Schengen borders as a system of lines of defence*, SCH/I (98) 86, 2a rev., Brussels, 24 November 1998.

[7] Council of the European Union, General Secretariat, DG H, *EU Schengen Catalogue. External Borders Control, Removal and Readmission*, February 2002, p. 11. A second and a third volume of the Schengen Catalogue were published in December 2002 ('Schengen Information System, Sirene: Recommendations and Best Practices') and in March 2003 ('Issuing of Visa: Recommendations and Best Practices') respectively; all three volumes are available on http://ue.eu.int/jai/default.asp?lang=en).

We shall return later to the implications of this multi-level 'European model' for border management, especially with reference to the forthcoming EU enlargement (section 3B). For the moment, however, this brief overview is sufficient to explain the reason for tackling the study of law and European policy on the subject of visas, borders, and immigration from a systemic perspective. Indeed, in the current European context visas and norms for immigrant admission constitute separate politico-legal domains which nevertheless form a system inasmuch as they are tightly interwoven and address common ends, or at the very least complementary ones. Such a system, which we shall call the 'EU entry control system', can be defined as a more or less co-ordinated set of norms, apparatuses, and administrative practices designed to control the entry into and settling of third-country nationals in the EU, and basing its selection on partially common criteria.

The EU entry control system is clearly neither established nor stable, whether from a political or a strictly legal point of view. Instead, it is a body with an uncertain and shifting profile which in recent years has entered a phase of radical transformation whose end result is still unclear at this moment in time. This strongly dynamic aspect of the EU entry control system suggests a two-part analysis: in the first ('The formation of the EU entry control system') we shall analyse the process behind the system's formation, and will try to highlight the key elements of continuity and discontinuity in the development from the intergovernmental framework created by the Schengen Convention to the scenario of partial and progressive communitarization broached in the Treaty of Amsterdam. The analysis of the formative phase of the EU entry control system will be developed from a number of perspectives. In section 2A, we will consider the political-conceptual foundations of the whole process. We will then turn to look at the actors involved in this process, focusing on the transition from a stage of general affirmation of community competence to one of specific definition and delimitation of this competence (section 2B). We will move subsequently to examine how different methods of normative integration have combined in grounding the legal basis to the EU entry control system (2C). Finally we address the structural gaps in the system, and in particular the delays in community action on matters of legal immigration (2D).

In the second part ('The current evolution of the EU entry control system') we will concentrate on three current lines of development, in order to identify their main implications and the main problem areas. We will refer in particular to: the current attempts to reinforce functional integration between national migration control apparatuses (3A); the geographic expansion of the European entry control system which will occur after EU enlargement (3B); and the possible impact on migration of the institutional reform process underway since the institution of the Convention on the Future of Europe, which is likely to end with the signing of a second Treaty of Rome (3C).[8]

Before beginning our analysis, however, it is worth further defining the scope of the investigation. What we define as the EU entry control system is just one component in a more complex and vast entity—an emerging common immigration and asylum policy—which itself can be described and analysed in systemic terms. Important sectors of this common policy lie outside the scope of this analysis: in particular, the norms and policies regarding family reunification, repatriation, integration of immigrants into the destination society, and the fight against organized crime such as smuggling and immigrant trafficking. Some of these arguments are dealt with in other contributions to this volume, which form therefore a strong complement to this chapter.

A further boundary has to be drawn: for reasons of space and coherence, this essay will not deal with those laws and policies relating to immigration which were already part of treaties prior to Amsterdam and which today form part of Title III ('Free movement of persons, services and capitals') rather than Title IV TEC. The two main areas excluded by this are the relatives of European citizens who are free to move within the EU,[9] and citizens of third countries who have signed accords with the EU and Member States on migration (*special migration regimes*). This last area in particular is quite a significant exclusion: as one author notes, '[m]ost people who are nationals of third countries and live in EU Member States are protected by rules of agreements concluded by the European Community with their country of nationality'.[10] Thus we will limit ourselves to the examination of *jus commune* on migration, through which the European Community and its Member States still regulate the conditions and means of access to and residency in its territory for the vast majority of the world's population.

[8] This chapter takes into account political and legal changes up to 4 October 2003.

[9] Recently, the Court of Justice, with its ruling relating to Case C–459/99 *MRAX* (25 July 2002), has considerably broadened the sphere of protection allowing foreign spouses of Community citizens to move freely, stating that 'a Member State may not send back at the border a third-country national who is married to a national of a Member State and attempts to enter its territory without being in possession of a valid identity card or passport or, if necessary, a visa, where he is able to prove his identity and the conjugal ties and there is no evidence to establish that he represents a risk to the requirements of public policy, public security, or public health'. In the same ruling, the Court held that 'a Member State is not permitted to refuse issue of a residence permit and to issue an expulsion order against a third country national who is able to furnish proof of his identity and of his marriage to a national of a Member State on the sole ground that he has entered the territory of the Member State concerned unlawfully'.

[10] A. C. Oliveira, 'Immigrants from Third Countries under EC External Agreements: the Need for Improvement', 4 *European Foreign Affairs Review* (1999) 215. By the author's own estimation, over 50% of the EU's resident immigrant population is subject to a special migratory regime.

2. THE FORMATION OF THE EU ENTRY CONTROL SYSTEM

A. The Driving Force: The Structural Interdependence between Internal Freedom of Movement and External Border Controls

In the development of the EU entry control system, as in other areas of European integration, identifying the *finalité politique* of the process is a delicate intellectual task, owing to the often elusive nature of the concepts involved, but it is nevertheless an essential one. As in other areas, the official strategic objectives of European co-operation on visas, borders, and immigration strongly determine the path of the legislative process. In a legal environment dominated by the subsidiarity principle, the wording and arguments of 'the objectives of the proposed action' (using the terminology of Article 5 TEC) represent one possible variable in any evaluation of legitimacy.

From a historical perspective, the need for dialogue and co-operation between European states on managing borders and migratory flows began to be recognized in the first half of the 1970s, when all the countries which imported foreign labour on a mass scale decided virtually simultaneously to block access to new economic migrants without any prior warning and with no co-ordination amongst themselves. The international repercussions of this chaotic 'rush to close' were significant, and not just for the obvious reasons of the countries of origin losing a vital 'safety-valve' for internal economic and social tensions. Other European countries, and in particular those which until then had never experienced significant migratory inflows, for instance Mediterranean Europe, were also affected.

Nevertheless, the intention to reduce the negative side-effects of the closed border policy would probably not have been sufficient to kick-start the integration process in this area, had it not been interlaced with another, even more powerful 'loop of interdependence'—namely, the Single Market. Subsequent to the ratification of the Single European Act in 1986, the EC became 'an area without internal frontiers in which the free movement of goods, persons, services and capital is ensured'. Indeed, as Jörg Monar notes:

> The provisions on free movement in the EC treaties had always had potentially major implications for justice and home affairs, but it was only with the move towards the completion of the internal market since the mid-1980s that they came to the forefront . . . It seems unlikely that without the constraints generated by the internal market programme, the Member States would have been willing to go so far with their co-operation on asylum and policing matters at that stage.[11]

[11] J. Monar, 'The Dynamics of Justice and Home Affairs: Laboratories, Driving Factors and Costs', 4 *JCMS* (2001) 754.

In those crucial years, the primary objective of European integration was the completion of the Single Market as in essence an area of free movement. But such a strategic aim could only partially be pursued within the Community context, with the consequence that Member States situated in the vanguard of the integration process were forced to engage in that early experiment in reinforced intergovernmental co-operation that was launched in 1985 in Schengen.

We shall return later to the problematic relationship between the two tracks along which European integration proceeded during this period: the community track and the intergovernmental one which Steve Peers has aptly termed 'black-market integration'.[12] What should be emphasized at this point, however, is that, even in Schengen, the main objective of co-operation between national executives was originally represented as the completion of the area of free movement by the removal of systematic police checks along borders between participating nations. This objective had a double *raison d'être*: it performed an important symbolic function, demonstrating tangibly the benefits of integration to increasingly sceptical public opinion; but perhaps more important, at least from the dominant technocratic point of view holding sway at the time, were the economic and trade dimensions which linked the scrapping of border controls with substantial savings for the European transport system and thus intra-European trade. The norms on external border controls and police/judicial co-operation—which assumed a central relevance in the 1990 Convention of Application—thus represent a '"spillover" effect ... of economic integration',[13] at least from the standpoint of its original aims and the rhetoric of official statements.

If, from a purely political point of view, the strengthening of external borders soon achieved similar prominence to the abolition of internal borders, the argument that the measures meant to achieve the former objective are no more than flanking or compensatory ones has survived in the Amsterdam Treaty:

> Article 61(1)(a): [W]ithin a period of five years after the entry into force of the Treaty of Amsterdam, measures aimed at ensuring the free movement of persons in accordance with Article 14, in conjunction with the directly related *flanking measures* with respect to external border controls, asylum and immigration, in accordance with the provisions of Article 62(2) and (3) and Article 63(1)(a) and (2)(a), and measures to prevent and combat crime in accordance with the provisions of Article 31(e) of the Treaty on European Union [emphasis added].

The paradox by which *security measures*—and in particular those relating to the reinforcement of external borders—are logically conditional upon yet in fact politically dominant over *freedom measures* (freedom of circulation, in particular) is also clearly evident in the wording of Declaration no. 15

[12] S. Peers, *EU Justice and Home Affairs Law* (London: Longman, 2000), at 81.
[13] Monar, *supra* note 11, at 754.

annexed to the Treaty of Amsterdam on the preservation of the level of protection and security provided by the Schengen *acquis*:

The Conference agrees that measures to be adopted by the Council, which will have the effect of replacing provisions on the abolition of checks at common borders contained in the 1990 Schengen Convention, should provide at least the same level of protection and security as the aforementioned provisions of the Schengen Convention.

This conceptual framework attributing a compensatory function to internal security in relation to free movement evidently affects the principles of subsidiarity and proportionality in this context. And undoubtedly the 'measures on the crossing of external borders of Member States' in Article 62(2) TEC should be linked to some extent with the demands stemming from the implementation of 'measures with a view to ensuring, in compliance with Article 14, the absence of any controls on persons, be they citizens of the union or nationals of third countries, when crossing internal borders' (Article 62(1) TEC). In other words, to employ terms already widely in use in other areas of community law, 'positive integration' consisting of various types of harmonization and common regulation of certain public functions (such as external border control) is justified and legitimized only as a counter-weight to 'negative integration' caused by the removal of obstacles to free movement.[14]

It may be easy to understand the treaties' aims at this elementary level, but it is difficult to agree on the actual means by which proportionality should operate in these cases. In particular, the level of discretionary powers which community institutions enjoy in defining the 'levels of security' necessary to counterbalance given 'levels of freedom' is controversial. Some authors heavily underline the difficulty (or indeed the impossibility) of measuring such levels, and present strong arguments in favour of particularly wide discretionary power for the European legislator.[15] Nevertheless, it is difficult not to agree with those who assert that this discretionary power has so far been exercised in such an unbalanced manner, that effects of harmonization 'to the bottom'—which positive integration should theoretically prevent—have instead been encouraged:

[14] For application of these concepts to the Dutch case see M. P. Vink, *Negative and Positive Integration in European Immigration Policies*, European Integration Online Paper (EIoP), vol. 6 (2002) no. 13, http://eiop.or.at/eiop/texte/2002-013a.htm.

[15] '[T]he argument has been raised that, under Community law, compensatory measures may only re-assert, but may not extend the level of security which existed before the abolition of internal border controls. However, security levels are not easily quantifiable and statistics may be manipulated. The effectiveness of measures aimed at establishing a high level of security may change under different political or social conditions. An evaluation of which compensatory measures are sufficient and effective must be left to the political actors. The assessment may be guided by the proportionality principle—both vis-à-vis the Member States

> [W]hat has happened is that the EU/EC have in some cases achieved a mix of positive and negative legal integration (harmonising some external borders and migration law along with the abolition of internal border controls between most Member States), but that positive legal integration has been unbalanced (in the direction of greater controls of migrants, with little done to encourage *their* legal integration).... With little negative legal integration allowing for greater free movement of third-country nations or positive legal integration strengthening their integration, the positive legal integration which has been achieved—strengthening controls on illegal immigration and admission—does not merely fail to prevent a 'race to the bottom' toward more unfavourable treatment of third-country nationals, but encourages or compels Member States to engage in such a race.[16]

Even in the presence of such distortions, the fundamental link between the abolition of internal controls and the reinforcing of external controls has for a long time acted as the driving force for European integration on visas and borders. In other words, the interdependence between these two strategies has worked not only as a source of legal legitimation but also as a political motor, of an indirect and functionalist kind, for the advances in these two areas.

Only in recent years, a change in approach has been seen which was already contained in embryonic form in the insertion of the maintenance and development of an area of freedom, security, and justice amongst the fundamental objectives of the EU (Article 2 TEU). After the European Council of Tampere (15–16 October 1999), the raising of internal security levels was made a political objective in itself, and not one directly associated with the creation of an internal territory without frontiers. From this point of view, of particular significance are the statements contained in point 6 of the Conclusions of the Finnish presidency, in the section which states the main principles of European activity in matters of justice and internal affairs, the so-called 'Tampere milestones': '[p]eople have the right to expect the Union to address the threat to their freedom and legal rights posed by serious crime. To counter these threats a common effort is needed to prevent and fight crime and criminal organisations throughout the Union.' It is true that such a statement of principle does not directly challenge, at a legal level, the principle of proportionality between freedom and security, which retains a central role in JHA. Nevertheless, the reference to a *collective right to security* by itself indicates a change in approach. Progress in European integration on matters of internal security and, consequently, also of external border controls is

which, by the public order clauses included in Title IV EC have the right to maintain internal security, and vis-à-vis the individuals concerned, whose human rights to security (on the one hand) and freedom of movement (on the other) set the parameters for determining compensatory measures. Accordingly, the Community institutions enjoy a margin of political discretion in implementing Articles 62 and 63 EC': K. Hailbronner, *Immigration and Asylum Law and Policy of the European Union* (The Hague: Kluwer, 2000), 78.

[16] Peers, *supra* note 12, at 6.

increasingly explained by use of direct reference to some security demand expressed by European citizens. One can thus see a progressive slipping from forms of indirect and 'technocratic' legitimation based, as we have seen, upon interdependence between the abolition of internal borders and the strengthening of external controls, towards direct and 'democratic' legitimation strategies hinging on the explicit invoking of the public will.[17]

B. The Institutional Game: From the Affirmation to the Delimitation of Community Competence

For many years, the development of European co-operation on visas, borders, and immigration was dominated by inter-institutional battles, and legal and judicial controversies over the distribution of competencies in these areas. It has only been with the insertion of the new Title IV in the Community Treaty—made possible by the decisive British opt-out—that the question has been resolved. Only the politicking carried out at the Amsterdam IGC could sort out the clash between incompatible definitions towards which the Court had always adopted a cautious approach.

It was only after the implementation of the new treaty that the Court finally ruled the old Article 7a EC (now Article 14) could not have direct effect since:

> [a]s long as Community provisions have not been adopted concerning controls at the Community's external borders, which would also entail common or harmonised rules on the conditions governing entry, visas and asylum—the exercise of the right conferred upon citizens of the union by Article 8a of the Treaty (now, after amendment, Article 18 EC) presupposes that the person concerned is able to establish that he or she has the nationality of a Member State.[18]

We should also realize that such a level of judicial pragmatism was perhaps inevitable, as it was observed:

> [t]he Court could not overlook the political impact of a ruling that would establish a general prohibition on internal border controls on persons. Effective and common or harmonised police and immigration policies still do not exist in the Union today, not to mention at 1993, the time of the facts before the Court. Besides, most

[17] We should also note, however, the increasingly difficult task of explaining and justifying the reinforcement of external controls through the abolition of internal borders, in a period when such internal controls have been to a great extent re-introduced—in air travel at least—even if this has not been for reasons of migration policy. The key to this is quite clearly the impact that the terrorist attacks of 11 September 2001 have had on movement of persons in Europe, as elsewhere. The strengthening of security controls on air travel has contributed to changing the shape of the EU entry control system, substantially weakening its emphasis on the freedom of internal movement.

[18] Case C–378/98, *Wijsenbeek* [1999] ECR I–6207. Only much more recently, within a substantially altered normative framework, has the Court finally been forced to recognize the direct applicability of norms of European citizenship (cf. the ruling in Case C–224/98 *D'Hoop*, 11 July 2002).

Members States' governments would be against that prohibition. Therefore, this judgement may be seen as a sign of judicial realism and caution.[19]

On visas too, the Court of Justice preferred to adopt a 'respectful' attitude, declining to force by judicial means the political process of communitarization set out in Maastricht and continued by Amsterdam. We are referring to the fate of Regulation 2317/95 on visas. Having been annulled due to non-consultation of the European Parliament after substantial modification of the Commission's original proposal by the Council,[20] the binding force of this measure was preserved until the adoption of the subsequent Regulation 574/1999 (for which the Council did not wait for a new proposal from the Commission), and was subsequently modified in 2001 and 2003.

The strategic caution of the Court of Justice is even more clearly visible in the case of the third pillar Joint Action on airport transit visas.[21] Faced with an action of annulment brought by the Commission with the support of the European Parliament on grounds of breach of Community competence as defined in Article 100C EC (Maastricht numbering), the Court in fact accepted the arguments of the Member States involved (Denmark, France, and the UK) stating that:

> [A]rticle 100c(1) of the EC Treaty applies only to visas which permit their holders to cross the external borders of a Member State at such crossing points (i.e., border control points) in order to stay or travel in the internal market during the period and subject to the conditions prescribed by the visas.[22]

The *fictio juris* upon which the Court based this ruling raised many doubts, because, as has been quite rightly noted, '[t]he territory of a State is legally defined by borders, not by border control points. A visa relates to the right of entry into a territory, even if the holder is not submitted to any border controls.'[23] However, even these perplexities should today be regarded as having been resolved, since there seems little doubt that the wording of Article 62(2)(b)(i) can be interpreted to include airport transit visas.[24] This

[19] A. Castro Oliveira, 'Workers and Other Persons: Step-by-step from Movement to Citizenship—Case Law 1995–2001', 39 *Common Market Law Review* (2002) 103.

[20] Case C–392/95 *EP v. Council* (visa regulation) [1997] ECR I–3213.

[21] 96/197/JHA, OJ 1996 L63/8.

[22] Case C–170/96, *Commission of the European Communities* v. *Council of the European Union* [1998] ECR I–2763, para. 24.

[23] A. Castro Oliveira, 'Commentary to Court of Justice, Case C–170/96, *Commission of the European Communities* v. *Council of the European Union*, 12 May 1998, [1998] ECR I–2763', 99 *Common Market Law Review* (1999) 153.

[24] For example, this is the opinion of Peers, *supra* note 12, at 78–9. Undoubtedly, though, one can still argue another case: on the basis of a rigid conceptualization of the complementary relationship between 'measures aimed at ensuring the free movement of persons in accordance with Article 14' and 'flanking measures' one could claim that airport transit visas are outside the scope of Article 62(2) TEC. Under this interpretation, however, an irresolvable

also seems to be the European Commission's point of view which, in its statement on its Scoreboard 'to review progress on the creation of an area of "freedom, security and justice" in the European Union',[25] gives notice of a regulatory proposal on airport transit visas, indicating April 2001 as the deadline (since put back substantially).

Today, therefore, there is no doubt about the existence of Community competence on visas, borders, and immigration, but doubts nevertheless persist as to the extent and limits of such competence. In particular, the Treaty of Amsterdam has left open important questions regarding (a) the contents of Community competence, i.e. the interpretation of the list of Community-related matters, and (b) the actual manner in which such competences should be exercised, especially regarding the limits of executive competence and external competence, even in matters upon which the general principle of a central core of Community competence is no longer open to discussion.

The Contents of Community Competence

Following the entry into force of the Treaty of Amsterdam, cautious attitudes prevailed, both within European institutions as well as in academic studies, in the delimitation *ratione materiae* of the new Community sphere of competence. This tendency was evident at two levels: at a broader level, the area of competence defined by the new Title IV TEC was generally described as a mosaic of *ad hoc* normative competences, to be realized through the adoption of 'measures', 'rules', 'criteria' and 'standards' (mainly 'minimum' ones) by specific deadlines. There was, therefore, an extreme reluctance, not only within the Council but also within the European Commission, to describe communitarization as the unfolding of a 'common policy' amongst the Fifteen on asylum and immigration. At a more detailed level, namely the definition of individual provisions of Title IV, 'wary' approaches also predominated, underlining gaps in the list of competences and encouraging restrictive interpretations. For example, one author stated that, in Article 63(3)(b), '[t]he term "repatriation" only refers to illegal residents. Whether

paradox appears, because it would be difficult to include transit visas within the third pillar (this now being restricted to 'police and judicial cooperation in criminal matters') as the Council did in adopting the common action in 1996. It is also doubtful whether, in adopting a restricted interpretation of the scope of Article 62(2), so that airport transit visas would be excluded from Community competence, these could instead be brought under the remit of Article 308 TEC which limits the implied reach of community competence to matters concerning the correct functioning of the common market. This does not apply in the case of transit visas, whose only aim is to prevent illegal immigration.

[25] The latest version of this biannual communication is COM(2003)291 final, 22 May 2003, at 88.

this power may be used to prescribe standards on expulsion and deportation is highly questionable.'[26] Another commentator notes that '[i]mportant areas missing are, for instance, occupational admissions, measures regarding the social integration of asylum seekers and immigrants and interior enforcement measures (against clandestine entries and visa overstays)'.[27]

However, with the passage of time and the start of the actual policy-making process, this general attitude has changed. More open interpretations have appeared, not just in the academic sphere[28] but also in the decisions and rulings of the institutions. Here, we are referring both to specific policy changes, such as the adoption of the Directive on mutual recognition of deportation orders,[29] which opened the way for potential further normative harmonization in the same area, and also to more general trends, such as the fact that the concept of a *common* policy on asylum and immigration is by now currently used not only by the European Commission but also by the Council and the European Council.[30] The fact that a broad interpretation of competences in immigration has been affirmed in the practice and the habits of the EU institutions has been endorsed by the recent conclusions of the Working Group on Freedom, Security and Justice of the Convention on the Future of Europe: 'the Group does not recommend substantive changes to the legal bases contained in Article 63(3) and (4) TEC[31] *on the understanding that these include action against illegal immigration*, including criminal sanctions' (emphasis added).[32]

[26] Hailbronner, *supra* note 15, at 86.

[27] J. Monar, 'Justice and Home Affairs in the Treaty of Amsterdam: Reform at the Price of Fragmentation', 4 *European Law Review* (1998) 320, at 323.

[28] Peers, *supra* note 12, at 100.

[29] Directive 2001/40/EC, 28 May 2001, OJ 2001 L149/34.

[30] 'The European Council is determined to speed up the implementation of all aspects of the programme adopted in Tampere for the creation of an area of freedom, security, and justice in the European Union. The European Council points here to the need to develop a European Union *common policy* on the separate, but closely related, issues of asylum and immigration.' (Seville European Council, 21–22 June 2002, Presidency Conclusions, item 26, emphasis added).

[31] The only exception, contained in the previous section of the document, consists of a recommendation that a legal basis be introduced into the Treaty 'to allow the Union to take incentive and support measures to assist Member States' efforts to promote the integration of legally resident third country nationals'.

[32] Final Report of Working Group X, 'Freedom, Security and Justice', CONV 426/02, 2 December 2002. Part A, sect. I.2. As we shall expound in greater details in sect. 3.C., the final Draft of the Treaty establishing a Constitution for Europe, handed by the Convention to the IGC, held it safer to specify that:
'1. The Union shall develop a common immigration policy aimed at ensuring, at all stages, . . . the prevention of, and enhanced measures to combat, illegal immigration and trafficking in human beings.
2. To this end, European laws or framework laws shall establish measures in the following areas: . . . (c) illegal immigration and unauthorised residence, *including removal and repatriation of persons residing without authorisation*' (Art. III–168, emphasis added).

The Limits of Community Competence

With the gradual assertion of an extensive interpretation of the role of Community competence in migration policy, attention has shifted to the means by which such competence should be exercised. Amongst the first problems to emerge was that of the distribution of executive competence on Community matters and in particular those governed by the Schengen *acquis* and its post-Amsterdam developments. The general rule would obviously be that the Commission should assume the function of executing norms adopted by the Council, preserving the entitlement of the latter to 'impose certain requirements in respect of the exercise of these powers' and to 'reserve the right, in specific cases, to exercise directly implementing powers itself' (Article 202 TEC). Recent events have quickly demonstrated, however, that in this particular area the exceptions envisaged in the Article have attained a high degree of prominence. The delicacy of executive functions on visas and border controls, and their close link with the historic basis to national sovereignty, could in fact push the Council repeatedly to invoke the exception clause, thereby overturning the Community approach 'from the inside' and thus instigating a potentially long-term point of friction with the Commission. In fact, this scenario already seemed to be playing out when the Council (wearing its agricultural hat) granted itself the power to amend a substantial part of the rules contained in the Common Consular Instruction and the Common Manual by a simplified method through the low-key adoption of two regulations on 24 April 2001.[33] These two acts which had already given rise to a contrary vote in the European Parliament and to a parliamentary reservation raised by the Dutch delegation in the Council, were finally made the subject of an act of annulment by which '[t]the Commission submits that the Council has . . . improperly and irregularly reserved implementing powers to itself and that, in any event, the Council has neither adequately nor properly attributed the said reservation of implementing powers to itself'.[34] The ruling of the Court on this question will undoubtedly have a forceful impact on the actual development of the European migration control system in years to come: if the judges in Luxembourg were to validate the disputed acts, this would lead to the confirmation (until eventual reforms on this point) of the principle that, on visa and border issues, the Community method is undergoing structural derogations which leave the major part of executive action under the control of Member States.[35]

[33] Regulations 789/2001 and 790/2001, OJ 2001 L116/2 and 5.

[34] Action brought on 3 July 2001 by the Commission of the European Communities against the Council of the European Union (Case C–257/01) (2001/C245/21), OJ C245/12 of 1 August 2001.

[35] An encouraging sign in this respect is contained in the Conclusions adopted without debate by the JHA Council of 19 December 2002, on the theme 'External border checks and

Similar doubts arise when one tries to delimit the sphere of external competence of Community institutions in this area. As has been noted, the IGC which was concluded in Amsterdam outlined a regime of exceptions to the general Community rule, laid out by the Court of Justice in its 1994 opinion on the GATS and TRIPS agreements, on the basis of which: '[o]nly in so far as common rules have been established at internal level does external competence become exclusive'.[36]

This principle is now affected by Protocol no. 8 annexed to the Treaty of Amsterdam, according to which the norms of Title IV TEC on matters of external border controls 'shall be without prejudice to the competence of Member States to negotiate or conclude agreements with third countries as long as they respect Community law and other relevant international agreements'. One further exception to general Community law doctrine on external competence seems to be suggested by Declaration no. 18, also annexed to the Treaty of Amsterdam, which allows Member States to negotiate and sign accords with third countries on matters of legal immigration (including family reunion) 'as long as such agreements respect Community law'. Amongst the main commentators,[37] there seems to be unanimity on the fact that these arrangements form an exception to Community law, allowing a certain room for manœuvre for Member States in the international arena; nevertheless, the implications of such an exception remain uncertain. Doubts especially arise on a certain type of international accord which has great

combating illegal immigration'. With reference to a specific technical problem dealt with by the Schengen Common Manual (the need to stamp the travel documents of all third-country citizens on entry to the EU and the consequences of not having such a stamp), para. 6 of the document states: 'the Council invites the Commission to clarify, before the next Justice and Home Affairs Council, the existing rules of the Schengen acquis and to reflect on amending the relevant rules accordingly. The consequences of a lack of entry stamps in travel documents should also be examined, including the question of presumption of irregular stay. In this regard, proposals could be submitted, if necessary, with a view to harmonise [*sic*] the practices of stamping of travel documents, also in the perspective of enlargement.' In relation to the theme in question, this seems to represent a full and spontaneous recognition of the Commission's executive prerogative.

[36] Court of Justice Opinion 1/94 of 15 November 1994, Competence of the Community to Conclude International Agreements Concerning Services and the Protection of Intellectual Property (GATS and TRIPS), [1994] ECR I–5267, para. 77. Despite a certain attenuation by the Court of Justice with regard to certain specific situations (Opinion 2/91, [1993] ECR I–1061; Opinion 2/92, [1995] I–521), the ruling given in the first aforementioned Opinion provides a basis for the consistent jurisprudence of the Court of Justice. It should be noted that Article 12(2) of the Draft Treaty establishing a Constitution for Europe (CONV 850/03, 18 July 2003) now proposes a slightly different approach:

'The Union shall have exclusive competence for the conclusion of an international agreement when its conclusion is provided for in a legislative act of the Union, is necessary to enable it to exercise its internal competence, or affects an internal Union act.'

[37] Hailbronner, *supra* note 15, at 65; Peers, *supra* note 12, at 79.

practical importance for migration management—*readmission agreements*. Since Article 63(3)(b) is mentioned neither in the Protocol nor in the Declaration cited above, it could be argued that, in matters pertaining to the repatriation of persons in irregular situations, the general principle that internal norms produce an exclusive external competence for the Community holds. The problem appeared in concrete form after the bestowal by the Council of a first 'package' of legal mandates to negotiate readmission agreements with certain third countries upon the Commission.[38] Since a Southern European Member State had already started negotiations on the same type of accords with one of the third countries specified, it appears from unofficial sources that the European Commission had made some preliminary moves to assess the possibility of ordering the Member State in question to interrupt these negotiations and, if necessary, to begin an infraction procedure. At this point, however, it seems that the Commission has decided to postpone action or even to renounce it, implicitly accepting that, even in matters of repatriation and readmission of foreigners in irregular situations, a regime of external competence split between the Member States and the Community institutions exists. From this perspective too, the institutional specificity of migration in the Community arena appears to be confirmed.[39]

C. Methods of Integration: The Difficult Balance between Mutual Recognition and Harmonization

Having tried to answer in the previous sections the questions *why* an EU entry control system was born and *who* (i.e. which institutions) has so far directed the formative process, it is worth asking *how* (i.e. via which regulatory methods) such a system has been structured. To answer this basic question, it is useful to start with some brief theoretical considerations of the legal dimension of European integration. The integration of a plurality of national legal systems within a common framework is an extremely complex process which was historically made possible by the flexible use of a multiplicity of different regulatory methods, according to the sector involved, and implying varying levels of convergence amongst national legal frameworks.

[38] Hitherto, the Council has bestowed such mandates for readmission agreements upon the Commission with regard to Albania, Algeria, China, Hong Kong, Morocco, Macao, Pakistan, Russia, Sri Lanka, Turkey, and Ukraine. The first 'European' readmission agreement was signed on 27 November 2002 with Hong Kong; on 30 May and 18 October 2002, the agreements with Sri Lanka and Macao respectively were initialled.

[39] Such a preliminary conclusion is now thrown into doubt by the recent news that the Commission was about to start an infraction procedure against Germany for analogous reasons ('UE/Immigration: La Commission s'apprêterait à lancer une procédure d'infraction contre l'Allemagne, pour un accord de réadmission signé avec la Chine', Agence Europe, *Bulletin Quotidien Europe*, no. 8542, 16 September 2003, at 9).

From this perspective, a 'methods of legal integration' scale can be drawn up with, at one end, no harmonization of legal norms (classically defined as norms of a general and abstract nature) being carried out and integration occurring exclusively via *mutual recognition* of administrative or legal provisions as defined by national authorities. One can subsequently identify various levels of *normative harmonization* which extend from the definition of minimum standards to which all national arrangements should conform to the adoption of a *common set of norms* which applies integrally in all Member States, thus eliminating the previous plurality of national standards in a given sector.[40]

It should also be noted that each of these regulatory methods can of course be applied more or less strictly: a system of mutual recognition, for example, can or cannot permit exceptions in certain cases; similarly a system of minimum standards or a set of common norms will have a very different profile and implications according to whether it is legally binding and judicially enforceable, or whether it simply takes the form of soft law.

To understand the current anatomy of the EU entry control system, it is useful to recall how the various regulatory methods were combined prior to the Treaty of Amsterdam. To do so, we need not spend time on the third pillar, as it was originally shaped by the Maastricht Treaty—we need only recall that it was a relatively simple and quite ineffective combination of soft law (most of it containing general principles and norms, with few detailed prescriptions) and some secondary norms packaged in those few conventions which were adopted. Of greater interest, because of the continued influence that it has over Community law-making even after Amsterdam, is instead the regulatory method used in the Schengen context, which is characterized by an original combination of mutual recognition and minimum standards. The migration control component of the Schengen system hinged upon two 'loops' of mutual recognition, which themselves were based upon a standard level of normative convergence; this was obtained through a set of minimum common standards complemented by a supranational mechanism for the control of their implementation at national level. More precisely, full members of Schengen committed themselves to mutual recognition of their respective decisions in two key arenas of migration control:

(a) national admission decisions formalized by the granting of a visa for a period of less than three months (short-stay uniform visas, Articles 9–17, Schengen Implementation Convention) or of greater duration (long-stay national visas, Article 18, Schengen Implementation Convention);

[40] Beyond these regulatory methods—which all affect, with varying intensity, the universe of *primary norms*, or norms which regulate the relationship between private individuals or those between public authorities and individuals—European legal integration obviously is also crucially dependent on a large body of secondary norms, of an organizational nature, whose fundamental function is to regulate relations between Member States.

(b) national non-admission decisions, for reasons of law and order or public safety, or based upon previous violations of national norms on entry and residence for foreigners (Article 96, Schengen Implementation Convention).

As we have already said, both these loops of mutual recognition presupposed a minimum level of harmonization of national norms on visas and border control. This common floor was scarcely to be found in the 1990 Convention. A more substantial source was provided by the standards contained in a body of law of uncertain legal standing and highly restricted contents—in particular the Common Consular Instructions and Common Manual.[41]

Even now that the communitarization process is underway, and following the incorporation of the Schengen *acquis* within EU law, this double loop of mutual recognition remains at the heart of the EU migration control system. Article 62 TEC may not limit Community competence on visas and border controls to the adoption of minimum standards (as it does in matters of asylum, as stated in Article 63), but the level of harmonization in this domain has nevertheless remained low, leaving the bulk of the responsibility to the mutual recognition mechanism. This specific combination of regulatory mechanisms—we might call it a 'regulatory strategy'—has a significant effect on the general anatomy of the EU entry control system and on its tangible implications, particularly from the point of view of the targets of these norms, namely the migrants or, more generally, third-country nationals who wish to enter the EU. In this regard, two general considerations are in order.

First, by its very nature, a regulatory system based on mutual recognition allows ample room for national discretion and thus differential treatment. In many areas, such heterogeneity poses no problems and, on the contrary, can work particularly well, both from a practical point of view—because it gives the system adaptive strength—and from a theoretical point of view—relating to the general rules of subsidiarity and proportionality. In migration matters, however, the risk that such heterogeneity turns into unjustified discrimination is especially high: as Ryszard Cholewinski states, somewhat polemically: '[a]lthough frequently not articulated in this way, discrimination between third-country nationals lies at the heart of the cross or mutual recognition exercise and it is difficult to see what reasons can be

[41] These two essential collections of operational norms, initially drafted by the Schengen Executive Committee, have now been transformed, with amendments, into Council documents (*Common Consular Instructions on visas for the diplomatic missions and consular posts*, 2002/C 313/01; *Common Manual*, doc. 8248/01 (both these documents have now finally been published, with the exclusion of certain reserved sections, in OJ C313)).

advanced for the differences in treatment short of deterring third-country nationals from entering the EU.'[42]

Such a view is reinforced by a second general consideration. Successive developments since the entry into force of the Treaty of Amsterdam have confirmed a tendency which was already previously evident: mutual recognition works much more easily 'negatively' (disfavouring immigrants, by generalizing the effect of negative acts or provisions) than 'positively' (by generalizing favourable effects). Examples are numerous, starting with the visa regulation which, as originally proposed by the Commission in December 1993, even foresaw a mechanism of mutual recognition for visas issued by a Member State, but which in its final Council-approved version[43] did not include such form of mutual recognition favourable to migrants. More recently, it is significant that, amongst the relatively few acts approved by the Council on the basis of the new Title IV TEC on matters of immigration policy, one finds Directive 2001/40[44] on reciprocal recognition of expulsion orders, rooted in an initiative by the French government and approved by the JHA Council of May 2001, despite the opposition of the European Parliament.

The regulatory strategy described—which steered the whole formative period of the EU entry control system, pre- and post-Amsterdam—is probably the most effective, from the point of view of the speed of decision-making. Indeed, this allows the drawn-out process of assessing the specific contents of norms on visas and borders to be dispensed with, limiting negotiations to the procedural aspect—in other words relative to the conditions and modes of reciprocal recognition. Nevertheless, this regulatory strategy—which, as we have seen, has already raised specific criticisms inspired by civil libertarian demands *vis-à-vis* third-country nationals[45]—has begun to reveal the practical limits relative to its effectiveness in terms of migration control. These limits are particularly evident in light of the imminent enlargement of the EU (cf. section 3.B).

[42] R. Cholewinski, *Borders and Discrimination in the European Union*, a report for the Immigration Law Practitioners' Association (ILPA) and the Migration Policy Group (MPG) (London-Brussels: 2002), at 35. In the report, Cholewinski also denounces an example of 'negative' mutual recognition encountered in practice: the 'proscription list' used to exclude persons informally assessed as suspect or *non gratae* from the allocation of entry visas, which would be shared by EU consulates in certain third countries (at 30). If confirmed, such practice would most likely be illegal.

[43] Reg. 2317/95.

[44] OJ 2001 L149/34.

[45] It is significant that the proposals on immigration and asylum presented following the implementation of the Treaty of Amsterdam by two of the main organizations for migrants' rights were based upon a fundamental methodological option favouring normative harmonization rather than mutual recognition (Immigration Law Practitioners' Association and Migration Policy Group, *The ILPA / MPG Proposed Directives on Immigration and Asylum*, (Brussels-London: ILPA & MPG, 2000)).

D. Structural Imbalances: The Belated Community Intervention on Legal Immigration

From a substantive perspective, a large number of the norms and measures which today make up the EU entry control system derive from the transfer of a pre-existing intergovernmental *acquis* into the Community arena. Of the three thematic blocs which make up this chapter—visas, borders, and immigration—only one actually represents a novelty in terms of the norms set out in the Schengen system. For this reason, whilst this is certainly not the right place to look systematically at the Schengen framework on matters of visas and border controls, it seems worthwhile dwelling briefly upon Community action on legal immigration. Article 63(3)(a) and Article 63(4)EC introduce certain novel elements into the EU entry control system and, even if these seeds have so far scarcely borne fruit, their very presence is of notable significance in the systemic framework which we have adopted.

In looking at Community action on regular immigration, it seems useful for us to begin once more with an inquiry into *la finalité politique*, or the basic motivations and objectives which have led to the communitarization of this domain. To this end, it is above all necessary to remember that, within Schengen, legal immigration policy, i.e. the power to organize admission and residence for periods greater than three months, was conceived of as an *almost* exclusive prerogative of sovereign states. Indeed, the 1990 Implementation Convention stated in the clearest of terms that '[v]isas for stays exceeding three months shall be national visas issued by one of the Contracting Parties in accordance with its national law' (Article 18(1)). The main limit to this national power, justified by the limited freedom of movement allowed to foreigners admitted in the Schengen space on the basis of a national visa, was stated by the first section of the subsequent Article 25 and was not absolute:

> Where a Contracting Party considers issuing a residence permit to an alien for whom an alert has been issued for the purposes of refusing entry, it shall first consult the Contracting Party issuing the alert and shall take account of its interests; the residence permit shall be issued for substantive reasons only, notably on humanitarian grounds or by reason of international commitments.
>
> If a residence permit is issued, the Contracting Party issuing the alert shall withdraw the alert but may put the alien concerned on its national list of alerts.

The preservation of this core of national sovereignty within the Schengen framework can basically be explained by the fact that what we have already defined as the 'politico-conceptual motor' of the EU entry control system's creation (section 2A)—that is, the interdependence between the abolition of internal controls and the reinforcement of external controls—did not involve (or hardly so) the policies and national legislation on legal immigration. As noted above, the freedom of movement allowed to foreigners with residency permits over three months was rigorously restricted to brief stays 'within the territories of the other Contracting Parties' (Article 21(1), Schengen Implementation Convention). The impact of such limited movement was further reduced, on paper at least, by the mutual readmission obligation which was rather understated in Article 23, but over time has been rendered more cogent by a network of bilateral agreements.

Although completely marginalized within the Schengen framework, the theme of legal immigration is to be found within the pre-Amsterdam third pillar in the form of six resolutions approved by the Council between 1993 and 1997.[46] The Commission drew upon this broad swathe of soft law when, a few months prior to the signing of the Treaty of Amsterdam, it presented an ambitious proposal for a Convention on admission and integration,[47] with the intention of 'marking out its territory' and possibly presenting it again as a Directive proposal after the instigation of the new treaty. If, on a political and conceptual plane, the aforementioned acts were of some significance, from a more strictly legal point of view the third pillar's output on regular immigration remains limited to a single joint action, relating to the format of residency permits.[48]

When the effects of the Treaty of Amsterdam began to be seen, therefore, the panorama of national normative frameworks on admission for periods over three months was extremely heterogeneous and marked by a deep divide between countries still formally adhering to a policy of 'zero immigration' and countries—particularly those in Southern Europe—with an explicit policy of economic migration. It was onto this starting point—clearly described in a study carried out on behalf of the European Commission in 2000[49]—that the cautious communitarization approach set out in Article 63(3)–(4) TEC was grafted.[50]

[46] For a summary analysis see Peers, *supra* note 12, at 84–90; see also Hailbronner, *supra* note 15, at 260 *et seq.*

[47] COM(97)387, 30 July 1997.

[48] Joint Action 97/11/JHA of 16 December 1996, published in OJ 1997 L7.

[49] Ecotec—Research and Consulting, 2000, *Admission of Third Country Nationals for Paid Employment or Self-Employed Activity*, study carried out on behalf of the European Commission (DG JHA) (Brussels-Birmingham-Madrid: Ecotec, 2000).

[50] It is worth emphasizing that, unlike almost all other aspects of Community policy on immigration and asylum, the measures on legal immigration policy are not subject to any deadline (Article 63, last section). As we have anticipated in sect. 2B, the particularly elastic nature of the communitarization process in this domain is also confirmed by Declaration no. 18, linked to the Treaty of Amsterdam, which states that 'Member States may negotiate and conclude agreements with third countries in the domains covered by Article 63(3)(a) of the Treaty establishing the European Community as long as such agreements respect Community law'. External competence of Members States on regular immigration is thereby expressly preserved.

What then is the rationale for these norms, given that they lie outside the original integration project developed in Schengen, so much so that they are not defined as 'directly related flanking measures' under Article 61(a)? The answer, which is vital to the understanding of current Community law-making process and to predicting its future developments, depends upon the institutional perspective which one adopts.

From the perspective of national executives which in 1997 signed up to these norms, the 'promise' of communitarizing legal immigration policy constituted by itself an important political result, destined to reinforce the legitimacy of European action on migration policy within the more progressive sectors of public opinion, without generating rigid strictures on subsequent political and normative actions.[51]

From the European Commission's point of view, the original objectives of this strand of communitarization were undoubtedly different, even if it is not easy to define what they were with any precision, in the absence of any clear, coherent, and exhaustive lay-out of the Commission's strategy on this matter. At various times, the Commission put forward different structural explanations of the necessity for communitarizing legal immigration policy without ever providing a single convincing framework to support that need. Many of the explanations provided, in particular those put forward in the Explanatory Memorandum on the directive proposal 'on the conditions of entry and residence of third-country nationals for the purpose of paid employment and self-employed economic activities',[52] seemed insufficient fully to justify the proposed action in light of the subsidiarity principle.[53] In the Commission's official statements, one can still find stronger arguments, even if these were not sufficiently developed and brought out; three in particular stand out as worthy of note here, given their relevance to a systemic analysis of EU law and policies on migration management:

[51] See *supra* note 47.

[52] COM(2001)386 final, 11 July 2001.

[53] In the abovementioned Explanatory Memorandum, the Commission explains, for example, its decision to promote convergence between national legislations and policies in admission matters with the necessity of 'providing procedural and transparency safeguards, in order to assure a high level of legal certainty and information for all interested actors', of 'providing a single national application procedure leading to one combined title, encompassing both residence and work permits within one administrative act, in order to simplify and harmonise the diverging rules currently applicable in Member States', of 'providing rights to third-country nationals while respecting Member States' discretion to limit economic migration', etc. For all that such objectives may be reasonable, one cannot help but note that all of them—except harmonization itself, which sometimes seems to be presented as an end in itself—can be effectively pursued at the national level and do not necessarily require a Community-level effort towards harmonization.

The Commission's Arguments: Preventing Irregular Migration

First, a certain degree of harmonization of admission policies has been presented as an effective tool for preventing clandestine and irregular immigration:

> Member States will be in a better position to address the problem of irregular migration if they are equipped with a broad range of migration management policies going beyond measures to curb the perceived or real misuse of their asylum systems. Opening up legal admission policies for labour migration will not completely prevent this, however, and they should be accompanied by both appropriate anti-smuggling measures and effective asylum adjudication systems.[54]

It should, however, be recognized that such a rationale, even if quite plausible (and shared by the author), nevertheless remains very controversial at the empirical level and does not seem sufficient to justify the body of action proposed in the light of the subsidiarity principle. Greater weight seems to have been given—particularly in supporting the two crucial (and tightly interwoven) proposals on the status of long-term resident third-country nationals[55] and on admission for economic reasons—to two essentially economic arguments.

The Commission's Arguments: Extending Freedom of Movement

In various arenas, the European Commission has seemed to reduce the harmonization of admission policies to some kind of secondary or derivative status where the primary objective of Community action would be the extension to third-country nationals legally resident in a Member State of the freedom of movement for work-related purposes. In particular, in the Explanatory Memorandum relating to the directive proposal on the status of long-term residents, the Commission stated that 'a genuine area of freedom, security and justice, a fundamental objective of the European Union, is unthinkable without a degree of mobility for third country nationals residing there legally, and particularly for those residing on a long-term basis'.[56]

But, despite the generic reference to the implications of establishing an area of freedom, security, and justice, the reasons presented in support of such a fundamental strategic choice are essentially economic:

[54] Communication from the Commission to the Council and the European Parliament, *On a Community Immigration Policy*, COM(2000)757, 22 November 2000, section 3.2.

[55] COM(2001)127, 13 March 2001.

[56] Commission of the European Communities, Proposal for a Council Directive concerning the status of third-country nationals who are long-term residents, COM(2001)127 final, 13 March 2001, para. 5.6.

The evolution of the employment market in the Union is highlighting employment shortages in certain sectors of the economy. Third-country nationals who are long-term residents may be ready and willing to relocate either in order to put their vocational skills to work in another Member State or to escape unemployment in the Member State where they reside. The mobility of long-term residents can thus make for better utilisation of employment reserves available in different Member States.[57]

But, if some degree of liberalization of intra-EU freedom of movement for foreign long-term resident workers were established, the actual interdependence among national laws and policies on admission would become much tighter. At that point—this was the reasoning of the Commission—a degree of harmonization even in the latter arena would be strongly needed, for political rather than technical reasons: to return to our previous categories (section 2A), *negative* integration of long-term resident status would impose *positive* integration on matters of admission.[58]

The Commission's Arguments: Increasing European Competitiveness

Finally, the Commission has rightly argued that, in order to increase European competitiveness in the global market of qualified labour capital, a simplification of admission procedures on a continental scale is desirable:

In an increasingly global labour market and faced with shortage of skilled labour in certain sectors of the labour market the Community should reinforce its competitiveness to recruit and attract third-country workers, when needed. This should be facilitated by administrative simplification and by facilitating access to relevant information. Transparent and harmonised rules on the conditions under which third-country nationals may enter and stay in the Community to pursue economic activities, and their right, should be laid down.[59]

This summary reconstruction of the Commission's arguments helps us to understand better the extent of Community action on legal immigration, as well as the reasons for the limited advance in this political and normative project.[60]

[57] Ibid., para. 5.8.

[58] This argument is supported elsewhere: for example, in the proposed Directive on long-term residency status, recital 12: 'Harmonisation of the terms for acquisition of long-term resident status promotes mutual confidence between Member States.... The possibility of applying more favourable national provisions is not excluded by the Treaty. However, for the purposes of this Directive, it should be provided that permits issued on more favourable and unharmonised terms do not confer the right to reside in other Members States.'

[59] Commission of the European Communities, Proposal for a Council Directive on the conditions of entry and residence of third-country nationals for the purpose of paid employment and self-employed economic activities, COM(2001)386 final, 11 July 2001, proposed recital 6, at 22.

[60] So far, the only act formally adopted in this domain (if we except Regulation 859/2003 on third-country nationals' social security which lies outside the strict scope of this essay) has

Through intensive intellectual and political work, the Community executive has conceived an integrated system regulating entry and legal residence of foreigners in the EU. The politico-normative nub of this system—whose guidelines are to be found in the Communication *On a Community Immigration Policy*[61]—was made up of the two cited proposals on long-term third-country residents and admission for economic reasons.[62] This normative architecture was completed by the directive proposal 'on the conditions of entry and residence of third-country nationals for the purpose of study and vocational training and for non remunerated purposes'.[63] Within the Commission's strategy, a crucial role towards the eventual functioning of the system was initially attributed to the *open method of co-ordination for the Community immigration policy*, proposed in Communication COM(2001)387 of July 2001.

Faced with such a broad and demanding plan, the first reaction of Member States has been tepid to say the least and the overall Commission's strategy did not find general support. Negotiations within the Council Working Groups on various aspects of this strategy have been carried out at different speeds and with different levels of effect. Eventually, the European Council of Seville formally 'dismantled' the comprehensive approach of the Commission, mentioning only the Directive on the status of long-term residents (and not that on admission for economic reasons) amongst the acts which the Council needed to approve 'without delay' and 'before June 2003'. Such a strong and targeted political backing did produce its intended results: the text on long-term residents was finally agreed at the June 2003 Justice and Home Affairs Council, although in a strongly diluted version compared to the original proposal.

The uncoupling of these two normative proposals which together formed the key axis of the European Commission's strategy cannot but generate some puzzlement. Even if the approach of DG JHA was in many ways debatable,[64] it at least had some internal coherence, given the combination of negative integration, looking to extend the freedom of movement to citizens of third

been the regulation which instigates a uniform model for residency permits given to third-country nationals (CE 1030/2002)—an essentially technical act with little innovative value.

[61] COM(2000)757, November 2000.

[62] We will limit ourselves to mentioning here the directive proposal on the right to family reunification (the most recent version of which is COM(2002)225 final, 2 May 2002, finally agreed upon at the 27–28 February 2003 JHA Council). This Directive certainly falls within the basket of Community actions on legal immigration, but it responds to a different logic from the other proposals cited in this essay, and constitutes the focus of another essay in this volume (by Steve Peers) for that very reason.

[63] COM(2002)1886, 7 October 2002.

[64] For a critique see F. Pastore and G. Sciortino, 'Immigration and European Immigration Policies: Myths and Realities', in J. Apap (ed.), *Extending the Area of Freedom, Security and Justice through Enlargement: Challenges for the European Union* (provisional title), forthcoming.

countries based in the EU, and positive integration through regulations governing admission for economic reasons. Once this parallel approach is abandoned, the general meaning and implications of Community action on legal immigration needs to be rethought.

The bold approach initially adopted by the Commission which *de facto* aimed at gradually shaping the Community as a unified space for legal immigration and for the circulation of third-country workers has been (temporarily, at least) abandoned. As was abruptly demonstrated by the last-minute insertion in the text of the draft EU Constitution of Article III–168(5),[65] some Member States are absolutely not ready for any form of harmonization in the field of admission, which would entail a potential weakening of their capacity to limit entries. The debate on a 'European quota system' launched by the Italian Presidency of the EU on the occasion of the informal JHA Council of 12–13 September 2003 could certainly bring interesting policy developments, but the substantive terms of the proposal are still far from clear and the political divergences among Member States far from surmounted.

For the time being, the structural imbalance which has characterized the entire formative period of the EU entry control system persists: the 'defensive' and control-oriented component of the system keeps growing in complexity and effectiveness whilst the component designed to promote civil and economic liberties remains little more than an intention.

3. THE CURRENT EVOLUTION OF THE EU ENTRY CONTROL SYSTEM

A. Deepening: Towards Common Structures for Immigration Control?

With regard to the framework set out so far, a series of recent events has produced changes of notable importance. In particular, we can distinguish three simultaneous processes transforming the EU entry control system: an acceleration towards a deepening of European co-operation on matters of migration control via the creation of new instruments and common structures; the broadening of the EU entry control system which will occur after the joining of ten new members on 1 May 2004; and the prospect of institutional reforms which, after the preparatory phase within the Convention on the Future of Europe, will be decided upon at the IGC on treaty reform opened in Rome on 4 October 2003. These three evolutions are closely

[65] According to which, the establishment of a common immigration policy 'shall not affect the right of Member States to determine volumes of admission of third country nationals coming from third countries to their territory in order to seek work, whether employed or self employed'.

interlinked and only a unified analysis can allow predictions as to the future of European mechanisms on migration control.

Since autumn 2001, a real 'race' to achieve technical and organizational innovation within the EU entry control system has started. During it, the European institutions and Member States (in particular the holders of the Union Presidency during this period) have been vying with one another for politico-conceptual leadership, or at least strong influence, in a phase of sectoral renewal which nevertheless has important general political implications. Unlike in the past, the Commission has also played a very significant orientation and co-ordination role in this period, in a clear and largely successful effort to avoid political marginalization.[66]

To give an idea of the intensity with which the technical and political drafting took place, it is useful to list the main documents—of variable form and institutional progeny—which marked the period in question. The Commission kicked off with its Communication to the Council and the European Parliament, 'On a common policy on illegal immigration',[67] presented on 15 November 2001. The suggestions contained in the Communication were largely endorsed by the 'Comprehensive plan to combat illegal immigration and trafficking of human beings in the European Union'[68] approved by the Justice and Home Affairs Council on 28 February 2002. Debate intensified with the Commission Communication to the Council and European Parliament on 'an integrated management of the external borders of the Member States of the European Union',[69] published on 7 May 2002.[70] A further contribution appeared with the presentation in Rome on 30 May 2002 of the final report of the *Feasibility Study for the Setting Up of a 'European Border Police'*, carried out by the governments of Italy, Belgium, France, Germany, and Spain with the support of the Odysseus Programme of the European Commission. The operational phase began fully with the approval of the *Plan for the management of the external borders of the Member States of the European*

[66] As we have already seen in detail, the fundamental lines of the EU entry control system do not derive from Commission initiatives, but rather from independent elaboration by Member States mainly carried out in the Schengen sphere. Following the communitarization of the Schengen *acquis*, the Community executive was slow to assume the role of a driving force in this sector (except, as we have seen, on matters of legal immigration—section 2D), despite the request contained in the 'Action plan of the Council and the Commission on how best to implement the provisions of the Treaty of Amsterdam establishing an area of freedom, security and justice' (Council Doc. 13844/98, 4 December 1998), which inserts the fight against illegal immigration among the measures to be adopted within two years (point 36 c iii).

[67] COM(2001)672 final.

[68] DOC. 6621/1/02.

[69] COM(2002)233 final.

[70] On this communication, see the European Parliament report (A5-0449/2002—*rapporteur*: Hubert Pirker), approved by the Assembly on 15 January 2003.

Union[71] by the JHA Council of 13 June 2002. Subsequent to the European Council of Seville (21–22 June 2002) giving further political impetus to this development, a detailed timeframe was drawn up by the Council with its approval of the 'Road map for the follow-up to the conclusions of the European Council in Seville—Asylum, Immigration and border control'.[72] The general proceedings were set down in two reports produced by the Council, a 'Status report on the follow-up to the Seville conclusions on asylum and migration'[73] and a more specific 'Progress report on the implementation of the Plan for the management of the external borders of the Member States of the European Union and the comprehensive plan to combat illegal immigration'.[74] Indeed, as the Commission points out, '2002 was certainly particularly productive in terms of political programming';[75] but the process did not slow down much during the following year. New documents were produced for the Thessaloniki European Council of 19 and 20 June 2003: one more progress report on the Seville agenda by the Greek Presidency and another Commission Communication 'on the development of a common policy on illegal immigration, smuggling and trafficking of human beings, external borders and the return of illegal residents'.[76] To complete the picture, it is worth adding that, to the complex strategy of the (then) Fifteen in the fight against illegal immigration and migrants' smuggling, also belong measures which go beyond the bounds of our analysis—in particular, the action plan adopted by the Council on repatriation of illegal migrants.[77] All these strands are then tightly connected with the ongoing reflection on the modes of integrating migration issues into the EU external relations system—and even within this new agenda, the fight against illegal immigration represents a central priority.[78]

Within this hectically busy policy field, in which the symbolic and rhetorical elements of policy-making often take precedence over substantive regulatory and operational activity, it is not easy to identify strands of innovation which relate specifically to the themes of this essay. An effort should be made on this, however, in order to bring together and highlight a series of structural transformations of the EU entry control system which have been shaped in the most recent period.

[71] DOC. 10019/02. [72] DOC. 10525/02, 2 July 2002.

[73] 14707/02, 25 November 2002. [74] 14708/02, 26 November 2002.

[75] COM(2003)323, 3 June 2003, p. 3. [76] COM(2003)323, 3 June 2003.

[77] There are two complementary documents: the first (doc. 14673/02, 25 November 2002) has general scope, whilst the second (doc. 15215/02, 4 December 2002) looks specifically at Afghan citizens within the EU. The Council's planning on repatriation policy is largely based upon the contents of the Green Paper presented by the Commission in April 2002 (COM(2002)175) and of the subsequent Communication (COM(2002)564).

[78] Commission of the European Communities, *Integrating migration issues in the European Union's relations with third countries*, Communication to the Council and the European Parliament, COM(2002)703 final, 3 December 2002. The Commission's Communication fostered the adoption of a specific set of Conclusions by the Council in May 2003 (doc. 8927/03).

With regard to a model of migration control whose basic architecture was still that envisaged by Schengen, the current changes respond to some fundamental demands which have been made in varying degrees and nuances by political elites and administrative and security bodies alike. These demands are threefold in nature:

(a) the demand for the extension of the area of control, by extending the number and categories of migrants and potential migrants subject to controls. This demand is inspired by the preoccupation with security, and not just migration policy, and has been particularly strongly felt since 11 September 2001;
(b) the demand for greater integration of national migration control systems in order to increase their effectiveness, but also to strengthen common monitoring mechanisms of control activities. This demand has been seen to increase in intensity with the imminent broadening of the EU entry control system, and in particular with the accession of states whose national control systems are in clear need of strengthening;
(c) the demand for greater integration of national migration control systems in order to redistribute the costs connected with external EU border control. Although made by some Member States for a long time, this demand too has acquired renewed intensity on the eve of enlargement.

How can these specific factors of change be translated into concrete reform? Amongst the many technical novelties in development, two merit particular attention for their undoubted systemic importance and for the significant implications they will have in the legal and institutional domains.

European Databases for Migration Control

The first such novelty consists of the generalization of the practice of common files (that is, European databases) on third-country citizens for the purposes of migration control, and of the bringing forward of the point in time when a migrant to the EU (or even a would-be migrant, as we will immediately see) is actually recorded. Hitherto, as has been noted, the storage of personal data for migration purposes has been carried out solely for categories classified as 'high risk'—in the context of a entry refusal or expulsion order; for the databank on 'non-admissible' foreigners within the Schengen Information System (Article 96(3), Schengen Convention); or subsequent to an asylum request or following an apprehension due to irregular crossing of an external border (under the Eurodac system, in force since 15 January 2003).[79]

[79] The protracted developmental phase of Eurodac (formally instigated by Regulation 2725/2000, OJ 2002 L62/1), long paralysed by divergences among Member States on the modes of implementation, finally bore fruit with the adoption of the initiation regulation (doc. 6328/ 02+6345/02 ADD 1) by the JHA Council in February 2002.

Hitherto, then, the EU migration control system has made use of extremely selective systems of integrated electronic filing which were triggered only at the moment of contact between a migrant and control authorities along an external border or within the EU. With the Action Plan approved on 28 February 2002, the Council agreed to provide a third electronic identification network for migration policy purposes alongside the two existing databases, provisionally called the European Visa Identification System (VIS). This new tool, which the Seville European Council decided to establish as quickly as possible 'in the light of a feasibility study to be submitted in March 2003 and on the basis of guidelines from the Council',[80] should take the shape of an extremely capacious and powerful database containing personal and biometric data relating to all third-country nationals who ask for a visa to enter the EU, regardless of the outcome of the visa application. The creation of this archive would be accompanied by a modification of the standard uniform visa, in order to guarantee a clear connection between a person's identity and the self-adhesive visa, via the incorporation of a photograph using specialized technology.[81] This new filing system should ensure the 'traceability' of each person who requests a visa; as a control mechanism, this would undoubtedly be useful in many ways—it would permit, for example, a clear distinction in practice between illegal entrants and illegal residents,[82] it would allow easy recognition of travel document frauds, and would facilitate readmission via duplication of travel permits hidden by migrants (but present in the database). It is expressly foreseen that the future VIS will be developed to allow the most effective interaction

[80] Conclusions of the Seville European Council (21–22 June 2002), point 30. The fundamental attitude of the Council towards the structure and role of the future VIS is to be found in Council of the European Union, *Guidelines for the introduction of a common system for an exchange of visa data*, doc. 9615/02, 5 June 2002.

[81] See the Commission's proposal for the amendment of Regulation 1683/95 (COM(2001)577 final, 9 October 2001). Regulation 1683/95 was first modified by Regulation 334/2002 (OJ 2002 L53/7). Further proposals, aimed at modifying Regulation 1683/95 on a uniform format for visas and Regulation 1030/02 on a uniform format for residence permits were presented on 24 September 2003 (COM(2003)558 final); in the words of the press communiqué by the European Commission, '[t]he two regulations provide only for the legal basis for Member States to store biometric data on the uniform format for visas and the residence permit for third country nationals. The implementation of such action is left to the Member States . . .' (http://www.europa.eu.int/comm/justice_home/news/intro/news_intro_en.htm).

[82] According to the terminology codified in the Annex to the Commission's Communication on a Community return policy on illegal residents (COM(2002)564) there is a distinction between 'illegal residents' ('Any person who does not, or no longer, fulfil the conditions for presence in, or residence on the territory of the Member State of the European Union') and 'illegal entrants' ('Any person who does not fulfil the conditions for entry in the territory of the Member States of the European Union').

possible with SIS II,[83] the new version of the Schengen Information System, already at an advanced developmental stage.[84]

Whatever the particular outcome of the technical definition of the VIS—which, in spite of recent acceleration,[85] looks like being a drawn-out and complex process—and whatever the relationship which is established between it and SIS II, the bringing forward of the recording of personal details of a (would-be) migrant to the time of the visa request will fundamentally transform the structure of the EU entry control system. Even though in terms of effectiveness the potential benefits of such an innovation are quite clear, we should think more deeply about the possible 'perverse' effects of such a spectacular broadening of the sphere of individuals who are subject to supra-national electronic and biometric filing for migration control purposes. Indeed, we might speculate that a third-country national, wishing or needing to enter the EU but uncertain about the outcome of any eventual visa request and worried about the multiplier effect of supra-national filing of a denial, may consequently decide to opt immediately for illegal entry.[86]

[83] 'This VIS structure will need to take account of the development of SIS II in creating synergies which can maximise the human and financial resources required' (Council of the European Union, *Guidelines for the introduction of a common system for an exchange of visa data*, Doc. 9615/02, 5 June 2002, para. II.2.). The need for a coherent approach, which 'would result in harmonised solutions for documents for third country nationals, EU citizen's passports and information systems (VIS and SIS II)', was strongly underlined by the Conclusions of the Thessaloniki European Council (point 11).

[84] The main objective of SIS II (to be developed on the basis of two Council acts—6 December 2001, Decision 2001/886/JHA and Regulation 2424/ 2001; OJ 2001 L328) is to provide a workable system within an enlarged EU, surpassing the original maximum technical capacity of 18 participating states. Nevertheless, it is likely that the technological upgrading will provide an opportunity to allow access to the information system to a broader range of European and national authorities, as well as the introduction of new categories of data (as originally suggested by the Belgian Presidency). At the current stage, new functions for the SIS II on matters of immigration and asylum are not openly foreseen, but neither explicitly excluded: 'The proposed Regulation and Decision concerning new functions for the SIS turned out to suggest no significant changes in relation to immigration or asylum. However, it is still possible that in future new powers will be agreed for the planned "SIS II" which could raise such concerns' (S. Peers, *EU Legislative Update*, in Immigration Law Practitioners' Association, *ILPA European Update*, September 2002, para. 1.3). More recently, concerns of an analogous nature have been expressed by the Joint Supervisory Authority of the European Union ('EU-wide database raises data protection concerns', euobserver.com, available at http://euobs.com/index.phtml?print=true&sid=22&aid=12950).

[85] The two Commission proposals which were presented on 24 September 2003 (see *supra* note 81), following the explicit urging of the Thessaloniki European Council, brought forward from 2007 to 2005 the deadline by which Member States should store biometric data on the uniform formats for visas and residence permits for third-country nationals.

[86] For some further critical remarks see: 'Biometrics—The EU takes another step down the road to 1984', Statewatch News Online, 25 September 2003, http://www.statewatch.org/news/2003/sep/19eubiometric.htm.

Joint Structures for Migration Control

The second development which merits highlighting concerns the means of migration control and more specifically the increasing integration of national apparatuses which in the future could lead to the creation of truly European control structures. This tendency is apparent at a number of levels: on visa policy, thought has been given to improving the efficacy of the system and simultaneously reducing the management costs via the creation of 'joint visa offices'. But, after the comprehensive plan to combat illegal immigration and trafficking in human beings adopted in February 2002 had foreseen that '[i]n the short term, any possible initiatives by the Member States on setting up joint offices or infrastructures could be carried out in Pristina as a priority pilot project', action in this area has made hardly any progress. In practical terms, the Pristina experiment was 'abortive',[87] probably also due to contingent reasons. But, from a more general point of view, such a slowing down should not surprise us: the centralization of visa-related administrative functions within Community structures is a major change which raises thorny problems at not only a practical but also a normative level. In particular, whilst it is not difficult to imagine how an EU joint visa office could work in providing Uniform Schengen Visas (short-stay visas: Articles 9–15 Schengen Implementation Convention), there are organizational and legal barriers to it providing National Visas (long-stay visas: Article 18 Schengen Implementation Convention) and visas with a restricted territorial validity (Article 16 Schengen Implementation Convention), especially in the absence of any progress on the harmonization of national entry norms. To some extent, then, the slowness of the communitarization process on legal immigration (section 2D) leaves very tangible obstacles to any overall rationalization of the European migration control system. This is particularly to be regretted because integration of national consular offices into the European framework would bring major benefits, not only in terms of efficiency and effectiveness, but also in terms of the equity of the whole system. Indeed, as has been noted:

> local consular co-operation, by its very nature, cannot lead to the development of a fully harmonised approach. In the absence of clear rules together with reduced control from the central visa issuing authority, the risk of discriminatory practices occurring on the local consular level and of unequal treatment of similar situated persons, who submit visa applications in different regions of the world, is increased considerably.[88]

The recent tendency towards pushing integration between national migration control systems is evident not only at the level of visa policy but also—and with greater intensity—in the field of external EU border

[87] This is the Commission's official assessment in COM(2003)323, para. 2.1.
[88] *Supra* note 42, at 31.

controls.[89] The move towards a European system of external border management is shaping up to be one of notable complexity, and certainly cannot be summed up by the partial and misleading slogan 'towards a common border police'. It serves no purpose here to list and analyse all the intended and ongoing technical actions in this area. It seems more useful to concentrate on the main existing dynamics, starting with the decisions taken and the deadlines fixed by the Seville European Council.

Heads of State and Government first took a fundamental decision of an organizational/institutional nature which consisted of the immediate instigation ('without delay', the Spanish Presidency conclusions read) on the part of the Council of a 'common unit of external-border practitioners, composed of Members States' heads of border control'. In implementing this decision, the SCIFA (the Council's Strategic Committee on Immigration, Frontiers and Asylum) in its meeting at Elsinore in Denmark on 22 July 2002 gave birth to SCIFA+. This new body—which combines the normal membership of the Strategic Committee with the Members States' heads of border control—was expected to provide, informally and rapidly, operational direction capable of being applied along all EU external borders. Although such a mechanism still raises questions about its capacity to guarantee acceptable levels of transparency and accountability,[90] from this very point of view it marks slight progress in comparison with a somewhat analogous organizational model, namely the Police Chiefs' Operational Task Force (PCOTF), set up in

[89] The integration process in this area is based upon a broad concept of 'management of external borders', which goes well beyond the specific area of migration policy and is functional to a wider process of conceptual and operational reform of European security policy. An analytical definition of the concept of management of external borders can be found in the *Plan for the management of the external borders of the Member States of the European Union*, approved by the Council on 14 June 2002. This definition is as follows:
'The activities carried out by public authorities of the Member States to:

—carry out checks and surveillance at external borders provided for by Articles 5 and 6 of the *Schengen Convention*;
—gather, analyse and exchange any specific intelligence or general information enabling the border guard to analyse the risk that a person, object or asset constitutes for the internal security of the common area of freedom of movement, law and order or the national security of the Member States, and for general compliance with Community legislation;
—analyse the development of the threats likely to affect the security of the external borders and to set the priorities for action by border guards accordingly;
—anticipate the needs as regards staff and equipment to ensure security at external borders'.

[90] In favour of a judicial control regime by the Court of Justice over SCIFA+, see D. Curtin and S. Peers (eds), *Joint Submissions by the Standing Committee of Experts in International Immigration, Refugee and Criminal Law* (the Immigration Law Practitioners' Association, Statewatch), and the European Council of Refugees and Exiles to Working Group X ('Freedom, Justice and Security') of the Convention on the Future of Europe, Utrecht–London, 14 November 2002, para. 6.4.

Tampere for the development of the third pillar.[91] Furthermore, we should take note of the important elaboration in point 47 of the Council's plan for the management of the external borders, which explicitly preserves the legislative and executive competences of the Commission:

In any event, whether in the short term or the longer term, the functions exercised by the common unit [i.e. the external borders practitioners unit] would include activities to improve the effective implementation of Union law but they would involve no legislative proposals and no implementing measures within the meaning of Article 202 of the EC Treaty. The first challenge of this common unit would be to launch its work systematically and to attain the respect and trust of the parties involved.

But the operational deficiencies of SCIFA+ proved to be even more formidable than the institutional perplexities raised by its creation. As the European Commission clearly stated only a few months after the beginning of activity of the new body:

Notwithstanding the work done by the SCIFA+ in approving these operations and projects, its limitations as a Council Working Party have been demonstrated, when co-ordinating and managing the joint operations and pilot projects raising therefore the need of alternative institutional solutions.... [C]ertain more strategic co-ordination tasks could remain with SCIFA+; the more operational tasks could be entrusted to a new permanent Community structure able to exercise this day-to-day management and co-ordination tasks and to respond in time to emergency situations. The status and legal basis of this operational Community structure remain to be defined given the present drafting of article 62 TEC.[92]

A first response to the Commission's remarks came from the JHA Council of 5–6 June 2003, which agreed that operational co-operation should be co-ordinated by the heads of national border control corps, meeting as 'the Practitioners' Common Unit' (PCU) and not as part of SCIFA+. The latter—it was decided by the Ministers of Interior—will continue to carry responsibility for the general strategy to set up an integrated border management system.[93]

[91] The Police Chiefs' Operational Task Force—whose legal and constitutional status has never been fully resolved—'was intended to concentrate on "three or four top priority organised crime problems" but after September 11 was given a series of operational roles covering: intelligence and information exchange; cooperation between national anti-terrorist units, security at airports, border management planning and operations and the coordination of para-military police units for EU Summits and international meetings. When *Statewatch* applied for access to minutes of their meetings they were told that the PCOTF did not come under the Council of the European Union and therefore the documents could not be supplied' (T. Bunyan, '"The War of Freedom and Democracy". An Analysis of the Effects on Civil Liberties and Democratic Culture in the EU', *Statewatch*, September 2002, http:// www. statewatch.org/news/2002/sep/04freedom.htm).

[92] COM(2003)323, para. 2.2.

[93] Council Conclusions on a more effective management of the external borders of the EU Member States, adopted by the Justice and Home Affairs Council, Luxembourg, 5–6 June 2003, doc. 9845/03.

These decisions by the Council may have solved some practical problems, but they have not eradicated more fundamental doubts about the most appropriate institutional architecture in this field. This is why the Thessaloniki European Council invited the Commission to 'examine in due course, drawing on experience by the Common Unit activities, the necessity of creating new institutional mechanisms, including the possible creation of a Community operational structure, in order to enhance operational cooperation for the management of external borders' (Presidency Conclusions, point 14). At the informal meeting of interior ministers which was held in September 2003 in Rome, the Commission announced that it would present a proposal for the creation of a European Border Protection Agency by the end of 2003; but without waiting for the formal Commission proposal, Interior ministers already discussed the subject at the JHA Council of 2–3 October 2003. The policy debate on this crucial point is undoubtedly entering a decisive phase.

Besides its institutional choices, the Seville European Council played an important role in defining the shape of the developing European system of external border management, by selecting and ordering political and operational priorities. The detailed agenda dictated by the Heads of State and Government is worth reproducing in its entirety:

> [The European Council] requests the Council, the Commission and the Member States, each within its respective sphere of responsibility, to implement the following:
>
> —before the end of 2002:
> - joint operations at external borders;
> - immediate initiation of pilot projects open to all interested Member States;
> - creation of a network of Members States' immigration liaison officers;
>
> —before June 2003:
> - preparation of a common risk analysis model, in order to achieve common integrated risk assessment;
> - establishment of a common core curriculum for border guard training and consolidation of European provisions concerning borders;
> - a study by the Commission concerning burden-sharing between member States and the Union for the management of external borders.

This agenda lends itself to a number of interesting considerations regarding the direction which the EU entry control system is taking. From a political point of view, first of all, we can see that the calendar defined in Seville represents the results of a compromise between an array of different approaches, with at one end the 'conservative' position, initially held by the Scandinavian countries and limited to some form of co-operation between national agencies,[94] and at the other a highly innovative position, set out in

[94] Agence Europe, *Bulletin Quotidien Europe* 8210, 13–14 May 2002.

the Commission Communication of 7 May 2002, which expressly looked to the creation of a 'European Corps' of border guards. The European Council and the Council have hitherto avoided taking a stance on the final outcome of the process, favouring instead an 'experimental' approach built upon a number of pilot schemes in which normative integration is reduced to a bare minimum.[95]

The absolute prominence of the operational dimension is quite evident from the report on the state of play of the two action plans (the one 'for the management of the external borders' and the other 'to combat illegal immigration and trafficking of human beings'), presented by the Council in November 2002[96]. This report describes seventeen initiatives for administrative co-operation, most of which were begun during the Danish Presidency and which, depending on their nature and duration, are classified as *ad hoc* projects, joint operations, and specialized centres.[97] This blossoming of pilot schemes can be seen as a positive development from a number of perspectives: as a means of confidence building amongst national control apparatuses, particularly in light of enlargement; as a tool for reinforcing controls along sections of external EU borders which are particularly 'exposed'; perhaps also as a communication strategy, designed to send reassuring signals to an overly worried public.[98]

Nevertheless, the Seville method is not free from criticisms. The first problem of this intensely experimental operational phase is that national officials in candidate, associate (Norway and Iceland), and Member States are asked to carry out delicate activities—in particular, land and maritime border surveillance—without sufficient legal basis to regiment their behav-

[95] An organic initiative for the recast of the Schengen Common Manual on external borders, which would transform it into a regulation, is still awaited. The Thessaloniki European Council invited the Commission to present, 'as soon as possible', proposals to that purpose (Presidency Conclusions, point 16). Until now, only very limited changes have been made to the Borders Manual (see for instance the Decision amending Part II, OJ 2002 L187/50); but, for a full list of the various initiatives aimed at reforming the Common Manual, see the latest revision of the Commission scoreboard 'to review progress on the creation of an area of "freedom, security and justice" in the European Union' (COM(2003)291 final, 22 May 2003).

[96] DOC.14708/02.

[97] A further joint operation, the eighteenth of the list, was launched under Italian supervision during the Summer of 2003; it was baptised 'Neptune' and is a pilot operation in the field of maritime surveillance against human smuggling in the Central Mediterranean (for an official account see http://www.interno.it/news/pages/2003/200307/news_000018610.htm).

[98] It must be noted, however, that the concrete operational results of some of the first pilot joint operations, mainly due to technical compatibility and communication problems among national agencies, do not seem particularly encouraging: 'UE/Immigration: Difficultés de la coopération aux frontières maritimes', Agence Europe, *Bulletin Quotidien Europe*, no. 8418, 12 March 2003, at 6; see also 'EU: Mediterranean joint patrols fail to stop migrants', http://www.statewatch.org/news/2003/mar/08med.htm.

iour.[99] From this perspective, the future proposal of the Commission for the recasting in a 'Community' format of the Common Borders Manual assumes particular importance.

The second weakness in external border management is the lack of clarity on the financing of European co-operation in this area. For many years, some geographically peripheral Member States, which bear particularly heavy responsibility for external border control—first and foremost Italy, then Greece—have tried to take the question of costs associated with such responsibilities to the European level. For a long time, the European institutions have reacted to these requests with generic statements of principle.[100] Gradually, however, the material dimension to this question has become increasingly difficult to avoid, due to the rising financial and political costs associated with external border control, particularly for maritime borders, and also because the principle of burden-sharing has in the meantime been recognized in other areas, some of which are closely connected with border management.[101]

[99] Ongoing common operations on external borders find general legitimation in Article 66 TEC; for all other aspects, the Schengen Common Manual provides the framework, but is superseded in many areas. As for the definition of legitimate means of limiting personal freedom, the only legitimate legal source is represented by the national law of the Member State where each operation takes place. The applicable law for operations in international waters is still an open and very delicate question. Analogous preoccupations are expressed, in very clear terms, by the House of Lords Select Committee on the European Union, in its excellent Report on 'Proposals for a European Border Guard' (HL Paper 133, Session 2002–03, 29th Report, 1 July 2003, at 19–20).

[100] See, for instance, the Action Plan of the Council and the Commission on how best to implement the provisions of the Treaty of Amsterdam on an area of freedom, security, and justice, adopted by the JHA Council on 3 December 1998 (OJ 1999 C19/1) which, listing the criteria for selecting the priorities in the creation of the area of freedom, security, and justice, stated that: 'the principle of solidarity among Member States and between them and the European institutions, should apply in facing the transnational challenges presented by organised crime and migration movements' (point 24, iii).

[101] We refer here to the creation of the European Refugee Fund, which contributes to the implementation of Article 63(2)(b) TEC as a measure 'promoting a balance of effort between Member States in receiving and bearing the consequences of receiving refugees and displaced persons'. More recently, the principle of 'balancing costs' has been applied in the 2001 Directive on mutual recognition of expulsion orders (Directive 2001/40, OJ 2001 L149/34), whose practical implementation was recently the focus of a proposed Commission decision (COM(2003)49; see Agence Europe, *Bulletin Quotidien Europe*, no. 8393, 5 February 2003, at 9). Of particular significance, if we look beyond the migration field, has been the setting up of a European Solidarity Fund, which made considerable resources (€728 million) available as compensation for damage caused in Central Europe by the floods of August and September 2002 (Council of the European Union, Decision adopted by the written procedure, 14519/02, 20 November 2002). All these developments make it difficult not to recognize that 'the case for financial burden-sharing [in the field of external border control] is inarguable' (this was also the conclusion of the House of Lords Select Committee on the European Union in its report on 'Proposals for a European Border Guard', HL Paper 133, Session 2002–03, 29th Report, 1 July 2003, at 17–18). The principle has finally been incorporated

Within the Action Plan for the management of the external borders, the Council has thus explicitly admitted the existence of the problem,[102] forecasting that '[t]he bases for a genuine sharing of the financial burden as regards the requirements in equipment and human resources for an integrated management of the external borders should be established at EU level, in full respect of financial perspectives'.[103] In the same document, the Council further specified that:

> National budgets should remain the principal resources directed to these expenses. Nevertheless, Community budget support could be used to establish a mechanism for financial redistribution between Member States as well as to finance in the longer term the acquisition of common equipment, in particular for the purpose of supporting joint operations.[104]

These steps forward within the JHA Council led the Seville European Council to give the Commission the difficult task of writing a 'report... on the effectiveness of financial resources available at Community level for repatriation of immigrants and rejected asylum seekers, for management of external borders and for asylum and migration projects in third countries',[105] together with 'a study... concerning burden-sharing between Member States and the Union for the management of external borders'.[106]

The Commission had already partially carried out this remit with the presentation of an interim report included in the December 2002 communi-

also in the Draft Treaty establishing a Constitution for Europe, which contains an important Article (III–169) providing that:

> 'The policies of the Union set out in this Section and their implementation shall be governed by the principle of solidarity and fair sharing of responsibility, including its financial implications, between the Member States. Whenever necessary, the acts of the Union adopted pursuant to this Section shall contain appropriate measures to give effect to this principle.'

102 'Financially speaking, the cost of staff and supplies [for the management of external borders] is borne by the national budget of each Member State. This can be extremely expensive for some of them, because of their geographical features, in particular for the surveillance of maritime borders' (Council of the European Union (doc. 10019/02), point 27). The European Commissioner for Justice and Home Affairs poses the problem in even more explicit terms: 'Luxembourg only guards its airport at external border; Germany and Austria control lengthy land borders; Greece surveys both external borders and very important sea borders; Italy also carries out a huge task in surveying its sea borders' (A. Vitorino, *Models of Co-operation within an Enlarged European Union*, Speech 03/31, Royal Institute for International Affairs, Brussels, 28 January 2003, available at http://europa.eu.int/futurum/documents/speech/sp280103_en.pdf).

103 Council of the European Union, *Plan for the management of the external borders of the Member States of the European Union* (doc. 10019/02), point 115.

104 Ibid., point 116.

105 Presidency Conclusions, para 38.

106 Ibid., para. 32.

cation on external dimensions of common migration policy,[107] whose second part is entitled 'Report on the effectiveness of financial resources available at Community level for repatriation of immigrants and rejected asylum seekers, for management of external borders and for asylum and migration projects in third countries'. But it was only with the June 2003 Communication 'on the development of a common policy on illegal immigration, smuggling and trafficking of human beings, external borders and the return of illegal residents' that the EU executive body formulated sufficiently precise options for the use of the limited resources available for the period 2004–2006, while deferring the 'real' decisions to the debate on the new post-2006 financial perspectives.[108] Under the Greek Presidency, the European Council has endorsed the Commission approach by inviting it to 'examine . . . the possibility of appropriating funds' (on the basis of an estimated need of €140 million):

> in order to address, during the period 2004–2006, the most pressing structural needs in this area and to cover a wide definition of solidarity that would . . . include inter alia Community support in the management of external borders, the implementation of the Return Action Programme and the development of the Visa Information System (VIS).[109]

As for the longer term, the Thessaloniki summit embraced the core of the Commission approach by stating that 'the post-2006 financial perspectives should reflect this political priority [i.e. the promotion of the area of freedom, security and justice in the light of the principles of solidarity and mutual confidence between Member States] of the Community'.[110] The stage is set, but the battle for the financial future of the AFSJ, and of the European Union's entry control system in it, is just in its early stages.

B. Widening: The Problems of Enlargement in the Field of Immigration Control

Since its official baptism, with the signing of the Schengen agreement and the subsequent implementation convention, the European system of migration control has been permeated by simultaneous dynamics of deepening and broadening. The progress and intensification of co-operation have generated

[107] Communication from the Commission to the Council and the European Parliament—Integrating Migration Issues in the European Union's Relations with Third Countries (COM(2002)703 final), presented on 3 December 2002.

[108] 'The preparation of the next multi-annual financial perspective offers indeed an important opportunity to shape the political project for the enlarged Union after 2006 in the light of the Convention work. The Commission is determined to fully recognise the development and maintenance of the area of freedom, security and justice as a priority objective of the Union' (COM(2003)323, para. 4).

[109] Thessaloniki European Council, 19–20 June 2003, Presidency Conclusions, point 23.

[110] Ibid. point 22.

a 'power of attraction' which has progressively extended the limits of common internal security and free movement area. From the original core made up of five bordering states, a vast integrated domain has emerged which today incorporates almost the whole continental segment of the EU, and extends to the North as well (subsequent to the association agreements with Iceland and Norway, adopted in May 1999), crossing the English Channel (with the partial participation of the UK and Ireland, decided in May 2000 and February 2002 respectively) and, in the future, may include Switzerland, with which the Council approved the opening of negotiations on 17 June 2002.

It has been written that this expansion would be the expression of a general evolutionary tendency in international security and control regimes:

> Security regimes have the tendency to be expansionist: they aim both at maximising control within their territory and at providing 'added' security by creating protective zones outside of their territory. There are examples galore both in past (such as the Roman Empire's strategies in border regions) and present (such as Israel's security zone in southern Lebanon). The Union's emerging AFSJ is no exception to that.[111]

In very general terms, this assessment is probably correct, but the expansion patterns of the European internal security regime—and, in particular, of the migration control system which represents a central component of this—appears quite distinctive and innovative. In the case of contemporary Europe, the aim of widening the common security space has largely been carried out, not by means of 'protective' or buffer zones, but through a much more complex and binding integration strategy.[112] The reasons for this approach have to do with the deepest historical roots of European integration, which can be seen as a grand experiment in the promotion of regional security via the creation of networks of economic, bureaucratic, and political interdependence. This is not the place to develop such arguments. Nevertheless, the premiss of deep integration helps us to understand why, in the European context in particular, '[t]he common security system is only as strong as its weakest point'.[113]

This statement of principle has particular relevance when ten states are preparing themselves for entry into the EU, substantially lengthening its external land border and extending it to coincide with the frontiers of three

[111] J. Monar, *Justice and Home Affairs in a Wider Europe: The Dynamics of Inclusion and Exclusion,* in ESRC, '*One Europe or Several?*', Programme Working Paper 07/00, pp. 12–13, available at http://www.one-europe.ac.uk/pdf/monarW7.PDF.

[112] From this perspective, the European internal security model distinguishes itself from most others, as the North American model, where the *core state*, i.e. the USA, has never renounced (and is currently ever less likely to renounce) a strategy based heavily upon national border surveillance, which rules out any 'strong' idea of regional integration on security.

[113] Council of the European Union, *Comprehensive Plan to Combat Illegal Immigration and Trafficking of Human Beings in the European Union*, doc. 6621/1/02, point 19.

states which emerged from the dissolution of another Union, namely the Soviet Union.

According to the perceptions of decision-makers and public opinion alike, the shifting eastwards of the external EU border today represents one of the most difficult challenges thrown up by enlargement. What is certain is that the moving of borders constitutes a very strong factor pushing for change in the EU entry control system. To avoid expansion causing a general weakening of the system, the EU has launched (although somewhat late in the day, given when Eastern enlargement was decided upon, as well as when the preparatory activities started in other areas) an impressive programme of institutional and capacity building.

In the case of the current enlargement, the incorporation of new members in the EU entry control system presents an even more arduous political, bureaucratic, and operational task than the past admission of 'border states' (such as Austria, Greece, and Italy) into Schengen. Indeed, in that case the new partners already enjoyed existing infrastructures and apparatuses for controlling borders and migration inflows. It was thus a matter of 'simply' reinforcing, modernizing, and rationalizing what already existed. In the case of the current candidates, and in particular of those which formerly made up part of the Communist *bloc*, the question is structurally different. The systems of international mobility control in these countries orbiting the USSR were designed with a very different aim in mind: besides military functions, the strategic priority of border controls was to dissuade and, if necessary, actively hinder its citizens from leaving countries where clandestine emigration was treated as one of the more serious crimes.

With the transition process, these notorious control networks were rapidly dismantled to the extent that Central and Eastern Europe at the beginning of the 1990s had turned into a space of considerable freedom of movement, in which traditional transnational links began to re-emerge and transnational markets and production systems began to spring back into life. In this context, border controls were virtually absent and national visa policies were drawn up mainly on the basis of each state's trade and foreign policy objectives. When the enlargement process began, it became immediately clear that these differences amongst the political, institutional, legal, and bureaucratic apparatuses of the two sets of countries (members and applicants) constituted a huge obstacle which for the purposes of membership would require a radical systemic overhaul.[114]

[114] The conversion of the candidate countries' control systems to satisfy the Schengen/EU *acquis* is a very complex process which this essay cannot begin to describe in detail. Nevertheless, it is useful to indicate three main strands in this conversion process, which also correspond to the three blocks of policies which form the object of this study, namely visas, borders, and immigration:

But, despite the early acknowledgement of the existence of such problems it was only in 1997 with the Amsterdam Treaty that the decisive choice was made, with the insertion in the Protocol integrating the Schengen *acquis* into the framework of the EU of Article 8, on the basis of which, '[f]or the purposes of the negotiation for the admission of new Member States into the European Union, the Schengen acquis and further measures taken by the institutions within its scope shall be regarded as an acquis which must be accepted in full by all States candidates for admission'. From the moment of its adoption, this disputed provision directed the entire convergence process of the twelve candidate countries which had opened negotiations. The importance of the norm lies in its having clarified that such convergence should be *integral* (with no room for later opt-outs such as those allowed to Denmark, Ireland, and the UK) as well as being *continual and progressive*, using the current *acquis* as its reference point, and not the *acquis* which held at the time of the opening of negotiations. We cannot run through here, even in a condensed way, the various events of the pre-accession and accession processes, nor can we set out the fervent and intense debates which accompanied these.[115] It is rather worth looking at the current state of the enlargement process, to try to highlight the principal problems which remain to be solved.

> (I) First, candidate countries have been asked to 'turn their borders around', in other words to adopt entry control systems (to replace the old exit control systems) with a view to the future abolition of internal borders with current Member States. This strand of structural reform is carried out mostly through the following actions: (a) professionalization and demilitarization of border guards, with consequent raising of salaries and fight against corruption; (b) technological improvement (starting with computerization and linking of border posts); (c) development of systematic collaboration with border control corps in adjoining countries.
>
> (II) The second strand of structural reform consists of the 'Europeanization' of national visa policies. Amongst the main actions in this sphere are: (a) the imposition of visa obligation even for short stays for 'migration risk' countries; (b) the abolition of the widespread practice to grant visas at border points; (c) organizational and technological improvement (beefing up and electronic interconnection of consular networks).
>
> (III) The systemic conversion lastly requires candidate countries to pass rigorous immigration legislation to avoid them becoming 'magnets' for migrants (legal and illegal) potentially interested in subsequently relocating to current EU Member States. Amongst the actions required in this regard are: (a) the adaptation to EU standards of norms and practices on refusal of entry and expulsion; (b) the stipulation of a network of readmission agreements with the main third-countries of provenance and transit; (c) improvement of norms and practices on legal immigration (generalized obligation to obtain residence permits; limits to the upgrading of short-stay permits to long-stay, etc.).

[115] The debate took two main directions: on the one hand, analyses and evaluation of the implications of enlargement for the functioning of the area of freedom, security, and justice abounded, and in particular on the implications for the European migration control system (the works by Jörg Monar epitomize this, for instance *Enlargement Related Diversity in EU Justice and Home Affairs: Challenges, Dimensions and Management Instruments*, Working Document W112, Scientific Council for Government Policy, Ministry of General Affairs,

Despite the enormous political, bureaucratic, economic, and cultural difficulties which the improvement to Schengen/EU standards represents for candidate countries, the membership negotiations on Chapter 24—dedicated to 'Justice and Home Affairs'—were completed with ten states, with few surprises or excessive tensions.[116] This provisional success was undoubtedly helped, as it had been in other areas of negotiations, by the preponderant attention given by EU negotiators to the normative dimension of the *acquis* rather than the implementation side. But the decisive factor in permitting the rapid conclusion of negotiations was the clarification by the European institutions, after some initial hesitation, of the nature and method of membership of the common space of security and free movement:

> The Schengen system will apply to all new Member States. Full participation in it will be based on a two-step process. The new Member States will first need to achieve a high level of external border control upon accession whereas the lifting of internal border controls with current Member States will take place only at a later stage, subject to a separate decision by the Council.[117]

Kingdom of Netherlands, December 2000; see also: House of Lords Select Committee on the European Union, *Enlargement and EU external frontier controls*, Session 1999–2000, 17th Report (October 2000)). On the other hand, many appraisals (mostly critical ones) appeared examining the more general consequences of the enlargement of the EU entry control system and the shifting of the EU's external border to the East—amongst the first studies of this kind are that of G. Amato and J. Batt, *The Long-Term Implications of EU Enlargement: The Nature of the New Border*, (Florence: Robert Schuman Centre for Advanced Studies of the European University Institute—Forward Studies Unit of the European Commission, 1999); more recently, see J. Apap and M. Anderson, *Police and Justice Cooperation and the New European Borders* (The Hague: Kluwer, 2002). Some of the most serious technical criticisms raised by these and other similarly inspired works obtained a convincing response by the European Commission, first with the proposed regulations establishing a Facilitated Transit Document and a Facilitated Rail Transit Document for persons transiting by land across future EU external borders in order to travel 'between two parts of the same third country via the territory of one or more Member States' (COM(2003)60; these proposed provisions for the time being address only the Kaliningrad situation) and more recently with the two draft regulations on the establishment of a regime of local border traffic at the external and 'temporary external' (i.e. internal land borders between old and new members, until the end of the Schengen transition period) land borders of the EU (COM(2003)502). With these important and innovative proposals, the Commission moved away from a rigid interpretation of the Schengen/EU *acquis* towards a more flexible attitude which conceives the *acquis* as 'continually under development' and where 'the EU's position should . . . be defined both by its legal obligations and by its own, *and the candidates*', political interests' (COM(2003)60, Explanatory Memorandum, para. 1, emphasis added).

[116] Negotiations on Chapter 24 were closed in this order: November 2001—Hungary; December 2001—Cyprus, Czech Republic, Slovenia; March 2002—Estonia, Malta; April 2002—Lithuania; June 2002—Latvia, Slovakia; July 2002—Poland.

[117] Commission of the European Communities, *Making a Success of Enlargement. Strategy Paper and Report of the European Commission on the progress towards accession by each of the candidate countries*, 2001, at 5. The Strategy paper is available at http://www.europa.eu.int/comm/enlargement/report2001/index.htm#paper2001.

The clarification of the fact that, as in preceding enlargements of the Schengen system, formal membership would not immediately imply full participation in European co-operation, nor the comprehensive application of the *acquis*, opened the way for an agreement. Organizing the enlargement of the EU entry control system as a two-step process in this sense represents a compromise from which both current members—who can postpone the delicate moment of internal border suppression—and new members—who can spread the political and financial costs of further convergence—can benefit. At the same time, the solution of two-step integration presents some risks: on the one hand, it gives to current partners the possibility of delaying *ad libitum* the moment of allowing full membership, and perhaps for political and even electoral, rather than technical, reasons.[118] On the other hand, the prospect of remaining for a long time in membership limbo could stimulate negative reaction in public opinion in new Member States and force their respective governments to adopt braking tactics or other unco-operative behaviour within the Community.

The political process during the transition period will depend in large part on the adequacy of the legal, organizational, and institutional solutions which are provided. From this perspective, recent months have seen some important clarifications. By the second half of 2001, the European Commission had already proposed the formal subdivision of the *acquis* into two categories, distinguishing between those dispositions to be fully applied as from accession and those which would only have to be applied at the moment of the abolition of the internal border controls with other Member States. This proposed division was subsequently discussed within the Council's Enlargement Working Group,[119] confirmed by Coreper in September 2001 and finally applied to the candidate countries.[120]

[118] Similar dynamics have been seen in the final phase of the Italian rush to full admission into Schengen. On this see F. Pastore, 'L'expérience italienne dans la mise en oeuvre de Schengen', in K. Hailbronner and P. Weil (eds), *Von Schengen nach Amsterdam. Auf dem Weg zu einem europäischen Einwanderungs- und Asylrecht* (Cologne: Bundesanzeiger, 1999); F. Pastore, *Border Countries in an Enlarging Union. Some Reflections on the Italian Case*, CEPS Policy Brief, no. 14, March 2002, available at http://www.ceps.be; see also an interesting report by the Italian Parliamentary Control Committee on the Implementation and Functioning of the Schengen Implementation Convention: Comitato parlamentare di controllo sull'attuazione ed il funzionamento della Convenzione di applicazione dell'accordo di Schengen, *Stato di attuazione della Convenzione di applicazione dell'accordo di Schengen*, Atti Parlamentari, XIII legislature, Indagini conoscitive e documentazioni legislative, 2 volumes, nos 3 and 3-A, Camera dei Deputati, Rome, 1997–1998.

[119] Doc. 12148/01 ELARG 214.

[120] For a more detailed account, cf. Ministry of Justice of Denmark, Presidency Secretariat, *Schengen and the enlargement*, background paper presented at the informal JHA Council in Copenhagen, 13–14 September 2002, p. 9, available on http://www.eu2002.dk. The division of the Schengen/EU *acquis* into two *blocs* has now been definitively confirmed in the Act of Accession which makes up part of the membership treaties which were signed on 16 April

A few months later, after the provisional completion of JHA negotiations with the ten future members, the Council further clarified the practical means by which the full *acquis* would be gradually adopted. As regards the first *bloc* of the Schengen *acquis* (and successive developments):

> The candidate countries must implement and apply the Category 1 provisions of the Schengen acquis directly upon accession to the European Union, without being subject to the Schengen evaluation process. The preparation and the monitoring of the implementation and application of the Category 1 provisions of the Schengen acquis will be carried out as a part of the application process.[121]

After accession, the daily application of the measures in this category will be subject to the normal monitoring and evaluation procedures implemented in the post-Schengen framework of co-operation:

> The new Member-States may—in accordance with the Schengen acquis—be subject to Schengen evaluations as participating Schengen States on the correct application of the Category 1 provisions. These evaluations could be conducted either as thematic evaluations covering certain topics in more than one participating Member State or, in principle, even as a country evaluation to be carried out in a geographically limited area.[122]

Concerning the measures belonging to the second category, the new Member States shall demonstrate after accession, from 1 May 2004, 'their capacity to comply with the relevant requirements of the Schengen acquis in a uniform, consistent and efficient manner'.[123] The crucial, and highly delicate, task of judging on the basis of these criteria the actual level of compliance is handed to the Schengen Evaluation Working Group of the Council. The procedure which this body of functionaries and experts needs to follow is regulated by the previously cited document. This foresees that the new Member State itself should trigger the evaluation process, which will be based on a number of tools including an 'extensive questionnaire' and 'inspection visits'. On this basis, the Working Group will produce a report for each country under scrutiny, which 'may include recommendations' and require a further phase of adaptation. At the end of this procedure, a final report will be submitted to the Council, which 'will make a separate decision for each new Member State'.[124]

As is clear from the above, the detailed regulation of the evaluation procedure introduces some significant elements of certainty and predictability, but

2003 in Athens (see Article 3 and Annexes, OJ 2003 L236 33); for a first comment see S. Peers, *Statewatch Analysis of the EU Accession Treaty*, Statewatch News Online, 18 February 2003, (http://statewatch.org/news/2003/feb/14accession.htm).

[121] Council of the European Union, *Process leading to the implementation and application of the Schengen acquis in full by new Member States following their accession to the European Union*, doc. 1544/02, 10 December 2002, point 4.

[122] Ibid., point 5. [123] Ibid., point 11. [124] Ibid., points 13–17.

it certainly does not prevent spurious variables from interfering in the process, and causing an undesirable element of politicization. To limit this risk and to make sure that the transition phase of the enlargement of the area of freedom, security, and justice comes to term within a reasonable length of time for *all* the new members, concrete progress at the implementation level is clearly crucial.

From this perspective, it is important to emphasize that even current Member States have certain obligations to carry out in the near future. Amongst the few *truly objective* obstacles to enlargement to twenty-five of the EU entry control system is the limited capacity of the Schengen Information System in its current state. The start-up of SIS II (see section 3A) is thus a necessary condition of the full admission of the ten new members to the common space of control and free movement. However, it is clear that from this point onwards it will take some years before the new computer system comes into operation: an initial estimate in a background paper circulated by the Danish Presidency on the eve of the informal JHA Council on 13–14 September 2002 stated that 'the new system . . . is currently estimated to become operational by the end of 2005 at the earliest'.[125] This indicative deadline has been confirmed in a speech by the European Commissioner for Justice and Home Affairs at the end of January 2003.[126] From the technical point of view, it is the EU which is currently unable to accept new members into the club, rather than vice versa.

Having underlined this oft-neglected aspect, we nevertheless should not ignore the challenges that the new Member States must confront. Despite the important advances in the last few years, there are still large gaps not only at the organizational (falling behind on demilitarization and professionalization of border guards) and implementation levels (lack of personnel and infrastructure, as well as suitable equipment) but also at the normative and policy level (especially in visa policy).[127] For the structural gap to be filled, or at least reduced to a significant extent, so as to ensure that the transition

[125] The paper, entitled *Schengen and the enlargement*, is available on the official Danish presidency site: http://www.eu2002.dk, p. 9.

[126] The speech is reported at http://www.europa.eu.int/comm/enlargement/docs/newsletter/latest_weekly.htm, downloaded on 5 February 2003.

[127] Gaps of this kind persist not only in Bulgaria and Romania, the two countries excluded from the next round of enlargement, but also for some of the countries that are meant to join on 1 May 2004. The 2001 Regular Report on Poland, for example, indicated with concern that: 'The intended visa introduction for Belarus, Russia and Macedonia has not yet taken place, due to the fact that the negotiations with the countries concerned have not been completed, and due to a lack of funding. Visas continue to be granted at borders in increasing numbers. This practice is not in line with the acquis' (*2001 Regular Report on Poland's Progress Towards Accession*, SEC(2001)1752, 13 November 2001, p. 85). The progress recorded in the 2002 Regular Report on this particular point is limited and not decisive (COM(2002)700 final, 9 October 2002, pp. 113–114).

phase does not carry on beyond 2006, heavy political and financial investment is indispensable. It is difficult to predict the strength and persistence of political will on either side. Nevertheless, the recent increase in economic aid decided upon by the current Member States is reassuring: besides the €541 million allocated between 1997 and 2001 under the PHARE programme for activities in the Justice and Home Affairs sector,[128] the package of financial aid for enlargement eventually launched by the Copenhagen European Council set aside over €850 million (286 for 2004, 302 for 2005 and 271 for 2006) to reinforce the 'Schengen facility'.[129]

In the coming years, then, the construction site of the expanding EU entry control system will be occupied by frenetic institutional and capacity building. Very substantial financial and manpower resources will be involved, to shape what will be the future external borders of an EU of twenty-five, twenty-seven or even more. It is certain that the enlargement of the European migration control system will interact heavily with the deepening that we described in the previous section (3B). It is difficult to predict the patterns and dynamics of this interaction. One of the hypotheses is that current Member States are increasingly making the financial support necessary for improving to Schengen/EU standards dependent upon the ceding of important tranches of national sovereignty on the part of the new 'border States', via the creation of common structures for the control of external borders and the strengthening of reciprocal control mechanisms and peer review. Such a trade-off between the costs of border management and sovereignty is to some extent inevitable. If well managed, this political exchange might ensure successful enlargement along one of its most vital yet delicate dimensions. But European institutions and the current Member States must proceed with caution, in order to avoid negative reactions on the part of states and civil societies which have only recently won back sovereignty over their own borders and the population flows across them, and so are unlikely to tolerate rigid diktats in this area.

C. Institutional Reforms and Immigration Control

A certain institutional fragility and ambiguity have burdened European co-operation on justice and home affairs from the start. The Treaty of

[128] Of which over €310 million have been invested in strengthening border controls (W. De Lobkowicz, 'L'Europe et la sécurité intérieure. Une élaboration par étapes', *Notes et Etudes Documentaires*, nos. 5144–5, December 2001, *La Documentation Française*, Paris, 2002, at 92).

[129] Copenhagen agreed a financial package defining maximum enlargement-related commitments for 2004–2006 for ten new Member States (Euro millions, 1999 prices), available at http://www.europa.eu.int/comm/enlargement/negotiations/pdf/financial_package.pdf. According to more recent calculations, the Schengen facility launched in Copenhagen would amount globally to €970 million (COM(2003)323, para. 5). Besides the Schengen Facility, the draft of the Act of Accession foresees a Transition Facility targeting *inter alia* the reinforcement of external border controls (doc. AA 3/03, 31 January 2003, Articles 34–35).

Amsterdam may have contributed significantly to clarifying the institutional framework within which co-operation takes place, but deciding to incorporate the Schengen *acquis* into the Union's structure has not allowed the elimination of all of the original vagaries of this sector of European integration. The five-year transition period foreseen in Title IV TEC is the principal mechanism introduced by Amsterdam to channel and manage this persistent constitutional uncertainty, in an attempt to orient itself towards finally overcoming these problems via complete communitarization.

As regards the particular themes of this chapter, the deadline for the transition period—1 May 2004—will automatically have an immediate impact upon visa policy. The effect of the fourth section of Article 67 TEC will be to subject the last vestiges of these policies still currently subject to unanimity decision-making to QMV and co-decision.

The only other certainty (or relatively so) relating to the institutional framework after the deadline of the transition period seems to derive from the protocol concerning Article 67 TEC annexed to the Treaty of Nice, which finally entered into force after various vicissitudes on 1 February 2003. In that brief text it is foreseen that '[f]rom 1 May 2004, the Council shall act by qualified majority, on a proposal from the Commission and after consulting the European Parliament, in order to adopt the measures referred to in Article 66 of the Treaty establishing the European Community'. The importance of such a step should not be missed, in a context in which—as we saw in section 3A—the evolution of the EU entry control system is most manifest in the operational sphere and within co-operation between national administrations, in contrast with its deliberately limited effect at the normative level. But it should also be recognized that the protocol mentioned here introduces a temporary but nevertheless substantial derogation as regards the 'normal' path set out in Article 67 EC, which contemplates a more incisive role for the Parliament via co-decision. In other words, this sets out a particularly fluid decision-making regime (qualified majority, *but without co-decision*) which may serve to favour the upgrading of the EU entry control system, but which, by perpetuating old institutional imbalances, may create the basis for new tensions and debates.

That said, it is clear that Article 67 leaves the way open for greater conversion of decision-making procedures upon which the Council should soon pronounce unanimously at the expiry of the five-year deadline. With respect to this decisive passage, a declaration annexed to the Nice Treaty (no. 5 relating to Article 67 TEC) provides some constraints whose legal nature and implications are, as always, somewhat dubious and controversial. In particular, it foresees that:

> the Council, in the decision it is required to take pursuant to the second indent of Article 67(2):

—will decide, from 1 May 2004, to act in accordance with the procedure referred to in Article 251 in order to adopt the measures referred to in Article 62(3) and Article 63(3)(b);

—will decide to act in accordance with the procedure referred to in Article 251 in order to adopt the measures referred to in Article 62(2)(a) from the date in which agreement is reached on the scope of the measures concerning the crossing by persons of the external borders of the Member States.

The bland specification follows that '[t]he Council will, moreover, endeavour to make the procedure referred to in Article 251 applicable from 1 May or as soon as possible thereafter to the other areas covered by Title IV or to parts of them'.

To sum up, we find ourselves faced with a solemn declaration by the High Contracting Parties that, at the expiry of the transition period, the Council will formally confirm that co-decision and QMV will apply to the regime of movement by third-country nationals for short periods within the EU (Article 62(3)) and all measures relating to illegal immigration and illegal residence (Article 63(3)(b)). As regards border control regimes (Article 62(2)(a)), however, the abandoning of unanimity has been delayed by a particularly hazy formulation to the moment at which agreement is reached (by what means and with which degree of specification is not clear) on the scope of measures to be adopted in this field.

It will consequently be a confused patchwork of different decision-making methods that, on the basis of existing treaties, will govern the development of the entry control system of the enlarged EU—which will be born (fortuitously, it seems) on the same day as the expiry of the five-year transition period, namely on 1 May 2004.

Naturally, this discomfiting scenario does not take into account further possibilities of institutional change discussed within the Convention on the Future of Europe. Initially, Justice and Home Affairs as such may have been absent from the Convention's agenda. Very quickly, however, this exclusion—the result of the initial methodological choice which wanted to deal first with the major horizontal questions, before moving to specific policy-fields—appeared inopportune and politically unsustainable. It was argued on many sides that the JHA sector in general and migration control policy in particular would be amongst the few sectors in which a general popular demand for 'more Europe' would emerge and that, consequently, the Convention could not, for fear of weakening its legitimacy, absolve itself from taking an explicit position on such matters.[130]

[130] In fact, the degree of popular support for deeper integration and stronger Community powers in the field of migration control turned out to be less homogeneous and solid than expected, according to an in-depth and broad survey recently conducted on behalf of the European Commission ('European Citizens and Freedom, Security and Justice', a qualitative survey of citizens of the 15 Member States and 13 applicant countries conducted by

This was the reason why, after an inaugural thematic debate in plenary session on the future of the space of freedom, security, and justice (6 June 2002), on 19 June Valéry Giscard d'Estaing proposed the creation of some new working groups within the Convention, including one dedicated to 'Freedom, Security and Justice'. In subsequent weeks, the new Working Group—the tenth, according to official counting—began its work on the basis of a mandate defined by the Praesidium, under the presidency of the former Irish Prime Minster, John Bruton.

After several months of intense activity, in December 2002, Working Group X adopted its concluding report, submitting it to the plenary Assembly. Without forgetting the obvious principle by which hypotheses on treaty reform should be evaluated in a unitary manner, considering the complex interdependence between the various elements of institutional and normative architecture in the Union, it nevertheless seems useful to extrapolate those findings and recommendations of the Working Group which are reflected in the Draft Treaty establishing a European Constitution finally approved by the Convention and which touch upon the future of the EU entry control system.

First, as far as the legal bases for Community action are concerned, the current framework has been largely retained (except for a few details being polished) in matters of immigration and visas, whilst on border management:

> The Seville European Council welcomed the objective of the gradual development of an integrated system of external border management. The Group recommends that the current Article 62(2)(a) TEC is redrafted in order to create a general legal base enabling the adoption of the measures needed to put in place this integrated system. This implies both legislation and operational co-operation.[131]

It seems that the implicit assumption contained in these lines—that the current norm would not provide sufficient basis for the creation of an integrated border management—is neither self-evident nor proven. It is evident, however, that the Convention judged it safer to make a very explicit reference to the Community competence of the Union to 'develop a policy with a view to . . . the gradual introduction of an integrated management system for external borders', that will enable the adoption of European laws and framework laws concerning 'any measures necessary for the gradual establishment of an integrated management system for external borders' (Article III–166 of the Draft Treaty establishing a Constitution for Europe).

OPTEM for the JHA Directorate General of the European Commission, March 2003, available at http://www.europa.eu.int/comm/justice_home/doc_centre/intro/docs/eurobaro_qualitatif_en.pdf).

[131] Final Report of Working Group X, 'Freedom, Security and Justice', CONV 426/02, 2 December 2002. Part A, para. I.4.

With such a broad and elastic legal foundation,[132] the margins for future Community action in this field seem to be firmly established and leave little scope for any major controversy.

An analogous clarification of the actual extent of Community competence has been operated with regard to illegal immigration and unauthorized residence, which now (more explicitly than in the Treaty of Amsterdam) include 'removal and repatriation of persons residing without authorisation' (Article III–168(2)(c)). Much more limited and cautious is the establishment of competence on integration of legally residing third-country nationals, where European laws and framework laws may only 'establish measures to provide incentives and support for the action of Member States' (Article III–168(4)).

One of the general 'golden rules' for the future of the AFSJ which the Working Group states in the introduction to its final report is that '[t]here should be clearer distinction between legislation . . . and reinforced co-ordination of operational collaboration at Union level'. It is obvious how this principle, restated and elaborated later in the document,[133] may be susceptible to particularly important applications (and be potentially controversial, particularly in relation to the executive role of the Commission) in the field of migration control. It must be noted, however, that the Working Group recommendation was only lightly reflected in the draft Constitution finally approved by the Convention which, for instance, entrusts the European Council with the crucial task to 'define the strategic guidelines' both for legislative *and* operational planning, thus preserving a debatable constitutional routine that has been set *de facto* in the last few years.

Also of great relevance to the subject of this essay is the recommendation made by the Working Group in very explicit terms 'to enshrine in the Treaty the principle of solidarity and fair sharing of responsibility (including its financial implications) between the Member States, applying as a general principle to the Union's asylum, immigration and border control policies.

[132] What is an 'integrated management system for external borders' and what is necessary for its gradual establishment is obviously not defined *a priori*, once and for all, but only step by step, depending on future technological and political developments. Therefore, this particular sphere of Community competence is formulated in a particularly flexible and 'progressive' way that should leave relatively little space for competence-limiting factors such as the subsidiarity and proportionality principles (in spite of the enhanced control powers granted to national Parliaments by Article III–160) and the traditional sovereignty clause of Article III–163.

[133] 'There is broad acknowledgement amongst members of the Working Group that current operational collaboration lacks efficiency, transparency and accountability' (Final Report of Working Group X, *supra* note 131, Part B). 'A clearer distinction between the Council acting in its legislative capacity and the Council exercising specific executive functions in this area would be advantageous' (ibid., Part B, para. I).

A specific legal basis should enable the adoption of the detailed policies necessary to give effect to this principle.'[134] The impact of the eventual constitutionalization of such a principle on the dynamics described in section 3A would clearly be very deep. From this point of view, we have already stressed above[135] the importance of the quite explicit and comprehensive final drafting of Article III–169 by the Convention, which opens the way for fundamental changes in the future financial architecture of the EU migration control system.

If we move to questions of general institutional design, provided they are accepted by the future IGC, the recommendations pertaining to the reinforcement of mutual evaluation mechanisms[136] and the new powers given to the Court of Justice[137] would produce significant effects on the EU entry control system, with a net improvement in transparency, the rule of law, and accountability. An equally strong impact could occur—in particular in certain fields such as legal immigration—from the eventual acceptance of the Convention's recommendation to move to the co-decision method (which should rise to the status of general 'legislative procedure'), using a new, fairer, and more transparent form of qualified majority vote (albeit not

[134] Ibid., Part A, para. I.1.

[135] *Supra* note 101.

[136] '[T]he "peer review" reports should be supplied to the European Parliament and to national parliaments' (Part C, para. I). The recommendations by WG X were largely accepted in the final text by the Convention which, at Article III–161, establishes:

> 'Without prejudice to Articles III–265 to III–267, the Council of Ministers may, on a proposal from the Commission, adopt European regulations or decisions laying down the arrangements whereby Member States, in collaboration with the Commission, conduct objective and impartial evaluation of the implementation of the Union policies referred to in this Chapter by Member States' authorities, in particular in order to facilitate full application of the principle of mutual recognition. The European Parliament and Member States' national Parliaments shall be informed of the content and results of the evaluation.'

Article III–160 significantly adds to this that 'Member States' national Parliaments may participate in the evaluation mechanisms contained in Article III–161'.

[137] The majority of the Working Group proposed the extension of full jurisdiction to the Court in the entire space of freedom, security, and justice, via the abolition of the limits set out in Article 68 TEC and Article 35 TEU. In particular, in referring to the crucial point of legal exclusion on matters of public order and safeguarding internal security, Working Group X notes:

> 'the jurisdiction of the Court is excluded concerning measures related to the maintenance of law and order and the safeguarding of internal security (control of persons crossing internal borders). Yet, . . . the very nature of these measures it to affect individual rights. To the majority of the Working Group it is difficult to justify a continuation of exemption from the jurisdiction of the Court for such measures especially taking into account that other measures relating equally to the maintenance of law and order (e.g. expulsion from one Member State to another of EU citizens) have always been subject to judicial control by the ECJ' (Part C, para. V).

until 1 November 2009), on all matters pertaining to current Title IV TEC. Provided this crucial reform is not diluted or delayed due to the stonewalling of some late defender of formal national sovereignty, the further development of EU common migration policy will be decisively boosted, in spite of the growing diversity of migration-related national interests that will emerge in an enlarged European Union.

This latter circumstance does not exclude the possibility that, even in a qualified majority decision-making context, the new constitutional provisions on enhanced co-operation (Articles I–43, III–322 to III–329) will find a particularly fertile testing ground precisely in the field of migration policy. The strengthening of the supranational dimension in the procedure to activate any new enhanced co-operation, via a reinforced role for the Commission and the European Parliament, makes this a more viable option than under the post-Amsterdam and post-Nice sets of rules.

Finally, it is worth giving some consideration to the 'constitutional outlook' for some of the specific policy issues treated above. With reference to practical solutions to adopt in the field of external border management, a prudent approach respecting traditional national prerogatives prevailed within the Working Group:

> Most members of the Group consider the possible creation of a common European border guard unit as a longer-term issue.[138] Some more immediate steps (such as enhanced co-operation, closer co-operation between Member States' services, common instruction and training, sharing of equipment, joint teams composed by officials from different Member States in order to make the control of the external borders more effective) could be taken first. Progress in this area would thus be gradual.[139]

It is interesting to note that similar prudence—even if it is inspired by the aim of safeguarding civil liberties, rather than national sovereignty—was shown by some of the most authoritative civil society groups which took part in the

The recommendation by WG X to establish full jurisdiction of the ECJ was fully accepted by the Convention and absorbed in the text of the draft Constitutional Treaty, as far as the subject matters of old Title IV TEC are concerned, if not in relation to old Title IV TEU (see Article III–283).

[138] A slightly more advanced position is stated in the document presented jointly by the French and German governments to Working Group X: 'A deadline will be fixed for the creation of a European Border Police with sovereign competence, and for the introduction, in the new constitutional treaty, of a relevant legal base' (European Convention, Working Group X, Working Document 32, 27 November 2002, para. III.2, at 6).

[139] Final Report of Working Group X, 'Freedom, Security and Justice', CONV 426/02, 2 December 2002, Part B, para. II. The caution towards the radical integration hypotheses of border control apparatuses is also reflected in the recommendation to maintain unanimity decision rules for the eventual setting up of a common border control corps, just as more generally for 'the creation of new Union bodies for the exercise of certain responsibilities currently performed at national level' (ibid., Part A, para II.3.b).

Convention debate. The essential neutrality of such organizations with respect to the eventual creation of a European Border Guard is nevertheless accompanied by some important substantive conditions:

> We do not take a view on whether or not a 'European Border Guard' should be established, but if a European Border Guard is established there should be adequate judicial and parliamentary control . . . This will be best assured if the European Border Guard is brought fully within what is presently the 'first pillar' of EC law. This is because the border is a place where persons crossing it exercise rights to do so under Community law relating to persons and services and where only a tiny percentage are eligible for refusal. It is this model which corresponds more closely to the reality of EU borders. The administrative body established to carry out the control should therefore be commensurate with this function—civilian in nature and with only such powers as are strictly necessary for the function to be performed.[140]

From the work of Working Group X of the Convention, and to a large extent from the text of the Draft Constitution, there emerges a synthetic image of an EU entry control system with stronger elements of integration and homogeneity, more effective in decision-making, but also more transparent, more respecting of fundamental rights, and more democratic. It will be up to the IGC to respond to these indications. But, beyond the next wave of institutional reform, the future of the EU entry control system is open and closely linked to other dimensions fundamental to the future of the Union. Much depends upon the evolution of common policy on visas, borders, and immigration; not only the opportunities for hundreds of millions of people to access the EU each year, but also, in some part at least, the economic and demographic future of the continent, the success of the enlargement process, and the degree of long-term stability within and around the enlarged EU, and, indeed, the very credibility of a Union which lists amongst its fundamental aims the guarantee and promotion—in equal measure—of freedom, security, and justice.

[140] Curtin and Peers (eds), *supra* note 90, para. 5.1.

4

Family Reunion and Community Law

STEVE PEERS

1. INTRODUCTION

Racism; sexism; homophobia; mistreatment of children; marginalization of the poor; and human rights abuses. EC law on family reunion has been accused of committing all of these offences. In fact, perhaps no other area of EC law has ever faced such a long charge sheet. Are these criticisms valid, particularly in light of substantial new case law and legislative developments in recent years? It will be seen that the criticisms were largely valid before these recent developments but have lost some of their force since. Nevertheless, many criticisms are still valid. In particular, EC family reunion law remains riddled with unjustifiable distinctions on grounds of nationality, resulting in indirect racial discrimination, which the European Court of Human Rights has shamefully and unjustifiably endorsed.

In this essay, I first set out the core features of family reunion as it is protected by international human rights law, focusing in particular upon the case law of the European Court of Human Rights. I then set out the EC rules governing family reunion.[1] The framework for analysis breaks down the issue of family reunion into its four core aspects. First, because there are major distinctions in family reunion rules depending on the status of the 'sponsor' (the person whom the family member is accompanying or joining), it is necessary to define who the 'sponsor' is before examining the substantive family reunion rules. This essay therefore examines the rules applicable in turn to those family members joining EC nationals, family members of persons covered by EC association agreements, and the general rules on family reunion for third-country nationals. It does not examine the special

[1] By 'EC law' I mean all Community law rules concerning family reunion with any persons residing within the EC. There has been a tendency to refer only to the rules concerning the family members of EC nationals exercising free movement rights as 'Community law', but this is clearly no longer an accurate phrase in light of rules in EC association agreements and the powers to adopt rules concerning third-country nationals in Title IV of the EC Treaty. The former category of rules is therefore referred to as 'EC *free movement* law'.

rules for those third-country nationals seeking or having a recognized need for protection. Furthermore, there are major subdivisions within these four broad categories, as well as certain cross-overs between those categories.

Secondly, the obvious issue at the heart of any rules on family reunion is the definition of 'family'. Thirdly, a critical issue for families seeking to reunite in practice is the conditions attached to family reunion. Is there a waiting period? Are there financial requirements? These conditions (and others) can make it impossible or significantly more difficult for many families to reunite. Finally, the treatment of family members after reunion (which I refer to as the issue of the 'status of family members') has major implications in practice.[2] For example, on what grounds can family members be expelled? Do they have access to education and employment? What happens in the event of divorce?

The second part of the essay examines the criticisms of EC legislation and case law, and further examines critically the case law of the European Court of Human Rights in this context.

There are several in-built tensions concerning the legal regulation of family reunion. The most obvious tension is between the goal of ensuring respect for family life, set out in human rights treaties, and the objective of immigration control. This tension is particularly strong for social conservatives, because they are strong believers in both objectives. But of course social conservatives only support family life as they define it, characterized by marriage *between persons of opposite sexes* and ideally including children and a mother outside the paid labour market. 'Foreign' ideas like extended families are not very welcome, at least if they involve the entry and residence of actual foreigners. Nor are 'non-traditional' families such as those led by a single parent (usually the mother), particularly if they require social benefits, or those involving unmarried couples, particularly same-sex couples. But within the European Union there are wide differences of opinion between Member States and within each Member State's population as to whether such non-traditional family lives are acceptable, and what the consequences for immigration law should be. This diversity in national approaches has inevitably made it difficult for the EU's legislative and judicial bodies to define a common approach.

Equally, although the family, notwithstanding the development of such non-traditional versions of it, is a conservative social construct, it is an inherently dynamic institution, even in the most conservative scenario. Put simply, children grow up and their legal and social relationship with their parents is bound to change as a consequence. The marital or other relationship between spouses and partners frequently breaks down and even if the

[2] For a survey of national law on this subject see S. Peers, R. Barziloy, K. Groenendijk and E. Guild, *The Legal Status of Persons Admitted for Family Reunion* (Strasbourg: Council of Europe, 2000) and subsequent Recommendation 2002/4 of the Council of Europe Committee of Ministers, online at: http://cm.coe.int/stat/E/Public/2002/adopted_texts/recommendations/2002r4.htm.

relationship is maintained for life, it is likely that one spouse or partner will pre-decease the other. Even while the family relationship subsists, its members are still independent persons who may have individual interests in pursuing employment, education, and other activities. This dynamism causes difficulties for immigration law, which prefers to deal with people in fixed categories, and creates a further tension between granting rights to collective units based on the inter-relationship between the individuals involved and then seeing those individuals as autonomous persons.

Finally, it should be kept in mind that as a result of the 'opt-out' rules applicable to the UK, Ireland, and Denmark within the scope of Title IV of the EC Treaty, which contains special rules on EC immigration and asylum law, there are differences of territorial scope as regards the measures discussed in this essay. The free movement rules apply to all Member States, as do the rules in association agreements, with the possible exception of the EC–Swiss treaty. The Council has purported to state that this treaty has no direct effect in the UK, Ireland, and Denmark, but rather only takes effect as an international law treaty. There are reasons to doubt the accuracy of this conclusion.[3] As for the general rules on family reunion for third-country nationals, they will not apply to the UK, Ireland, and Denmark. However, the UK and Ireland have respectively opted into all and some of the EC legislation specifically concerning asylum and other forms of protection,[4] although those rules are not examined in this essay.[5] The complications resulting from the distinctions of scope are not explored here in detail.[6]

2. HUMAN RIGHTS AND FAMILY REUNION

The international human rights regime protects the right to 'family life' and recognizes the family as a fundamental unit of society in a number of

[3] See E. Guild and S. Peers, 'Out of the Ghetto? The Personal Scope of EU Law' in N. Rogers and S. Peers (eds), *EU Immigration and Asylum Law: Text and Commentary* (The Hague: Martinus Nijhoff, forthcoming).

[4] The general family reunion Directive also applies to family reunion for refugees, to some extent setting out special rules governing their position.

[5] Also the rules on responsibility for asylum-seekers, which impact upon family reunion, apply between Denmark and the other Member States in the form of the original Dublin Convention. The revised responsibility rules agreed by the Council (Reg. 343/2003, OJ 2003 L50/1) will not apply to Denmark until conclusion of a treaty between the EC and Denmark requiring their application.

[6] For example, the discussion of the cross-over between the general family reunion rules for third-country nationals and association agreements (see sect. 5D below) is not relevant to the UK, Ireland or Denmark. The UK and Ireland will apply EC rules on the status of family members of persons *accompanying* refugees when they entered, but not the rules in the general family reunion Directive concerning those who *join* refugees later.

universal and regional treaties.[7] Of these, the case law of the European Court of Human Rights on the European Convention of Human Rights (ECHR) is best known and most influential within the EU, particularly because the Court of Justice treats the ECHR as having a special place as a source of guidelines for the human rights forming part of the general principles of EC law.[8] The core relevant provision of the Convention is Article 8, which guarantees the right to respect for private and family life. In turn, Article 8(2) ECHR allows interference with that right on a number of grounds, including public safety, national security, the economic well-being of the country, and the prevention of disorder or crime.[9]

The relevant cases can be broken down between those judgments concerning admission and those governing removal. A further distinction can be drawn in the latter category between those to be expelled on public safety or public security grounds and those to be expelled in the economic interests of the host State. The admission cases are relatively few; here the Strasbourg Court has consistently ruled that there is in principle no interference with the right to respect for family life if it is possible for the family to live elsewhere. This even applies in cases where the mother of the child has died and the father (after some years of residence abroad) wishes the child to join him, or where the parents have difficulty leaving a host State because of the illness of the mother.[10] States are entitled to have a separate regime for persons with special links with that State that treats such persons more favourably as compared to other sponsors, but a distinction between men and women as regards family reunion is a breach of Articles 8 and 14 ECHR (guaranteeing equality in respect of the rights set out in the Convention).[11] However, the Convention can entail a right of admission in some cases: the Court has ruled that where some children are living in the host State with their parents and some have been left in the country of origin, the latter must

[7] See generally, R. Cholewinski, *Migrant Workers in International Human Rights Law* (Oxford: OUP, 1997), at 68–70, 171–173, and 335–336; and R. Cholewinski, 'The Protection of the Right of Economic Migrants to Family Reunion in Europe', 43 *ICLQ* (1994) 568. On the UN International Covenant on Civil and Political Rights see S. Joseph, J. Schultz, and M. Castan, *The International Covenant on Civil and Political Rights: Cases, Materials and Commentary*, 2nd edition (Oxford: OUP, 2004), at 360–363 and 448–453.

[8] Case 222/84 *Johnston* [1986] ECR 1651. See also Art. 6(2) TEU.

[9] For a detailed analysis, see P. van Dijk, 'Protection of "Integrated" Aliens against Expulsion under the European Convention on Human Rights', in E. Guild and P. Minderhoud (eds), *Security of Residence and Expulsion: Protection of Aliens in Europe* (The Hague: Kluwer, 2001) 23; C. Harvey, 'Promoting Insecurity: Public Order, Expulsion and the European Convention on Human Rights', in ibid., at 41; P. Marin and J. O'Connell, 'The European Convention and the Relative Rights of Resident Aliens', 5 *ELJ* (1999) 4; and H. Storey, 'The Right to Family Life and Immigration Case Law at Strasbourg', 39 *ICLQ* (1990) 329.

[10] See *Ahmut* v *Netherlands* (Reports 1996–VI) and *Gul* v *Switzerland* (Reports 1996–I).

[11] *Abdulaziz and others* v *UK* (Series A, no. 94).

be reunified in the host State of their parents if it is impractical for their siblings to leave school there.[12]

As for expulsion, in principle there is an interference with family life where any State seeks to expel persons who have established family life in that State.[13] Where a State simply wishes to expel persons solely in the economic interest of that State, the Court is unwilling to accept an interference with family life, ruling that the State's interest was outweighed by the interest of an active father in continuing a relationship with his young daughter.[14] Also, where a father showed signs of wishing to develop a relationship with his child but faced difficulties due to the opposition of the child's mother, the State could not pre-empt the conclusion of the family law proceedings by expelling the father before those proceedings were properly completed.[15]

The position changes in cases where the State wishes to expel a person following a criminal conviction for a serious crime. In such cases, there must be a balancing test, which takes into account on the one hand the extent, timing, and seriousness of the criminal offences committed and, on the other hand, the difficulties that expulsion from that State would cause for the family life of the person concerned.[16] This aspect of the test entails assessing whether a family life could be maintained in the State of origin, taking into account such factors as the number of family members living in the State of origin as compared to the host State, along with the language skills and other connections with the State of origin which the expellee still maintains. A recent line of case law suggests that a particular test must be applied where the spouse of the expellee is not a national of the State of origin, which takes into account the particular difficulty that such a spouse may have integrating into the foreign spouse's country of origin and the likely severe impact on their marriage.[17] There also seem to be special considerations for children, as it is not permissible to return them alone to a State of origin where they have no close family and there has been recent fighting when they have only committed a less serious crime.[18] Moreover, there are minimum procedural requirements for Member States where Article 8 rights may be involved; they cannot simply disrupt family life without considering objections by the individuals concerned, even in supposed 'national security' cases.[19] The concept

[12] *Sen* v *Netherlands*, judgment of 21 Dec. 2001, not yet reported.

[13] The same applies to those who have established a 'private life' there, but that issue is not directly relevant to the issue of family reunion.

[14] *Berrehab* v *Netherlands* (Series A, no. 138).

[15] *Ciliz* v *Netherlands* (Reports of Judgments and Decisions, 2000–VIII).

[16] Case law beginning with *Moustaquim* v *Belgium* (Series A, no. 193).

[17] Case law beginning with *Boultif* v *Switzerland*, judgment of 2 June 2001, not yet reported. Specific factors include the existence and age of children, the length of the marriage, and the spouse's knowledge of the criminal activity before the start of the marriage or relationship.

[18] *Jakupovic* v *Austria*, judgment of 6 Feb. 2003, not yet reported.

[19] *Al-Nashif* v *Bulgaria*, judgment of 10 June 2002, not yet reported.

of family member for the purposes of the ECHR appears to be broad, encompassing not just the nuclear family but also co-habitees (at least in cases involving children), parents' relationship with children (and vice versa) after divorce or separation from the parent carer, or adulthood of the children, and siblings, aunts, and uncles.[20]

It has been argued that foreign nationals should not be subject to expulsion when nationals are not, and that EU Member States should not subject nationals of non-EU States to discrimination as regards expulsion compared to nationals of EU States. But the Strasbourg Court has rejected these arguments, on the grounds that in principle a State's nationals cannot be expelled at all, and that the EU has created a 'special legal order', so there is an 'objective and reasonable justification' for treating them better than persons from non-EU States.[21] A subsequent judgment updates this conclusion by referring to the subsequent creation of citizenship of the Union, failing to take account of the fact that 'citizens' of the Union outside their Member State of nationality can be expelled from other Member States, unlike the citizens of the relevant Member State.[22] The refusal to condemn discrimination on grounds of nationality as regards family reunion is crucial, as we shall see, to the highly differentiated system of family reunion rights constructed by the European Community. It should be noted, however, that it contradicts the conclusion of the same Court in the cases of *Gaygusuz* v *Austria* and *Poirrez* v *France* that nationality discrimination as regards the rights set out in the Convention cannot easily be justified.[23]

The potential links between EC law on family reunion and the ECHR rules have not been fully explored by the Strasbourg Court. In several judgments the Court has examined whether a non-EU national could move with an EU spouse to another EU country other than that wishing to expel the non-EU spouse,[24] but it has never drawn the obvious connection with EC free movement law in such cases. In fact, it might be questioned whether the crimes committed in these particular cases would be serious enough to permit another Member State to refuse the entry of such persons.[25] The Court has

[20] See, for example, *Abdulaziz* (*supra* note 11), *Moustaquim* (*supra* note 16) and *Yildiz* v *Austria*, judgment of 31 Oct. 2002, not yet reported.

[21] See *Moustaquim*, *supra* note 16.

[22] *C* v *Belgium* (Reports 1996–III).

[23] Reports 1996–IV and judgment of 30 Sept. 2003, not yet reported.

[24] See particularly *Mehemi* v *France* (Reports 1999–VI), where the spouse of the expellee was actually a national of Italy, not France. In *Amrohalli* v *Denmark* (judgment of 11 July 2002, not yet reported), the Court rejected the possibility that the expellee could live in Greece or Turkey on grounds of insufficient links there, not considering the prospect of the Danish spouse exercising free movement rights to live in Greece. On the links between the ECHR and EC free movement law see also the Commission's report on the derogations from free movement law (COM(1999)372, 19 July 1999), at 7–9 and 20–21.

[25] See discussion of the relevant EC rules in sect. 3D below.

instead focused in these cases on the extent of family life enjoyed by the expellee in the host Member State. In cases involving admission of a non-EU national to live with an EU national, free movement law could also be relevant.[26] In future, the possibility of free movement of long-term resident third-country nationals of the EU could also be relevant to family reunion cases. Also, there has already been a Strasbourg judgment involving application of an EC agreement with a non-EU country, in which the Court of Human Rights left it to national courts to determine whether the association agreement with Turkey had been correctly applied.[27] Perhaps the Strasbourg Court would be more willing to consider EC law issues if and when the Community or Union becomes a contracting party to the ECHR.[28] Conversely, the Court of Justice has on a number of occasions referred to the right to family life when ruling on family reunion cases governed by EC law, often referring to Article 8 ECHR and even, in two cases, to Strasbourg Court judgments.[29]

3. FAMILY MEMBERS OF EU NATIONALS

A. Sponsors

Lawyers speak of free movement or immigration of *workers*; but in reality it would usually be more accurate to speak of movement or migration of *families*. Nonetheless, the starting point of EC free movement law is to find an individual who is exercising an activity covered by that law. Only if that individual meets the conditions for exercising free movement do we

[26] See the cases discussed in sect. 3A below, particularly the *Akrich* case.

[27] *Yildiz, supra* note 20. If the expellee had acquired rights under the EC–Turkey agreement, he would have been covered by the rules limiting expulsion discussed in sect. 4D below, which would surely have prevented his expulsion given the minor theft and road traffic(!) offences involved. In fact, the Austrian courts apparently failed to consider whether he was the 'family member' of his cohabitee, a Turkish national who was possibly a worker herself (see the *Eyup* case, discussed in sect. 4A below). Presumably the Human Rights Court would equally have left alone a judgment by the Court of Justice concerning interpretation of the agreement. In *Boultif* (*supra* note 17), the Court rejected the prospect of the expellee living in Italy with his Swiss wife, although in this case the expulsion decision (and the Strasbourg judgment) pre-dated the entry into force of the EC–Swiss agreement on free movement of persons (see sect. 4 below) which would have permitted them to move there.

[28] See Art. I–7 of the proposed EU Constitution agreed by the EU Convention in July 2003 (OJ 2003 C169/1), which would permit EU accession to the ECHR.

[29] See Case 249/86 *Commission* v *Germany* [1989] ECR 1263; Case C–60/00 *Carpenter* [2002] ECR I–6279 (applying the *Boultif* judgment); Case C–459/99 *MRAX* [2002] ECR I–6591; Case C–413/99 *Baumbast and R* [2002] ECR I–7091; Case C–257/00 *Givane* [2003] ECR I–345; and judgment of 23 Sept. 2003 in Case C–109/01 *Akrich*, not yet reported (referring to *Boultif* and *Amrohalli*).

consider that person's family, whose legal position is ancillary to the free movement rights of the individual sponsor.

As noted in the introduction, the basic distinction here is between those EC nationals who exercise free movement rights and those who do not. This distinction was first confirmed by the Court as regards family reunion in the *Morson and Jhanjan* judgment,[30] and further applied to an aspect of the status of family members (equal working conditions) in *Uecker and Jacquet*.[31] The importance of the distinction is that at present EC free movement law regarding family reunion *only* applies to those who have exercised a free movement right, so national law alone applies to the families of those who have exercised no such right. However, the Commission has twice suggested equalizing the rules between the two categories, so that those joining 'non-moving' EU citizens will be in the same position as those who join 'movers'. The first such suggestion was its proposal for a Convention on migration in 1997,[32] and the second was its proposal for a general directive on family reunion with third-country nationals in 1999.[33] But the Commission dropped this suggestion from a revision of its proposal in 2002, on the ground that EC free movement legislation was being revised, although it intends to return to the issue later.[34]

In any event, where Member States choose to extend the EC free movement rules to internal situations, the Court of Justice is willing to rule on their application of those rules.[35] Although the Court apparently suggested later that Member States 'cannot' extend the free movement rules to internal situations,[36] this can surely only have meant that Member States are not obliged to do so,[37] for the EC legislature (still less the Court) lacks the

[30] Joined Cases 35/82 and 36/82 *Morson and Jhanjan* [1982] ECR 3273.

[31] Joined Cases C–64/96 and 65/96 [1997] ECR I–3171.

[32] COM(1997)387, 30 July 1997; OJ 1997 C337/9. On the family reunion issues in this proposal see M. Hedemann-Robinson, 'From Object to Subject? Non-EC Nationals and the Draft Proposal of the Commission for a Council Act Establishing the Rules for Admission of Third-Country Nationals to the Member States', 18 *YEL* (1998) 289 at 317–326 and S. Peers, 'Raising Minimum Standards or Racing to the Bottom? The Commission's Proposed Migration Convention', in E. Guild (ed), *The Legal Framework and Social Consequences of Free Movement of Persons in the European Union* (The Hague: Kluwer, 1999) 149 at 159–164.

[33] COM(1999)638, 1 Dec. 1999; OJ 2000 C116 E/66. The proposal was maintained in the revised proposal of 2000, following the EP's vote (COM(2000)624, 10 Oct. 2000; OJ 2001 C62 E/99).

[34] COM(2002)225, 3 May 2002; OJ 2002 C203 E/136.

[35] See Joined Cases C–297/88 and 197/89 *Dzozdi* [1990] ECR I–3763.

[36] See *MRAX*, *supra* note 29, para. 39.

[37] In other words, what the Court meant to say more precisely was that the EC free movement rules cannot automatically be applied to internal situations.

competence to prevent Member States from doing this.[38] It should in any event be emphasized that the third-country national family members of *all* EU citizens, regardless of whether those citizens have exercised free movement rights, could eventually qualify for the status of long-term resident under EC legislation.[39] Also, where a national of one Member State moves to another Member State to become part of the family of an EU citizen sponsor who has not exercised free movement rights, EC free movement law *does* apply because the family member has exercised free movement rights.[40]

In the absence of EC rules governing family reunion with 'non-moving' EC nationals, it is necessary to define a distinction between those who exercise free movement rights and those who do not. The key case here is *Singh*, in which the Court held that an EC national who exercises free movement rights (in this case, the right of establishment) must still be treated as exercising those rights when he or she returns to the home Member State.[41] This was an application of long-standing case law concerning the application of free movement law to 'returnees'.[42] Subsequently, in its judgment in *Carpenter*, the Court made clear that where the free movement of services is concerned, an EC national could invoke the EC rules even when living in his host Member State, if he was providing services to another Member State. Therefore the *Treaty* (rather than secondary legislation) conferred the right to ensure the continued residence of a family member, because the removal of that person would affect the conditions under which the sponsor exercised his free movement right.[43] Logically, this ruling should apply equally to

[38] The free movement legislation and Treaty rules do not purport to have this effect; nor could they, as the EC can only regulate free movement using these powers. It might be arguable that Title IV family reunion legislation could have this effect, but no family reunion measure had been adopted at that time. In any event, as noted above, the latest proposal did not suggest regulating the issue at all, and even the earlier proposals from the Commission took the opposite approach to this issue. Also, this approach contradicts the cases in which the Court is flexible about ruling on cases where the free movement rules might be applicable internally: see Case C–448/98 *Guimont* [2000] ECR I–10663; Joined Cases C–321–324/94 *Pistre* [1997] ECR I–2343; Joined Cases C–515/99, 519–524/99 and 526–540/99 *Reisch and others* [2002] ECR I–2157; Case C–300/01 *Salzmann* [2003] ECR I–4899; judgment of 11 Sept. 2003 in Case C–6/01 *Anomar*, not yet reported; and Case C–281/98 *Angonese* [2000] ECR I–4139, which concerned the free movement of persons. See particularly para. 23 of the *Guimont* judgment and para. 26 of the *Reisch* judgment, in which the Court expressly accepted the power of Member States to extend free movement rules to internal situations and its willingness to answer requests for a preliminary ruling in such cases.

[39] For details see sect. 3D below.

[40] See the Commission's interpretation of the rules in COM(1999)127 and the Opinion in Case C–413/01 *Ninni-Orasche*, judgment of 6 November 2003, not yet reported.

[41] Case C–370/90 [1992] ECR I–4265.

[42] See particularly Case C–378/97 *Wijsenbeek* [1999] ECR I–6207 and Case C–234/97 *Fernandez de Bobadilla* [1999] ECR I–4773.

[43] *Supra* note 29.

admission of family members, because the refusal to admit would equally be detrimental to the conditions for the exercise of free movement rights.

Should the 'returnees' rule be limited to those sponsors who exercise economic free movement rights? Although *Singh* concerned sponsors exercising such rights, the 'returnees' rule should not be limited to those groups, as the Court's recent judgments applying the 'returnee' principle require a broad application of that principle.[44] So logically all those exercising any form of free movement right are covered by *Singh* as regards family reunion. But what if the motivation for exercising free movement rights was purely to take advantage of EC free movement law rules on family reunion, in place of national law rules? In its judgment in *Akrich*, the Court ruled that such behaviour was not an 'abuse' of EC free movement law, but that where a family member had not complied with the migration law of the first Member State, he or she could be denied return to that Member State with the sponsor.[45] The judgment could also potentially be interpreted to mean that there was no EC free movement law right for the family member to enter the second Member State in such circumstances, or even that the initial formation of a family in the second Member State is not governed by free movement law in any circumstances. With the greatest respect, the Court of Justice wholly lacked the jurisdiction to consider these issues, since it was limited to answering the question whether the application of EC free movement law is being 'abused' in such circumstances. The national court solely considered the question of abuse, its questions relate solely to the question of abuse, and all of the observations in the written procedure and at the hearing (including from the UK government) relate solely to the question of abuse.[46] Moreover, with great respect, the Advocate-General was wrong to examine the issue from the perspective of Title IV of the EC Treaty, not only because the national court declined to approach the issue from this angle but also because the national court *could* not do so, as the UK is not bound in principle by Title IV but only by the particular measures it opts into, and in any event because the referring court is not a final court entitled to send questions concerning Title IV to the Court.[47] Further-

[44] See *Wijsenbeek* (*supra* note 42) and particularly Case C–224/98 *D'Hoop* [2002] ECR I–6191, which applies the principle to EU citizens' right to move and reside freely.

[45] *Supra* note 29.

[46] See the order for reference, dated 3 Oct. 2000, and the Report for the Hearing. I am grateful to Don Flynn for supplying these documents and information about the oral hearing.

[47] I have argued elsewhere that a lower court can refer Title IV questions where a Title IV question is inextricably linked with 'normal' EC law questions, and that the Court of Justice should be able to interpret 'normal' EC law questions in light of Title IV acts ('Who's Judging the Watchmen?: The Judicial System of the Area of Freedom, Security and Justice', 18 *YEL* (1998) 337 at 397–399). But this case does not fall within either category, as there is no Title IV legislation involved and Title IV itself does not expressly state that Member States are required to screen all family reunion in the way the Advocate-General suggests. For examples of possible family reunion issues where the principle might apply, see sect. 4D below.

more, there were serious errors of fact and law in the Opinion, which may have swayed the Court: it is not true that all Member States apply restrictive rules to admission of family members to join their own nationals,[48] or that all Member States have repeatedly restricted primary immigration in recent years.[49] Finally, it is even more questionable in the absence of questions from the national court for the Court to rule (if it was intending to do so) that EC free movement law does not govern family formation and that the Member State to which a person moves in the *Singh* or *Akrich* case could refuse entry to the family members.[50] Again with respect, it has apparently been forgotten in this judgment that the system of preliminary rulings was designed as a mechanism for co-operation between the national courts and the Court of Justice. Since there was no fresh hearing allowing for any discussion of the points raised by the Advocate-General on his own initiative and at least partly accepted by the Court, the judgment also appears to be a flagrant breach of Article 6 ECHR.

EC free movement law determines different categories of EC national sponsors who, as we shall see, enjoy different rights of family reunion. The free movement of workers is guaranteed by Article 39 EC, with further detail of this right (including the right of family members) found in Regulation 1612/68 and Directive 68/360.[51] Freedom of establishment (including of the self-employed) is guaranteed by Article 43 EC, supplemented by Directive 73/148.[52] Free movement of services is ensured by Article 49 EC, also supplemented by Directive 73/148. Students have the right to move freely to take up vocational training;[53] this right is supplemented by Directive

[48] The Council's internal documents concerning the Commission's 1999 proposal on family reunion indicate that only three Member States out of twelve participating in discussions (Germany, Finland, and the Netherlands) objected to the Commission's proposal to extend EC free movement family reunion rules to EU citizens who have not exercised free movement rights (Council doc 8209/01, 2 May 2001). It is well known that Belgium extends the free movement rules to its own citizens not exercising free movement rights (see *Dzozdi*, *supra* note 35 and *MRAX*, *supra* note 29); the same applies in sect. 49 of the Austrian Aliens Act 1997 (following earlier national court rulings) and the Spanish Aliens Act. I am grateful to Professor Kees Gronendijk for this information.

[49] Most pointedly, the UK has considerably liberalized the rules for admission of economic migrants: see, for example, Home Office press release 67/2003, 11 Mar. 2003, referring to a policy of 'actively encouraging properly managed economic migration' and a planned 50% increase in work permits processed over two years (online at: http://213.121.214.245/n_story.asp?item_id=397).

[50] Again the national court in the UK *could not* have asked questions about the legal position in Ireland. This essay assumes that the Court only intended to rule on the issue actually referred to it (the status of Mr. Akrich upon his return to the UK).

[51] OJ Spec. Ed. 1968 L257/2, p. 475 and OJ Spec. Ed. 1968 L257/13, p. 485.

[52] OJ 1973 L172/14.

[53] Case C–357/89 *Raulin* [1992] ECR I–1027. On the broad definition of 'vocational training', which includes nearly all post-secondary education, see Case 293/83 *Gravier* [1985] ECR 593 and Case 24/86 *Blaizot* [1988] ECR 379.

93/96.[54] Legislation also governs the position of persons who retire after taking up employment or self-employment in another Member State, or who retire in another Member State without any such recent economic activity.[55] Finally, there is 'default' legislation giving the right to move to any EU citizens not covered by other legislation or Treaty rules, subject to certain conditions.[56] The relevant secondary legislation, including all of the provisions on family members, would be consolidated and amended if a directive proposed by the Commission in 2001 were agreed.[57]

Furthermore, the EC Treaty provides for further free movement of both sponsors and family members. The right of EU citizens to 'move and reside freely' in Article 18 EC is a directly effective right which gives EU citizen sponsors the right to move in at least a few further cases besides those set out expressly in the Treaty and secondary legislation.[58] It is not known whether this entails associated rights for the family members of such citizens. But, as noted above, at least some of the Treaty provisions on free movement of persons also grant rights to family members, as the Court stated in *Singh* and confirmed in *Carpenter*. In the former case, the impact was limited, as the Court required 'returnees' from the host Member State to be assimilated to nationals of other Member States exercising free movement rights there. But *Carpenter* is potentially more radical (or more limited), as the Court did not suggest an assimilation with those exercising free movement rights. Since we do not know much yet about which family members are covered by the *Carpenter* rule, or about their status or conditions for their reunion, it is possible to argue that the rules on these points are wider than those normally applying to family reunion with EC nationals. If the rules are wider, then we can see the obvious importance of the Court potentially taking a further step, and concluding that family reunion can be based on the Treaty free movement rules, not just where there is a Treaty right to free movement not implemented by secondary legislation, but even where secondary legislation applies. That would mean that EC national sponsors could rely on the Treaty directly to avoid restrictions in the legislation on the definition of family member, on family status and on conditions for reunion found in secondary legislation.

In any event, even if *Carpenter* does not apply to such 'overlap' cases, it could still apply to cases besides those where a person is providing services to other Member States while still normally resident in his or her home Member State. It could also apply to what might be called 'frontier returnee' cases,

[54] OJ 1993 L317/59.

[55] Reg. 1251/70 (OJ Spec. Ed. 1970 L142/24, p. 402), Dir. 75/34 (OJ 1975 L14/10), and Dir. 90/365 (OJ 1990 L180/28).

[56] Dir. 90/364 (OJ 1990 L180/26).

[57] COM(2001)257, 23 May 2001. See sect. 3E below.

[58] *Baumbast and R*, *supra* note 29.

where someone is employed (or otherwise exercising an activity) in his *home* Member State while residing in another Member State. This is distinct from what might be called the 'classic' frontier case, where someone is residing in his or her home Member State while exercising activities besides provision of services in another Member State. Traditionally the Court ruled that the persons exercising activity in their home Member State while residing in another Member State (for example, a German national resident in France but working in Germany) had not 'moved' within the Community and so were not covered by the free movement rules.[59] With respect, this is an unconvincing legal fiction, which sits uneasily with the Court's long-standing application of the free movement rules to fully-fledged returnees. But it is now arguable that Directive 90/364 and/or the rules on EU citizenship, which clearly apply to fully-fledged returnees, governs the situation of the frontier returnees.[60] Such an interpretation should be supported, as it would fit literally within the definition of the right to *move* and reside freely.

As for the 'classic' frontier cases where a person resides in his or her home Member State and pursues activities in another one, the Court has held that at least some such cases fall within the scope of the free movement rules.[61] This must mean that the free movement rules on family reunion apply. For workers, the wording of Regulation 1612/68 does not rule out the application of the family reunion rules in the Regulation to frontier workers, as Article 10 of the Regulation applies wherever a person is *employed* in another Member State; there is no condition of residence in another Member State.[62] As for self-employment, the *Meeusen* judgment was based purely on the Treaty as far as self-employment was concerned, and moreover concerned issues of family status. For services, it could be suggested that *Carpenter* was simply applying the classic frontier case law, although the Court did not suggest this in its judgment. As for other forms of free movement, the Court has not yet been asked to rule whether the classic 'frontier' rule applies. Logically it should, even though the relevant legislation in these cases only grants a right of residence to family members in the Member State where the relevant activity takes place, because, as we have seen, the rights in 'frontier' cases appear to be based on the Treaty, not simply on secondary legislation. Also, there seems no reason to distinguish between cases where the main thrust of activity is in the other Member State or where that activity is merely ancillary. This would contradict the approach in *Carpenter* and the right to

[59] See particularly Case C–112/91 *Werner* [1993] ECR I–429.

[60] See the Opinion in *Werner* and in Case C–107/94 *Asscher* [1996] ECR I–3089.

[61] On workers see Case C–57/96 *Meints* [1997] ECR I–6689 and Case C–35/97 *Commission* v *France* [1998] ECR I–5325. On the self-employed see Case C–337/97 *Meeusen* [1999] ECR I–3289, which partly concerned issues of family members' status.

[62] On the subsequent status of such family members see sect. 3D below.

'double establishment' of professional activity in multiple Member States guaranteed by Article 43 EC.

The practical implications of applying family reunion rules to frontier and frontier returnee cases as regards all forms of free movement could be considerable, wherever family reunion rules in the host Member State are significantly more restrictive than the rules of EC free movement law. For example, the Danish national law preventing family reunion where persons are married before the age of 25 could not apply to those Danish citizens who live in the Swedish town of Malmö but exercise activities in Copenhagen *or* vice versa.

Also, the *Carpenter* rule could apply in any other case where the right to move and reside freely applies, rather than a specific free movement right. The Court did not examine this point in *Baumbast and R*, the only case to date to address a free movement right (as distinct from a social benefit) derived from Article 18 EC, presumably because the national court had not addressed questions on it and the family members had status based on the rules on workers.[63] But in another case, the Court will have to examine the issue, as it will obviously be hard for any citizens to exercise the right to move and reside fully in the absence of any connected family reunion rights.

Finally, it is necessary to examine which comparator should be used for EC national returnees. In *Singh*, the Court required comparison between the returnee and an EC national who has exercised a free movement right. However, in *D'Hoop*, it required a comparison between the returnee and the home State nationals who had not moved. The difference could obviously be crucial for family reunion cases. A useful illustration of the distinction is the UK case law following *Singh*, in which UK returnees, having taken advantage of the more favourable family reunion rules offered to EC nationals, then sought to rely on the more favourable rules on the status of family members applied to UK nationals who had not exercised free movement rights. The UK courts took the view that since the sponsors had relied on a comparison with migrant EC nationals to get their family members into the UK, they could not insist on a switch to a comparison with non-migrant UK nationals in order to obtain a better status for those family members later.[64] But while *Singh* requires the first comparison, *D'Hoop* requires the second.

[63] The *extent* of that status is examined in sect. 3D below.

[64] *Zeghraba and Sahota* [1997] 3 CMLR 576 and *Boukssid* [1998] 2 CMLR 281. See T. Connor, 'Non-Community Spouses: Interpretation of Community Residence Rights', 23 *ELRev.* (1998) 194 and 24 *ELRev.* (1999) 99. The relevant rules ensure easier access to long-term resident status for family members of UK nationals who have not moved, as compared to UK nationals who move or other EC citizens who move to the UK. For more detail, see the Opinions and judgments in *Kaba I* and *Kaba II* (Case C–356/98 [2000] ECR I–2623 and Case C–466/00 [2003] ECR I–2219), discussed further in sect. 3D below.

The only way to explain the apparent contradiction is to look for the underlying rule which the Court is seeking to defend: the avoidance of obstacles to free movement. Following that logic, the UK returnees should be able to switch between comparators, and similar cases should be decided on the same basis.

It should also be noted that special transitional rules concerning family members of EU nationals applied to the Spanish and Portuguese accession, as well as to the accession planned for May 2004. These rules relate solely to the status of family members, and so are considered further below.[65]

B. Family Members

The principal source for the definition of 'family members' is secondary legislation relating to free movement. First, Article 10 of Regulation 1612/68 gives two groups the right to install themselves with the worker: the spouse and their descendants who are under 21 *or* dependent, and dependent relatives in the ascending line of the worker and the worker's spouse. Member States are also obliged to 'facilitate' the admission of any other family member if dependent on the worker or living under the worker's roof in the country the worker came from. Directive 73/148 applies very similar rules to family members of the self-employed and service providers or recipients, except that the legislation instead requires admission of the children of the sponsor (rather than the joint children); admission of all children (rather than all descending relatives) under 21 is required without a dependency test; and Member States are required to facilitate the entry of the family members of the sponsor or spouse who was dependent on one or the other.[66] The same definition of family members applies after retirement of workers or the self-employed.[67] As for other categories of free movement, pensioners and the self-sufficient can bring spouses and dependent ascending and descending relatives, while students can bring spouses and dependent children.[68] It should be noted that not all family members of all sponsors need to be 'dependent' in order to join the sponsor. In particular, spouses *never* have to fulfil this requirement.

The Court of Justice has defined 'spouse' to mean only a person joined by marriage to a sponsoring worker.[69] Presumably this definition applies to all of the free movement rules, and it seems unlikely in light of the judgments in *Grant* and *D* v *Council* that the Court will take a wider view of the concept of

[65] See sect. 3D.

[66] Art. 1(1)(c), 1(1)(d) and 1(2) of the Directive (OJ 1973 L172/14).

[67] Art. 1 of Reg. 1251/70 and Art. 1 of Dir. 75/34 (both *supra* note 55).

[68] Art. 1(2) of Dir. 90/364 (*supra* note 56); Art. 1(2) of Dir. 90/365 (*supra* note 55); and Art. 1 of Dir. 93/96 (*supra* note 54).

[69] Case 59/85 *Reed* [1987] ECR 1283.

'spouse' in the near future.[70] However, these judgments did not concern free movement law, so it is still possible that the Court would rule that denying entry to an unmarried partner is an obstacle to free movement. Moreover, the judgments involved same-sex couples, not opposite-sex couples, although the obstacle to free movement would still exist regardless of the sexual orientation involved. But, more positively, the Court has ruled that a 'spouse' remains a spouse until a marriage is fully dissolved, regardless of the separation of the spouses (within the same Member State) or the state of divorce proceedings.[71] It is assumed that the status of 'spouse' ceases when a divorce has become final.[72] However, according to the *Reed* judgment, it is open to sponsoring workers to argue for admission of unmarried partners on the same basis as a host Member State admits entry of unmarried partners of its own nationals as a 'social advantage' for workers. Although the secondary legislation governing other sponsors does not require equal treatment for 'social advantages', it is likely that the Court would rule that all other sponsors are entitled to equal treatment with nationals as regards admission of unmarried partners.[73]

As for children, in *Baumbast and R* the Court stated expressly that step-children are covered by the legislation on free movement of workers whether the sponsor or the spouse is the parent,[74] even though the wording of Regulation 1612/68 suggests that the child in question must be the joint child of the worker and his or her spouse. Given this judgment and the underlying objective of eliminating obstacles to free movement of persons, it logically follows that step-children and adopted children must be considered to be 'children' under all the rules applying to different categories of sponsor. Similarly, a single parent must be able to bring his or her child under the relevant conditions when exercising a free movement right. There is no case law on other relatives, although logically ascending relatives can only be related to the sponsor *or* the spouse, since the sponsor and spouse cannot have the same parent(!),[75] and the marriage of first cousins is not generally common or permitted within the EU.

[70] Case C–249/96 [1998] ECR I–629 and Joined Cases C–122/99 and 125/99 [2001] ECR I–4319.

[71] See *Singh*, *supra* note 41 and Case 267/83 *Diatta* [1985] ECR 567.

[72] See the UK case of *Sandhu* [1982] 2 CMLR 553 (High Court); [1983] Imm. AR. 61 (CA). The Court of Justice has never ruled expressly on the point, although its judgment in *Baumbast and R* (*supra* note 29) clearly assumed that divorce will end the residence status of family members unless they have some other ground to stay. The status of family members in such cases is explored further in sect. 3D below.

[73] This would be based on the ban on discrimination on grounds of nationality set out in Art. 12 EC. For the self-employed, the Court has already assumed that equal treatment in 'social advantages' is ensured by Art. 43 EC: see *Meeusen* (*supra* note 61).

[74] Para. 57 of the judgment, *supra* note 29.

[75] However, a step-*parent* is presumably considered to be a family member, by analogy with the position of step-children.

Sooner or later the Court of Justice will be asked to consider cases where a marriage, adoption, or custody (parental responsibility) decision taken in one Member State might not necessarily be recognized in the host Member State. The most sensible approach here would be to apply the usual test for 'public policy' derogations from free movement rules, in which Member States must justify measures taken by showing that they have a legitimate aim and that the methods taken to achieve that aim are necessary and proportionate, taking account of measures to achieve the same aim already applied in the other Member State. It might be tempting for private international lawyers to assert that only the rules of private international law apply, but this approach fails to take account of the central importance to the EC legal order of ensuring free movement of persons. But where relevant EC legislation exists, it can be used to address this issue in place of the general test for derogations from free movement rules.[76] Interpreted in light of free movement rules, this legislation can be used to facilitate free movement.[77]

Finally, it should be recalled that the judgment in *Carpenter* opened the possibility that rights to movement of family members could be based directly on the Treaty, arguably even where secondary legislation already sets out which family members can join the sponsor. This could entail a requirement to let in wider categories of family members.[78] The judgment in *Carpenter* ruled simply that the separation of family members was detrimental to the exercise of a free movement right, without suggesting that there had to be a direct link between the presence of the family member and the exercise of the relevant freedom. So there is no reason to exclude children, for example, from the scope of the *Carpenter* rule just because they do not add economic value to the activities of the person exercising free movement rights.

Also, the prospect of EU citizenship rights entailing an increase in the scope of family members who can join a citizen has yet to be explored. In any event, it should always be kept in mind that where family members are themselves EU citizens, they may always be able to find a way to enter another Member State using free movement law in their own name, not only (obviously) where they take up work or self-employment, but even if they are dependent on another EU citizen. For example, there is nothing to preclude the use of Directive 90/364 by the dependent unmarried partner of an EU citizen to live with that citizen in another Member State, as long as the sponsor (who may be in the host Member State in any capacity permitted by

[76] See Reg. 1347/2000 (OJ 2000 L160/19) and now the wider reg. on responsibility and access issues (Reg. 2201/2003, OJ 2003 L338/1).

[77] For example, if there is an obligation to ensure simplified cross-border recognition of access orders, it is harder to justify a restriction on the parent with custody or responsibility leaving the country on the grounds of the right to access of the non-custodial parent.

[78] See further sect. 3A above.

EC free movement law) can fund sickness insurance and sufficient resources for his or her partner in order to meet the criteria in the Directive.[79]

C. Conditions

There are no conditions for family members to join EU national workers, self-employed persons, or service providers or recipients except an accommodation requirement as regards workers and a 'dependence' requirement as regards certain family members. Article 10(3) of Regulation 1612/68 requires workers to have housing suitable for the family as long as this requirement is not applied in a discriminatory fashion as compared to national workers. In *Commission* v *Germany*, the Court ruled that this condition could only be applied to the initial admission of family members, not when the family expanded later.[80] However, in addition to this requirement, there is a financial test built in where the sponsors are workers or self-employed persons, for they must qualify for that status in the first place. While the Court of Justice has taken a wide approach to the definition of 'worker',[81] as well as a parallel approach to the definition of 'establishment' of the self-employed,[82] this wide interpretation has its limits, as the sponsor must be undertaking some form of market activity.

After the end of employment or self-employment, family members can stay with the retired or disabled sponsor (or following the death of the sponsor) on the condition that the sponsor has exercised activity there for a sufficient period. Alternatively, if the sponsor dies during his or her working life, the family members can stay if the sponsor spent two years there before his or her death, died as a result of an occupational accident or disease, or if the surviving spouse is a national of the host Member State or only lost such nationality due to marriage.[83] However, in the *Givane* judgment, the Court ruled that the first criterion could only be satisfied by two years' residence immediately before the death of the sponsor, not residence at some prior period.[84]

[79] On the application of this Dir. to EU citizen family members to join a national of the host Member State see sect. 3A above.

[80] *Supra* note 29.

[81] For the core definition see Case 53/81 *Levin* [1982] ECR 1035 and Case 66/85 *Lawrie-Blum* [1986] ECR 2121; see particularly further Case 139/85 *Kempf* [1986] ECR 1741; Case 196/87 *Steymann* [1988] ECR 6159; Case C–27/91 *Le Manoir* [1991] ECR I–5531; *Raulin* (*supra* note 53); and Case C–3/90 *Bernini* [1992] ECR I–1071 on inclusion of persons receiving public funds, working in a collective, working as a trainee, with a short-term contract or working for few and irregular hours. See now opinion and judgment in Case C–413/01 *Ninni-Orasche* (*supra* note 40) and opinion of 19 February 2004 in Case C–456/02 *Trojani*, pending.

[82] For the definition of 'establishment', linking the concept to the undertaking of even a modest level of economic activity, see Case C–268/99 *Jany* [2001] ECR I–8615, paras 32 and 33.

[83] Art. 3 of Reg. 1251/70 and of Dir. 75/34 (both *supra* note 55).

[84] *Supra* note 29.

For other persons exercising free movement rights, the sponsor must meet conditions of sickness insurance in the host State and sufficient resources for the family members as well as himself or herself. In the case of pensioners, the latter requirement takes the form of showing receipt of a sufficiently large pension. Moreover, for both pensioners and persons covered by the 'default' Directive 90/364, Member States are expressly obliged to take account of the family members' financial position when considering whether the sponsors have sufficient funds. Presumably this could work both ways, making it harder for a sponsor to enter if the family members are his or her dependants, but easier to enter if the family members are contributing or can contribute to the family income. For students, the requirements can be demonstrated by a declaration, while other sponsors must show proof of meeting the conditions, although there are limits on Member States' power to insist that certain forms of documents be used.[85] The simplified procedural position of students explains the lack of an obligation for Member States to examine their family members' financial position.[86]

The Court has hinted strongly that sickness insurance in the home Member State will satisfy the requirement of having sickness insurance in the host Member State, due to the rules on EC social security co-ordination.[87] However, the Court of Justice rebuffed the Commission's argument that a distinction between pensioners and persons governed by Directive 90/364 as regards the resources condition was automatically suspect.[88] It should also be kept in mind that EU citizenship imposes limits in certain cases upon a Member State's ability to apply these conditions, and this might have some impact upon the application of the conditions to family members.[89]

Furthermore, the ability of spouses and dependent children to take up work or self-employment pursuant to these Directives means that the family members are able to provide the means for the sponsors to meet the sufficient resources test and to pay for sickness insurance.[90] It may seem odd that persons with an 'ancillary' right can create the means for their sponsors to exercise the primary right, but the Directives do not set out any conditions concerning the source of the sponsor's funds. This interpretation would obviously best respect the goal of ensuring free movement of persons and

[85] Case C–424/98 *Commission* v *Italy* [2000] ECR I–4001.

[86] The same applies to the resources requirement, which is less specific in the case of students. See *Commission* v *Italy* (ibid.).

[87] See *Baumbast and R* (*supra* note 29), para. 89. The Court was referring to Dir. 90/364, but the point is logically valid for all three Dirs. imposing a sickness insurance requirement.

[88] *Commission* v *Italy*, *supra* note 85. It is not clear whether the Court rejected this argument on substantive or procedural grounds.

[89] See Case C–184/99 *Grzelczyk* [2001] ECR I–6193 and *Baumbast and R* (*supra* note 29).

[90] On this right for family members see further sect. 3D below. Logically this is only relevant for third-country national family members, since family members who are EU citizens would be exercising primary free movement rights in this scenario.

would moreover acknowledge that the family is to some extent a collective institution, not solely a group of atomized individuals.[91] It would mean that to a certain extent the spouses are mutually dependent in a 'chicken and egg' scenario, with the 'market' spouse providing the financial means to allow the 'non-market' spouse to exercise free movement rights, which in turn enables the latter to bring the former into the country.

This brings us to two conditions that apply to all categories of sponsor: the condition of dependence and the requirements of public policy, public security, and public health. On the first condition, it should be kept in mind that not all family members are subject to a dependence test, and that the application of this test to different family members varies depending on the category of sponsor. For example, workers can bring all children under 21 without needing to satisfy a dependence requirement, while students must show dependence of any children they wish to bring with them.[92]

The definition of 'dependence' for the family members of workers was examined in *Lebon*, where the Court ruled that 'dependence' was a factual concept which applied whenever the sponsor assists the person in question. The concept is not based on whether there was a legal obligation of the sponsor to assist the 'dependent'; the status is not lost if the 'dependent' claimed social benefits; the reasons for support are irrelevant; and the prospect of whether the dependent could support himself or herself is equally irrelevant.[93] There is no reason to doubt that this ruling is equally applicable to the concept of 'dependence' as regards other categories of sponsor.

The entry and stay of all family members is also subject to the requirements of public policy, public security, and public health. Since these requirements apply to expulsion as well as admission, they are considered further below along with other aspects of the status of family members.

Finally, what conditions may apply to cases covered by the rule in *Carpenter*? As noted above, the only test applicable is whether separation of the family members would be a detriment to the sponsor.[94] This suggests that no further conditions for reunion should apply.

D. Status

There are two express provisions on family members' status in Regulation 1612/68. Article 11 gives the worker's (or self-employed person's) spouse and the worker's children who are under 21 or dependent the right to take up any

[91] It is also the interpretation of the Commission, which argues that there is no requirement that the sponsor's resources must be generated by the sponsor: see second report on the 1990 and 1993 Directives (COM(2003)101, 5 Mar. 2003), p. 11.

[92] For details of the distinctions see sect. 3B above.

[93] Case 316/85 [1987] ECR 2811.

[94] See sect. 3B above.

employment in the territory of the Member State in which the worker is employed. The right to work entails a continued right to reside as long as the family relationship subsists,[95] along with a corresponding application of all the provisions of Title I of the Regulation ensuring equality as regards access to employment and other EC legislation concerning mutual recognition of qualifications.[96] However, the application of Article 11 could be anomalous where the sponsor is a frontier worker (or pursues self-employment across a frontier), as the spouse and children do not have an express right to take up employment in the State of residence.

Article 12 specifies that the children of any worker who is or has been employed in the territory of another Member State must be 'admitted' to 'general educational, apprenticeship, and vocational training courses' under the same conditions as the host State's nationals, if the children reside in the territory, although this condition has been interpreted liberally. Also, Member States have to 'encourage all efforts to enable such children to attend these courses under the best possible conditions'. The Court has ruled that this Article applies to finance for such courses,[97] and that children are entitled to remain after a parent/worker has left the Member State in order to continue their education.[98] This applies to all levels of education, and entails a corollary right for a parent carer to remain there even if he or she is divorced or separated from the worker.[99] There is no age or dependency condition placed on children for the purposes of Article 12.[100] The territorial requirement for the children set out in Article 12 prevents application of that Article to the children of frontier workers (if they are living with the worker); moreover, there is no corresponding right to education in the State of the parent's residence in such cases.

In addition, the Court has held that the right to equal treatment in 'social advantages' for workers provided for in Article 7(2) of the Regulation applies also to family members, where the benefit for them can be considered as a benefit for the worker.[101] The EC's Regulation on social security

[95] *Diatta* (*supra* note 71).

[96] Case 131/85 *Gül* [1986] ECR 1573.

[97] Case 9/74 *Casagrande* [1974] ECR 773; Case 235/87 *Matteucci* [1988] ECR 5589 (equal treatment as regards financial support for education in other Member State under bilateral treaty); Case C–308/89 *Di Leo* [1990] ECR I–4185 (equal treatment as regards financial support for education in home Member State); Case C–3/90 *Bernini* [1992] ECR I–1071; and *Meeusen* (*supra* note 61).

[98] Joined Cases C–389/87 and 390/87 *Echternach and Moritz* [1989] ECR 723. This also entails continued equal treatment as regards study finance.

[99] See *Baumbast and R* (*supra* note 29); *Echternach and Moritz* (*supra* note 98); and Case 76/72 *Michel S.* [1973] ECR 457.

[100] Case C–7/94 *Gaal* [1995] ECR I–1031.

[101] See case law starting with Case 32/75 *Christini* [1975] ECR 1085, applied to third-country national family members in Case 94/84 *Deak* [1985] ECR 1873. Note that Art. 7(2) can be used as regards education benefits, with the result that the territorial requirement of

co-ordination also applies to the family members of workers and the self-employed;[102] indeed in 1996 the Court dropped an old rule that prevented family members from receiving social security benefits in their own name,[103] although the rule has been maintained for unemployment benefits.[104] However, the Court has twice held that there is no discrimination where a Member State gives family members of its own nationals who have not exercised a free movement right better treatment than the family members of EU citizens who exercise a free movement right in that Member State as regards access to long-term residence status.[105] This finding is unconvincing for the simple reason that the Court has chosen the wrong comparator in these cases, failing to compare the position of the family members, rather than the sponsors.[106] A comparison of the sponsors might be reasonable in other cases, but not where the right at issue is the right *to autonomous status* of the family member: the whole point in such a case is that the link between the sponsor and family member is being broken.

For other sponsors, the three Directives on non-economic movement each grant the spouse and dependent children of the sponsor the right to take up employment or self-employment in the host Member State.[107] One obvious question here is whether the family members, if they are third-country nationals, are entitled to equal treatment with EC nationals as regards access to employment (as in the *Gül* case) and self-employment. In the absence of any wording to the contrary, and given the similarity between the wording of this right and the right in Regulation 1612/68, it should follow that they do. This interpretation would certainly best facilitate free movement. For the same reasons, it should follow that, as in the *Diatta* case, the relevant family members can become separated from the sponsor and will not lose status as long as the family relationship subsists and the sponsor is exercising free movement rights in that Member State.

As for education for children and the right to equal treatment in social advantages, the Court assumed in its *Meeusen* judgment that the latter right applied equally to family members of the self-employed, pursuant to Article

Art. 12 will not apply (although a requirement of age or dependency will): see *Bernini* and *Meeusen* (*supra* notes 97 and 61). Presumably this also means that access to education extends beyond children of the worker to other family members. Art. 7(2) normally does not apply once the sponsors and their family members have returned to the Member State of origin: Case C–33/99 *Fahmi and Cerderis-Anhero* [2001] ECR I–2415.

[102] Reg. 1408/71, amended and updated by Reg. 2001/83 (OJ 1983 L230/6).

[103] Case C–308/93 *Cabanis-Issarte* [1996] ECR I–2097. The Reg. does not extend to access to education benefits (*Fahmi*, *supra* note 101).

[104] Case C–189/00 *Ruhr* [2001] ECR I–8225.

[105] *Kaba I* and *Kaba II*, *supra* note 64.

[106] For details of this argument see S. Peers, 'Dazed and Confused: Family Members' Residence Rights and the Court of Justice', 26 *ELRev.* (2001) 76.

[107] Art. 2(2) of each Dir. (*supra* notes 54 and 56).

43 EC.[108] Since the Court has ruled that some form of equal access to state benefits applies where services are being provided pursuant to Article 49 EC, it might reasonably be assumed that the right to equal treatment for family members' social advantages applies also.[109] The position of the remaining sponsors as regards family members' social advantages is not governed by EC free movement legislation, which does not govern the sponsor's position as regards such benefits either, except to rule out using Directive 93/96 to obtain maintenance grants for students.[110] However, the sponsor's equal access to social benefits is implicitly ruled out by the conditions for admission in these cases, although the Court has ruled that these conditions are not absolute, and the Court has a tendency to support broader access to social benefits as a consequence of EU citizenship.[111] It is not plausible to argue that the family members can circumvent the limits on access to social benefits imposed on the sponsors by the legislation, but any rights which can be obtained on the basis of such sponsors' citizenship of the Union could potentially be extended to family members.

The issue of education takes on added importance given the ruling in *Baumbast and R* that parent carers can stay as a corollary of the education right of migrant workers' children. There are no education rights for children in any other free movement legislation, and this issue has not been explored in the case law to date. But the equality right of EU citizens suggests strongly that the children of any EU national exercising free movement rights have equal access to any level of the education system, with a corollary right for a parent carer to stay with them if need be.[112] By analogy with the case law on vocational training, EU national children can exercise the right to obtain education in another Member State in their own name,[113] and can exercise a

[108] *Supra* note 61.

[109] For example, see Cases 63/86 *Commission* v *Italy* [1988] ECR 29; 305/87 *Commission* v *Greece* [1989] ECR I–1461; 186/87 *Cowan* [1989] ECR 195; and C–45/93 *Commission* v *Spain* [1994] ECR I–911.

[110] Art. 3 of the Dir. (*supra* note 54).

[111] See *Grzelczyk* (*supra* note 89) on the conditions in the Dir., and more generally *D'Hoop* (*supra* note 44) and Case C–85/96 *Martinez Sala* [1998] ECR I–2691.

[112] The Court did not examine whether the children at issue in the *Givane* judgment (*supra* note 29) were exercising the education right of children of migrant workers when their father died. Perhaps the Court began from the assumption that Reg. 1251/70 is *lex specialis* as regards death of a worker and so *Baumbast and R* issues do not apply in such a case.

[113] In *Raulin* (*supra* note 53), the Court combined Arts. 12 and 150 EC to find a right to move to another Member State to take up vocational training on a basis of equal access (apart from study finance and maintenance). Arts. 12 and 149, concerning education, could similarly be combined to find a parallel right to take up any course of education in another Member State. The Court has accepted by implication that moving to another Member State to obtain secondary school education is an exercise of citizenship rights (*D'Hoop*, *supra* note 44), and has also emphasized the importance of the education provisions of the Treaty and expressly stated that there is nothing to preclude students from the scope of the rules on

corollary right to bring their parent carers of any nationality with them.[114] Alternatively the rules on citizenship of the Union or Directive 90/364 could apply, if the children have sufficient funds and sickness insurance (by virtue of their parents' support).

One issue not explored yet is the status of third-country national family members who are allowed to enter or stay on various grounds, but where their status is not expressly set out in secondary legislation. Examples of this can be seen in *Reed*, *Carpenter*, *Singh*, and *Baumbast and R*. Are the spouses or parents who are allowed to stay in these cases (still) able to enjoy access to employment or social advantages?[115] In *Reed*, since admission of the unmarried partner was a social advantage to the worker to start with, it should follow that equal treatment of the partner is still a social advantage to that worker. Bringing *Reed* and *Baumbast and R* together, the position of a parent carer is equally a corollary of the child's education regardless of whether that parent was married to the other parent or not. In the *Singh* judgment, the Court's stress on assimilation of the returnees' family members with the family members of EC nationals moving there suggests strongly that the rules of Regulation 1612/68 apply. This would also mean that after divorce, the third-country national parent carer of a migrant worker's child could stay in returnee cases as well (bringing *Singh* and *Baumbast and R* together), although this again raises the question of the status of the carer in such cases. The best answer to this question is that the carer must at least have continued access to employment and social advantages, because his or her status is a corollary of the child's access to education and such access would be a further example of enjoying access to education under the best possible conditions. What about the position of a returnee with an unmarried partner (*Reed* and *Singh*), in particular following the break-up of the relationship (*Reed*, *Singh* and *Baumbast and R*)? Applying the principles in the case law, the position of the returnee's partner (assuming he or she had no independent free movement right) would depend on the treatment of unmarried partners by the home State of the returnee; if partners were recognized, then *Singh* and *Baumbast and R* should apply as set out above *mutatis mutandis*.

citizenship of the Union (*Grzelczyk*, *supra* note 89). Most recently, the Court explicitly stated that children benefit from the non-discrimination rights and citizenship rights in Arts. 12 and 18 EC (judgment of 2 Oct. 2003 in Case C–148/02 *Avello*, not yet reported).

[114] Questions on this point are pending in Case C–200/02 *Chen and Zhu*, not yet decided.

[115] Another question is whether the sponsor must continue the same activity for the family members to retain their rights (see L. Woods, 'Family Rights in the EU—Disadvantaging the Disadvantaged?' 11 *CFLQ* (1999) 17). It could also be questioned whether family members can accompany a work-seeker (Case C–292/89 *Antonissen* [1991] ECR I–745) and, if so, what their status is; but it appears that *de facto* this issue is now subsumed by Dir. 90/364. See now the Opinion of 10 July 2003 in Case C–138/02 *Collins*, para. 61.

As for *Carpenter* cases, refusing access to employment and social advantages would, just like expulsion, affect the basis on which the sponsor exercises his or her rights to free movement. It might be tempting, on the facts of *Carpenter*, to suggest that the family member's role in looking after the sponsor's child and thus freeing up the sponsor to undertake more economic activity is the critical factor in justifying her stay. However, such a post-feminist attempt to recognize the contribution made by unpaid carers to the family's welfare would have a pre-feminist result, as it would mean that Member States could prevent the carers from considering the option of paid employment if they wished. In any event, the Court examined Mrs. Carpenter's carer role when assessing the extent of her family life, not the extent of her contribution to her husband's ability to exercise free movement rights. Bringing *Baumbast and R* and *Carpenter* together, again the role of a parent carer as a corollary to the child's right of access to education suggests that her access to employment and social advantages should continue.[116]

Family members of EC nationals will also be able to rely on the Directive on long-term resident third-country nationals, adopted by the Council in November 2003.[117] This Directive will confer long-term resident status on any third-country national legally resident in a Member State for five years, with the exception of students, diplomats, persons authorized to take up only short-term employment, and most persons seeking or receiving protection status (although recognized refugees would be covered). This status will be autonomous, and will confer equal treatment as regards a number of issues (including access to employment and self-employment), enhanced protection against expulsion and the right to move to other Member States. While Member States will be free to set higher standards for the acquisition of long-term residence under their domestic law, such a decision would not confer free movement rights.

Although the initial proposal suggested that family members of EC nationals could not obtain the status of long-term resident until they had obtained 'permanent residence' status under the free movement rules,[118] a reference to the proposal for a consolidated directive on the free movement rights of EU citizens,[119] this proviso has been dropped during negotiations, without excluding the family members of EC nationals from the scope of the proposal.[120]

[116] It might be difficult to apply this to cases such as *Carpenter* where the third-country national is a step-parent to the relevant children and has no joint children with the sponsor, unless the step-parent is awarded custody.

[117] For the original proposal see COM(2001)127, 13 Mar. 2001. For the final Directive 2003/109, see OJ 2004 L16/44.

[118] Proposed Art. 3(3).

[119] See sect. 3E below.

[120] See the final Directive (*supra* note 120). The impact of the agreed Dir. on family reunion is considered in detail in S. Peers, 'Implementing Equality? The Directive on Long-Term Resident Third-Country Nationals' (forthcoming *ELRev.*).

It should also be recalled that the Directive will apply to the third-country national family members of *any* EC nationals, not just those who have exercised free movement rights.

Finally, as noted above, the requirements of public policy, public security, and public health can be imposed on the admission and continued residence of family members. These conditions apply equally to EU national sponsors, although logically they cannot apply to returnee sponsors, given the absolute immigration status which citizenship of a State usually confers.[121] The detailed application of these principles is set out in Directive 64/221,[122] which expressly applies to all family members falling within the scope of EC free movement legislation,[123] bar a merely partial application to students and their families.[124] But the latter are logically covered by principles similar to all the provisions of the Directive in any event, since their right to move to other Member States derived initially from the Treaty (rather than legislation),[125] and EC law contains a principle of effective remedies. It might be argued that the creation of citizenship of the Union subsumes the old students' rights based directly on the Treaty, and so, due to the wording of Article 18, EC legislation alone now governs students' position (and that of their families) as regards public policy, public security, and public health.[126] However, it is not plausible to assume that the creation of EU citizenship had the effect of reducing the rights of any category of EU citizens. Although it could be argued that third-country national family members of students are only governed by the legislation, the principle of effective remedies must equally apply to them as a limited application of Directive 64/221 would inevitably impact upon the sponsor's free movement rights.

While the Court had held on two occasions that residence permits are declaratory for family members,[127] just as they are for workers,[128] the

[121] A few Member States have created inferior classes of citizenship, with the result that this is not true of all of their 'citizens': see Case C–192/99 *Kaur* [2001] ECR I–1237.

[122] OJ Spec. Ed. 1963–64 117. For discussion see E. Guild, 'Security of Residence and Expulsion of Foreigners: European Community Law' in Guild and Minderhoud (eds), *supra* note 9, at 59.

[123] See Art. 1(2) of the Dir., *supra* note 122 (sponsors who are employed, self-employed or receiving services); Dir. 72/194, OJ 1972 L121/32 (sponsors retiring after employment); Dir. 75/35, OJ 1975 L14/14 (sponsors retiring after self-employment); and Art. 2(2) of Dirs 90/364 and 90/365 (*supra* notes 55 and 56).

[124] Art. 2(2) of Dir. 93/96 (*supra* note 54) only refers to the application of Arts 2 and 9 of Dir. 64/221.

[125] See *Raulin*, *supra* note 53, in which the Court referred expressly to possible public policy limits on students' free movement rights (at para. 40).

[126] The Court has certainly held that students are citizens of the EU (see *supra* note 113), but it has not ruled out the prospect that they could still rely directly on other provisions of the Treaty.

[127] See *Echternach and Moritz* (*supra* note 98) and *Commission* v *Germany* (*supra* note 29).

[128] See Case 48/75 *Royer* [1976] ECR 495. The same holds true for students (see *Raulin*, *supra* note 53) and presumably other categories of sponsor.

more recent judgment in *MRAX* has explored the issue more fully.[129] In this case the Court ruled that Member States could not refuse entry to family members at the border if they had proof of their family status; that the obligation to offer the 'facility' to obtain a visa required the issue of visas without delay, if necessary at the border; that expulsion of family members following unlawful entry or lawful entry (but with an expired visa) was not permissible, as residence permits were merely declaratory, even for third-country national family members;[130] and that family members still had remedies against expulsion as provided for by Directive 64/221 in such cases.

Also, it should not be forgotten that in cases of expulsion or even (in rare cases) admission, the status of family members of EU citizens could be covered by the ECHR.[131]

Finally, as noted above, certain accession treaties set out separate rules on the status of family members of EU citizens for a transitional period, affecting solely access to employment by the family members.[132] In the first case, Spanish and Portuguese workers' and self-employed persons' family members were not entitled to take up employment for five years after accession in 1986, unless they had already been admitted to a Member State before the date of accession (subject to the possibility for Member States to limit this by reference to the date of prior bilateral agreements). Those entering after accession had to wait three years for access to employment, although this wait was restricted to eighteen months from 1 January 1989. As for the eight eastern Member States joining the Union in 2004, there is a more generous approach. Family members of workers who have been previously admitted may have immediate labour market access, unless the worker had only been admitted for a period of less than twelve months. Family members entering during the seven-year transition period for free movement of workers have access to the labour market after eighteen months or from three years after accession, whichever is earlier.

E. Proposed Changes to Free Movement Legislation

The Community is now on its third attempt to revise EC free movement law. A first attempt in 1988 fizzled out after several years of negotiation.[133]

[129] *Supra* note 29.

[130] Similarly, an application for a residence permit should not be refused on the ground that the entry visa had expired. Sanctions falling short of expulsion could be applied in such cases, as they could to EC nationals. It might now be questioned how to distinguish this judgment on this point from the later judgment in *Akrich* (*supra* note 29), which makes no reference to it.

[131] See sect. 2 above.

[132] See, for example, Art. 57 of the 1985 Accession Treaty and para. 8 of the provisions on derogation from free movement of workers in Annex XIV of the 2003 Accession Treaty (OJ 2003 L236/1).

[133] COM(88)815, 29 Mar. 1989, revised in COM(90)108, 9 Apr. 1990.

A second initiative in 1998 never got off the ground,[134] because successive Council Presidencies simply refused to discuss it. These two attempts would merely have amended the rules on workers, but the third attempt, dating from 2001, would, if agreed, consolidate all free movement rules into one directive.[135] It is also an ambitious attempt to enhance those rules, particularly as regards family members. At the time of writing, the European Parliament had adopted a first reading position on the Directive, and the Council adopted a Common Position in December 2003.

But since the EP and the Council take different approaches to many key issues, the final text of the directive (or even its adoption) is still uncertain. However, it is worth outlining the changes that would result from the original proposal. If agreed, the proposed directive would set out a single wider definition of family members entitled to join all EC national sponsors, comprising the spouse, unmarried partner (in accordance with *Reed*), and descending and ascending relatives of the sponsor or the spouse or unmarried partner, with no condition of dependence.[136] As for the conditions for reunion, the accommodation requirement for family members of workers would be dropped, and the conditions for non-economic sponsors to migrate (with their families) in the first place would be relaxed.[137] There would be specific rules for the first time on the position of family members after family breakdown, and more favourable rules in the event of death, disability or retirement.[138] After four years, family members would gain the right of permanent residence, which would prevent expulsion on any ground whatsoever.[139] Finally, family members would be subject to the same broad equal treatment rule as sponsors.[140] It seems unlikely that the Council will agree to all of these changes, but the application of qualified majority voting in the Council and the co-decision procedure with the European Parliament will very likely ensure that the text is closer to the Commission's proposal than at least some Member States would like.

[134] COM(98)394, 15 July 1998.

[135] *Supra* note 57.

[136] Art. 2(2). Member States must 'facilitate' the admission of other family members (Art. 3(2)).

[137] Arts. 7 and 8(3), which requires only a declaration to be made in all cases.

[138] Arts. 12, 13, 15 and 16.

[139] Art. 14.

[140] Art. 21. See also Art. 20 on access to employment or self-employment.

4. FAMILY MEMBERS OF THIRD-COUNTRY NATIONALS UNDER ASSOCIATION AGREEMENTS

A. Sponsors

The Community's association agreements are very diverse. Some contain no rules at all on the movement or status of natural persons and others contain no rules specifically relating to family members. The treaties relevant to family members are the EEA (European Economic Area) with Norway, Iceland, and Liechtenstein;[141] the agreement on free movement of persons with Switzerland;[142] the Association Agreement with Turkey;[143] the Europe Agreements with ten Central and East European countries;[144] the Stabilization and Association Agreements with Western Balkan countries;[145] and the Euro-Mediterranean agreements with three North African States.[146] As we shall see though, the content of these agreements varies dramatically, with

[141] OJ 1994 L1/1.

[142] OJ 2002 L114/6.

[143] OJ 1977 L361/60. For comments see S. O'Leary, 'Employment and Residence for Turkish Workers and their Families: Analogies with the Case Law of the Court of Justice on Article 48 EC', in *Scritti in Onore di Giuseppe Federico Mancini* (Milan: Giuffrè, 1998) 731; M. Hedemann-Robinson, 'An Overview of Recent Legal Developments at Community Level in relation to Third-country Nationals Resident within the European Union, with Particular Reference to the Case Law of the European Court of Justice', 38 *CMLRev.* (2001) 525; and N. Rogers, *A Practitioners' Guide to the EC–Turkey Association Agreement* (The Hague: Kluwer, 2000).

[144] OJ 1993 L347 (Hungary); OJ 1993 L348/1 (Poland); OJ 1994 L357/1 (Romania); OJ 1994 L358/1 (Bulgaria); OJ 1994 L359/1 (Slovakia); OJ 1994 L360/1 (Czech Republic); OJ 1998 L26/1 (Latvia); OJ 1998 L51/1 (Lithuania); OJ 1998 L68/1 (Estonia); and OJ 1999 L51/1 (Slovenia). For comments, see Hedemann-Robinson (*supra* note 143) and E. Guild, 'Movement of Persons', in A. Ott and K. Inglis (eds), *Handbook of European Enlargement* (The Hague: T.M.C. Asser Press, 2002), at 439–440.

[145] Art. 44 of the agreement with the former Yugoslav Republic of Macedonia (COM(2001)90) and Art. 45 of the proposed agreement with Croatia (COM(2001)371). The former treaty entered into force on 1 April 2004, and the latter is being ratified by Member States.

[146] See initially OJ 1978 L263/1 (Algeria); OJ 1978 L264/1 (Morocco); OJ 1978 L265/1 (Tunisia). Replacement agreements with similar provisions are in force or being ratified: OJ 2000 L70/1 (Morocco); OJ 1998 L97/1 (Tunisia); COM(2002)157 (Algeria). The case law on these agreements comprises Case C–18/90 *Kziber* [1991] ECR I–199; Case C–58/93 *Yousfi* [1994] ECR I–1353; Case C–103/94 *Krid* [1995] ECR I–719; Case C–126/95 *Hallouzi-Choho* [1996] ECR I–4807; Case C–113/97 *Babahenini* [1998] ECR I–183; Case C–314/96 *Djabali* [1998] ECR I–1149; Case C–179/98 *Mesbah* [1999] ECR I–7955; *Fahmi* (*supra* note 101); and order in Case C–23/02 *Alami* [2003] ECR I–1399. All of these cases involve the 1978 agreement with Morocco except *Krid* and *Djabali*, which concern the 1978 agreement with Algeria.

only the EEA and Swiss treaties providing for a core family reunion right. The other treaties are concerned solely with certain issues relating to the status of family members.

The EEA simply extends the EC rules for family reunion with EC nationals, as set out in the EC Treaty free movement rules and connected secondary EC legislation, including provisions on family members, has been made a full part of the agreement, although there is no ECJ or EFTA Court case law on the interpretation of these provisions. However, since EU citizenship does not apply to the EEA, any rights for family members that derive from this principle do not apply to nationals of the non-EU EEA states. For this reason, it might be difficult to establish precisely which provisions of the proposed directive on EU citizens' movement and residence rights will apply to those States.[147] The treaty with Switzerland contains very similar rules to EC free movement law, although provision of services is more limited.[148]

As for the other association agreements, the rules adopted pursuant to the Ankara Agreement only apply to family members of Turkish workers. This concept of 'Turkish worker' has been extensively defined in the case law on such workers' access to employment (under EC–Turkey Association Council Decision 1/80)[149] and social security (under EC–Turkey Association Council Decision 3/80).[150] The concept of Turkish 'worker' is very similar, perhaps even identical, to the definition of EC national 'workers' as regards employment or social security. However, the association agreement rules do not in any way govern the initial entry and access to employment of Turkish workers into the territory of a Member State,[151] or govern their movement between Member States.[152] Nor do they affect the power of Member States to govern the initial family reunion for Turkish workers.[153] Family reunion cannot be accomplished by means of entry as a worker, because the goal of

[147] *Supra* note 57.

[148] For detail see S. Peers, 'The EC-Switzerland Agreement on Free Movement of Persons: Overview and Analysis', 2 *EJML* (2000) 127, at 129 and 134.

[149] See particularly Case C–434/93 *Bozkurt* [1995] ECR I–1475; Case C–98/96 *Ertanir* [1997] ECR I–5179; Case C–36/96 *Gunaydin* [1997] ECR I–5143; Case C–1/98 *Birden* [1998] ECR I–7747; and Case C–188/00 *Kurz* [2002] ECR I–10691.

[150] See particularly Case C–262/96 *Sürül* [1999] ECR I–2685. It should be kept in mind that the concept of 'worker' is different when applied to social security co-ordination and is distinct from free movement of workers, in both EC free movement law and under the EC–Turkey association agreement.

[151] However, their *return* to a Member State's territory after residing there and acquiring rights pursuant to the Ankara agreement is governed by the association rules: see *Kurz, supra* note 149.

[152] Case law starting with Case C–171/95 *Tetik* [1997] ECR I–329.

[153] Again the subsequent return after initial acquisition of rights under the Agreement is governed by the association rules: see Case C–351/95 *Kadiman* [1997] ECR I–2133 and Case C–329/97 *Ergat* [2000] ECR I–1487.

free movement of workers set out in the Ankara Agreement is not directly effective and has not been realized by secondary decisions of the Association Council yet.[154]

Similarly, the rules in the North African agreements, the Europe Agreements and the Stabilization and Association Agreements are all relevant only to those who join workers with the nationality of the relevant non-EU States. There is no indication in the agreements of what the concept of 'worker' means under any of these agreements or any case law to clarify this issue yet, except for the finding that a 'worker' under the social security provisions includes former workers who had to leave employment because one of the risks covered by the social security rules materialized.[155] However, since the concept of 'social security' in the North African agreements and the concepts of 'establishment' (as regards the types of activity covered by that concept) and 'working conditions' in the Europe Agreements are apparently identical to the EC free movement concepts, it is arguable that the concept of 'worker' has the same meaning also.[156]

Under all these treaties, there is a question whether refugees of the relevant nationality can also rely on the association agreement, or can instead only rely on rules relating to refugees. So far the Court has not been asked to answer this important question.[157]

B. Family Members

Because the EEA Treaty extends EC free movement rules, the concept of 'family' is the same as for EC nationals. The EC–Swiss agreement has a 'facilitation' requirement for additional family members applying to sponsors exercising non-economic free movement rights, and such sponsors can also bring with them children who are under 21 *or* dependent, not just dependent.[158] The Europe Agreements and the Stabilization Agreements refer to 'spouses and children', with declarations stating that 'children' are defined by the national law of the host States. For their part, Article 7(1) of

[154] Case 12/86 *Demirel* [1987] ECR 3719.

[155] See the case law *supra* in note 146.

[156] On the concept of 'social security' and the North African agreements see particularly *Kziber*, *Yousfi* and *Krid*, *supra* note 146. On the concept of 'establishment' under the Europe Agreements, see *Jany* (*supra* note 82); but note that the concept is not identical as regards the absence of prior immigration control on self-employed persons (on this, see *Jany* and further Case C–63/99 *Gloszczuk* [2001] ECR I–6369; C–257/99 *Barkoci and Malik* [2001] ECR I–6557; C–235/99 *Kondova* [2001] ECR I–6427; and opinion of 19 February 2004 in Case C–327/02 *Panayotova*, pending).

[157] The issue should have been referred with Joined Cases C–95/99 to 98/99 *Khalil and others* and C–180/99 *Addou* [2001] ECR I–7413, but was not. See comments by Peers in a case note on the judgment, 29 *CMLRev.* (2002) 1395, at 1402–1403.

[158] Peers, *supra* note 148, at 138. Compare with EC free movement rules in sect. 3B above.

EC–Turkey Association Council Decision 1/80 and the North African agreements refer only to 'family members' of workers, and so it has fallen to the Court to interpret these concepts. There is also a special rule for the children of Turkish workers, subject to certain conditions, in Article 7(2) of Association Council Decision 1/80.

In the case law concerning the EC–Turkey agreement, it was accepted without question that a spouse and a child (even following adulthood) could be considered 'family members' under Article 7(1) of Decision 1/80.[159] But in *Eyup*, the Court was faced with a more difficult question concerning the definition of 'family member': did it extend to a couple who had been married, divorced but continued to cohabit, and then remarried?[160] The Court found that in the particular circumstances of that case, the couple in question remained 'family' for the entire period. This leaves open the possibility that cohabitees could be considered to be 'family members' in other, less unusual circumstances, a prospect explicitly considered in light of Strasbourg case law by the Advocate-General's Opinion in this case. In two pending cases, the Court has to decide whether a stepson aged under 21 and a person born in the territory to a Turkish worker are family members.[161] The answer to the latter question may appear obvious, but since the Association Council Decision refers to persons 'authorised to join' the Turkish worker the literal position appears to be that those children born in the territory are worse off. This wording obviously results from an assumption that Turkish workers would eventually leave the country, an outmoded assumption even by 1980. In both cases, applying the obligation to interpret the Decision consistently with EC free movement case law as far as possible, stepsons and children born in the territory are covered by the rules.[162] As for social security, Association Council Decision 3/80 applies to workers' family members, a concept presumably defined in the same way as under EC free movement law.[163]

[159] See *Kadiman* and *Ergat*, *supra* note 153.

[160] Case C–65/98 [2000] ECR I–4747. In *Kurz* (*supra* note 149) the Court was asked whether a Turkish worker's child who was adopted as an adult by a German couple still fell within the definition of 'family member' in Decision 1/80, but neither the Court nor the Advocate-General answered this question because it was unnecessary as he fell within the definition of 'worker'.

[161] Cases C–275/02 *Ayaz* and C–467/02 *Cetinkaya*. Presumably the answer to the first question is equally relevant to the position of graduate children under Art. 7(2) of the Decision, but the answer to the second question is not because they do not need to have been 'authorised to join' the worker to be covered by this provision: see Case C–355/93 *Eroglu* [1994] ECR I–5113.

[162] This obligation dates from the *Bozkurt* judgment (*supra* note 149) and has been applied many times since. On the application of EC free movement law to persons born in the territory, see *Avello*, *supra* note 113. On the application of the EC free movement law to step-children, see the *Baumbast and R* judgment (*supra* note 29).

[163] See *Sürül*, *supra* note 150.

As for the Euro–Mediterranean Agreements, the Court has ruled that the concept of 'family member' includes descending relatives and ascending relatives who normally live as part of the worker's household, including potentially mothers-in-law.[164] Other cases have involved children and spouses of workers, even after the death of the worker.[165]

C. Conditions

Since there is no right to family reunion under the agreements with Turkey, North Africa, the Europe Agreements or the Stabilization and Association agreements, there is no need to consider which conditions can apply to family reunion. Under the EC–Swiss agreement, there is no obligation to waive fees for families' visas, so the position is more restrictive than under EC free movement law.[166]

D. Status

Although the EC–Turkey rules were primarily designed to regulate access to employment of workers and family members, the Court has ruled that a right to residence is a corollary of access to employment for both groups.[167] The rules state that once a family member has been 'authorised to join' the sponsor, he or she may have access to employment in the host State after three years and access to any job, without priority for EC nationals, after five years. Here, the Court has ruled that the requirement of being 'authorised to join' the worker means that, unlike in the *Diatta* case, family members must stay with the worker during an initial period, except where there are 'objective reasons' to live separately, such as education and employment reasons.[168] The Court might have been intending to suggest that *subjective* factors, such as the abuse and mistreatment Mrs. Kadiman complained of at the hands of her husband, could not justify separation, but it is understood that the national court in this case allowed Mrs. Kadiman to stay in any case.

After three years have passed, then, there is a right to independent status in connection with liberalized access to the employment market, even if the family member has employment difficulties.[169] Even before that point,

[164] *Mesbah, supra* note 146.

[165] All of the cases to date have involved family members except *Yousfi* and *Alami, supra* note 146; on the application after the worker's death: see for example *Krid, supra* note 146.

[166] Peers, *supra* note 148, at 138.

[167] On Art. 7(1), see *Kadiman, supra* note 153; on Art. 7(2), see *Eroglu, supra* note 161. It is also clear that residence permits are only declaratory of the rights of Turkish workers' family members (see particularly *Ergat, supra* note 153), like EC sponsors' family members (see sect. 3D above).

[168] See *Kadiman, supra* note 153.

[169] *Ergat, supra* note 153.

it is possible for the family member to gain status as a Turkish worker under Article 6 of the Decision, although that will depend on whether Member States permit the family member to take up employment early.[170] Of course, this option will only be available to those family members with Turkish nationality.[171] Similarly it is possible for Turkish nationals admitted for the purpose of family reunion with a non-Turkish sponsor to gain the status of 'worker' pursuant to Article 6 of Decision 1/80, with the result that a divorce is irrelevant once they have acquired that status.[172]

Article 7(2) of the Decision gives full access to the labour market on graduation from a course of vocational training if at least one parent has worked in that Member State as a Turkish worker for at least three years. It is assumed that 'vocational training' has the same broad meaning that it does in EC free movement law; and the Court has ruled that since the rule assumes a separation between parent and child, the parent need no longer be resident in the host Member State when the right is exercised.[173] As for Article 9, it gives a right of equal treatment in education to children of Turkish workers and its scope is unclear, although it is surely directly effective.[174] But by analogy with *Baumbast and R*, it might be argued that equally the primary carer of a Turkish child should be allowed to stay as a corollary of the child's right to education, where the carer has no other right to stay under Decision 1/80 or the family reunion Directive.

[170] This conclusion can be derived from the judgments in *Eroglu* and *Kadiman* (*supra* notes 161 and 153), in which the Court examined Art. 6 status before Art. 7 status, and also from *Kurz* (*supra* note 149), in which the Court found it unnecessary to examine Art. 7 after its conclusions on Art. 6.

[171] It is assumed that family members can hold any nationality to qualify for treatment under Art. 7 of Decision 1/80: S. Peers, 'Towards Equality: Actual and Potential Rights of Third-Country Nationals in the European Union', 33 *CMLRev.* (1996) 7, at 25. The argument for this is that Art. 7 does not state the opposite and the principle of interpreting the Decision in line with EC free movement law 'as far as possible' (see *supra* note 162 and accompanying text) supports this interpretation.

[172] See Case C–237/91 *Kus* [1992] ECR I–6781. This case involved a marriage to a national of the host Member State, but there is no reason to suggest the result would be different if the Turkish national had married a national of any other country residing in the host Member State, including a national of another Member State exercising a free movement right. Of course, in such cases the rules regarding initial admission and access to employment might be different.

[173] On the former point, see *Eroglu*, *supra* note 161, particularly the Opinion; on the latter point, see Case C–210/97 *Akman* [1998] ECR I–7519 and exploration of the impact in case note by Peers, 36 *CMLRev.* (1999) 1027.

[174] See further the Court's reference to Art. 9 in *Akman* and analysis in my case note (ibid.). The scope of Art. 9 is at issue in Case C–374/03 *Gürol*, pending.

Family members are governed by the restrictions on expulsion set out in Article 14 of the Decision, which the Court has held guarantees equivalent protection to that governing EC nationals and their family members.[175] This protection should logically cover family members from the moment they join the Turkish worker, for the Court has held that there are directly effective rights to reside from that point.[176] Finally, it should be noted that Article 13 of the Decision imposes a standstill on any new restrictions on access to employment as regards Turkish workers and their family members. The Court has held that this right is directly effective,[177] and it is arguable that it extends to new restrictions on residence, given that residence is a corollary of the employment rights in the Decision.

As for the Maghreb agreements, the Court has ruled in favour of a broad definition of 'social security' based on EC free movement law, but has strictly applied the condition that the family members must reside in the Community in order to receive the social security benefits.[178]

Finally, the provisions on access to employment of spouses and children in the Europe Agreements and Stabilization Agreements are surely directly effective, based on a comparison between these provisions and the directly effective freedom of establishment and right to equality in working conditions in the Europe Agreements.[179] As compared to the EC–Turkey agreement, these agreements do not expressly state that the family members have *equal* treatment as regards access to employment; but the same could be said of the provisions of Regulation 1612/68, which did not prevent the Court from ruling that family members had full equal treatment.[180] Since the case law on the Europe Agreements requires those agreements to be interpreted consistently with the EC Treaty free movement rules in most cases,[181] it should follow that the family members' rights of access to employment have the same broad scope.

[175] See particularly Case C–340/97 *Nazli* [2000] ECR I–957; para. 46 of the *Ergat* judgment, *supra* note 153; and order of 19 Sept. 2000 in Case C–89/00 *Bikaci* (unpublished), which expressly applies Art. 14 of the Decision to family members covered by Art. 7.

[176] *Kadiman*, *supra* note 153, at para. 29.

[177] Case C–192/89 *Sevince* [1990] ECR I–3641. See now the judgment of 21 October 2003 in Joined Cases C–317/01 and C–369/01 *Aksatay and others*, not yet reported.

[178] See respectively the relevant case law (*supra* note 156) and *Fahmi* (*supra* note 101).

[179] See respectively the case law on establishment (*supra* notes 82 and 156) and Cases C–162/00 *Pokrzeptowicz-Meyer* [2002] ECR I–1049 and C–438/00 *Deutscher Handbattbund* [2003] ECR I–4135.

[180] See *Gül*, *supra* note 96.

[181] See the cases referenced *supra* in note 179.

5. FAMILY REUNION FOR THIRD-COUNTRY NATIONALS: GENERAL RULES

The EU Ministers of Home Affairs first adopted a Resolution on family reunion in 1993.[182] Subsequently, in 1997, the Commission proposed a convention on migration that would have contained, *inter alia*, rules on family reunion.[183] Following the entry into force of the Treaty of Amsterdam, the Commission proposed a family reunion directive in 1999,[184] then revised this proposal following the EP's Opinion in 2000.[185] Negotiations in the Council were fraught, and so the Commission issued a revised proposal in May 2002, suggesting (closely following Council discussions) a significantly lower level of protection for family reunion rights.[186] After further detailed discussion in Council bodies, the JHA Council reached a 'general approach' on the proposal in February 2003 and formally adopted the Directive in September 2003.[187]

A. Sponsors

It should be recalled throughout the following discussion that the family reunion Directive will only set minimum standards. Member States are free to set higher standards in their domestic law.[188] The Directive is also without

[182] For the text see E. Guild and J. Niessen, *The Developing Immigration and Asylum Policies of the European Union: Adopted Conventions, Resolutions, Recommendations, Decisions and Conclusions* (The Hague: Kluwer, 1996), at 250–257. For comments on the Resolution, see ibid., at 257–273; S. Peers, 'Building Fortress Europe: The Development of EU Migration Law', 35 *CMLRev.* (1998) 1235, at 1239–1242; M. Hedemann-Robinson, 'Third-Country Nationals, European Union Citizenship and Free Movement of Persons: A Time for Bridges rather than Divisions?', 16 *YEL* (1996) 321, at 324–325; K. Hailbronner, 'Migration Law and Policy Within the Third Pillar of the European Union', in R. Bieber and J. Monar (eds), *Justice and Home Affairs in the European Union* (Brussels: European Interuniversity Press, 1995); and P. Boeles *et al.*, *A New Immigration Law for Europe: the 1992 London and 1993 Copenhagen Rules on Immigration* (Utrecht: Nederlands Centrum Buitenlanders (NCB), 1993). For the negotiating history, see ch. 19 of Rogers and Peers, *supra* note 3.

[183] *Supra* note 32. For the comments of Member States, see Rogers and Peers, *supra* note 3.

[184] *Supra* note 33. For comments on this initial text see P. Boeles, 'Directive on Family Reunion: Are the Dilemmas Resolved?', 3 *EJML* (2001) 61, and G. Brinkmann, 'Family Reunion, Third-Country Nationals and the Community's New Powers' in E. Guild and C. Harlow (eds), *Implementing Amsterdam: Immigration and Asylum Rights in EC Law* (Oxford: Hart, 2001) 241, at 252–263. For an alternative proposal for a dir., drawn up by NGOs, see *The Amsterdam Proposals* (ILPA/MPG, 2000).

[185] Ibid.

[186] *Supra* note 34.

[187] Dir. 2003/86 (OJ 2003 L251/12).

[188] Art. 3(5). However, the standstill proposed by the Commission in its 2002 proposal was not accepted by the Council.

prejudice to more favourable treaties concluded before or after its adoption by the Community or the Community with its Member States, or to the Council of Europe Social Charter and Convention on the Rights of Migrant Workers.[189]

The Directive on family reunion applies to all third-country national sponsors residing legally in a Member State and holding a residence permit for over a year's validity who have 'reasonable prospects' of obtaining 'permanent residence' status.[190] However, the Directive will not apply where the sponsor is an asylum seeker or has temporary or subsidiary protection (or is seeking either of those forms of protection).[191] There is no indication of what 'permanent' residence means or what a 'reasonable' prospect of obtaining it is.

While it is simply astounding that the Council has adopted such a poor approach to legislative drafting, we can surely consider what these two core requirements could mean. Surely we can assume (in the absence of evidence to the contrary) that different EC immigration directives are intended to be applied coherently. Therefore the best definition of 'permanent' residence is that the concept includes the acquisition of either long-term resident status under the Directive on long-term resident third-country nationals, *or* the acquisition of status under a more generous national regime for long-term residence, which that Directive will permit.[192] 'Permanent' residence cannot mean an absolute right to stay in any circumstances, since even EU citizens exercising free movement rights lack that.[193]

The concept of 'permanent' residence must surely include at least those Turkish workers who have qualified for full status to take up any employment after four years' work under the EC–Turkey Association Council Decision. It is also arguable that those who have passed the three-year point (allowing them to take up any employment within the same occupation) have a reasonable expectation of gaining permanent residence. It could even be argued that those past the one-year point (allowing them to stay with the same employer) have a reasonable expectation of such status if they are still with that employer, given the structure of the Decision. The Ankara Agreement rules could also be relevant to the self-employed on this point, given the directly effective standstill on creating new restrictions on freedom of establishment.[194]

189 Art. 3(4).

190 Art. 3(1); Art. 3(3) makes clear that the dir. does not apply to citizens of the Union or to their family members. In 1999, the Commission had originally proposed covering all EU national sponsors who had not exercised a free movement right (see sect. 3) along with all third-country nationals authorized to stay for over a year.

191 Art. 3(2).

192 See Art. 13 of Directive 2003/109, *supra* note 117.

193 See *Kaba I*, *supra* note 64.

194 Case C–37/98 *Savas* [2000] ECR I–2927.

There are several arguments for an alternative interpretation. In the absence of an EC-wide definition provided by the Directive, it could be suggested that the concept of 'permanent' residence should be defined by national law. However, the Directive refers to 'national law' expressly in Articles 4(1), 4(6), 5(4), 7(2), 8 and 15(4) and implicitly in Article 18. This suggests *a contrario* that the concept of 'permanent residence' is intended to have a Community meaning. Moreover, there were attempts during the negotiations of the two Directives to keep both texts consistent.[195] Also, this definition ensures greater uniformity in the application of the family reunion Directive. A uniform interpretation is also justified by the overall context of EC migration law, because many persons who enter the EU pursuant to the family reunion Directive will ultimately be able to obtain the status of long-term resident and move to other Member States.

As to whether there is a 'reasonable' prospect of obtaining that status, it follows from the express 'right' to family reunion and the right to mount a legal challenge to the authorities' refusal to permit family reunion that the national authorities do not have full discretion to interpret this concept. At the very least, therefore, it is arguable that family reunion must be granted where the sponsor can show on the balance of probabilities that he or she will probably obtain permanent residence status. There are other ways to interpret the concept of 'reasonable', but in the absence of contrary indications from the text of the Directive, the well-established civil law standard of proof would provide for the application of a familiar test for determining when the Directive applies. As for the burden of proof, it follows from the creation of a 'right' by the Directive that it is for the national authorities to show that the expectation of permanent residence is not reasonable, once an applicant has shown *prima facie* evidence that a sponsor is likely to obtain such status. It might be argued that the application of the concept of 'reasonable' likelihood is up to national law, but again in the absence of a reference to national law the context of the Directive suggests that a uniform approach should apply.

Whichever definition applies, it is obvious that the Directive applies to a far narrower scope of sponsors than does EC free movement law, which grants family reunion rights to any EU citizens meeting free movement conditions, no matter how long their residence in the host Member State.

[195] The provision on derogations for public security, *et al.* in the long-term residence Directive (Directive 2003/109, *supra* note 117) was expressly aligned with the family reunion Directive. Also, in the Commission's explanatory memorandum to the revised version of the family reunion Dir. in 2002 (*supra* note 34), it was expressly stated that Arts. 13 and 15 of the proposal were being aligned with the long-term residents' proposal.

B. Family Members

The family reunion Directive specifies that Member States must admit the sponsor's spouse and the minor children of the sponsor and of his/her spouse, including 'children adopted in accordance with a decision taken by the competent authority in the Member State concerned or a decision which is automatically enforceable due to international obligations of that Member State or must be recognised in accordance with international obligations'.[196] There is no condition of dependence for admission of either the spouse or joint children. Where only the sponsor or the spouse is a parent of minor children, reunion is also required, subject to the condition that the relevant parent has custody and the children are dependent on that parent.[197] Admission of children in cases of joint custody is optional for Member States, and is dependent upon the consent of the other person sharing custody.[198] All children must be under the age of majority and unmarried, and Member States may apply legislation existing on the date of implementing the Directive to insist that children over 12 have to meet a condition of 'integration' in national law. A recital in the preamble states that the purpose of this derogation is to reflect children's early capacity for integration and ensure that they acquire language and education skills at school.

The admission of another three categories of family members is only optional. First, Member States may admit first-degree direct dependent ascending relatives of the sponsor or spouse, if they 'do not enjoy proper family support in the country of origin'.[199] Secondly, they may admit adult unmarried children of the sponsor or spouse, if they are 'objectively unable to provide for their own needs on account of their state of health'.[200] Thirdly, they may admit the 'unmarried partner' of the sponsor in a 'duly attested stable long-term relationship' with the sponsor or a person in a 'registered partnership' with the sponsor. In this third case, the Member States may admit also unmarried minor children, including adopted children, of the sponsor and the partner, as well as the adult unmarried children who are objectively unable to provide for their own needs on account of their state of health, of such persons.[201] It is also open to Member States to treat registered partners the same as spouses. A clause in the preamble asserts that Member States can refuse to admit all these optional categories in the event that the

[196] Art. 4(1)(a) and (b).

[197] Art. 4(1)(c) and (d). Adopted children are expressly covered here; presumably adoption has the same meaning as in Art. 4(1)(b).

[198] Ibid.

[199] Art. 4(2)(a).

[200] Art. 4(2)(b).

[201] Art. 4(3). Again 'adoption' presumably has the same meaning as in Art. 4(1)(b). It is not clear whether the children of only one of the partners are included, and if so what conditions apply to their admission.

sponsor wishes to move to another Member State of the EU as a long-term resident. Note that the *Reed* principle does not apply here as such: there is no test whether Member States treat unmarried partners and married couples the same as regards their nationals, but simply a discretion for Member States to admit the partners.

There are three possibilities for derogation by Member States, which presumably apply to any case of family reunion within the scope of the Directive. First, Member States 'shall not' admit any additional wives in the case of polygamy, when one wife already lives in a Member State. There is an option to admit the children of the additional wives in such a case. Secondly, Member States can set a minimum age requirement (21 maximum) for the sponsor or spouse as a condition for admission. This is 'in order to ensure better integration and to prevent involuntary marriages'. Finally, Member States can apply existing legislation on the date of implementing the Directive and insist that applications for minor children must be submitted before the age of 15. If applications for older children are submitted, the Member State concerned 'shall authorise' their entry on grounds other than family reunification, so presumably different conditions for entry and different rules on status will apply.

Compared to EC free movement law, the scope of family members entitled to join the sponsor is more precise but also more limited. At first sight, there is one case where the scope of family members is wider: unmarried partners are included regardless of the status of the sponsor, whereas the application of EC free movement law to such family members is uncertain if the sponsor is not a worker.[202] However, unlike EC free movement law, there are two levels of discretion in the family reunion Directive: even if a Member State chooses to treat unmarried partners the same as married couples, it still has an option whether or not to admit them. As for extended family members, their admission is not only wholly optional but in any event subject to certain conditions, although presumably Member States may waive those conditions if they choose since this is a 'minimum standards' Directive. This compares unfavourably to EC free movement law, except for EC students; but third-country national students will not be covered by the Directive in any case. Yet even in the 'core' family, Member States have options to set age limits at both ends as regards children; the Directive simultaneously assumes that teenagers could be considered too mature to integrate yet not mature enough to decide whether to get married. The Directive thus permits substantially greater limits to be placed on admission of children as compared to EC free movement law. Also, it takes no account of the Strasbourg ruling in *Sen* v *Netherlands* on the circumstances in which the ECHR requires the admission of children.[203]

[202] See sect. 3B above.
[203] *Supra* note 12.

C. Conditions[204]

The family reunion Directive contains a procedural requirement to submit documentary evidence as well as certified copies of travel documents. Member States may carry out interviews and conduct other investigations. There are particular provisions on examining the applications submitted for reunion with unmarried partners.[205] An application must usually be submitted and examined while the family members are outside the relevant Member State's territory, but Member States may opt to consider in-country applications.[206] Member States are in principle obliged to make a decision on the application within nine months, but in 'exceptional circumstances' there can be an indefinite extension of this period and it is up to Member States to determine the consequence of a failure to observe time limits, although there is an obligation to give reasons if the application is rejected.[207] In the event of rejection, a sponsor or family member has the right to 'mount a legal challenge' in accordance with the procedure set out in the relevant Member State. Compared to EC free movement law, far more documentation is required for applications, in-country residence during the application is only an option for Member States, there is no six-month upper limit on processing the application and the right to a remedy is less detailed.[208] Indeed, the absence of any upper limit and the weak reference to 'mounting a legal challenge' appear incompatible with the obligation to offer an effective remedy for ECHR rights set out in Article 13 ECHR, although it would be possible to interpret the legal challenge proviso to the effect that it requires a court review of the merits of a refusal.

As with EC free movement law, Member States may reject applications for entry and residence of family members on grounds of 'public policy, public security or public health'. Several provisions provide further explanation of these concepts. First, persons cannot be removed on the sole ground of illness or disability suffered after entry.[209] Secondly, a recital in the preamble asserts that 'public policy and public security covers also cases in which a third-country national belongs to an association which supports the international terrorism, supports such an association or has extremistic aspirations'. Thirdly, decisions to expel must consider on the one hand the 'nature and

[204] For a critical view of the conditions to be permitted in the *earlier* stages of discussion of the Dir., see R. Cholewinski, 'Family Reunification and Conditions Placed on Family Members: Dismantling a Fundamental Human Right', 4 *EJML* (2002) 271.

[205] Art. 5(2).

[206] Art. 5(3).

[207] Art. 5(4).

[208] Compare with Arts. 3(1) and 4 of Dir. 68/360 and Arts. 5, 8, and 9 of Dir. 64/221 (*supra* notes 51 and 122).

[209] Art. 6(3). This proviso is very similar to a rule of EC free movement law: see Art. 4(2) of Dir. 64/221 *supra* note 122.

solidity of the person's family relationships', 'the duration of his residence in the Member State' and 'the existence of family, cultural and social ties with his/her country of origin' and on the other hand the 'severity or type of offence against public policy or public security committed by the family member, or the dangers that are emanating from this person'.[210] These provisos are obviously based on the ECHR case law, but they do not take account of the principles fleshed out in recent judgments.[211] Finally, a further statement in the Council minutes asserts that the provisions on public policy *et al.*, are without prejudice to the provisions that may appear in other EC immigration legislation. Perhaps this is a reference to the attempts by some Member States to insert a 'threat to international relations' criterion for family reunion, which was rejected after a Council legal service opinion that presumably objected to the suggestion.[212]

Comparing the 'public policy' requirement with the rules of EC free movement law, the core test is the same but there is no equivalent to the clarifications offered by Directive 64/221.[213] However, it is arguable that substantive equal treatment is required nonetheless in the absence of wording to the contrary. The case for this is that the Council has taken care to insert additional grounds for admission of third-country national family members or different wording regarding their conditions of entry in a number of cases, including different wording on the procedures to dispute an expulsion or a refusal to admit. Logically the failure to insert additional or different wording as regards the public policy exception implies that that exception has the same substantive meaning as under EC free movement law. In fact, while the ban on expulsion for deterrence of others and the requirement of a serious present threat are not expressly mentioned in ECHR case law, those standards do not contradict the ECHR principles. It could also be argued that the EC free movement principles are a logical extrapolation of the ECHR principles.

Next, the host Member State may impose requirements concerning accommodation, sickness insurance, and stable and sufficient resources.[214] Compared to EC rules on free movement of workers, the first requirement applies to all categories of third-country national sponsors, and lacks a prohibition of discrimination. In turn, when compared to EC free movement legislation on admission of 'non-economic' EC nationals, the latter two requirements are similar, although under the Directive, a Member State is not expressly obliged to consider resources as sufficient if they are higher than the minimum social security pension for nationals or to consider the circum-

[210] Arts. 6(2) and 17.

[211] See sect. 2 above.

[212] The obvious argument against such a criterion is that it is not in the exhaustive list of grounds in Art. 8(2) ECHR permitting interference with family life.

[213] Arts. 2(2), 3, 4(1) and (3) of the Dir. (*supra* note 122).

[214] Art. 7(1).

stances of the family members. These conditions are also extended under the Directive to economically active sponsors; here the 'sickness insurance' requirement is clearly an additional obligation as compared to EC nationals, although some form of 'sufficient resources' requirement is built in for EC nationals exercising economic activity. Nevertheless, it should be recalled that an EC national can still qualify as a 'worker', and thus enjoy the right to family reunion on favourable grounds, even if he or she is receiving top-up social assistance,[215] a prospect clearly ruled out by the Directive.

Member States may also require third-country nationals to comply with national 'integration measures'.[216] The timing of this requirement is left open, but presumably, for obvious practical reasons, non-resident family members cannot be required to comply with this condition in advance. Of course, no such condition applies to any category of EC nationals.

What if the conditions are not met after entry? It is clear that the 'sufficient resources' criterion can justify subsequent termination of residence, but the Directive is ambiguous as to whether breaches of the other conditions can be invoked to justify expulsion after entry.[217] At least in the case of a later lack of 'sufficient resources', the Directive also specifies that the Member State must 'take into account' family members' contributions to household income. Since there is no 'public policy' limitation in Article 8(2) ECHR, an interference with family life could only be justified on economic grounds, which would cover recourse to public welfare, housing, or health assistance. Even in these cases, in light of the ECHR case law, removals on purely economic grounds in the absence of criminal activity by the family member are very difficult to justify.[218] Failure to 'integrate', or housing considered inadequate without a demand for public funds, could never justify expulsion under the ECHR.

Finally, Member States may impose a waiting period for family reunification of two years' maximum, with an extension to three years where existing national law on the date of *adoption* of the Directive permits it.[219] There is no possibility whatsoever to impose quotas on admission of family members or to set priorities within the categories of those covered by the Directive.

D. Status

The Directive obliges Member States to accept the entry of family members, giving them 'every facility' for obtaining the necessary visas.[220] The latter rule compares to EC free movement law, where the same provision requires

[215] *Kempf, supra* note 81. [216] Art. 7(2). [217] Art. 16(1)(a).

[218] See sect. 2 above.

[219] Art. 8. Note that the two other references to existing national law, both in Art. 4, refer instead to national law at the date of *implementation* of the Dir.

[220] Art. 13(1).

Member States to issue visas immediately or at the border.[221] However, there is no requirement to issue visas free of charge.[222] Member States must give family members a renewable residence permit of at least one year's duration, but 'in principle' the family member cannot have a permit going beyond the date of expiry of the sponsor's residence permit.[223] This compares to an obligation under EC free movement law to give family members a document having the same validity as the sponsor's.[224]

Member States must give family members the same access as the sponsor to education, employment and self-employment, vocational guidance and training.[225] However, Member States may set a waiting period of up to a year before authorizing access to employment or self-employment, and may furthermore restrict access to employment by ascending relatives or adult children indefinitely.[226] There are no further rights to social benefits by family members, and the extension of EC social security co-ordination rules to them only assists them in cases involving more than one Member State.[227]

As for autonomous status of family members, the Directive requires Member States to issue a separate residence permit for the spouse, unmarried partner, or child who has reached majority, if those persons were admitted on grounds of family reunion. However, Member States may limit the grant of such a permit only to spouses or unmarried partners in the event of family breakdown.[228] The grant of such permits to adult children and family members in the ascending line is only optional.[229] In the event of widowhood, divorce, separation, or death of direct ascending or descending family members, Member States have an option to issue a residence permit; and they 'shall' do so 'in the event of particularly difficult circumstances'.[230] Presumably this clause covers situations not covered by the preceding rules. Finally, the Directive specifies that the conditions of the granting and duration of the autonomous permit are set out in national law.[231] Logically this provision cannot, in the absence of clearer wording to that effect, mean that Member States could apply conditions which negate their mandatory substantive

[221] Art. 3(2) of Dir. 68/360 (*supra* note 51); see discussion of the *MRAX* judgment in sect. 3D above.

[222] Art. 9(2) of Dir. 68/360 (*supra* note 51). The rule applies to all sponsors.

[223] Art. 13(2) and (3).

[224] Art. 4(4) of Dir. 68/360 (*supra* note 51). The rule applies to all sponsors.

[225] Art. 14(1).

[226] Art. 14(2) and (3).

[227] On this limitation see *Khalil and Addou* (*supra* note 157) and Reg. 859/2003 (OJ 2003 L124/1), in force 1 June 2003.

[228] Art. 15(1).

[229] Art. 15(2).

[230] Art. 15(3).

[231] Art. 15(4).

obligations set out in the rest of this Article. Their national discretion must therefore apply only to procedural matters such as setting a time period to apply for the permit and time periods to reply. Even then, the procedural conditions could logically not be so stringent as to make it impossible or excessively difficult for family members to exercise the substantive rights which the Directive provides for.

It is clear that the wording of the Directive leaves Member States free to limit their obligations to grant autonomous status only to cases of family breakdown for spouses and unmarried partners (and even then only after five years) and to 'particularly difficult circumstances'. There is also no indication whether family members with an autonomous permit will have (continued) access to employment, as the Directive does not appear to regulate their status beyond the obligation to grant them an autonomous residence permit. Also, the Directive clearly limits Member States' obligations to issue autonomous permits to cases where persons were admitted on grounds of family reunion; a case like *Eroglu*, where autonomous status followed admission as a student because a parent also happened to be employed in the host Member State, could therefore not happen under the Directive.[232] It would be possible in principle to argue that a *Baumbast and R* rule applies where a child is in education and the parent carer has not yet got autonomous status, but it could equally be argued that the Article on autonomous status is *lex specialis*.

The importance of autonomous status is underlined by Article 16 of the Directive, which permits Member States to withdraw or refuse to renew the residence permit of a family member if the sponsor's residence ends and the family member lacks autonomous status, where the sponsor and family members are no longer in 'a full marital or family relationship' or where the sponsor or partner is married or in a 'stable long-term relationship' with someone else. In comparison with EC free movement law, there is a free-standing right to autonomous status in the Directive that does not depend on the family member either having EC nationality and meeting the criteria for exercising free movement in his or her own name, or remaining to care for a child exercising the right to education. But family members of sponsors pursuant to free movement law do not have to reside with the sponsor during separation and there is no time limit on their ability to obtain an autonomous right where this is possible for them. Moreover, the ability of family members who are EC nationals to 'switch' status under free movement law could be essential in practice for many of them who wish to remain. Compared with the EC–Turkey Association agreement, the waiting period for obtaining autonomous status is longer under the Directive, and again the right to switch status could be significant for many family members under the EC–Turkey rules.

[232] See *supra* note 161.

However, the limits on autonomous status set out in the Directive are not the end of the story. Directive 2003/110 on long-term residents' status also permits qualification for the autonomous status of long-term resident after five years' legal stay in most capacities.[233]

It is also worth pointing out that the link between the sponsor's status and the family members' status created by the Directive will often mean a link to other rules of EC law. This will particularly be the case for those joining long-term resident third-country nationals and those third-country nationals allowed to enter for employment or self-employment (once the relevant Directive is adopted), where Member States do not take the option of applying higher standards for persons covered by those Directives. It will also be the case as soon as the Directive is applied for the family members of Turkish workers, who will be able to claim the same status as their sponsor as regards access to employment, self-employment, education, and training. As regards employment, this obviously improves on the position under Article 7(1) of Association Council Decision 1/80, where there is a three-year wait for any access and a five-year wait for equal treatment.[234]

Where the Turkish worker sponsor has a full right of access to the workforce on an equal basis with EC nationals pursuant to Article 6 of Decision 1/80, a family member entering pursuant to the Directive will be able to begin work either immediately, or after one year at the latest, with the same level of workforce access as the sponsor. In contrast, a Turkish graduate meeting the conditions of Article 7(2) of Decision 1/80 will not need to rely on the Directive as regards access to employment, since the latter puts the graduate in no better position.[235] But graduates can still use the Directive to gain equal treatment with the sponsor as regards access to self-employment, education, and training. It would also follow that family members joining a Turkish worker with full access to the EC workforce will have a right to autonomous status immediately (or after one year at the latest), since they will also enjoy full access to the workforce with a corollary right of residence. However, there will be a complication if the Directive applies (as argued in section 5A above) to those Turkish workers who have not yet obtained full status under Decision 1/80. In those cases the family members who claim

[233] For further details see sect. 3D above.

[234] See sect. 4D above.

[235] At best the graduate is in the same position under both instruments, but he or she will be in a worse position under the Dir. if the host Member State imposes a waiting period for access to employment, or if the sponsor does not have full access to the workforce under Art. 6 of Decision 1/80. The latter is a possible scenario since the parent need only have worked in the host Member State for three years for Art. 7(2) to apply; even a parent who has been there for longer could have changed jobs so frequently that Art. 6 does not apply to him or her. Art. 7(2) also applies in situations not covered by the Dir., where the graduate was not admitted on grounds of family reunion (see *Eroglu*, *supra* note 161) or where the parents have left the country (*Akman*, *supra* note 173).

equality with the sponsor are claiming the right to stay with the 'same employer' or to take up any job within the 'same occupation'. But even if the family members share the same occupation as the sponsor or (implausibly) the same employer (perhaps a multinational company), they will not normally have been exercising that employment or occupation within the host Member State.[236] So it is arguable that such family members will instead be able to take up a job with *an* employer or within *an* occupation (depending on the stage that the worker is at), and that the family member will immediately have the same period of 'acquired rights' as the worker for the purpose of qualifying for the more advanced rights under the Decision.

Logically, when the family members of Turkish nationals are themselves Turkish and wish to take up self-employment, they will be covered by the directly effective standstill provision of a Protocol to the Ankara Agreement, which prevents Member States imposing new restrictions on the freedom of establishment of Turkish nationals.[237]

Finally, there is a procedural point. Given the current limits on the jurisdiction of the Court of Justice as regards 'Title IV' cases, there could be complications for a lower court that wants to ask a question about the link between the Directive and the Association Council Decision, because it will have jurisdiction to send references only about the latter issue, not the former.[238] However, I have argued elsewhere that lower courts can send questions on all aspects of such cases of 'mixed jurisdiction' to the Court of Justice, because there is an inextricable link between the Title IV issues and the other EC law issues.[239]

6. ASSESSMENT

As noted at the outset, EC rules on family reunion have been criticized for racism, class bias, sex discrimination, human rights breaches, homophobia, and violation of children's rights. In light of the recent adoption of the Directive on family reunion for third-country nationals and the important recent case law on family reunion under EC free movement law, EC association

[236] There might be some cases where the family members were already present in the host Member State on other grounds (for example as a student or trainee), and the Member State authorizes them to remain on grounds of family reunion instead (probably following a marriage to another resident of that Member State).

[237] *Savas*, *supra* note 194.

[238] Since the Council is obliged to 'adapt' the provisions on the Court of Justice by 1 May 2004 (see Art. 67(2) EC), this issue could be resolved by the time that Member States have to implement the Dir. in Oct. 2005.

[239] See Peers, *supra* note 47.

agreements, and the ECHR, it is an opportune time to revisit these arguments.

Taking these points in turn, although there is clearly no direct *race discrimination* in EC family reunion law, critics of EC family reunion law have argued that indirect race discrimination resulted from the exclusion of third-country national sponsors (and EC national sponsors who have not exercised free movement rights) from EC free movement law rules on family reunion.[240] Following the agreement on the family reunion Directive, this argument is no longer valid. However, the highly graduated distinctions between sponsors on grounds of nationality, still evident after the agreement on the family reunion Directive, clearly results in indirect race discrimination, although this is tempered somewhat by the extension of the scope of EC free movement rules in *Carpenter* and *Baumbast and R.* Following the classic definition of indirect discrimination, there are more white people falling within the categories of sponsors with privileged family reunion law and more non-white people falling within the non-privileged categories. The EC's Council knows this full well, otherwise it would not have believed it necessary to exempt certain immigration matters from the scope of the EC's race discrimination Directive.[241] But what of the Strasbourg Court's rejection of the race discrimination argument in the *Abdulaziz* case, along with later rejections of Article 14 ECHR arguments in *Moustaquim* and *C*?[242] In *Abdulaziz*, the Court only compared the general rules for admission to the rules applicable to those sponsors with close links to the UK. It did not examine whether the UK could have different rules for different countries. In *Moustaquim* and *C*, the Court did accept that EU Member States could not just maintain different rules regarding nationals and non-nationals, but also regarding EU citizens and non-EU citizens, at least as regards expulsion. But it should be recalled that the Court condemned nationality discrimination strongly in the *Gaygusuz* judgment.[243] Let us examine the arguments regarding admission and expulsion in turn.

As for admission, the Court argued in *Abdulaziz* against a finding of race discrimination on the ground that the relevant UK rules were an attempt to restrict primary immigration. They were not directly discriminatory, and could not be regarded as discriminatory merely because more non-white people were affected than white people; this was simply the consequence of more non-white people wanting to immigrate to the UK. This finding was not affected by a favourable rule for those with UK ancestry, as these were

[240] See T. Hervey, 'Migrant Workers and their Families in the European Union: the Pervasive Market Ideology of Community Law' in J. Shaw and G. More (eds), *New Legal Dynamics of European Union* (Oxford: OUP, 1995) 91.

[241] Art. 3(2) of Dir. 2000/43 (OJ 2000 L180/22).

[242] *Supra* notes 16 and 22.

[243] *Supra* note 23.

considered exceptions for the benefit of those with close links with the UK, which do not affect the tenor of the general rules. This ruling confuses the separate issue of the rules on primary immigration (not as such covered by human rights law) with the family reunion rules which fall within the scope of Article 8 ECHR; surely it is not beyond the powers of any court to distinguish between these two sets of rules. The reasoning as regards indirect discrimination does not follow the usual approach, which is to examine possible justifications once a differential effect is clearly made out. Nor is it clear why a specific part of the national rule should simply be disregarded. The underlying question evaded here was why two sets of sponsors should be in a different position as regards the enjoyment of their right to family life.

A clearer answer to this question was offered in *Moustaquim* and *C*, based on the distinctions between sponsors who are home State or EC nationals on the one hand and all other sponsors on the other. Certainly there are distinctions between the sponsors, but can that justify distinctions as regards the enjoyment of family life? In *Abdulaziz*, the Court expressly noted that the sponsors did not have a secure right of residence in the host State. Obviously such sponsors cannot be compared with host State nationals or even EC nationals coming for a short stay, since the latter have the right to 'switch' to other free movement categories and to stay indefinitely if they meet the relevant conditions.[244] But there is far less distance between the status of long-term residents and the position of home State or EC nationals. In fact, at Tampere the EU resolved to treat long-term residents the same as EC nationals 'as far as possible'. It could even be said that the EC's approach to long-term residents is part of its 'special legal order'. Alternatively, it is hard to see why the 'special legal order' criterion exists at all, unless it simply refers to the enhanced immigration status of EC national sponsors. Otherwise EU Member States would have *carte blanche* to justify any form of unequal treatment between EU and non-EU nationals as regards any of the rights in the Convention, including such matters as detention, fair trials, and freedom of religion. It may even be questioned whether this concept is now implicitly overruled by the more recent judgments bringing the activity of EU Member States implementing EC law within the scope of the Convention. Even if the 'special legal order' justification still exists, there is still insufficient distinction in the immigration status of EU citizens (considering that their citizenship status does not confer absolute prohibition of expulsion in all Member States) and long-term resident third-country nationals to justify any distinction as regards expulsion *or* admission of family members. This interpretation would also better respect the critical view of nationality discrimination expressed in

[244] This is a separate question from the question whether the sponsors are the correct comparator at all when the right at issue is an autonomous right of residence for the *family member* (see text *supra* at notes 105 and 106).

Gaygusuz. The Strasbourg Court cannot take such a strong, principled position against nationality discrimination and at the same time shrug off any such discrimination the EC chooses to practise with the excuse that the EC is a 'special legal order'.

Next, critics argue that EC rules contain a *class distinction* as regards family reunion, because the sponsors must exercise an economic activity or have sufficient funds in order to exercise their rights.[245] This argument is less valid in recent years, given the willingness of the Court of Justice to rule that EU citizenship confers a right to social benefits, in at least some circumstances.[246] But the focus on the particular circumstances of the citizens in these judgments and the Court's references to the possible legitimacy of refusing benefits in other cases suggest that citizenship still does not entail a fully-fledged right to move to another Member State and obtain social assistance from that State as a sole source of income. So there still remain distinctions based on wealth and income, even for EU citizens and their families. Taking race and class together, third-country nationals with a need for social assistance will be entirely prevented from family reunion (unlike those EC nationals with some earned income supplemented by top-up benefits), and those with irregular and unstable work will (unlike EC nationals) have difficulty qualifying for family reunion. Moreover, there is a greater risk of family reunion being terminated later for third-country nationals since access to social assistance after family members enter will more likely lead to possible termination of their reunion rights.

As for *sex discrimination*, critics have argued that women are vulnerable after divorce if they are not EC nationals exercising economic activities, particularly since EC free movement law refuses to recognize unpaid caring or voluntary work as 'work'.[247] In the case of EC free movement law, this objection has been answered to some extent by the *Baumbast and R* judgment which expressly recognizes the position of carers, although certain important issues (the position following divorce from other sponsors or where children are too young for education, the status of the family members in question) are still unresolved and the case would not benefit women who do not have children to care for. Access to social security by family members

[245] See Hervey, *supra* note 240.

[246] See sect. 3D above.

[247] See Hervey, *supra* note 240; L. Ackers, 'Citizenship, Gender and Dependency in the European Union: Women and Internal Migration', in D. O'Keeffe and T. Hervey (eds), *Sex Equality Law in the European Union* (Indianapolis, Ind.: Wiley, 1995) 221; T. Hervey, 'A Gendered Perspective on the Right to Family Life in European Community Law', in N. Neuwahl and A. Rosas (eds), *The European Union and Human Rights* (The Hague: Kluwer, 1995) 221; I. Moebius and E. Szyszczak, 'Of Raising Pigs and Children', 18 *YEL* (1998) 125; and L. Ackers, 'Women, Citizenship and European Community Law: The Gender Implications of the Free Movement Provisions', 4 *JSWFL* (1994) 391.

has also been improved,[248] and the broader access to social assistance as a result of the case law on citizenship rights may also be relevant in such cases.

But the position of Turkish women is weaker, in that they cannot usually separate (never mind divorce) from the family they were authorized to join for three years unless they can attain worker status in their own right, unusual facts such as those in *Eyup* apply, or a *Baumbast and R* principle applies to the EC–Turkey agreement. As for the family reunion Directive, there would be a clear autonomous right to stay after a certain period but with many limits and *caveats*; however, the long-term residents' Directive has improved the position somewhat. Since there is no automatic possibility to switch to the sponsor's status, as there is for EC nationals and Turkish family members of Turkish workers, the dependence of the spouses upon the sponsor will be even further exaggerated. The Community has thus set up a graduated system of sex discrimination, with the position worsening in stages the further the sponsor and the family member get from the EU national 'norm'.

It should not be forgotten, however, that men can face immigration difficulties, too.[249] The situation of divorced men compared to divorced women has worsened following *Baumbast and R*, as men will rarely be able to claim the status of carer, although overall men will usually be more likely to maintain their immigration status through workforce participation, given their lesser share of family responsibilities and (for third-country nationals) enhanced access by the sponsor to the labour market. Having said that, in practice a significant percentage of women exercising EC free movement rights exercise the right to participate in the workforce, although a greater percentage of them curtail such participation due to maternity.[250]

Is EC family reunion law guilty of *human rights* breaches, due to defining the 'family' too narrowly, or failing to recognize the humanity of former spouses after divorce?[251] On the first point, certainly the definition of 'family'

[248] *Cabanis-Issarte*, *supra* note 103.

[249] A number of the ECHR cases (*Berrehab* and *Ciliz*) in sect. 2 concern the possible expulsion of fathers following family breakdown; *Singh* (sect. 3) concerned a man facing expulsion due to divorce proceedings; and *Kus* (sect. 4) concerned a man facing expulsion following divorce.

[250] Ackers, 'Citizenship', *supra* note 247, at 228–237.

[251] For the first argument, which is sometimes confined to arguing that the concept of family is too narrow without suggesting an ECHR breach, see Hervey, *supra* notes 240 and 247; Ackers, 'Women', *supra* note 247; K. Lundstrom, 'Family Life and the Free Movement of Workers in the European Union', 10 *IJLPF* (1996) 250; and H. Stalford, 'Concepts of Family Under EU Law—Lessons from the ECHR', 16 *IJLPF* (2002) 410. For the second argument, which obviously crosses over with the sex discrimination argument, but does not confine itself to the position of women, see J. H. H. Weiler, 'Thou Shall Not Oppress a Stranger: On the Judicial Protection of the Human Rights of Non-EC Nationals—A Critique', 3 *EJIL* (1992) 65. I leave aside Weiler's critique of the *Demirel* case as it does not

in EC family reunion law is narrower than that found in human rights law, where siblings and extended relatives and particularly unmarried partners (at least where a joint child exists) are considered to be family members. But it should not be forgotten that despite this wide definition, family *reunion* under the ECHR is only protected in limited cases as far as admission is concerned. So the definition in EC law is more problematic when it comes to expulsion, where it is clear from ECHR case law that an unmarried partner has protection from expulsion, at least as a parent. Within EC free movement law, this position is unexplored, although it has been suggested above that if the partner were allowed entry, the principles in the *Baumbast and R* judgment would apply.[252] As for admission, it would follow from Strasbourg case law that the limited obligation to admit family members could also apply to unmarried partners in the right case.

Apart from the definition of 'family', the EC free movement rules and association agreement rules are in many respects more generous than the human rights rules, not just as regards the clear right of admission under the free movement rules but also as regards issues of family members' status, which are not dealt with under the ECHR except as regards expulsion. Even the family reunion Directive goes further than the Strasbourg case law regarding admission in some respects, although it does not fully take on board the latest case law, and it appears to allow Member States to apply conditions on family reunion, such as waiting periods and certain limits on the children allowed to enter, which have not been accepted by the Strasbourg case law. Similarly it does not take on board recent cases as regards expulsion and remedies, so the compatibility of the Directive with human rights law can in several respects be doubted. While it might be argued that this is begging the question, since a minimum standards Directive leaves Member States free to apply higher standards if necessary to meet their human rights obligations, it is submitted that the obligation to respect human rights based on the ECHR as general principles of Community law, set out in Article 6 ECHR, cannot mean that EC legislation can permit lower standards than the ECHR standard even on a discretionary basis. This could lead to confusion in Member States as to which standards they must follow and surely cannot be described as 'respecting' human rights obligations. In light of this, the European Parliament appears to have a sound case against the Council in its challenge to the validity of the family reunion Directive on human rights grounds, brought at the end of 2003.[253]

concern substantive human rights law, but rather the *scope* of human rights protection in EC law. Woods, *supra* note 115, covers both arguments.

[252] See sect. 3D.

[253] Case C–540/03 *EP* v *Council*, pending.

The more fundamental problem here is not with the EC rules, but with the family reunion judgments of the Strasbourg Court. There is no justification for that Court's conservatism regarding the admission of family members as seen in the *Ahmut* and *Gül* judgments. In particular, the argument that the refusal to admit family members is not in principle an interference with family life is unsustainable. Since the ECHR also requires respect for private life and includes the right to marry and found a family, the right to respect for family life should entail an obligation in principle to accept the private decisions of families as to where to carry out family life, in particular in the case where one of the family members is a national of or a long-term resident in an ECHR Contracting Party. In that case, an obligation to leave that State in order to enjoy a family life would clearly entail a refusal to respect the right to private life as defined by the Court, or (in the case of nationals) a breach of the right to live in one's own country as implied by the Fourth Protocol to the ECHR. This approach to the issue would still leave States the right to apply Article 8(2) ECHR in particular cases where the entry of a specific family member would cause a difficulty, and would still leave States discretion as regards primary immigration intact.

On the second argument, the failure to respect the dignity and humanity of former spouses (or potentially grown-up children, particularly if they are third-country nationals) requires, as noted in the introduction, a shift from a focus on the protection of family life to the protection of individuals. Certainly the failure in EC free movement law to provide expressly for the acquisition of autonomous status results in such a lack of respect. It cannot be argued that the 'right to human dignity' is not recognized in EC law, as the right is expressly set out in the EU Charter of Fundamental Rights and the Court has also explicitly accepted its existence as part of the general principles of EC law.[254] As set out above in the discussion of sex discrimination critiques, there is a limited move toward providing for autonomous status in the recent case law and legislation, but it is still ambiguous or insufficient.

As for *homophobia*,[255] it is true that the Court of Justice rejected in the 1980s the inclusion of any relationship outside formal marriage as a 'spousal' relationship, and the recent judgments in *Grant* and *D* v *Council* appear to consider that partnerships and presumably marriages between same-sex couples recognized by the law of a Member State cannot be considered as 'marriages' by EC law.[256] Here again, as in the case of race discrimination, EC discrimination law has attempted to protect immigration law against

[254] Case C–377/98 *Netherlands* v *EP and Council* [2001] ECR I–7079.

[255] See Lundstrom, 'Family Life' and Stalford, 'Concepts of Family', both *supra* note 251. For an exploration of the issue before the judgments in *Grant* and *D* see K. Waaldijk, 'Free Movement of Same-Sex Partners', 3 *MJ* (1996) 271.

[256] *Supra* note 70.

allegations of discrimination based on sexual orientation.[257] However, the *Reed* principle requiring equal treatment between home State national workers and EC national workers exercising free movement rights as regards entry of unmarried partners presumably applies equally to same-sex relationships between unmarried partners (or persons in a registered partnership). It is arguable that the principle applies to other categories of EC free movement law beyond the movement of workers,[258] and the principle definitely now applies in the general family reunion Directive, although only as an option for Member States. But the situation remains uncertain even for EC nationals and the option permitted Member States as regards third-country nationals leaves the position for them entirely up to national discretion. Sooner or later, the Court will be forced to choose between its support for abolishing obstacles to free movement of persons and its apparently unchangeable conservative instincts as regards same-sex and opposite-sex partners alike.

Finally, as for *children*, critics argue that they have not been given autonomous rights within the free movement rules of the EC.[259] But, as noted above, there has been in recent case law recognition of children's autonomy at a later stage, upon entry into or graduation from vocational training.[260] The Court of Justice also implicitly accepts that secondary school pupils who move are exercising EU citizenship rights,[261] and the logic of the *Baumbast and R* judgment is that a parent carer and migrant worker's child are mutually dependent on each other—with the child taking a lead role in the perspective of EC free movement law. There is an excellent argument that even schoolchildren can be sponsors under EC free movement law, which the Court will soon have a chance to rule on if a pending reference is maintained.[262] Finally, the *Avello* judgment has now expressly accepted children's status as EU citizens and their corresponding right to non-discrimination on grounds of nationality, although it remains to be seen what effect this has beyond the facts of that judgment.[263] However, the family reunion Directive clearly treats third-country national children as secondary to sponsors, with only a limited prospect that *Baumbast and R* might apply or that they might otherwise attain autonomous status. Furthermore the education and training

[257] Art. 3(2) of Dir. 2000/78 (OJ 2000 L303/16).

[258] See sect. 3B above.

[259] H. Stalford, 'The Citizenship Status of Children in the European Union', 8 *IJCR* (2000) 101.

[260] On entry into vocational training, see particularly *Grzelczyk*, *supra* note 89, confirming that students have citizenship rights; on the status after vocational training, see particularly *Akman* and my case note examining this issue, *supra* note 173.

[261] *D'Hoop*, *supra* note 44.

[262] *Chen and Zhu*, *supra* note 114.

[263] *Supra* note 113.

rights in the Directive are weak and the Directive provides for no other social benefits for children as members of families.

7. CONCLUSIONS

The EU's legislators and judiciary have taken some tentative efforts to address the criticisms of EC family reunion law. It cannot now be said that third-country nationals are not covered by any EC rules, that former spouses will always face expulsion after divorce, that unmarried partners will never be successful in obtaining entry, that only the already economically successful can ever rely on free movement law or that children are fully ignored as autonomous agents by EC law. However, on many of these points, EC law still has a long way to go. As far as we know, there is still no right at present to bring unmarried partners to all Member States when exercising free movement rights, regardless of the impact on free movement law or the indirect discrimination on grounds of sexual orientation which results. Neither are divorced spouses, in particular men, always going to be protected in the event of family breakdown. Nor will the economically less advantaged always be able to rely on the concept of citizenship of the Union to surmount the obstacles which EC free movement law places upon them. But in each of these cases, the position would be ameliorated if the family consisted entirely of EU nationals, since access to autonomous status is inherently far easier to accomplish. The fundamental distinction between EC nationals and third-country nationals still remains, despite the agreement on a family reunion Directive, because of the extremely low standards set by that Directive. It has been accentuated by the EU's decision to give preference to its wealthy neighbours as regards free movement of persons. And the stark result of that distinction is that many non-white people in the European Union cannot enjoy the human right to respect for their family life in the same way as the white majority, even if they are long-term residents of a Member State. This unethical situation, has, to its lasting shame, been endorsed by the European Court of Human Rights. It can only be hoped that greater judicial courage and political will may result in narrowing and eventual abolition of this unjustifiable distinction in the years to come.

Part Three

Police and Judicial Co-operation in Criminal Matters

5

Eurojust and the European Public Prosecutor in the *Corpus Juris* Model: Water and Fire?

CHRISTINE VAN DEN WYNGAERT

1. INTRODUCTION

It has become a commonplace to say that crime does not stop at national boundaries and that crime in today's society has to a large extent become international. The result of this is that states, if they rely on their domestic law making and law enforcing institutions alone, cannot protect their citizens against crime. In the European Union, where internal borders between the Member States have disappeared, this problem becomes all the more apparent. Closer co-operation between the states is an obvious response to this phenomenon.

On this particular point, the European Union and the European Communities are at a crossroads in their history. The 'European Convention', under the chairmanship of Mr. Valéry Giscard d'Estaing, has drafted a new Constitution for Europe in which the institutions and the legislative instruments of the EU and EC are to be merged into a new structure with a new name, perhaps the 'United States of Europe'.[1] The question of the objectives, tasks, and powers to be conferred upon these 'United States of Europe' in the field of the criminal law is a crucial point in the continuing debate. In nearly all the Member States, crime control is a central theme in national elections and is therefore high on the political agenda of governments. The 'European Convention' and the subsequent Intergovernmental Conference have had

[1] This was one of the suggestions made during the Convention's deliberations. In the final analysis, Art. 1 of the draft Constitutional Treaty of July 2003 opted for 'European Union' (see OJ 2003 C169/8, and in particular the sections on the Area of Freedom, Security and Justice in Part III, Chapter IV, Arts III–158–178). Of course, the draft Treaty is not necessarily the final word, its fate depending upon the Intergovernmental Conference which started under the Italian Presidency of the EU in October 2003, and, thereafter, upon the success or otherwise of national ratification processes in the various Member States.

to address whether crime control will remain a purely national power, or whether it will, for certain crimes, be 'communitarized'. It has also had to address the institutional context in which these powers, if any, will be exercised.

The traditional way in which states have always co-operated in criminal matters has been by entering into international co-operation agreements in criminal matters in various forms, ranging from extradition through mutual assistance to transfer of criminal proceedings and execution of foreign criminal sentences. The institutional *habitat* in which these co-operation mechanisms developed has been, since the Second World War, the Council of Europe, not the EC or the EU. The Council of Europe was also the regional framework in which the European Convention and the European Court of Human Rights were developed.

Only in recent times has the EU decided to develop its own rules and mechanisms in these fields, sometimes as a substitute, sometimes as a complement to the existing Council of Europe conventions. As early as the 1970s, speaking of terrorism, the then French President Valéry Giscard d'Estaing, launched the idea of a European Legal Space (*espace judiciaire européen*), mistaking—so it seems—the Council of Ministers of the Council of Europe for the Council of Ministers of the EU.[2] This led to the 1977 European Convention on the Suppression of Terrorism, adopted within the framework of the Council of Europe.[3]

Meanwhile, the EU has been creating a legal space of its own. As from the 1980s, Member States of the EU have felt the need to develop co-operation rules that are more far-reaching than those already existing in the Council of Europe and have adopted a host of conventions for this purpose.[4] These

[2] B. Legendre in *Le Monde* of 6 December 1979: see C. Van den Wyngaert, 'L'espace judiciaire européen: vers une fissure au Conseil de l'Europe?', *RDP* (1981) 511, at 514.

[3] European Convention on the Suppression of Terrorism, Strasbourg, 27 January 1977, *European Treaty Series*, No. 90.

[4] Agreement on the application among the Member States of the European Communities of the Council of Europe Convention on the transfer of sentenced persons, Brussels, 25 May 1987; Agreement between the Member States of the European Communities on the simplification and modernization of methods of transmitting extradition requests, San Sebastian, 26 May 1989; Agreement between the Member States on the transfer of proceedings in criminal matters, Rome, 6 November 1990; Convention between the Member States of the European Communities on the enforcement of foreign criminal sentences, Brussels, 13 November 1991. None of these conventions has entered into force. Some states, the so-called Schengen states, have entered into a closer co-operation scheme in the Schengen Convention of 19 June 1990, applying the Schengen Agreement of 14 June 1985 between the Governments of the States of the Benelux Economic Union, the Federal Republic of Germany and the French Republic, on the Gradual Abolition of Checks at their Common Borders, International Legal Materials, 1991, 84. In 1997, with the Treaty of Amsterdam, the Schengen Convention has been integrated into the EC and in the EU.

conventions were, at first, elaborated within the loose framework of European Political Co-operation among the Member States of the European Communities. However, the Treaty of Maastricht (1992) establishing the European Union introduced a formal structure for the development of these rules. It created the so-called third pillar, which is now the framework in which Member States convene when they draft legislation on the subject of co-operation in criminal matters. Since then, the distinction has been made between the first pillar (EC Treaty) and the third pillar (EU Treaty).

In the Treaty of Amsterdam (1997), the EU Member States elevated co-operation in criminal matters into an objective of the EU (Article 2 TEU, 4th indent, and Article 29 TEU): henceforth, the Union's objective is 'to provide citizens with a high level of safety within an area of freedom, security and justice'. This objective, often referred to as the European legal area, is to be achieved through closer co-operation between police forces and judicial authorities and by approximation, where necessary, of the rules on criminal matters in the Member States (Article 29 TEU).[5]

In addition, the Treaty of Amsterdam created new legislative instruments to achieve this objective. Until then, the typical instruments on which co-operation was based were international conventions, subject to the general rules and principles of the law of treaties, in particular ratification and implementation. An example is the Europol Convention of 1995, which entered into force in 1999 and the Convention for the Protection of the Financial Interests of the European Communities, drawn up in 1995[6] and entering into force only in 2002. All the other conventions in the field of co-operation in criminal matters between the Member States of the EU failed to enter into force because they lacked the necessary number of ratifications.

The Amsterdam Treaty now provides two new instruments: framework decisions and decisions. *Framework decisions* can be made for the purpose of the approximation of the laws and regulations of the Member States, *decisions* can be adopted for any other purpose consistent with the objectives of Title IV of the TEU, i.e. the creation of a European legal area. Examples include the 2002 Framework Decision on the European Arrest Warrant[7] and the 2002 Decision setting up Eurojust.[8] In just a few years since the entry into force of the Treaty of Amsterdam in 1999, a host of framework decisions have

[5] See, generally, G. de Kerchove and A. Weyemberg (eds), *Towards a European Judicial Criminal Area* (Brussels: Institut d'études européennes, 2000). For the separate but complementary 'first pillar' aspect of the new Area of Freedom, Security and Justice, see Title IV of the EC Treaty (Visas, Asylum, Immigration and other Policies Related to Free Movement of Persons).

[6] *Infra*, note 31.

[7] Council Framework Decision of 13 June 2002 on the European arrest warrant and the surrender procedures between Member States, OJ 2002 L190/1.

[8] Council Decision of 28 February 2002 setting up Eurojust with a view to reinforcing the fight against serious crime, OJ 2002 L63/1.

been proposed in the field of the criminal law, some of which have been adopted.[9] Although EU framework decisions and decisions, unlike EC regulations, have no direct effect in the Member States, they are binding upon them (Article 34 (2)(b) and (c)). This is a fundamental difference with international conventions, which bind states only upon ratification. A disturbing element, obviously, is that national parliaments lose their control over matters that relate to criminal law and procedure, which may be problematic from a democratic perspective.

Judicial co-operation in criminal matters has now become a third pillar matter and has been integrated into the abovementioned general EU objective of creating an area of freedom, security, and justice. However, the legal instruments governing international co-operation in criminal matters between the EU Member States are still, in the first place, Council of Europe instruments. EU legislation is usually drafted as a complement to existing Council of Europe conventions. For example, the European Convention on mutual assistance in criminal matters (2000)[10] is built on the *acquis* of the Council of Europe's convention on the same subject (1959).[11]

Yet, the European Union seems to be steering in another direction since the Tampere Council of 1999. In the 'milestones' adopted at the end of this conference, the Heads of State and Government declared that the principle of mutual recognition should become the cornerstone of judicial co-operation in the EU.[12] This will eventually lead to EU instruments that will replace the Council of Europe conventions, rather than complement them. An example is the EU Framework Decision on the European arrest warrant,[13] which will

[9] See, for example, Council Framework Decision of 15 March 2001 on the standing of victims in criminal proceedings, OJ 2001 L82/1; Council Framework Decision of 28 May 2001 combating fraud and counterfeiting of non-cash means of payment, OJ 2001 L149/1; Council Framework Decision of 26 June 2001 on money laundering, the identification, tracing, freezing, seizing, and confiscation of instrumentalities and the proceeds of crime, OJ 2001 L182/1; Council Framework Decision of 6 December 2001 amending Framework Decision 2000/383/JHA on increasing protection by criminal penalties and other sanctions against counterfeiting in connection with the introduction of the euro, OJ 2001 L329/3; Council Framework Decision of 13 June 2002 on combating terrorism, OJ 2002 L164/3; Council Framework Decision of 13 June 2002 on joint investigation teams, OJ 2002 L162/1; Council Framework Decision of 19 July 2002 on combating trafficking in human beings, OJ 2002 L203/1.

[10] Convention on Mutual Assistance in Criminal Matters between the Member States of the European Union, Brussels, 29 May 2000, OJ 2000 C197/1; Additional Protocol to the Convention on Mutual Assistance in Criminal Matters, 16 October 2001, OJ 2001 C326/1.

[11] European Convention on Mutual Assistance in Criminal Matters, Strasbourg, 20 April 1959, *European Treaty Series*, No. 30.

[12] Tampere European Council (15 and 16 October 1999): Presidency conclusions, retrievable at: http://europa.eu.int/council/off/conclu/.

[13] Council Framework Decision of 13 June 2002 on the European arrest warrant and the surrender procedures between Member States, OJ 2002 L190/1.

replace the Council of Europe Convention on Extradition (1957)[14] as between the EU Member States.[15]

In 2000, at the Intergovernmental Conference in Nice, there were two proposals aiming at achieving closer judicial integration in Europe: there was a radical proposal, by the European Commission, to introduce a *European Public Prosecutor* for fraud crimes into the EC Treaty,[16] and a less radical proposal to introduce *Eurojust* for a limited number of crimes into the EU Treaty. The Intergovernmental Conference adopted only the second, not the first proposal and wrote Eurojust into the TEU (Articles 29 and 32).

Meanwhile, as already noted, the 'European Convention' has drafted the new European Constitution. This draft has produced a consensus to merge the first and the third pillars of the Union, and to provide a more democratic and transparent legislative process in an attempt to reduce the democratic deficit in the Union.

The place to be occupied by Europol, Eurojust, and a possible European Public Prosecutor for fraud crimes is to a large extent predicated on how the treaty and the ensuing Intergovernmental Conference resolve to organize the general institutional structure of the 'United States of Europe'. It also depends on what will be the objectives, tasks, and powers that are conferred upon European institutions and upon national institutions respectively in the field of crime prevention and suppression. In the process, it will have to define the position of the European Union *vis-à-vis* the Council of Europe, in respect both of human rights protection and of inter-state co-operation in criminal matters.[17] At the time of writing, the question is still unresolved.

Whether the European Public Prosecutor will also be introduced is still an open question. In its final report of 2 December 2002, Working Group X of the European Convention considered the possible creation of a European Public Prosecutor or a Public Prosecutor's Office, without making concrete proposals in this respect.[18] At least two Member States seemed to support the

[14] European Convention on Extradition, Paris, 13 December 1957, *European Treaty Series*, No. 24.

[15] See generally G. de Kerchove and A. Weyemberg (eds), *La reconnaissance mutuelle des décisions judiciaires pénales* (Brussels: Institut d'études européennes, 2001), at 255; and *L'espace pénal européen: enjeux et perspectives* (Brussels: Institut d'études européennes, 2002), at 305.

[16] Additional Commission contribution to the Intergovernmental Conference on institutional reforms—*The criminal protection of the Community's financial interests: A European Prosecutor*, 29 September 2000, COM(2000)608.

[17] See the Council of Europe's memorandum submitted to Working Group X of the European Convention: *Freedom, Security and Justice in the whole of Europe. Involving the Greater Europe in the realisation of an area of freedom, security and justice*, SG/Inf (2002)42, referring to the Council of Europe as a truly pan-European organization.

[18] European Convention, Final Report of Working Group X, 'Freedom, Security and Justice', 2 December 2002, CONV 426/02, at 20, retrievable at: http://register.consilium.eu.int/pdf/en/02/cv00/00426en2.pdf.

idea of a European Prosecutor.[19] Subsequently, the text of the draft Treaty itself kept the question open, contemplating the possibility of the establishment of a European Public Prosecutor's Office starting from Eurojust, but only if such a proposal were made unanimously by the Council of Ministers after obtaining the consent of the European Parliament.[20]

This essay discusses and compares Eurojust and the proposal to introduce a European Public Prosecutor. It examines whether they are as mutually exclusive as they seem to be at first sight.

2. EUROJUST

A. What is Eurojust?

Eurojust is the European Judicial Co-operation Unit of the European Union. Its primary mission is to facilitate and co-ordinate co-operation between the Member States of the EU. It is not an institution of the European Community but a third pillar organ serving the purpose of improving intergovernmental co-operation. It does not create a centralized judicial enforcement system.[21]

Eurojust is the judicial counterpart of Europol, the European Police Organization that is also an intergovernmental body, not a Community organization.[22] It is a complement to the European Judicial Network, set up by a Joint Action in 1998 and composed of national judicial contact points in the fifteen Member States.[23] Like Eurojust, the European Judicial

[19] European Convention, Contribution by Mr. Joschka Fischer and Mr. Dominique de Villepin, members of the Convention: 'Joint Franco-German proposals to the European Convention on an area of freedom, security and justice', Brussels, 28 November 2002, CONV 435/02, CONTRIB 156.

[20] *Supra* note 1, Art. III–175.

[21] S. Brammertz and Berthelet, 'Eurojust et le réseau judiciaire européen: concurrence ou complémentarité', *Revue de Droit Pénal et de Criminologie* (2002), 389; Berthelet and C. Chevallier-Govers, 'Quelle relation entre Europol et Eurojust? Rapport d'égalité ou rapport d'autorité?', 450 *Revue du Marché commun et de l'Union européenne* (2001) 468; D. Flore, 'Eurojust ou Ministère Public Européen: un choix de politique criminelle', 28 *Agon* (2000) 9; S. Brammertz, 'Eurojust: parquet européen de la première génération?', in de Kerchove and Weyembergh (eds), *supra* note 5, at 105; D. Flore, 'D'un réseau judiciaire européen à une juridiction pénale européenne: Eurojust et l'émergence d'un système de justice pénale', in de Kerchove, and Weyembergh (eds), *L'espace pénal europeéen: enjeux et perspectives, supra* note 15, at 9; S. White, 'The European Prosecutor: Extension of Eurojust or "Prolongation" of the *Corpus Juris* Proposals?', in ibid., at 47.

[22] Council Act of 26 July 1995 Drawing up the Convention based on Article K.3 of the Treaty on European Union, on the Establishment of a European Police Office, OJ 1995 C316/1. See also W. Bruggeman, 'Europol et Interpol', in de Kerchove, and Weyemberg (eds), *supra* note 5, at 97.

[23] Joint Action of 29 June 1998 on the Creation of a European Judicial Network, OJ 1998 L191/4.

Network facilitates co-operation, not from a central point (The Hague), but from the fifteen capitals of the Member States. The secretariat of the European Judicial Network forms part of the secretariat of Eurojust.

B. Sources

The idea of creating Eurojust was first formulated by the European Council of Tampere (1999) and written into the TEU by the Intergovernmental Conference of Nice in 2000. The new version of Article 29 TEU, which states the objective of creating an area of freedom, security, and justice, now adds that this objective is to be achieved through:

> Closer co-operation between judicial and other competent authorities of the member states *including co-operation through the European Judicial Co-operation Unit (Eurojust)* [emphasis added].

The general powers of Eurojust are described in Article 32 TEU. Eurojust is (1) to enable and facilitate proper co-ordination between Member States' national prosecuting authorities (Article 32(2)(a)); (2) to promote support of criminal investigations in cases of serious cross-border crimes, taking into account the analyses carried out by Europol (Article 32(2)(b)); and (3) to facilitate close co-operation between Eurojust and the European Judicial Network, particularly in order to facilitate the execution of letters rogatory and the implementation of extradition requests.

Before the entry into force of the amended version of the TEU, a provisional Eurojust unit ('pro-Eurojust') was set up in 2001 and started functioning as from 1 March of that year. The Council Decision of 28 February 2002 further defines its objectives, tasks, structure, and competences.[24]

C. Status and Composition

Eurojust is a body of the EU with legal personality. It is composed of fifteen members, who are seconded to it by the Member States (Article 2 of the Council Decision of 28 February 2002). These members can be prosecutors, judges, or police officers with equivalent competence. In practice, most Eurojust members are public prosecutors, with the exception of the members of the two states who do not recognize the continental *ministère public* institution in their national legal orders: Ireland and the UK. These states have seconded members of the Director of Public Prosecutions' office to Eurojust.

The status of *Eurojust members* is not determined by EU legislation but by the national law of the Member States who second them: national law

[24] See *supra* note 8.

(Article 9(a)) determines their appointment, salary, term of office, and so on. The nature and extent of their judicial powers in the territory of the Member States that seconded them is also determined by national law, as well as their powers to act in relation to foreign authorities (Article 9(c)). As a result, the powers of individual Eurojust members may vary considerably from one state to another.

Together, the fifteen Eurojust members form the *Eurojust College.* This college consists of all the national members, who each have one vote (Article 10). The voting rules within the College are set out in Eurojust's rules of procedure, which are adopted by the EU Council on a proposal adopted unanimously by the Eurojust College. The Eurojust College elects its own president and the two vice presidents, subject to the approval of the Council (Article 28(2)).

Eurojust has divided itself into five working groups: group one focuses on operational work; the second group contributes to the discussions of the working party on Eurojust; group three is in charge of the relations with European Institutions (Commission, Council, European Judicial Network, and European Parliament); group four is responsible for relations with police agencies (Europol, Interpol, FBI, and DEA); group five deals with international relations.[25]

Eurojust's seat has been, provisionally, located in The Hague, where Europol also has its seat. It has its own administrative staff, headed by an administrative director (Article 29), who is appointed unanimously by the College. One member of staff is appointed to the function of *data protection officer* (Article 17). A *Joint Supervisory Body*, composed of judges appointed by the Member States, supervises data protection within Eurojust. Unlike the presidency of the Eurojust College, the presidency of the Joint Supervisory Body rotates with the presidency of the EU Council.

D. Crimes for which Eurojust is Competent

1. Competence Ratione Materiae

The crimes for which Eurojust is competent are listed in Article 4 of the Council Decision of 28 February 2002. Eurojust is competent for the same crimes as Europol (Article 2 of the Europol Convention and Article 4(1)b of the Council Decision). This list originally covered a restricted range of crimes (unlawful drug trafficking, trafficking in nuclear and radioactive substances, illegal immigrant smuggling, trade in human beings, and motor vehicle crime). It has since been expanded by the EU Council and now includes terrorism, cybercrime, and counterfeiting the euro. In 2001, the EU Council

[25] Pro-Eurojust, Report, July 2001, 5 (unpublished).

extended Europol's competence to all the crimes listed in the Annex to the Europol Convention. As a result, very broad categories of crime came under Europol's, and therefore also under Eurojust's, competence: crimes against life, limb, or personal freedom (e.g. murder, grievous bodily injury, kidnapping); crimes against property or public goods including fraud (organized robbery, illicit trafficking in cultural goods, swindling and fraud, counterfeiting and product piracy, corruption); and illegal trading and harm to the environment (illicit trafficking in arms, in endangered species, environmental crime, and illicit trafficking in hormones).

In addition to the 'Europol crimes', Eurojust has a number of its own competences, which are listed in Article 4(1)b of the Council decision and which in part overlap with the crimes listed above: computer crime, fraud and corruption including EC fraud, money laundering, environmental crime, and participation in a criminal organization.

Eurojust is also competent in the case of other offences committed together with the types of crime and the offences referred to in Article 4(1)a and b (Article 4(1)c).

Finally, Eurojust may act in respect of types of offences other than those referred to in Article 4 of the Decision each time a competent authority in one of the Member States asks Eurojust's assistance (Article 4(2)).

2. Competence Ratione Loci*: 15 = 15*

Eurojust, acting either through its individual members or through its college, has no powers of direct action on the territory of the Member States except in cases where the national Eurojust member has, by his national law, been empowered to act on his national territory. Eurojust members may also have operational powers when acting within a joint investigation team. Generally speaking, however, Eurojust members do not have Union-wide powers and the European Judicial Area unlike in the *Corpus Juris* model, is not a single juridical unit (15 = 1). Even if the objective of mutual recognition, set by the Tampere summit, were attained, it would not give Eurojust members powers to act on the territory of the Member States. It would not mean that authorities of Member State A would be empowered to act on the territory of state B, only that state B would have to execute the judicial decisions rendered in state A, on the latter's request.

E. Powers and Tasks of Eurojust

Eurojust's powers must be seen in the light of its general objectives, which are set out in Article 3 of the Council Decision of 28 February 2002. Generally speaking, Eurojust is a co-ordinator and facilitator of investigation and prosecution of crime. The real 'players' remain national investigative, prosecutorial, and judicial authorities. Eurojust is, as such, not a player but only a co-ordinator and facilitator. Individual Eurojust members may, however, have operational powers on the territory of the Member State by which they are seconded. These powers, should they exist, derive from their mandate under national law, not from EU law.

Eurojust's tasks are defined in Articles 4, 5, and 6 of the Council Decision of 28 February 2002. They differ according to whether Eurojust acts through its members or as a college. When fulfilling its tasks, it must always indicate whether it is acting through its national members or as a college (Article 5).

1. General Objectives (Article 3)

Eurojust's objectives set out under Article 3 envisage three types of situations: (1) bilateral or multilateral cases between Member States, (2) cases involving a Member State and a third state, and (3) cases involving a Member State and the Community.

In *bilateral or multilateral cases* (cases involving two or more Member States), Eurojust's objective is to assist Member States in the investigation and prosecution of serious crime by stimulating and improving the co-ordination between the competent authorities of the different Member States, to improve co-operation between the competent authorities of the Member States or to support them in other ways calculated to render their investigations and prosecutions more effective (Article 3(1)).

Eurojust can also assist in *investigations and prosecutions concerning one Member State and a non-member state*. This can only be done where a special co-operation agreement has been concluded with the non-member state or where, in the specific case, there is an essential interest in providing assistance (Article 3(2)).

The third type of situation in which Eurojust can act is *investigations and prosecutions concerning one Member State and the Community*, on the request of either that Member State or the Community. As an example of the latter, one could think of cases that are investigated by OLAF (the European Anti-Fraud Office).

2. Tasks of Eurojust Acting through its National Members (Article 6)

Acting through its national members, Eurojust has a number of tasks that are set out in Article 6 and that can be summarized as follows: (1) addressing requests to the Member State, (2) ensuring that the authorities of the Member States inform each other of ongoing investigations and prosecutions of which they have been informed, and (3) assisting, in various ways, with co-operation requests.

Requests addressed to the Member States (Article 6(a) (i)–(v)) can be the following. Eurojust members can ask their respective states to start an investigation or prosecution of specific acts. They can ask them to consider accepting that one Member State may be in a better position to undertake an investigation or prosecution, which is sometimes called the 'concentration' of proceedings in one Member State. They can offer to co-ordinate between the competent authorities of the Member States concerned and can propose the establishment of joint investigation teams. They may ask a Member State to consider providing Eurojust with any information that is necessary to carry out its tasks.

All information exchanged between Eurojust and Member States, including requests of the kind described above, must be directed through the national member (Article 9(2)). National members shall have access to national criminal records in the same way as stipulated by their national law in the case of judges, prosecutors, police officers, or other authorities (Article 9(4)) and may contact the competent authorities of their Member State directly.

In order to facilitate communication between Eurojust members and the authorities of the Member States that seconded them, Member States may put in place or appoint one or more national correspondents (Article 12(1)). These national correspondents have their place of work in the Member State concerned, and may be the same as the contact points of the European Judicial Network (Article 12(2)). This shall not preclude direct contacts between Eurojust members and the competent national authorities.

As explained above, the powers of national members of Eurojust depend on the powers they have actually been given by their respective states. At the time of writing, Member States still need to indicate the powers of their respective national Eurojust members in accordance with Article 9(3). Some national members of Eurojust may have operational powers to 'act' personally on their national territories (e.g. initiating an investigation, performing certain investigative acts or prosecuting directly, lodging requests for mutual assistance), whereas others may have more limited powers (formulating requests only). This is likely to result in an asymmetrical situation, where some Eurojust members have more powers than others, creating a potential discrepancy between 'super members' and other members.[26] At least, however, national members of Eurojust must be given the power to contact the competent authorities directly.

3. *Tasks of Eurojust Acting as a College*

Eurojust can act as a college when so requested by one or more of its national members, when the case involves investigations and prosecutions with potential effects at Union level or in Member States other than the ones directly

[26] See generally Flore, 'D'un réseau judiciaire européen à une juridiction pénale européenne: Eurojust et l'émergence d'un système de justice pénale', in de Kerchove and Weyemberg (eds), *supra* note 21.

concerned. It can also act when a general question relating to the achievement of its objectives is involved (Article 5). One such general question will certainly be the definition of priorities and the development of a criminal justice policy concerning investigation and prosecution of crime (*politique criminelle*).

Like the individual members, Eurojust acting as a college can address requests to a Member State in the same cases as those listed above. The points listed under this heading in Article 7(a) are almost identical to those listed in Article 6(a) referred to above and applicable to individual Eurojust members. There are, however, two important points of difference.

First, when addressing a request under Article 7(a), the Eurojust College must give reasons. Secondly, there is no obligation on Member States to comply with the request. Where the Member State to which the request is addressed decides not to comply with it, however, it must give reasons for non-compliance, unless it is unable to do so for security reasons or for fear of jeopardizing the success of investigations under way or the safety of individuals (Article 8).

Other tasks of Eurojust acting as a college are enumerated in Article 7 (b)–(g) and also correspond to the tasks of Eurojust acting through its members: Eurojust as a college shall ensure that the authorities of the Member States inform each other of ongoing investigations and prosecutions of which it has been informed and assist, in various ways, with co-operation requests. It may supply logistical support in a number of cases, which may include assistance for translation, interpretation, and the organization of co-ordination meetings (Article 7(g)).

Eurojust as a college co-operates and consults with the European Judicial Network (Article 7(e)) and may assist Europol, in particular by providing it with opinions based on analyses carried out by Europol (Article 7(f)).

4. *Applicable Law*

For its practical operation, Eurojust does not need harmonized legislation defining offences, sanctions, and procedures to investigate and prosecute them. All this remains determined by national law as applied by national authorities, who remain the real players in this respect. The main instruments to be applied are those on international co-operation through e.g. extradition and judicial assistance. These fields, which are traditionally regulated in international conventions, will increasingly be dealt with in EU framework decisions or their equivalent under the new European Constitution.[27] Since the Tampere milestones, the emphasis has shifted from double criminality

[27] The term suggested in the draft Constitutional Treaty is 'European framework law'. See *supra*, note 1, Art. I–32.

towards mutual recognition, which is now considered as the cornerstone of judicial co-operation between the Member States.[28] Framework decisions implementing this policy have already been adopted in the field of extradition, which is replaced by the European arrest warrant.[29] New legislation is under examination.[30] That being said, the formulation of harmonized legislation in certain areas would probably facilitate the operation of Eurojust.

F. Data Protection

Several articles in the Council Decision of 28 February 2002 setting up Eurojust are devoted to data protection. Eurojust may set up its own database and must take the necessary measures to ensure compliance with the Data Protection Convention of 1981 (Article 14). Eurojust must appoint a Data Protection Officer who acts under the direct authority of the Eurojust College (Article 17) and is monitored by a Joint Supervisory Body composed of judges who are not members of Eurojust, appointed by the Member States.

G. Relations with Partners and Exchange of Information with Partners

In the course of the past decade, several organs and bodies have been set up in an attempt to fight crime in general or certain offences in particular. Examples are Europol, the European Judicial Network, OLAF (and its predecessor UCLAF), liaison officers, liaison magistrates. Avoiding duplication, ensuring co-ordination, and, where possible, co-operation is necessary. The Decision of 28 February 2002 contains a provision to that effect: it regulates Eurojust's relations with partners (Article 26).

The first obvious partner of Eurojust is its counterpart police organ, *Europol,* which is competent for the same crimes as Eurojust. Duplications should be avoided (Article 26(1)). Eurojust must establish and maintain close co-operation with Europol, in so far as it is relevant for the achievement of its purposes. Both EU bodies have concluded an agreement spelling out the essential elements of such co-operation.

The second obvious candidate for partnership with Eurojust is the *European Judicial Network*, which links fifteen national central contact points that co-ordinate and facilitate bilateral co-operation between judicial authorities

[28] *Supra* note 12.

[29] *Supra* note 13.

[30] Draft Framework decision on execution of European of orders to freeze evidence and property, text available on the website of the European Parliament. (http://www.eurloparl.eu.int/meetdocs/committees/libe/20020514/698069en.pdf). See also the Commission's non-paper on mutual recognition of orders to obtain evidence, Brussels, 12 December 2002.

of the Member States. Eurojust has privileged contacts with the European Judicial Network, whose secretariat is integrated into the Eurojust secretariat. Eurojust has access to the centralized information of the European Judicial Network (including the European Judicial Atlas) and to its telecommunications network. If invited, national members of Eurojust may attend meetings of the European Judicial network and vice versa (Article 26(2)).

Another organ with which close co-operation must be ensured is OLAF, the Commission's anti-fraud office, a specialized body responsible for the investigation of crimes against the financial interests of the European Communities ('EC fraud') under several EC regulations[31] and an EU Convention.[32] Belonging functionally to the European Commission, OLAF is a 'first pillar organ' with, however, cross-pillar competences that may coincide and overlap with the competences of Eurojust. To avoid duplication, Eurojust shall maintain close co-operation with OLAF. The latter may contribute to Eurojust's work of co-ordinating investigation and prosecution procedures in EC fraud cases. This may happen either on the initiative of Eurojust or at the request of OLAF where the competent national authorities concerned do not oppose such participation.

Eurojust may also establish contacts and exchange experiences of a non-operational character with other bodies, including in particular international organizations (Article 26(5)). Examples one could think of are the International Criminal Court, which is a specialized international organization, or the Yugoslavia and Arusha Tribunals, which are organs of the United Nations. Article 27 of the Council Decision on Eurojust allows Eurojust to exchange information and to set up co-operation agreements with third states, with 'bodies competent by virtue of provisions adopted within the framework of the Treaties' and with international organizations or bodies. These agreements must be approved by the Council. They may contain provisions concerning arrangements for the secondment of liaison officers or liaison magistrates to Eurojust. This is the judicial counterpart to the powers given to Europol (Article 42 of the Europol Convention), which have been used to conclude agreements with candidate Member States and with the USA.

[31] Council Regulation (EC, EURATOM) 2988/95 of 18 December 1995 on the protection of the European Communities' financial interests, OJ 1995 L312/1; Council Regulation (EC, EURATOM) 2185/96 of 11 November 1996 concerning on-the-spot checks and inspections carried out by the Commission in order to protect the European Communities' financial interests against fraud and other irregularities, OJ 1996 L292/2; Regulation (EC) 1073/1999 of the European Parliament and of the Council of 25 May 1999 concerning investigations conducted by the European Anti-Fraud Office (OLAF), OJ 1999 L136/1.

[32] Convention on the Protection of the European Communities' Financial Interests, Brussels, 26 July 1995, OJ 1995 C316/48.

3. THE EUROPEAN PUBLIC PROSECUTOR IN THE *CORPUS JURIS* MODEL

A. What is the European Public Prosecutor?

The European Public Prosecutor does not yet exist. If such an office were to be established, it would be a judicial body of the European Community (not of the European Union) with direct enforcement authority, not just powers to facilitate and co-ordinate the action of the Member States. The European Public Prosecutor would be responsible for the investigation and prosecution of financial crimes against the EC, including EC fraud, corruption, and money laundering. The office would have the power to investigate and prosecute these crimes throughout the whole European Union, which, for that purpose, would constitute a single European jurisdictional unit. That is to say, the European Public Prosecutor would plead the case for the prosecution in national courts. Where the court pronounced sanctions, the European Public Prosecutor would also oversee the enforcement of these sanctions, not only in the state where they were imposed but also elsewhere in the European Union.[33]

The European Public Prosecutor system would thus fundamentally differ from the current system of co-operation in criminal matters, which is *horizontal* in structure. Traditional co-operation is based on the co-operation between sovereign states acting on the basis of reciprocity, through mechanisms such as e.g. extradition, legal assistance, and the transfer of criminal proceedings, which all require the consent of the requested state. The European Public Prosecutor, on the contrary, would be based on a *vertical* enforcement system in which the European Public Prosecutor would be hierarchically superior to national prosecutorial and investigative authorities. The latter would be obliged to co-operate with the European Public Prosecutor. Traditional co-operation procedures would be substituted by direct action by the European Public Prosecutor on the territory of the Member States, and consequently there would be no need for procedures such as extradition, judicial assistance, and so on. Orders of the European Public Prosecutor, or warrants delivered by national judges on the request of the European Public Prosecutor, would be directly enforceable throughout the European Community. There would, in the vertical system, be no grounds for refusal or for non-execution, as they exist in the case of horizontal co-operation between states, even in the post-Tampere era where mutual recognition is becoming the rule.

B. Background to the Proposal

The idea of a European Prosecutor was developed in 1997 by a group of academics of different Member States who, after conducting various studies

[33] Flore, 'D'un réseau judiciaire européen à une juridiction pénale européenne: Eurojust et l'émergence d'un système de justice pénale', in de Kerchove and Weyemberg (eds), *supra* note 21.

for the European Commission (Directorate General of the Budget) and the European Parliament, came to the conclusion that the current system of purely national investigation and prosecution of crimes against the financial interests of the EC ('EC fraud') was totally inadequate. They proposed the introduction of a *Corpus Juris* for certain financial crimes against the Community. The *Corpus Juris* defines these crimes and states a number of general principles of criminal law relating to these crimes as in penal codes. It also contains detailed rules of procedure that would govern the operation of a European Public Prosecution service, such as a code of criminal procedure.

The *Corpus Juris* as proposed by the experts leaves the national court systems intact, but 'Europeanizes' the function of the public prosecutor. The idea is not to have European criminal courts, but only a European Public Prosecutor. The first version of the *Corpus Juris* was published in 1997[34] and subjected to a feasibility study in the fifteen Member States in the next two years. In 1999, at a scientific conference held at the European University Institute in Florence, the proposal was finalized in the so-called '*Corpus Juris* 2000'.[35]

It was taken up by the Committee of Independent Experts who, after the collective resignation of the European Commission in 1999, proposed the European Public Prosecutor as part of its recommendations for reform.[36] The Committee of Wise Persons (Dehaene, Simon, and von Weizsäcker) in its 1999 report written in preparation of the 2000 Intergovernmental Conference, called for consideration of this recommendation.[37] The European Commission formally proposed the creation of a European Public Prosecutor in its Additional Communication to the Intergovernmental Conference of 29 September 2000 in which it called for an amendment to the EC Treaty (a new Article 280(a)) which would form the legal basis for the European Public Prosecutor.[38]

Meanwhile, the European Council of Tampere (1999) had proposed the introduction of Eurojust and, unsurprisingly, the Intergovernmental Conference in Nice (December 2000) did not accept the Commission's more ambitious proposal to introduce a European Public Prosecutor in the EC Treaty (Article 280(a)). It decided to go forward with Eurojust instead, duly incorporating it in Articles 29 and 32 of the Treaty on European Union.

[34] M. Delmas-Marty (ed), *Corpus Introducing Penal Provisions for the Purpose of the Financial Interests of the European Union* (Paris: Editions Economica, 1997).

[35] M. Delmas-Marty and J.A.E. Vervaele (eds), *The Implementation of the Corpus Juris in the Member States, Penal Provisions for the Protection of European Finances* (Groningen: Intersentia, 2000–2001).

[36] European Parliament, Committee of Independent Experts, Second Report on Reform of the Commission. Analysis of current practice and proposals for tackling mismanagement, irregularities and fraud, 10 September 1999.

[37] Para.2.2.6 of the Report, European Commission, Secretariat General, SEC(1999)2000.

[38] See *supra* note 16.

This did not mean that the idea of a European Public Prosecutor had been abandoned. In December 2001, the Commission published a Green Paper on the Criminal Law Protection of the Community's Financial Interests and the Establishment of a European Public Prosecutor,[39] and in May 2002, the Commission reiterated its proposal to introduce a European Public Prosecutor in its Communication to Working Group X of the 'Convention' presided over by Mr. Valéry Giscard d'Estaing.[40] In its final report, Working Group X mentions that several of its members were in favour of introducing a European Public Prosecutor. Two governments expressed their support of the idea,[41] and, as we have seen, it is given tentative backing in the draft Constitutional Treaty.[42]

C. Sources

At this stage, the European Public Prosecutor is only a proposal, not part of positive law. The following paragraphs describe the proposal and explain how the European Public Prosecutor would operate in practice.

The sources referred to below are two-fold: first, *Corpus Juris 2000*, which is a doctrinal proposal, and secondly, the *European Commission's formal proposals* as expressed in the 2000 Communication to the Intergovernmental Conference, the 2001 Green Paper and the 2002 Communication to the 'Convention'.[43]

Corpus Juris 2000 is conceived of in the same general manner as national penal codes and codes of criminal procedure. It starts by defining the offences (part I—criminal law, special part), and setting out the rules of general criminal law governing these offences (part II—criminal liability and sanctions). It goes on to formulate the rules of criminal procedure governing the European Public Prosecutor in the preparatory stage of the proceedings and in the judgment stage (part III). The final part is on the complementarity of the *Corpus Juris* and national criminal law (part IV).

Translating this doctrinal proposal into draft Community legislation, the European Commission proposes the following approach. The essential

[39] Commission of the European Communities, Green Paper on criminal-law protection of the financial interests of the community and the establishment of a European prosecutor, 11 December 2001, COM(2001)715 final.

[40] Communication from the Commission, forwarded by Mr Barnier and Mr Vitorino, members of the Convention: 'Communication from the Commission to the Convention, 22 May 2002: A project for the European Union', 3 September 2002, CONV 229/02, CONTRIB 78, p. 13.

[41] See *supra* notes 18 and 19.

[42] *Supra* note 1.

[43] See also C. Van den Wyngaert, 'The Protection of the Financial Interests of the EU in the Candidate States. Perspectives on the Future of Judicial Integration in Europe', 3 *ERA-Forum* (2001) 2.

characteristics of the European Public Prosecutor should be laid down in the EC Treaty, by introducing a new Article 280a, just after the current Article 280 EC on fraud and other illegal activities affecting the Community's financial interests. The general conditions governing the performance of the functions of the European Public Prosecutor are to be further defined in secondary legislation, particularly the facts constituting criminal offences relating to fraud, the rules of procedure applicable to the European Public Prosecutor, the rules governing the admissibility of evidence, and the rules applicable to the judicial review of procedural measures taken by the European Public Prosecutor (draft Article 280a(3)). These points are further elaborated in the Commission's Green Paper of 2001.

D. Status and Composition

The European Public Prosecutor would be the specialized judicial body, independent of the Commission and the Member States (Article 18 of the *Corpus Juris* and paragraph 4.1.1. of the Green Paper). It would be composed of the Chief Public Prosecutor with a centralized staff in Brussels, and of Deputy European Public Prosecutors in the national capitals.

The *Chief European Public Prosecutor* would be appointed by the Council acting by qualified majority, on a proposal from the Commission, and with assent of the Parliament. His term of office would be a non-renewable term of six years. In case of serious misconduct in the performance of his functions, he could be removed from office by the European Court of Justice, on application by the European Parliament, the Council, or the Commission (draft Article 280a EC). The European Public Prosecutor would thus be a 'first pillar' organ.

Deputy European Public Prosecutors would be appointed by the Chief European Public Prosecutor on nomination of their state of origin. Candidates for that function would be national public prosecutors. Whether Deputy European Public Prosecutors would retain their national status as prosecutors or whether they would obtain an autonomous Community status is still an open question. Concomitantly, the question remains whether the office of Deputy European Public Prosecutor could be combined with a function as a domestic public prosecutor (Green Paper, paragraph 4.2.1.).[44]

The deputy prosecutors would be integrated in the national criminal justice systems and would actually bring the cases to trial. They would be subordinate to the European Chief Public Prosecutor within the organizational hierarchy. As a whole, the European Public Prosecution service would be *indivisible* in the sense that acts, undertaken by members of the European Public Prosecutor's service would be deemed to have been undertaken by the

[44] See also *infra*, p. 223, sect. 3G.

chief European Public Prosecutor (Article 18(3) a *Corpus Juris*). They would also be *inter-dependent* in the sense that deputy public prosecutors would be obliged to assist each other (Article 18(3)b).

E. Crimes for which the European Public Prosecutor is Competent

1. Competence Ratione Materiae

Under the current proposals, the mandate of the European Public Prosecutor and his deputies would be a limited number of offences against the Community's financial interests. It relates, not to offences committed *in* the European Community, but to offences committed *against* the European Community.

In the *Corpus Juris* these offences are: (1) fraud affecting the financial interests of the European Communities and assimilated offences; (2) market rigging; (3) money laundering; (4) conspiracy; (5) corruption; (7) abuse of office; and (8) disclosure of secrets pertaining to one's office. Some of these offences had already been defined in the *acquis communautaire*, for example EU fraud, money laundering, and corruption; others, like market rigging and abuse of office, are new.

Draft Article 280a EC as proposed by the Commission does not describe or enumerate the financial offences that would come under the European Public Prosecutor's jurisdiction but leaves this to secondary legislation (see paragraph 3(a) of draft Article 280a). In its Green Paper, the Commission refers to the same offences as those listed above, adding euro counterfeiting to the list.

The reason why the jurisdiction of the European Public Prosecutor is limited in such a way is that the research mandate of the group of academics that drew up the *Corpus Juris* was itself limited to financial offences only. The mandate emanated from the (Directorate General for the Budget of the) European Commission and the European Parliament and arose from the concern over major fraud circuits affecting the Community budget and remaining unpunished for technical or political reasons. The elaboration of a legal mechanism for the Community to protect its own financial interests in a more direct manner was considered as a priority as well as a duty to the European citizen. Respect for the subsidiarity principle was another reason to limit the research project and the recommendations that flew from it to financial offences only.

2. Competence Ratione Loci*: 15 = 1*

The European Public Prosecutor's competence *ratione loci* would extend to the whole territory of the Union: for the purposes of investigation, prosecution, trial, or execution concerning *Corpus Juris* crimes, the territory of the Member States of the Union constitutes a single legal area. Accordingly, prosecutions for such crimes can be brought before the courts of any of the Member States of the Union. The criteria determining the choice of the state where the case will actually be tried are set out in Article 26 of the *Corpus Juris*, which states that each case is judged in the Member State which seems appropriate in the interests of the good administration of justice. Article 26(2) sets out the principal criteria for the choice of the jurisdiction, which are (a) the state where the greater part of evidence is found; (b) the state of residence or of nationality of the accused (or the principal persons accused); and (c) the state where the economic impact of the offence is the greatest.

Conflicts of jurisdiction between two or more Member States are settled by the European Court of Justice on a request of the European Public Prosecutor or a national judicial authority or the accused (Article 28(1)(c) and (d) respectively).

F. Powers and Tasks of the European Public Prosecutor

The European Public Prosecutor would act not as a mere facilitator or co-ordinator of inter-state co-operation, but as a real player in the criminal procedure. He would be a central steering mechanism with operational powers in the investigation and prosecution of EU crimes. The *Corpus Juris* system 'Europeanizes' investigation and public prosecution of EU crimes, which means that the European Public Prosecutor has all the investigative and prosecutorial powers that would normally fall to a national public prosecutor. His powers are set out in Articles 20–24 of the *Corpus Juris.* They include investigation and prosecution of EU crimes and the execution of sentences imposed for such crimes. Draft Article 280a EC as proposed by the Commission does not describe the powers of the European Public Prosecutor but leaves this to secondary legislation (see paragraph 3(b) of draft Article 280a)). The Commission's Green Paper further discusses the question.

1. *Investigation*

Under the *Corpus Juris* system, the European Public Prosecutor has to be informed by national judicial and administrative authorities of all acts that could constitute one of the crimes for which he is competent. The European Public Prosecutor can also be seised of a case as a result of denunciation or of notification by the European Commission (Article 19(1)). The European Public Prosecutor would be responsible for overseeing investigations and their delegation to the Deputy European Public

Prosecutors. He would co-ordinate investigations undertaken by the Deputies as well as by national investigative authorities. He would have the right to call in cases (Article 20(2)). In general terms, the European Public Prosecutor would have a power to perform all investigative acts that do not require coercion. Accordingly, the European Public Prosecutor and Deputies could exercise a number of powers autonomously, without a judicial warrant. Examples are the questioning of the accused, the collection of documents or computer-held information and the hearing of witnesses who agree to co-operate with the law (Article 20(2)(a), (b) and (e)).

Coercive measures would need the authorization of a judge, as it is in most national criminal justice systems. In the *Corpus Juris*, this judge is called the *judge of freedoms*. The idea would be for each Member State to identify the judicial authority that would be competent to deliver warrants at the request of the European Public Prosecutor or Deputies. Depending on the legislation of the Member State concerned, this could be an investigating judge, a pre-trial court or a judge especially appointed for that purpose. As explained above, the 'Europeanization' of functions would be limited to the prosecutorial functions. Judges, also in the stage of pre-trial investigations, would remain national.

Throughout investigations carried out by the Public Prosecutor and Deputies, the judge of freedoms would control the legality and the regularity of the measures requested and ensure that the principles of necessity and proportionality are respected (Article 25(2)). If coercive measures need to be taken, the European Public Prosecutor or Deputy must apply for a warrant of the national judge of freedoms. Examples are arrest warrants (Article 25(3)) and searches and seizures (Article 20(2)(d)). To obtain the warrants, the European Public Prosecutor and Deputies may directly invoke the jurisdiction of the competent national authority. Warrants issued by the judge of freedoms can be enforced throughout the whole territory of the Union (Article 24(1)(b)). This power of direct action is the cornerstone of the European Public Prosecutor system. It is the feature that distinguishes it from the traditional, 'horizontal' co-operation systems, where states cannot proceed to investigative acts on the territories of other states: they need to follow the procedure of letters rogatory, which may be time-consuming and unsuccessful. The European Public Prosecutor's powers of direct action would make letters rogatory redundant.

When this system was proposed in 1997, it was quite revolutionary. It still is to the extent that direct action would emanate from a European judicial officer and his deputies. Yet it is less revolutionary today with regard to direct enforcement of orders emanating from national authorities, for in the meantime there has been a shift from traditional co-operation to mutual recognition and direct enforcement in the aftermath of Tampere. The European

Arrest Warrant[45] and, *de lege ferenda*, European orders to freeze evidence and property and European orders for obtaining evidence introduce direct enforcement into horizontal co-operation.[46] From this perspective, the gulf between the European Public Prosecutor and the legal framework of Eurojust has probably narrowed.

2. *Prosecution*

The decision whether or not to prosecute in a particular case is taken by the European Public Prosecutor (Article 19 of the *Corpus Juris*). In the *Corpus Juris* proposal, the European Public Prosecutor would always prosecute where it appears that one of the *Corpus Juris* crimes has been committed. The *Corpus Juris* thus adopts the principle of *legality* of prosecutions. Only in a few cases, which are enumerated in Article 19(4), could he decide not to prosecute.

When the investigation has come to an end, it is for the European Public Prosecutor to decide whether or not to bring the case to court (Article 21(1)(1)). The decision to bring a case to court is verified by a judge of liberties. It is that judge who actually seises the trial court before which the accused is brought (Article 25(3)(2)).

As the *Corpus Juris* 'Europeanizes' only the function of the prosecutor, the courts to which the cases are referred will be national courts. The composition of these courts and the proceedings will be determined by the national law of the state where the case is brought to court. The law to be applied by these courts will be the *Corpus Juris*, where necessary supplemented by national law (Article 35—complementarity of national law).

3. *Applicable Law*

Whereas Eurojust does not need harmonized legislation defining offences, sanctions, and procedures to investigate and prosecute them, the European Public Prosecutor, on the contrary, would require unified legislation in the limited field of the crimes over which he has jurisdiction: uniform definitions of crimes and penalties would be necessary, as well as principles of general criminal law relating to these crimes (liability of legal persons, attempt, complicity, accumulation of sentences).

The *Corpus Juris* offers an example of how these notions could be defined. In practical terms, they could be introduced, as in the Commission's proposal for a new Article 280(a), in EU legislation such as regulations or directives (or their equivalent in the new European Constitution). While this has the disadvantage of requiring legislative time and energy, the advantage is that all courts throughout the Union will, for Eurocrimes, apply the same concepts of

[45] *Supra* note 7. [46] *Supra* note 30.

crime and the same sanctions. The result is a greater transparency for Euro-crimes. The unified parts of the law would, quite obviously, not cover the whole field of criminal law and criminal procedure. National courts applying '*Corpus Juris* law' would still apply their national laws in areas that are not covered by the *Corpus Juris* (Article 35).

The Green Paper and the *Corpus Juris* also address the question of evidence. The burden of proof is, quite obviously, with the prosecution. The accused, whose innocence is presumed, is not obliged to contribute, directly or indirectly, to establishing his own guilt (Article 31 of the *Corpus Juris*). Normally, the evidence must be presented at the trial court, during a public hearing. The *Corpus Juris*, however, introduces a number of means of evidence that can be used instead of direct testimony by witnesses or defendants at their trial, i.e. the 'European deposition' and the 'European Interrogation Report', which is admissible evidence throughout the Union. In other words, the law of evidence would be unified on this particular point. A *European deposition* is the testimony of a witness recorded by the European Public Prosecutor who is examined before a judge in the presence of a defence lawyer who must be given the opportunity to ask questions. This deposition must be recorded on video. A 'European interrogation report' is a video-recorded examination of the accused in the presence of his lawyer (who has received the investigation file prior to the examination) (Article 32).

As observed above in relation to investigation, all this is less revolutionary today than when it was proposed in 1997. In the post-Tampere era, direct enforcement will probably be introduced into horizontal co-operation. Examples are the European Arrest Warrant and the proposal to introduce European orders for obtaining evidence.

Evidence illegally obtained must be excluded. This is evidence obtained in violation of the fundamental rights enshrined in the European Convention of Human Rights, in violation of *Corpus Juris* rules or in violation of applicable national law. Exclusion is not mandatory, but will apply only when the admission of the evidence would undermine the fairness of the proceedings.

G. Hybrid Cases

As noted above, the *Corpus Juris* and the Commission's Green Paper on a European Public Prosecutor do not propose the establishment of European criminal courts, only of a European public prosecutor. Prosecutions for EU crimes would still be brought before national courts. As the European Public Prosecutor would be hierarchically superior to national prosecutorial officers, all cases would have to be deferred to him and the decision whether or not to prosecute would be his.

However, the superiority of the European Public Prosecutor does not resolve all problems. What to do with hybrid cases, i.e. cases in which a person faces charges, not only for '*Corpus Juris* Crimes', but also for national crimes? For example: a person could be suspected of subsidy fraud for having fraudulently obtained, for one and the same economic activity, national and European subsidies. Or a person accused of VAT fraud could be charged with both national tax fraud and EU tax fraud, as VAT duties always comprise a national (99 per cent) and a European part (1 per cent). In practice, the majority of cases are likely to be hybrid cases; 'purely' European crimes would be the exception rather than the rule.

National courts would, in hybrid cases, apply both EU law and national law. But who would prosecute the case, i.e. who would plead the case for the prosecution in a trial before a national judge? There is an obvious need for distributing such cases between the European Public Prosecutor and national prosecution authorities. How this should be done is still an open question. Clearly, double jeopardy should be avoided: the same conduct should not give rise to more than one prosecution.[47] Also, conflicts of jurisdiction between different national courts hearing cases in parallel should be avoided, not only for reasons of fairness but also for the sake of effectiveness.

But even assuming that both parts of a hybrid case could be brought in one and the same proceeding before one trial judge, who should be the prosecutor: the European Public Prosecutor, the national public prosecutor, or both? How are conflicts between national and European authorities concerning the prosecution policy to be adopted in fraud cases to be avoided? The Commission's Green Paper discusses a number of possible answers but does not yet take a position. One answer would be to have one of the two levels (national and European) refer the case to the other, depending on whether the offence affects principally national or European interests. Another solution could be a joint prosecutions scheme, in which national and European public prosecutors would share the prosecution.

4. EUROJUST AND THE EUROPEAN PUBLIC PROSECUTOR: ARE THEY COMPATIBLE?

A. Which is the Better Model: Eurojust or the European Public Prosecutor?

Eurojust has been functioning for only a very short time, and the European Public Prosecutor only exists on paper. The comparison between the two can therefore only be theoretical. The success of Eurojust will depend on the powers that its members actually receive from the Member States. These are likely to vary from one state to the other, with the risk of a distinction

[47] See also Art. 50 of the Charter of Fundamental Rights in the European Union.

growing between 'super members' and other Eurojust members. Eurojust will also be dependent on the practical input it will receive from states. It will have no autonomous powers of investigation, nor is there an obligation on Member States or EU institutions to communicate information to Eurojust. In cases that have not been brought to Eurojust's attention by one of the Member States, its powers will be very restricted. Eurojust's college, which may decide on priorities and policies to follow with respect to the crimes coming under its jurisdiction, will only be able to do so if it has a general picture of the investigative and prosecutorial needs, which it will only have if all Member States supply it with the necessary information.

Eurojust cannot oblige states to co-operate. It can ask Member States to act in a particular way, but has no powers to oblige them to do so: it is still for national authorities, not for Eurojust, to decide whether or not to investigate and prosecute a case. Even requests emanating from Eurojust acting as a college do not bind the Member States: refusal is still an option, but the Member State concerned must give reasons. Negative injunctions (orders not to prosecute) issued by national governments would still be possible. In the case of fraud offences and corruption involving politicians, such injunctions have seriously impeded horizontal co-operation in the past. Under Eurojust, which operates on the basis of the current instruments on international co-operation (e.g. extradition, judicial assistance, transfer of proceedings), the traditional exceptions to these co-operation schemes would still apply. States may continue to rely on conditions (e.g. double criminality) and grounds for refusal (e.g. political offence exception, nationality exception, exception for fiscal offences, *ordre public* exception, *sub judice* exception) to refuse co-operation with other states, even where this co-operation is brokered by Eurojust.

All this would not hinder the European Public Prosecutor. He would not have the 'input problems' because national judicial and prosecutorial authorities would be obliged to communicate information about crimes coming under his jurisdiction. It would be for the European Public Prosecutor to decide whether or not to take on a case, which would allow him to develop a policy determining which cases are to be investigated and prosecuted on a domestic level and on a European level respectively. The European Public Prosecutor and his delegates would not base their activities on the current co-operation schemes, and would therefore not be hampered by the conditions and grounds for refusing co-operation by states. He would have operational powers: he would, together with his deputies, decide whether or not to investigate or prosecute cases. The European Public Prosecutor would have direct investigatory powers and could directly prosecute suspects in the territory of all the Member States. As observed above, post-Tampere developments towards direct execution of European Orders, e.g. the European

Arrest Warrant[48] and the European Freezing Order,[49] would lessen the gulf between the EPP model and Eurojust.

In terms of effectiveness, the European Public Prosecutor seems to be the better model, at least in theory. It would, however, presuppose that governments are willing to give up a great portion of their sovereignty and that national investigation and prosecution authorities are willing to co-operate with the European Public Prosecutor.

B. Is there a Need for a European Public Prosecutor?

It is premature to assess the functioning of Eurojust today and to say whether or not it is an appropriate instrument in the fight against crime. In the wake of the Tampere milestones,[50] many conditions and obstacles to classic international co-operation schemes are in the process of being reduced or abandoned. The European Arrest Warrant is an example of legislation giving effect to number 35 of the Tampere milestones,[51] and so is the Framework Decision on Joint Investigation Teams (Tampere milestones, number 45).[52] Meanwhile, the Commission's deliberation in preparation of draft legislation on the mutual recognition of orders to obtain evidence is another step in the direction of Tampere (number 36 of the milestones).[53] Eurojust could play an active part in the practical operation of this legislation, for example by brokering joint investigation teams and perhaps also by supervising their execution.[54] Only time can tell whether there is a real *added value* in Eurojust, as compared with already existing co-operation schemes such as the European Judicial Network and the liaison magistrates. It will also show whether Eurojust will live up to expectations, or whether there is, for some crimes such as fraud and terrorism, a need to proceed in the direction of judicial integration between the Member States.

The European Public Prosecutor model is an obvious step in this direction. The crucial question is whether there is a need for such a radical reform at this moment in time. According to some, this need exists and is established by empirical data. Others dispute it. Judging from the public hearings on the Commission's Green Paper,[55] many governments seem to oppose the very

[48] *Supra* note 7.

[49] *Supra* note 30.

[50] *Supra* note 12.

[51] *Supra* note 7.

[52] Council Framework Decision of 13 June 2002 on joint investigation teams, OJ 2002 L162/1,

[53] *Supra* note 30.

[54] See *infra*, sect. 4D.

[55] Conclusion of the Public Hearing on the European Public Prosecutor, 17 September 2002, IP/02/1315. See also the contributions at: http://europa.eu.int/comm/anti_fraud/

idea of a public prosecutor on a Union-wide level.[56] Therefore, although it was ultimately included in the draft Constitutional Treaty prepared by the European Convention,[57] the chances of the system being introduced in the new European Constitution seemed initially to be rather faint. Nevertheless, practitioners speaking at the same Commission hearings seem to hold a more nuanced view and tend to think that, in the medium term, a European Public Prosecutor would be a step forward. As a matter of fact, the very idea of creating a European Public Prosecutor originates from an outcry of practitioners publicly complaining that the current international co-operation mechanisms are insufficient to investigate and suppress financial crimes efficiently: the first was the Geneva appeal of 1 October 1996, followed by the Strasbourg manifesto of 20 October 2002 and the Trier Declaration of 15 September 2002.[58]

It may well be that in the years to come, as a result of increased economic and political integration between the Member States, the need for introducing a European Public Prosecutor will be clearer than it is today.

C. Combining the Two?

In theory, Eurojust and the European Public Prosecutor could function alongside one another. In terms of jurisdiction *ratione materiae*, they could be complementary: Eurojust would co-ordinate and facilitate intergovernmental co-operation for 'Eurojust crimes', the European Public Prosecutor would have direct investigation and prosecution powers for '*Corpus Juris* crimes' or other crimes to be added to this list, e.g. terrorism and trade in human beings. In practice, however, setting up yet another organ in addition to the already existing ones (Eurojust, the European Judicial Network, Europol, OLAF, and so on) would only add to the proliferation of institutions and bodies of the EU and therefore does not seem to be a step in the right direction. It would only increase the risk of turf wars between the various institutions and would require consultation and co-ordination. Too much time and energy would be wasted in co-ordinating the co-ordinators.

Would it be possible, then, to combine Eurojust and the European Public Prosecutor in one single institutional agency? This is clearly the option contemplated by the draft Constitutional Treaty, which envisages the

green_paper/public_hearing/index_en.html; European Parliament, Committee on Budgetary Control, Hearing on the Green Paper on the protection under criminal law of the financial interests of the Community and the establishment of a European Prosecutor, 5 November 2002.

[56] But not all: see the joint communication of the French and German governments, *supra* note 19.

[57] *Supra*, note 1.

[58] Quoted in the Commission's Green Paper, *supra* note 39.

establishment of a European Public Prosecutor's Office 'from Eurojust'.[59] Yet this, too, seems to be difficult, because its status is completely different. Eurojust's powers, as an intergovernmental body, depend on what powers the Member States attribute to their respective national members. Eurojust members remain national magistrates, owing obedience to the national authorities of their respective states. Their status, term of office, salary, and so on are determined by national law. The European Public Prosecutor, on the contrary, would be a judicial office of the European Union with a status determined by EU law and with powers based on European law. This office would act in the general interest of the EU and would take no instructions from national authorities, or from the European Commission.

One could perhaps think in terms of a graduated solution, such as the one proposed in 1999 by the Commission of Independent Experts in their report after the collective resignation of Santer's Commission. In this report, the experts proposed to introduce a European Public Prosecutor in three stages.[60] Building along the lines of this proposal, and taking into account the fact that in the meantime Eurojust has been introduced, this three-stage approach could be construed as follows.

In a *first* stage, the European Public Prosecutor could be set up with a limited competence, only comprising 'internal' EC fraud (i.e. financial crimes such as fraud, corruption, and money laundering by European civil servants). This European Public Prosecutor could share his secretariat with Eurojust (in the same way as the European Judicial Network has its secretariat incorporated in Eurojust).[61] In a *second* stage, Eurojust members would, while retaining their status as national prosecutors, also act as European prosecutors with special competence for the crimes for which Eurojust is competent. These national prosecutors would co-operate with the European Public Prosecutor and have operational powers in their respective territories, i.e. each Eurojust member in the Member State by whom he has been seconded. For practical purposes, they would act through their respective national contact points who could, depending on the state, be the national European Judicial Network member or the national correspondent of the Eurojust member. In a *third* stage, Eurojust members would become part of the European Public Prosecutor's Service, and would have jurisdiction over the whole EU. The European Public Prosecutor could become the General Prosecutor presiding over a service composed of the (former) Eurojust members. The national correspondents in the Member States could become

[59] *Supra* note 1.

[60] See *supra* note 36. W. Van Gerven, 'Constitutional Conditions for a Public Prosecutor's Office at the European Level', 3 *European Journal of Crime, Criminal Law and Criminal Justice* (2000) 296. See also S. Brammertz, 'Eurojust: parquet européen de la première génération?', *supra* note 21.

[61] *Supra*, sect. A.

the deputy European Public Prosecutors. An empirical example of such a gradual introduction of a centralized prosecution service can be found in Belgium. In the late 1980s, the need arose for a better co-ordination of the national prosecutorial services (which are twenty-seven in total) and a new institution was set up, the 'national magistrates' (1997). The task of these national magistrates was one of co-ordinating investigations that were carried out by prosecutors of more than one district. They had no operational powers of their own; they could only facilitate and co-ordinate the actions of the local public prosecutors in the same way as Eurojust can do today. In 2002, implementing a political agreement made in 1998, the national magistrates were abolished and substituted by a 'federal public prosecutor' and his deputies.

The federal prosecutor retains the powers of co-ordination and facilitation of his predecessors, but also has direct investigative and prosecutorial competences throughout Belgian territory. The law lists a number of crimes for which the federal prosecutor is competent, but this does not mean that these crimes are always investigated and prosecuted on a federal level. If they can be investigated and prosecuted locally, it will be for the local prosecutor to handle the case (subsidiarity principle). The federal prosecutor will, in principle, only intervene in cases involving more than one district or in cases that require specialized investigative skills that are not present in the local prosecutorial services (speciality principle). Although the federal prosecutor is not superior to the local prosecutor in the judicial hierarchy, he nevertheless has the right to call in cases (right of *evocation*).[62] *Mutatis mutandis*, Eurojust could, in the course of time, be gradually transformed into a European Public Prosecutor's office.[63]

D. Eurojust, the European Public Prosecutor, and National Sovereignty

Eurojust is, quite clearly, the more modest of the two models. It does not require Member States to change their domestic legislation and it is based on the *acquis* of the already existing instruments of the Council of Europe (e.g. extradition, judicial assistance) and of the European Union (e.g. European arrest warrant, joint investigation teams). It does not imply a transfer of sovereign powers (investigation and prosecution of crimes) to the EU. Quite

[62] Code of Civil Procedure, art. 144(3)(3).

[63] S. Brammertz and Berthelet, 'Eurojust et le réseau judiciaire européen: concurrence ou complémentarité', *Revue de Droit Pénal et de Criminologie* (2002) 389; Berthelet and Chevallier-Govers, *supra* note 21; Flore, *supra* note 21; Brammertz, 'Eurojust: parquet européen de la première génération?', *supra* note 21; D. Flore, 'D'un réseau judiciaire européen à une juridiction pénale européenne: Eurojust et l'émergence d'un système de justice pénale', in de Kerchove and Weyembergh (eds), *supra* note 15, at 9; S. White, 'The European Prosecutor: Extension of Eurojust or "Prolongation" of the *Corpus Juris* proposals?', in ibid. at 47.

obviously, the introduction of a European Public Prosecutor would be a radical departure from state sovereignty in the field of the criminal law. Many Member States would have to change their constitutions for that purpose.[64] This is a political choice to be made by the Member States. It would require a willingness to proceed towards further judicial integration, possibly in the context of a federation rather than an intergovernmental organization. Meanwhile, the 'European Convention' is divided on the sort of constitution that Europe needs, a (more) federal or a (more) confederal constitution.

The question of transferring sovereignty to a body of the European Community or European Union in the field of the criminal law has two sides. First, there is the question of the human rights protection in criminal investigations and prosecutions. Secondly, there is the state's power to decide whether or not to prosecute certain criminal offences. Often, the two are conflated with an emphasis on the former.

The protection of the individual's procedural rights is, obviously, part of the larger debate on human rights protection in criminal matters in the European Union. The proposition that the rights of defendants are better protected under national law is not necessarily correct, and may flow from a certain degree of chauvinism that states have about their own criminal justice systems. Even though human rights protection mainly occurs in the domestic legal order as opposed to the EU legal order, it does not follow that this protection could not be shared with or transferred to the EU legal order. All depends on what human rights one is talking about and what institutions (national or European) are the most protective of the rights in question. This question is intertwined with the more general debate about whether the European Union should become a party to the European Convention on Human Rights.[65]

The state's power to prosecute certain criminal offences and, more particularly, *not* to prosecute is the more delicate dimension in the debate about sovereignty. In certain Member States, high-ranking politicians have shielded themselves against corruption charges by ordering the prosecution to drop the case, by providing special procedures, or by adopting amnesty statutes to block prosecution.[66] All this would no longer be possible for EU crimes, were the European Public Prosecutor to be introduced for these crimes. On the contrary, the system as it is proposed would be based on the legality of

[64] Some states have changed their constitutions in order to become parties to the Rome Statute for an International Criminal Court, which also has an international public prosecutor. See the example of France: Loi constitutionelle n° 99–568 du 8 juillet 1999 insérant, au titre VI de la Constitution, un article 53–2 et relative à la Cour pénale internationale, *Journal Officiel*, n° 157, 9 July 1999.

[65] See further *infra*, sect. 4E.

[66] Italy and France are examples. See *The Economist* of 20 July 2002, at 27.

prosecutions (as opposed to the principle of 'opportunity'): as a matter of principle, all (EC fraud) crimes that are brought to the attention of the European Public Prosecutor would be investigated and prosecuted. Again, the answers to the questions raised in this section depend on the political choice that states will make in the 'Convention' and in the Intergovernmental Conference that will follow.

E. Eurojust, the European Public Prosecutor, and Democratic Legitimacy

A crucial concern is that of the democratic legitimacy of the European Public Prosecutor. Most states that have a public prosecutor have made provisions in their constitutions concerning the prosecutor's status. In some states, the prosecutor belongs to the executive state power, in others the public prosecutor is a judicial authority.[67] In the discussion about Eurojust and the European Public Prosecutor, this question is part of the general constitutional debate on the division and allocation of powers in the new European Constitution.

At the crux of this debate is of course the question whether the European Public Prosecutor would be completely independent. The European Public Prosecutor proposed in the *Corpus Juris* and in the Commission's Green Paper (paragraph 4.1) would be independent from national governments and Community institutions, yet accountable to the European Parliament and liable to dismissal by the European Court of Justice where he neglects his duties or abuses his powers. This status of total independence is not as analogous to national systems as it may seem. In many states, public prosecutors have to obey their government's instructions, which may go either way: orders to prosecute (positive injunctions) and orders not to prosecute (negative injunctions). For these states, a transfer of powers to the European Public Prosecutor would have far-reaching political implications.

Would a European Public Prosecutor be less 'democratic' than a unit of national prosecutors like Eurojust? As with all the questions raised here, the answer depends on the general institutional architecture of the Union and the outcome of the 'Convention' and the IGC. Will the Union be an intergovernmental organization, a confederation or a federation, or something in between?

In a recent essay on the search for legitimacy in EU constitutional arrangements, Professor K. Lenaerts draws upon a useful distinction between output legitimacy and input legitimacy. This distinction is very useful

[67] See, generally, C. Van den Wyngaert, C. Gane *et al.* (eds), *Criminal Procedure Systems in the European Community* (London/Brussels/Dublin/Edinburgh: Butterworth, 1993).

for the present debate. *Output legitimacy* refers to 'the extent to which citizens see their interests and desires mirrored in the outcomes of the public processes and therefore accept and support the political order as "right" .... *Input legitimacy* addresses the question of direct legitimisation of political powers through the participation of the citizens or their elected representatives in transparent decision-making and constitution-making processes'.[68]

In matters of criminal law, *input legitimacy* is of course crucial because it coincides with the principle of legality of crimes and sanctions, which is recognized in all international[69] and European Human Rights instruments,[70] including the European Human Rights Charter.[71] It requires the intervention of a democratically elected body in the creation of criminal offences and sanctions. *Nullum crimen, nulla poena sine lege.* From that perspective, there is a clear deficit in the European Union, as it exists today, especially in the field of justice and home affairs. There is a need for a greater role for national parliaments and/or the European Parliament in the legislative process, all depending on the centre of gravity that the new structure will have: more intergovernmental or more European.

The other aspect of democratic legitimacy, *output legitimacy*, may be of more direct relevance to the debate. It raises the question which of the two, Eurojust or the European Public Prosecutor, is the more effective in reaching the objective of creating a space of freedom, justice, and security in the European Union. It is impossible to answer this question at this moment in time. In theory, however, the European Public Prosecutor seems the more effective of the two models. Meanwhile, it remains to be seen whether Eurojust will be an adequate instrument in the prevention and suppression of crime in the European Union, and will fulfil the expectations (interests and desires) of citizens claiming protection against crime in the European Union. It may well be that Eurojust lacks the powers that are necessary to attain this objective. From that perspective, the European Public Prosecutor may, in terms of output legitimacy, be more legitimate than Eurojust.

[68] K. Lenaerts and Desomer, 'New Models of Constitution-Making in Europe: The Quest for Legitimacy', 39 *Common Market Law Review* (2002) 1217. See also K. Lenaerts, 'Comment Simplifier les Instruments d'action de l'Union?/How to Simplify the Instruments of the Union?', Groupe de travail/Working Group IX '"Simplification" de la Convention européenne/Simplification of the European Convention', 17 October 2002, WG IX -WD 07. For an earlier use of this distinction which inspired Professor Lenaerts' analysis see F. Scharpf, *Governing in Europe: Effective and Democratic?* (Oxford: OUP, 1999).

[69] International Covenant on Civil and Political Rights, 16 December 1966, Art. 15.

[70] European Convention on Human Rights and Fundamental Freedoms, Art. 7.

[71] Charter of Fundamental Rights of the European Union, Art. 49.

F. Eurojust, the European Public Prosecutor, and Human Rights Protection

Like the question of democratic legitimacy, the answer to the question of Human Rights protection under both systems (Eurojust and the European Public Prosecutor) is predicated on the outcome of the general debate in this respect. Will the Union have a complete catalogue of Human Rights in its Constitution that goes beyond the Charter adopted in 2000, or will it continue to take the Convention on the Protection of Human Rights and Fundamental Freedoms of the Council of Europe as its primary legal basis in the field of human rights protection? Will the Union as such adhere to the Council of Europe's Convention, and will the EU be justiciable before the European Court of Human Rights in Strasbourg? There is no room here to analyse or even summarize this debate for the purposes of this essay.[72] It is, however, very relevant for both Eurojust and the European Public Prosecutor.

Under the classic horizontal co-operation system in criminal matters, only states are accountable before the European Court of Human Rights in Strasbourg. Today, Eurojust operates under this system. This means, here and now, that human rights violations under the horizontal co-operation model, as facilitated by Eurojust, may only give rise to applications against the Member States, not against the relevant European institutions or bodies (e.g. Europol, Eurojust, OLAF). For example, if a human rights question were to arise in relation to the European arrest warrant of 2002[73] in a case which had been co-ordinated by Eurojust, applications of individuals claiming that there has been a violation would require to be lodged against the Member States concerned (issuing and/or enforcing state), not against Eurojust or its parent organization, the European Union.

Under the European Public Prosecutor model, the problem of accountability would arise in a different way because the EPP would have direct operational powers throughout the Union. It would be inappropriate to hold Member States accountable for human rights violations resulting from the direct action of the European Public Prosecutor in their territories. The better solution would probably be the European Union's accession to the ECHR, which would make it directly accountable in Strasbourg for acts emanating from one of its institutions. Human rights questions arising under the operation of Eurojust would probably be the same as those arising in the context of inter-state co-operation. They would arise from the current conditions and obstacles to such co-operation, some of which are partly human rights-inspired. Examples are the double criminality test, the death penalty exception, the political offence exception, and the nationality

[72] See K. Lenaerts and E. de Smijter, 'A Bill of Rights for the European Union', 38 *CMLRev.* (2001) 273.

[73] *Supra* note 7.

exception. These conditions and exceptions may or may not coincide with current human rights in positive international law. For example, the right not to be extradited to a state where the requested person may be subjected to torture or other forms of inhuman or degrading treatment or punishment clearly flows from Article 3 of the ECHR.[74] On the other hand, international human rights instruments do not guarantee the principle of non-extradition of nationals. The human rights status of other traditional conditions and exceptions, such as the double criminality principle and the political offence exception, is not always very clear.[75] In certain cases, the Charter of Fundamental Rights of the European Union offers a wider human rights protection than the ECHR. An example is the international *non bis in idem* protection, which is provided by the Charter (Article 50) but not by the ECHR. Another example is the prohibition of the death penalty (EU Charter, Article 2(2)), which was a prominent point in the negotiations between the EU and the USA concerning a treaty of extradition and mutual assistance in criminal matters.[76] This being said, general human rights provisions are made for national, not for international, criminal proceedings. There may be a need for more specific legislation, such as a framework decision on the protection of human rights in transnational European Proceedings.[77]

Human rights questions arising from the operation of the European Public Prosecutor system would not be the same, because the conditions and obstacles to inter-state co-operation would not be applicable. As the EPP would have direct operational powers, the human rights questions raised in this context would rather resemble the human rights questions arising from the operation of national criminal justice systems. They would turn on the right to personal liberty (Article 5 of the ECHR—Article 6 of the European Charter), the right to a fair trial (Article 6 of the ECHR—Article 47 of the European Charter) and the right to privacy (Article 8 of the ECHR—Articles 7 and 8 of the European Charter). The sources of law to be applied in the future (separate charter for the EU or return to the Council of Europe's instruments) will depend on the outcome of the proceedings of the 'European Convention' and the IGC.

[74] See Eur. Ct. H.R. *Soering* case, judgment of 7 July 1989, Series A No. 161 and C. Van den Wyngaert, 'Applying the European Convention on Human Rights to Extradition: Opening Pandora's Box?', *Int. & Comp. LQ* (1990) 757.

[75] See, generally, J. Dugard and C. Van den Wyngaert, 'Reconciling Extradition with Human Rights', 92 *American Journal of International Law* (1998) 187.

[76] Agreement on Extradition between the European Union and the United States of America, Washington, 25 June 2003, OJ 2003 L181/27; Agreement on Mutual Assistance in Criminal Matters between the European Union and the United States of America, Washington, 25 June 2003, OJ 2003 L181/34.

[77] See the Commission's Consultation Paper on Procedural Safeguards for suspects and defendants in criminal matters, available on the website of the European Commission.

G. Eurojust, the European Public Prosecutor, and the Police

The relations between investigative and prosecuting authorities are governed by national law, not by international law. International human rights norms are therefore not directly relevant in this context, although some soft law is emerging on the subject.[78]

National criminal justice systems have ways to control the police that vary from one state to the other. In states that boast a public prosecutorial system, the police are often monitored and controlled by the public prosecutor during criminal investigations. In other states, the police act autonomously. Examples are Ireland and the UK, who have a Director of Public Prosecutions, but no *ministère public* in the continental sense.[79] This may, depending on the overall structure of the criminal justice system, be counter-balanced by procedural guarantees in the course of the criminal process. There may be a *judicial* control at the end of the investigation, by the trial court. The problem is to know whether these counter-balances that may exist domestically also work internationally. This raises the question about how international police co-operation will operate in Europe, in the present and in a future European Union comprising more than twenty Member States.[80]

Within the general area of justice and home affairs, co-operation between police services has been the most 'successful'.[81] International co-operation between national police forces in the EU and within institutions such as Europol (Third Pillar) and OLAF is essential in the fight against cross-border crime, including financial crime, and can only be welcomed. However, the question of the counter-balancing of this co-operation by judicial (at trial) or quasi-judicial control (during the investigation) has hardly been addressed. Theoretically, judicial control always exists *a posteriori*, when investigations have come to an end, and a case is put before a trial court. This trial court will test the evidence and, in doing so, test the police practices that are behind the gathering of this evidence. The exclusionary rule will do its work. In practice, however, this control often does not materialize because many police investigations do not lead to criminal proceedings. And if they do, it may not always be possible to test before the courts of state A whether police investigations in state B were conducted in a legally acceptable way.

[78] See the United Nations Code of Conduct for Law Enforcement Officials, 17 December 1979 and the Council of Europe's Recommendation Rec(2000)19 of the Committee of Ministers to Member States on the role of public prosecution in the criminal justice system, 6 October 2000, available on the internet: http://cm.coe.int/ta/rec/2000/2000r19.htm.

[79] Van den Wyngaert *et al. supra* note 67.

[80] See C. Van den Wyngaert, 'The Protection of the Financial Interests of the EU in the Candidate States. Perspectives on the Future of Judicial Integration in Europe', ERA-Forum 2001, no. 3, pp. 2–60.

[81] See W. Bruggeman, 'Policing in Europe: a New Wave?', in M. Den Boer (ed.), *The Implementation of Schengen* (Maastricht: EIPA, 1997) 172.

Also, much depends on the choice of the forum—the place where a case will be tried if investigations have been successful. In practice, this is often determined by the place where the suspects are arrested. Indirectly (or directly), the police may, by proceeding to arrest at one particular point rather than another, determine where the trial shall be conducted and thus choose the forum.[82] In addition, police investigations may affect the rights of third persons (other than suspects) who may never be aware of the fact that investigations were conducted. For those persons, judicial control *a posteriori* would not work.

The existing European investigative authorities are not monitored by anyone except, in the case of Europol, their national authorities, and, in the case of OLAF, by a surveillance committee. This monitoring is very limited and does not take the form of direction and surveillance of the investigations. Eurojust's powers do not include the direction and monitoring of Europol. Both agencies have to co-ordinate their activities and to avoid duplication,[83] but Eurojust has not been given a position of directing or monitoring Europol. The *Corpus Juris* and the Commission's Green paper on a European Public Prosecutor are silent on the matter.

Thus far, the problem has hardly arisen in practice because Europol has no operational powers of its own and, therefore, the risk of Europol violating human rights has been relatively small. All this may change. Europol is likely to acquire operational powers in the near future, for example in the framework of joint investigation teams. It needs to be controlled, not only by national prosecutorial authorities, but also at the European level.

Looking at the type of cases that are likely to be handled by Europol and Eurojust, namely trans-European organized crime (financial and otherwise), the policing methods that are likely to be used will include so-called 'special investigation techniques'. These include systematic observation with sophisticated technological equipment, the use of informers, covert investigations (e.g. the use of undercover agents infiltrating criminal organizations), and controlled deliveries. European rules governing some of these methods have been elaborated, *inter alia*, in the European Convention on Mutual Assistance in Criminal Matters of 2000[84] and in the Framework Decision on Joint Investigation Teams of 2002.[85]

However, despite this legislation, national law and police ethics may vary on questions such as where to draw the line between observation and provocation and whether undercover agents may themselves commit criminal offences. I believe that, in addition to the European legislation that already exists, European and national police officers co-operating in trans-European investigations and acting in joint investigation teams should be subject to a

[82] See further *infra*, sect. 4H. [83] *Supra*, at sect. 3. [84] *Supra* note 10.
[85] *Supra* note 11.

European monitoring system by a public prosecutorial authority, be it Eurojust or the European Public Prosecutor. It is highly regrettable that Eurojust has not been given any powers and responsibilities in this respect.

H. Eurojust, the European Public Prosecutor, and the Choice of the Forum: Towards a European Pre-trial Court?

Nobody proposes, at this stage, the introduction of a European federal court system. Under both models, crime investigations that have been co-ordinated (Eurojust) or steered (European Public Prosecutor) by a transnational agency will eventually lead to criminal procedures before national courts which would, at least in part (even under the European Public Prosecutor model), apply their national laws. The choice of forum may therefore be a crucial decision, especially in cases where the courts of more than one Member State are equally competent to hear the case. In the case of Eurojust, individual Eurojust members and Eurojust acting as a college may ask states to accept that one of them may be in a better position to undertake an investigation or prosecute specific acts (the so-called concentration of prosecutions). Although it is not stated explicitly, this amounts to saying that Eurojust can propose the choice of the forum. In the *Corpus Juris*, the choice of the forum is, also indirectly, made by the European Public Prosecutor: by determining in what state he seises a judge of liberties for a coercive measure in the pre-trial stage, he will *de facto* also decide where the case will be prosecuted.

Consequently, in cases with Eurojust as well as the European Public Prosecutor model, it is the prosecutor who chooses the forum. This corresponds to the situation in many Member States, where it is also the prosecutorial authorities that determine before which court the case will be brought where several courts within one state are competent to try the same case. However, in a national context, the forum choice does not imply a choice about the law that will be applied to the case (substantive and procedural). In an international context, on the contrary, it may make a great difference for the parties to a case in what state the proceedings will be brought. In cases with accused of different nationalities, and perhaps victims of still other nationalities, there may be divergent views as to the forum that is the most appropriate to try the case.

As long as there is no full harmonization of the criminal justice systems of the Member States, the choice of the forum is likely to have an impact on all the parties in a criminal proceeding: police, prosecutors, defendants, victims. There will be a need for further development of the criteria guiding the choice of the forum, and also for a judicial control of the choice, if it is left, as it is today, to the (prosecutorial) authorities of states (in a horizontal model) or to the European Public Prosecutor (in a vertical model). The forum choice should be in the interests of a fair and efficient administration of justice. To avoid duplication, prosecutions should be concentrated in one state only and individuals should not face different parts of the same case in different trial courts in different Member States. For *Corpus Juris* crimes, criteria have been provided in Article 26. These criteria could be further elaborated in policy guidelines, to be adopted by *Eurojust* or the European Public Prosecutor and which would build on the Council of Europe convention on mutual assistance in criminal matters as well as Article 26(2) of the *Corpus Juris*.[86]

The choice of the forum should be decided by Eurojust or, if the *Corpus Juris* were to be introduced, by the European Public Prosecutor, not by the police. It is therefore important that Eurojust (and the European Public Prosecutor) should oversee the activities of the police. To protect the parties (defendants, victims) against *forum shopping*, there may well be a need for a judicial control of the choice of the forum at a European level, preferably by the European Court of Justice. One proposal could be to create a chamber of this Court that would function as a European Preliminary Chamber, following the example of pre-trial chambers in international criminal courts such as the International Criminal Tribunal for the Former Yugoslavia[87] or the Permanent International Criminal Court.[88] This Preliminary Chamber would oversee the choice of the forum.

In my view, this would be a *nihil obstat* procedure rather than a *fiat* procedure: only if one of the parties wanted to challenge the forum choice of the prosecutor (Eurojust or European Public Prosecutor) would there be a decision of the court. This task could be part of a more general function to be attributed to this court, i.e. the task of committing cases for trial and of validating settlement agreements and perhaps also deciding disputes about the validity of pre-trial investigative acts. I believe that a European Preliminary Chamber is a necessary complement to concurrent jurisdiction in the European legal area and, as such, is a minimum requirement for judicial integration in a Union that will soon consist of twenty-five Member States or more.[89]

[86] See also the European Commission's discussion paper on Mutual Recognition of Decisions in Criminal Matters among the Member States and Jurisdiction, Discussion paper with questions for experts, 15 May 2002, available on the Commission's website.

[87] Rules of Procedure and Evidence of the International Criminal Tribunal for the Former Yugoslavia, The Hague, 11 February 1994, latest version to be consulted at http://www.un.org/icty/legaldoc/index.htm.

[88] Rome Statute of the International Criminal Court, Rome, 17 July 1998, ILM 1998, p. 999, Art.39.

[89] C. Van den Wyngaert, '*Corpus juris*, parquet européen et juge national: vers une chambre préliminaire européenne?', in de Kerchove and Weyemberg, *supra* note 5, at 131; Delmas-Marty, 'Combating Fraud—Necessity, Legitimacy and Feasibility of the Corpus Juris', 37 *CMLRev.* (2000) 247; W. van Gerven, 'Constitutional Conditions for a Public Prosecutor's Office at the European Level', 3 *European Journal of Crime, Criminal Law and Criminal Justice* (2000) 296.

S. FINAL OBSERVATIONS

Eurojust and the European Public Prosecutor have different objectives and it is not possible, in the abstract, to say which model is the best. All depends on the institutional background under which the models operate. With his powers of direct investigation and prosecution in the whole European Judicial Area, the European Public Prosecutor would probably be the more effective institution. But it would imply a transfer of sovereignty for which governments do not seem to be fully prepared at this stage in time.

The two are not totally incompatible. Yet I would not favour the idea of having two prosecutorial institutions that would function alongside each other and would thus contribute to the proliferation of institutions and norms. This would not serve the objective of clarity and simplification on which both federalists and anti-federalists in the 'Convention' agreed. While a majority of the current Member States still seems to oppose the idea of the immediate introduction of a public prosecutor, the need for such an institution may become more readily apparent from practice and it may well be that Eurojust will, in the course of time, be given new powers that go in the direction of a European Public Prosecutorial Service. This, indeed, is why the drafters of the European Constitution have provided for the possibility of Eurojust transforming itself into a European Public Prosecutorial service in the years to come. Meanwhile, the potential problems concerning human rights protection of suspects and witnesses need to be addressed. The EU should make up its mind about whether or not it will accede to the Council of Europe's Convention on the Protection of Human Rights. European police co-operation, both national (e.g. under the Schengen Agreement) and European (Europol), needs better supervision. Both Eurojust and the European Public Prosecutor could play an important role in this respect. Finally, the risk of forum shopping (also by Eurojust) needs to be addressed, for example by the attribution of the powers of a Pre-trial Chamber to the European Court of Justice.

6

Police Co-operation and the Area of Freedom, Security and Justice

CYRILLE FIJNAUT

1. INTRODUCTION

The European Union is frequently portrayed as the façade of a Greek temple resting on three columns. The first pillar encompasses broadly the European Community; the second is related to the 'common foreign and security policy' of the Member States; and the third, according to Title VI of the Treaty on European Union (TEU), deals with 'police and judicial cooperation in criminal matters'.

The purpose of the so-called third pillar is not to create an 'area of freedom, security and justice' of the territory of the European Union (EU). The objective of this pillar is not that ambitious: citizens are guaranteed a 'high level of safety' in this area. The text of Article 29 of the TEU is very clear in this regard. What is not clear is how high a 'high level' is or how high it should be. The Article refers to only two means by which that vague objective should be reached: 'by developing common action among the Member States in the fields of police and judicial cooperation in criminal matters' and by 'combating racism and xenophobia'.

This essay is principally concerned with police co-operation as it is presented in the context of the third pillar with a focus on the set objective of development. Judicial co-operation will be examined only to the extent that this is necessary for a good understanding of police co-operation. This will also be the case with respect to police co-operation under the first and second pillars. These will only be considered in the light of police co-operation under the third pillar. However, just how the EU would generally like to see the police engaged in the 'area of freedom, security and justice' will not be considered at all. After all, a discussion of this would require that both the organization and the activities of the police systems in the Member States be included in the analysis. Such an undertaking would not be possible within the scope of an essay such as this.[1]

Given the wide variety of lines of approach available, a great deal can be said about police co-operation under the third pillar. Thus, one cannot avoid making choices. The choices made for this essay are each linked to its overall objective: an evaluation of the future plans of the Convention on the Future of Europe (hereafter the European Convention) and the European Commission (hereafter the Commission) with respect to police co-operation in the EU on the basis of an analysis of its current development. Therefore, the essay will begin by considering what place police co-operation is assigned in general under the third pillar: within what limits must it be organized? What forms can and may it take? What concrete purpose or purposes must these forms of co-operation serve? Without an accurate definition of the institutional framework within which this co-operation is required to unfold, no well-balanced judgement can be made regarding the advances that have or have not been made.

Secondly, on the basis of this general definition, the question regarding the development police co-operation has undergone within the context of the third pillar in recent years will be examined at a formal level: the level of the conventions between the Member States and the decisions of the Council and the Commission.[2] In answering this question, particular attention will be paid to the increasing operationalization of cross-border co-operation, the growing interweaving of police and judicial co-operation, and the branching of police co-operation towards the first and third pillars. The choice of these three issues is based on the consideration that they provide a good demonstration of the institutional dynamics of police co-operation under the third pillar and also that they reflect the difficulties with which its development has had to struggle on the formal level.

Thirdly, the phenomena that are to be addressed by means of police co-operation in accordance with Article 28 TEU, namely various forms of crimes, organized and otherwise, will also be reviewed. The questions that will be raised in this connection each have a bearing not only on the nature, the scope, and the development of these crime problems, but also on the relationship between these problems and police co-operation as it is currently

[1] Among the publications that consider, comparatively or otherwise, the present police forces in the Member States of the European Union are: A. Semerak and G. Kratz, *Die Polizeien in Westeuropa* (Stuttgart: Richard Boorberg Verlag, 1989); J.-C. Monet, *Polices et Sociétés en Europe* (Paris: La Documentation française, 1993); J.M. Erbès *et al., Polices d'Europe* (Paris: L'Harmattan, 1993); J.-J. Gleizal *et al., La Police; le Cas des Démocraties Occidentales* (Paris, Presses Universitaires de France, 1993).

[2] See also for a general overview of legal developments, C. Chevalier-Govers, *De la Coopération à l'Intégration Policière dans l'Union Européenne* (Brussels: Bruylant, 1999), and M. Sabatier, *La Coopération Policière Européenne* (Paris: L'Harmattan, 2001).

organized under the third pillar: does the co-operation in fact bring the objective of a 'high level of safety' in relation to these problems closer? In comparison with the earlier formal question raised in this regard, it is here rather a matter of a substantive or content-oriented question: has this co-operation in fact added value in the concrete transnational fight against organized crime in the EU?

Finally, in connection with the answer to this last question, this essay will examine how the European Convention and the Commission perceive the organization of police co-operation between the Member States in their recent plans regarding the future of the EU. In discussion of this point, it will of course be acknowledged in particular whether they take account of the problems that exist at the formal and the substantive levels with respect to this form of mutual co-operation. In addition, in what follows from this, it is of course impossible to avoid the question whether these plans, to the extent that they address the relevant problems, also suggest solutions.

2. POLICE CO-OPERATION UNDER THE THIRD PILLAR: A GENERAL CHARACTERIZATION

The third pillar, like the second pillar, is often compared to the first pillar of the EU. In this comparison, the first pillar is often characterized as the Community pillar and the other two pillars are described as intergovernmental pillars. In addition, this comparison also expresses a great deal about this latter characterization. It is not without reason that the title of Chapter VI TEU reads 'Provisions on police and judicial co-operation in criminal matters' and in Article 29 this designation is specified in terms of police and judicial co-operation between the EU Member States and not, for example, between the Member States and the Commission. Further, one should not lose sight here of the fact that Article 34(2) provides that the Council shall act unanimously when taking measures, so ensuring that the sovereignty of the Member States is respected in the decision-making process as regards policy; thus, none of the Member States can in this regard be overruled by the other Member States. The recognition of national sovereignty is also found in Article 33 TEU: the provisions of this title 'shall not affect the exercise of the responsibilities incumbent upon Member States with regard to the maintenance of law and order and the safeguarding of internal security'. Further, Article 32 is relevant here, stating that the Council 'shall lay down the conditions and limitations under which the competent authorities ... may operate in the territory of another Member State in liaison and in agreement with the authorities of that State'. In the case of police and judicial co-operation, in other words, each Member State remains in ultimate control of its own affairs.

By contrast, however, especially as a result of the amendments to the TEU brought about by the Treaty of Amsterdam, *communautaire* institutions like the Commission, the Court of Justice, and the European Parliament play more important roles than those provided in the Treaty of Maastricht. Through these changes the Commission has been given the right to take the initiative in developing policy to be sent to the Council (Article 34(2)). The Court of Justice has acquired the jurisdiction, subject to conditions, to give preliminary rulings on the validity and interpretation of, for instance, the framework decisions and Council decisions (Article 35(1)). And the European Parliament must in a number of cases be consulted regarding measures that the Council wishes to adopt (Article 39(1)). The third pillar, therefore, can only with difficulty still be called one of the two intergovernmental pillars of the EU. During the 1990s, this pillar assumed more of a dual nature. The hard core of Member State sovereignty was under this column gradually surrounded by the soft shell of the Community institutions.[3]

Nevertheless, the extent to which the notion of sovereignty still governs the third pillar is underlined by the manner in which police co-operation under Article 30 TEU is elaborated. The unarticulated hard core in the relevant provisions is that no executive power was provided for police agents involved in cross-border co-operation, still less was such power transferred to intergovernmental police agencies. The sovereignty of the Member States, therefore, remains completely intact in the field of public order and security. Accordingly, at home, the police remain the primary embodiments of the monopoly that is characteristic of the modern state: the monopoly over force. If the Member States had created or otherwise transferred such transnational powers, then this would instead have been a significant infringement of their monopoly over force and thus over their sovereignty. As is evident from Articles 32 and 33, it was precisely this that they did not want in any circumstances. Their only objective was to promote the conditions for cross-border operational co-operation between their police departments. What, then, does the key article concerned, Article 30 TEU, cover with regard to police co-operation?

First, paragraph 1 refers to police co-operation between the Member States in general: operational co-operation with respect to 'the prevention, detection and investigation of criminal offences', the 'collection, storage, processing, analysis and exchange of relevant information', 'co-operation and joint initiatives in training, the exchange of liaison officers, secondments, the use of equipment and forensic research', and the 'common evaluation of particular

[3] For a more detailed discussion of the character of the third pillar see the contibutions of E. Regan ('Overview of the New Third Pillar') and D. Walsh ('How the Third Pillar Works') in E. Regan (ed.), *Cooperation against Crime in the European Union; the New Third Pillar* (Dublin: Brunswick Press, 2000), at 1, and S. Peers, *EU Justice and Home Affairs Law* (Harlow: Pearson, 2000), at 8.

investigative techniques in relation to the detection of serious forms of organised crime'. Secondly, paragraph 2 specifically addresses co-operation through Europol. It provides that the Council shall promote co-operation through Europol and especially—within five years from the date of entry into force of the Treaty of Amsterdam (1 May 1999)—shall enable Europol 'to facilitate and support the preparation, and to encourage the co-ordination and carrying out, of specific investigative actions by the competent authorities of the Member States, including operational actions of joint teams comprising representatives of Europol in a support capacity'; shall adopt measures 'allowing Europol to ask the competent authorities of the Member States to conduct and to co-ordinate their investigations in specific cases and to develop specific expertise which may be put at the disposal of Member States to assist them in investigating cases of organised crime'; shall promote 'liaison arrangements between prosecuting/investigating officials specialising in the fight against organised crime in close cooperation with Europol' and shall establish 'a research, documentation and statistical network on cross-border crime'. Each of these provisions indeed has nothing to do with the delegation or transfer of executive power to police agents from the Member States or Europol personnel. Most of the provisions turn on the creation or the improvement of the conditions according to which such power can be exercised by the police agents from the Member States or can otherwise be better exercised. Only a few are directly involved in the operational execution of cross-border criminal investigations, possibly with the assistance of Europol.

The question that then arises is what purpose does this form of co-operation between the Member States serve? The answer in Article 29 is that it is intended to guarantee citizens a 'high level of safety' in an 'area of freedom, security and justice'. As far as this is concerned, it has already been noted that nowhere in the Treaty is there an explanation of what is to be understood by a 'high level of safety'. Thus, this objective is fairly rhetorical in nature, especially if one considers it in the light of the crime problems described earlier in Article 29 as those apt for co-operation, in particular: 'crime, organised and otherwise, in particular terrorism, trafficking in persons and offences against children, illicit drug trafficking and illicit arms trafficking, corruption and fraud'.[4] These are not inconsiderable problems and, more particularly, not problems whose nature, scope, and development are easily measured quantitatively or qualitatively. Thus, how can it ever be established that in relation to these problems a certain level of safety has been reached, and, what is more, a 'high' level? The debates over what 'high'

[4] By way of a decision on 6 December 2001, the Council established that Europol could carry out its tasks in relation to all offences that are taken up in the appendix to the Europol Convention (OJ 2001 C362/1).

in this context means are potentially inexhaustible. A closely connected question is how effective are the available means of realizing this high level? To what extent—leaving aside judicial co-operation and customs co-operation—can police co-operation as elaborated under Article 30 provide an important contribution to the fulfilment of this goal?

If one were to consider the action plans that the Council has adopted in past years, then it is possible to draw the conclusion that in its sphere doubt has also slowly been raised in relation to the effectiveness of police co-operation under the third pillar. This was very clear at the Tampere Council summit on 15 and 16 October 1999. Not only was it proposed that a working group comprising European chiefs of police—the EU Police Chiefs' Task Force—be established to organize more and better operational approaches to transnational crime problems, but it was also proposed that there should be an immediate move towards establishing joint investigation teams for the fight against drug trafficking, trafficking in humans, and terrorism.[5] The nature of these two decisions demonstrates where, in police co-operation in particular, the EU was lacking in 1999—at least according to the members of the Council: namely multinational cross-border co-operation, which, in the fight against organized crime, is operationally critical. Apparently, they considered that the working out of the forms of co-operation articulated in Article 30 had become bogged down in setting up general facilities for the fight against organized crime and had palpably failed in the business of conversion into concrete action to deal effectively with cross-border crime.

In connection with the foregoing, it is necessary to indicate the policy that was set up after the attacks of 11 September 2001 for the promotion of, for instance, police co-operation between Member States with respect to terrorism.[6] This policy can indeed be seen as the Council's first serious attempt, since the TEU entered into force, to reconstruct this form of co-operation in a specific area and do so directly on all points using a more operational model. This is not so surprising, of course, given the nature of these attacks and the urgent imperative to undertake joint action against Islamic terrorism. What did this new domain of action involve? Aside from organizing meetings of the chiefs of intelligence services of the Member States and the chiefs of their 'counter-terrorist units' and the co-ordination of consultation between Europol, pro-Eurojust, and the EU Police Chiefs' Task Force, it includes in particular, the following two measures:

[5] Tampere European Council, 15 and 16 October 1999, *Presidency Conclusions*, SN 200/99 EN.

[6] European Council, 25 September 2001, *Conclusions Adopted by the Council (Justice and Home Affairs)*, 12156/01, JAI 99. For comprehensive comment on the anti-terrorism policy see, for example, F. Pastore, 'The Asymmetrical Fortress: the Problem of Relations between Internal and External Security Policies in the European Union', in M. Anderson and J. Apap (eds), *Police and Justice Co-operation and the New European Borders* (The Hague: Kluwer, 2002), at 59.

—Establishing a 'team of counter-terrorist specialists' within Europol responsible for collecting relevant information and intelligence and for setting up a threat analysis;
—Giving the Europol director the task of keeping the Council informed about the information that the Member States submitted to Europol with a view to integrating it into its work files on terrorism.

This operational approach is not entirely unprecedented. With a view to the introduction of the euro, a team of experts has also been created within Europol.[7] In particular, the team was charged with collecting information on attempts at or cases of counterfeiting of the new money. It is fair to say, however, that the anti-terrorist initiative is the most developed example of the new approach.

3. THREE IMPORTANT ISSUES IN THE CURRENT DEVELOPMENT OF POLICE CO-OPERATION

As stated in the introduction, this section will discuss three issues. First, the growing tendency to organize cross-border police co-operation increasingly according to an operational model will be examined at greater length. Secondly, attention will be given to the growing entanglement of police and judicial co-operation. Thirdly, this section will consider the branching of police co-operation toward the first and the third pillars. The choice of these three issues was explained in the introduction. They are suitable for demonstrating what formal progress police co-operation has made under the third pillar, and they also paint a picture of the substantive problems that arise in the development of this form of co-operation between the EU Member States. Furthermore, it is important to reveal both sides of the development because otherwise it would be difficult to give a balanced answer to the question whether the plans that are now being made in the framework of the European Convention and the Commission over the future of police co-operation, in both the positive and the negative sense, mesh with its current development at the formal level.

A. Making Cross-border Police Co-operation Work

If one looks far enough into the past of international police co-operation in Europe, the evidence suggests that such co-operation has always had a strongly operational character. Whether it was directed at controlling political opposition or clearing up serious criminal offences, the objective was

[7] Council Decision of 6 December 2001 on the Protection of the Euro against Counterfeiting, OJ 2001 L329/1.

always 'to get things done' by collecting or exchanging information, gathering material evidence, hearing witnesses (or allowing them to be heard), etc.[8] It should be emphasized in this connection, however, that states were traditionally not at all prepared to relinquish any of their sovereignty. Even the police co-operation agreements concluded by small countries like Belgium and the Netherlands before World War II offered no or very little room for cross-border action by their police officers.[9] The fact that the larger countries were also unprepared to surrender any of their autonomy on this point is apparent from the European Convention on Mutual Assistance in Criminal Matters of 1959 (hereafter European Convention 1959).[10] In that Convention, for instance, the presence in criminal investigations of police agents from the requesting state in the requested state remains within the gift of the requested state (Article 4). By contrast, the provisions concerning police co-operation in the Benelux Treaty on Extradition and Mutual Assistance of 1962 are a vast improvement (Articles 26–28). They not only allow the possibility for police agents to be of assistance in an advisory sense in implementing requests for mutual assistance but also conditionally permit cross-border pursuits and surveillance. In this way police co-operation was, for the first time in Europe, put into practice in the form of cross-border powers.[11]

The explanation for regulating these forms of police co-operation in the Benelux Treaty 1962 is found in the fact that the three countries concerned were of the opinion that one of the consequences of the creation of an economic union, namely, the abolition of internal border identity checks, would have to be counterbalanced by a strengthening of, among others, the co-operation between them in criminal matters.[12] This also explains why, midway through the 1980s, Germany, France, and the Benelux countries took advantage of European Community plans to integrate the domestic market and so abolish border controls to conclude in Schengen an agreement on measures designed to flank this political-economic process.[13] The result of

[8] M. Deflem, *Policing World Society: Historical Foundations of International Police Cooperation* (Oxford: OUP, 2002), at 45–77, 124–152, and C. Fijnaut, 'The International Criminal Police Commission and the Fight against Communism, 1923–1945', in M. Mazower (ed.), *The Policing of Politics in the Twentieth Century* (Oxford: Berghahn Books, 1997), at 107.

[9] C. Fijnaut and G. van Gestel, 'De Politiële Samenwerking in het Belgisch-Nederlandse Grensgebied', in C. Fijnaut (ed.), *De Reguliere Politiediensten in België en Nederland* (Antwerp: Kluwer, 1992), at 175.

[10] Council of Europe (ed.), *International Co-operation in Criminal Matters* (Strasbourg: Council of Europe, 1997), at 47–61.

[11] R.C.P. Haentjes, *Nederlandse Instrumenten van Internationale Rechtshulp in Strafzaken* (Arnhem: Gouda Quint, 1992), at 44–59.

[12] M.J. Constant, *Le Traité Benelux d'Extradition et d'Entraide Judiciaire en Matière Penal* (Nivelles: Imprimerie Administrative, 1962).

[13] C. Fijnaut, 'Naar een "Gemeenschappelijke" Regeling van de Politiële Samenwerking en de Justitiële Rechtshulp', in C. Fijnaut *et al.* (eds), *Schengen: Proeftuin voor de Europese Gemeenschap?* (Antwerp: Kluwer, 1992), at 91–95.

this agreement was reflected in the 1990 Convention Implementing the Schengen Agreement of 13 June 1985 (hereafter 1990 Schengen Convention). Chapter 1 of Title III of this Convention ('Police and security') relates to police co-operation. It not only lays down in detail the modalities according to which cross-border pursuit and surveillance can take place but also provides for more facilities to exchange information within well-specified limits, to second liaison officers, and to adjust means of communication with each other. Moreover, Article 73 binds the Parties to create conditions for allowing 'controlled deliveries' in the context of the fight against drug trafficking. In addition, Titles IV and V of this Convention brought the Schengen Information System into being. This system gives the Parties the opportunity to inspect specific data regarding persons and goods under conditions that meet, notably, the standards in the European Convention for the Protection of Individuals with regard to the Processing of Personal Data of 1981.

It is difficult to describe the 1990 Schengen Convention as a breakthrough on all points in the organization of police co-operation in Europe. In certain respects—cross-border pursuit and surveillance—it was no more than a refined version of the Benelux Treaty 1962 and—where controlled deliveries are concerned—of Article 11 of the United Nations Convention against Illicit Traffic in Narcotic Drugs and Psychotropic Substances of 1988.[14] What was new was its embedding of cross-border powers in a comprehensive system of police co-operation and the fact that a body of important European countries accepted this system with open arms. The result is well known. Over the years, the majority of the EU Member States has ratified the 1990 Schengen Convention and this agreement, along with the rest of the so-called Schengen *acquis*, has been integrated into the EU through a special protocol to the Treaty of Amsterdam.[15] Another striking feature of the Schengen system is its indication that the EU, at least its third pillar, has been shaping the institutional framework for cross-border operational co-operation between its Member States in a *bottom up* fashion, even if Article 30 TEU itself does not in any way provide for such a development. Yet this does not mean that Schengen constitutes a violation of the TEU, since Articles 43–45 concerning 'enhanced cooperation' in fact make it possible for developments of this type as part of the internal dynamic of the EU.

While the integration of the 1990 Schengen Convention can be described as a *bottom up* cross-border operationalization of police co-operation in the EU, the intention to include Europol more closely—in particular through joint teams—in criminal investigations of Member States in the field of organized crime can be called a *top down* attempt at cross-border operationalization of

[14] http://untreaty.un.org/English.

[15] European Council (ed.), *The Schengen Acquis Integrated into the European Union* (Luxembourg: Office for Official Publications of the European Communities 1999).

police co-operation in the EU. During the preparation of the Treaty of Maastricht, the Member States indicated clearly that under no circumstances did they want anything to do with a Europol whose staff had executive powers—even in the long term. For them, Europol was acceptable only if it were no more than an intergovernmental 'clearing house for information'.[16] Accordingly, this is what it became. The description of the objective of Europol, its terms of reference, and its organization, in the Convention on the Establishment of a European Police Office of 1995, left no misunderstanding on this point. Soon after the Convention was signed, and thus long before it entered into force in the Summer of 1999, the Member States nevertheless came to realize that such a Europol was too remote from the national police corps and their practical actions against organized crime to be able to contribute added value convincingly to the fight against this problem in the EU. This can be inferred from the *Action Plan to Combat Organized Crime*, which was passed by the Council on 28 April 1997.[17] It provides that Europol should in early course be given the increased operational powers—powers that were indeed soon to be incorporated into the Treaty of Amsterdam. This point was again hammered home in the *Action Plan on How Best to Implement the Provisions of the Treaty of Amsterdam in an Area of Freedom, Security and Justice* of 3 December 1998: Europol would have to play an even more operational role in the EU and the powers intended for this purpose should one way or another be made available.[18] In 1999, this desire was once again emphatically voiced at the meeting of the Tampere European Council, and it appears again—almost dutifully—in the action plan *The Prevention and Control of Organized Crime: a European Union Strategy for the Beginning of the New Millennium* of 2000.[19] However, it was not until November 2002 that an agreement would be reached within the Council regarding the manner in which a more operational role for Europol could be achieved. On 28 November 2002 the Council took the decision, through a new protocol, to change the Europol Convention in accordance with the provisions of Article 30 of the TEU.[20] A new Article 3a provides that 'Europol officials may participate in a support capacity in joint investigation teams' and a new Article 3b provides that 'Member States should deal with any request from Europol to initiate, conduct or co-ordinate investigations in specific cases and should give such requests due consideration'. With respect to the participation of Europol in joint teams, the future Article 3 further provides that:

[16] C. Fijnaut, 'The "Communitization" of Police Cooperation in Western Europe', in H. Schermers *et al.* (eds), *Free Movement of Persons in Europe* (Dordrecht: Martinus Nijhoff Publishers,1993), at 81.

[17] OJ 1997 C251/1.

[18] OJ 1999 C19/1.

[19] OJ 2000 C124/1.

[20] OJ 2002 C312/1.

—Europol personnel shall 'assist in all activities and exchange information with all members of the joint team', within the limits of the law of the Member State where the team is taking action and in accordance with the agreement concluded between the director of Europol and the authorized national authorities; and
—the staff will perform their duties 'under the leadership of the leader of the team' and, under certain conditions, the other members of the team may be supplied with 'information from any of the components of the computerised system of collected information' at Europol.

Since the Member States have yet to ratify this protocol, it could take a few years before these two powers can also in fact be used. The *top down* operationalization of cross-border police co-operation through Europol, therefore, is moving very slowly, even if, as in this case, it is not related to the assignment of executive powers.[21]

In the 1997 action plan on organized crime, reference was made not only to the need to follow an operational model for Europol but also to the plan to conclude an EU Convention on Mutual Assistance in Criminal Matters (hereafter 2000 EU Convention) in an extension to the European Convention 1959. The Member States signed this convention on 29 May 2000 and most must still ratify it.[22] In this convention, a few forms of mutual assistance were included, which can likewise be considered as just so many attempts to broaden the possibilities for cross-border operationalization of police co-operation. As regards the regulation under Article 12 concerning controlled delivery, it is not so much its originality that stands out. Indeed it constitutes nothing more than an extension of the regulation already provided under Article 73 of the 1990 Schengen Convention. The difference is that under the 2000 EU Convention, the application of this mechanism is not limited to a certain offence or a certain form of crime. In addition, one should not overestimate the importance of the possibilities provided under Articles 10 and 11 of this Convention allowing for persons to be heard by video and/or telephone. In any event, much more important is the regulation under Title III of the Convention for international interception of telecommunications. Such a detailed and far-reaching regulation will not be encountered in any other mutual assistance treaty.

However, the regulation for 'covert operations' under Article 14 and the regulation for 'joint investigation teams' under Article 13 are also particularly important for the operationalization of cross-border co-operation. As regards

[21] What Europol's supporting task as regards 'joint investigative teams' could involve was stated in the Council Recommendation of 30 November 2000, OJ 2000 C357/7.

[22] OJ 2000 C197/1. For detailed comment see G. Vermeulen, *Wederzijdse Rechtshulp in Strafzaken in de Europese Unie: naar een Volwaardige Eigen Rechtshulpruimte voor de Lid-Staten* (Antwerp: Maklu, 1999).

the actions mentioned first, the intention is that the Parties have the ability to assist one another in criminal cases by exchanging police infiltrators ('officers acting under covert or false identity'), the deployment of whom is to be set out in a contract for each occasion. This Article repeatedly stresses that their deployment can only occur in compliance with the law of the state in which they are to set up their operations. The creation of joint investigation teams—which, as we have seen, is further elaborated in the new Protocol to the European Convention—must likewise take place on the basis of a contract entered into by the parties concerned regarding the objective of the investigation, the composition of the team, the conditions according to which the deployment of the team members by national authorities is governed, and so on.[23] Furthermore, it should be clearly stated that the team is bound by the law of the Member State where it undertakes its operations. This, however, does not mean that only the team members from the state where the team is operating may carry out criminal investigations. Indeed, paragraph 6 explicitly provides that the team leader can assign the performance of certain criminal investigations to other team members—seconded from other Member States. This provision is more important than it appears, and this for the simple reason that it constitutes a complete reform of the regulation of cross-border investigation. Indeed, never before has a treaty such as this made it possible for police agents from one Member State to perform their duties on the territory of another Member State for such a long period of time for the purposes of carrying out criminal investigations without—through a request for mutual assistance, for example—a prior determination of which proceedings it involves and/or without the proceedings being based on a form of co-operation that is specifically provided for in a treaty, for example cross-border pursuit. This regulation is thus just as innovative as the regulation under paragraph 7, which makes it possible for seconded members directly to ask their own competent authorities to conduct, or have someone conduct, criminal investigations in their respective states, as the former regulation obviates in cases of a joint team the need to submit requests for mutual assistance for every possible eventuality.

The observation that can ultimately be made from the foregoing is that with the previously mentioned Convention the EU has in fact now assumed the pioneering role that had traditionally been played by the Council of Europe in the field of mutual assistance in criminal matters. This changing of the guard was already anticipated in the 1990 Schengen Convention. In that convention, certain forms of police co-operation—cross-border pursuit and

[23] For that matter, one must not lose sight of the fact that the Council in its Framework Decision of 13 June 2002 with a view to the fight against terrorism, has already made the establishment of 'joint investigative teams' possible (OJ 2002 L162/1). In its considerations on this decision, the Council also expressly refers to the possibility of Europol personnel taking part in these teams.

surveillance—were regulated which until then did not appear to be achievable within the Council of Europe. That the EU has recently taken over the pioneering role from the Council of Europe on the issue of co-operation in criminal matters is only reinforced by the fact that the Second Protocol to the (Council of Europe) European Convention 1959, which was opened for signature in November 2001, is to a great extent a copy, in the domain of police, of the relevant provisions in the 1990 Schengen Convention and the 2000 EU Convention.[24]

For all their limitations, then, the achievements of the EU, as regards the conversion of formal frameworks into further operationalization of cross-border police co-operation should not be underestimated. This co-operation goes to the heart of state sovereignty, and so by definition is a very demanding matter. To then develop over no more than ten years through treaties that must be negotiated by more and more Member States an entire spectrum of more and more operational forms of co-operation is certainly considerable. In a longer historical view, indeed, this can be interpreted as a great success. Before 1990, police co-operation in Europe was for the most part an informal, even a secret, affair that often remained limited to the exchange of information.

Yet this does not alter the fact that it can still take a great deal of time to translate policy plans into workable agreements. Often this demands years of negotiations at the EU level, which is then followed by years of decision-making in the states themselves. As far as this is concerned, the establishment, coming into force, implementation, and amendment of the Europol Convention can still, without exaggeration, be viewed as a long-winded affair.

B. The Entanglement of Police Co-operation and Judicial Co-operation

The backlog accumulated by the Council of Europe over recent years in the domain of police co-operation is to a degree a result of the choice that was made in the establishment of the European Convention 1959. On the authority of experts, it was then indeed decided not to regulate this form of co-operation in the treaty: 'They thought it best not to force the existing practice of the police into a rigid mould, besides which, the Statute of the International Criminal Police Organisation (Interpol) already regulated mutual assistance between police authorities'.[25] Thus, very deliberately, only regulations regarding judicial co-operation were adopted. However, later attempts within the Council of Europe to rectify this choice and still make room for important forms of police co-operation in the treaty under consideration failed. With so many more countries than the EU Member States coming to the bargaining table, it appeared as though reaching a

[24] http://conventions.coe.int. [25] Ibid.

consensus on this matter would prove impossible. This was another indirect indication that this politically highly sensitive domain of interstate co-operation can only be organized with countries which have a great deal in common politically, economically, and culturally and which intend among themselves to expand further their union in these fields.[26] Be that as it may, however, until the 1980s the multinational organization of police co-operation in Europe followed a completely different route from that of judicial co-operation.

These two routes were for the first time expressly channelled toward one another in the Schengen Agreement and the 1990 Schengen Convention. Indeed Title III of this Convention deals with both police co-operation (Chapter 1) and judicial co-operation (Chapters 2–5). In this respect, the Convention was an innovation in the overall organization of assistance in criminal matters in Europe. Furthermore, Article 39 (Chapter 1) clearly states where the boundary between the two forms of co-operation in criminal matters lies. Indeed, paragraph 1 states that police co-operation is only possible 'in so far as national law does not stipulate that the request has to be made through the judicial authorities and provided that the request or the implementation thereof does not involve the application of measures of constraint by the requested Contracting Party'. Paragraph 2 adds a third criterion to these two, namely, that information that is exchanged between police departments on the basis of paragraph 1 cannot be used 'as evidence of the criminal offence other than with the consent of the competent judicial authorities of the requested Contracting Party'. The line drawn here between police and judicial co-operation therefore lies above all in the application of compulsory measures and in the use of evidence.

Now, if we look at the 2000 EU Convention in this light of the 1990 Schengen Convention, it can be stated, first, that no distinction is drawn here between police and judicial co-operation, and, secondly, that forms of co-operation regulated here can often be considered as much forms of police co-operation as forms of judicial co-operation. One may think, for example, of controlled delivery and the deployment of police infiltrators. In the Second Protocol to the European Convention 1959, which was cited above with regard to these matters, both the relevant forms of cross-border police co-operation from the 1990 Schengen Convention and those from the 2000 EU Convention are adopted. For its part, therefore, the new protocol to the 1959 Convention also indicates that police co-operation and judicial co-operation in Europe are becoming increasingly interconnected.

[26] C. Fijnaut, 'Transnational Organized Crime and Institutional Reform in the European Union: the Case of Judicial Cooperation', in P. Williams and D. Vlassis (eds), *Combating Transnational Crime: Concepts, Activities and Responses* (London: Frank Cass, 2001), at 276.

It is possible to speculate on the reasons for this. One factor is certainly the cases brought before the European Court of Human Rights pursuant to Articles 6 and 8 of the European Convention on Human Rights. This case law has increasingly raised the issue that criminal investigation practice must be taken into consideration when deciding whether the suspect has had a fair trial. Consequently, the public prosecution department and sometimes also the examining magistrate—who traditionally in some manner or form has authority over the performance of judicial tasks by police departments in continental Europe—must increasingly, and certainly in extensive and complicated criminal cases, satisfy themselves from the outset of the lawfulness of the criminal investigation.[27]

This entanglement of the two forms of co-operation in criminal matters and the related convergence of police and justice institutions need not of itself be a problem in cases of multinational co-operation based on the 1990 Schengen Convention and the 2000 EU Convention. Both Conventions, using terms like 'competent authorities', are so openly formulated that they are applicable in the most divergent institutional relationships between police and justice in the Member States. In addition, while the requested state may on the basis of Article 4(1) of the 2000 EU Convention be required to adhere to 'the formalities and procedures expressly indicated by the requesting Member State, unless otherwise provided in this convention', the subsequent condition—'provided that such formalities and procedures are not contrary to the fundamental principles of law in the requested State'—again limits the scope of this duty considerably. Thus the provisions of this Convention, like those of the 1990 Schengen Convention, do not impair the relationship of authority between the public prosecution department—and possibly the examining magistrate—on the one hand, and police departments on the other hand, as it has evolved in the Member States throughout history and as is specified in criminal and police legislation. In a certain sense, then, the provision under Article 13 of the 2000 EU Convention (regarding the establishment of a joint investigation team), that the leader of a team must be 'a representative of the competent authority participating in criminal investigations from the Member State in which the team operates' and that he/she will work 'within the limits of his or her competence under national law', is therefore unnecessary. However, the drafters of this Convention evidently did not want to leave any room for doubt on this point.

It is different in cases of police co-operation where Europol is involved. Europol is perhaps the most controlled police agency in Europe. Besides the internal management, there are now two important agencies based on the Convention that monitor the goings-on within Europol: the 'management board', which chiefly performs management tasks, and the 'joint supervisory

[27] J. Pradel and G. Corstens, *Droit Pénal Européen* (Paris: Dalloz, 1999), at 347.

body', which monitors the observance of the regulations for the protection of personal data. However, these two agencies do not operate independently but rather merely represent extensions of national authorities and organs. The members of the 'management board' are representatives of the Member States and fall as such under the ministerial responsibility of their respective ministers. Their actions can thus be monitored in this way. The 'joint supervisory body' is composed of representatives from those authorities in the Member States that have the right to verify for themselves whether Europol has properly handled the personal information that originates from their country. Furthermore, in many Member States, the public prosecution department ultimately decides which information can be transferred to Europol and under what conditions. As a result of the great distrust that existed at the beginning of the 1990s in many Member States with respect to the establishment of Europol, there is truly no deficiency in the monitoring of the organization.[28] This same distrust is also responsible for Europol having been placed at so great an initial distance from the actual criminal investigations in the Member States that it has subsequently required a great deal of effort to involve it still to any extent, as has already been shown above. At the beginning of the 1990s, most of the Member States wanted nothing remotely to do with even a subordinate 'executive Europol'.

What then does the discussion on monitoring Europol concentrate on? It concentrates on the question whether, aside from the existing structures of control, direct judicial control of this organ must also be provided. The European Parliament has long been a proponent of this and sees in a European prosecutor in particular the figure who in the future must take responsibility for judicial control of Europol.[29] However, as long as the very institution of such a prosecutor remains highly controversial, the idea that he or she must be made responsible for the control in question is not a realistic option.[30] Thus, this proposal can be safely left outside of consideration for the moment. Eurojust is another matter. This new organ under the third pillar should perhaps be able to fulfil such a function subject to conditions.

[28] Amongst the most recent analyses of Europol in Europe are those of G. Aschmann, *Europol aus Sicht der Deutschen Länder* (Frankfurt: Peter Lang, 2000) and of T. Petri, *Europol: Grenzüberschreitende Polizeiliche Tätigkeit* (Baden-Baden: Nomos Verlagsgesellschaft, 2001). See also European Commission, *Democratic Control over Europol*, Brussels, 26 February 2002, COM(2002)95 final. For what is meant in particular by the protection of information see P. de Hert and J. Vandenborght, *Informatieve Samenwerking over de Grenzen heen* (Brussels: Politeia, 1996), ii, at 427–462, 503–588, and S. Sule, *Europol und Europäischer Datenschutz* (Baden-Baden: Nomos Verlagsgesellschaft, 1999).

[29] European Parliament, *Working Document on the Green Paper on Criminal-law Protection of the Financial Interests of the Community and the Establishment of a European Prosecutor*, Brussels, 26 June 2002, PE 315.771.

[30] C. Fijnaut and M. Groenhuijsen, 'Een Europees Openbaar Ministerie; Kanttekeningen bij het Groenboek', 77 *Nederlands Juristenblad* (2002), at 1234.

The Council, and thus the Member States, however, anticipates nothing here for the moment, as it clearly appears from the relevant provisions in the TEU. Article 31, as amended by the Treaty of Nice, provides that the Council shall encourage judicial co-operation through Eurojust as regards assistance in criminal investigations into serious cross-border crime 'by promoting Eurojust ... particularly in the case of organised crime, taking account, in particular, of analyses carried out by Europol'. There is no way to understand these words as meaning that there should be a relationship of authority between Eurojust and Europol. Further, that such a relationship cannot be read into the legal text can also be inferred from the description of the duties of Eurojust in the Council Decision of 28 February 2002—by which this agency was properly established after a brief trial period.[31] Article 7 provides that Eurojust, established in the form of a board, 'may assist Europol, in particular by providing it with opinions based on analyses carried out by Europol'. Eurojust must, according to the European Commission, thus be considered the 'judicial counterpart of Europol' for the time being. At this stage, the word 'counterpart' would not 'refer to judicial supervision of Europol but to the fact that Europol's activities need to be backed up and complemented by co-ordination of prosecutions. Europol not only might need legal advice on certain judicial questions but its activities will also have to be supported by co-ordination of the relevant activity of national prosecuting authorities.'[32]

The position taken by the Council and the Commission is not rejected in the literature. As long as Europol does not acquire executive powers and so cannot conduct criminal investigations in its own name on the territory of the Member States, it has been considered unnecessary by several authors that a specific organ should exercise judicial control over Europol's performance of duties. On the other hand, it is a broadly held belief that the implementation of the powers that Europol is given in the Treaty of Amsterdam—especially of course for supportive participation in multinational criminal investigations—must be accompanied by the partial abolition of the immunity enjoyed by Europol personnel so that they may, in concrete cases, justify themselves before the national judge for their part in the investigations.[33] The Council agrees with this. An amendment to Article 8 of the Protocol on the Privileges and Immunities of Europol was also provided for in the same decision in which the protocol that led to the amendment of Article 3 of

[31] Council Decision of 28 February 2002, OJ 2002 L63/1.

[32] European Commission, *On the Establishment of Eurojust*, Brussels, 22 November 2000, COM(20000)746 final, at 10–11.

[33] See, for example, S. Glesz *et al.* (eds), *Justitielle Einbindung und Kontrolle von Europol* (Freiburg: Edition Iuscrim, 2001), ii, at 607–638, and T. Schalken and M. Pronk, 'On Joint Investigation Teams, Europol and Supervision of Their Joint Actions', 10 *Eur.J Crime Cr.L Cr.J* (2002) 1, at 70.

the Europol Convention was accepted. This change provides that employees of Europol enjoy no immunity 'in respect of official acts required to be undertaken in fulfilment of the tasks set out in article 3a of the convention regarding the participation of Europol officials in joint investigation teams'. This amendment, in the author's opinion, is also wholly in keeping with the intergovernmental position and the duty to provide assistance that Europol has on the basis of the Europol Convention.

C. The Branching of Police Co-operation toward the Second and First Pillars

In the debate surrounding police co-operation in the EU, this form of co-operation is usually treated exclusively as a matter that plays a role only under the third pillar. This approach, however, overlooks the branching of police co-operation toward the second and first pillars. These connections between the pillars are important because their operation determines for the most part to what extent the objective of police co-operation under the third pillar can be attained. Therefore, they certainly cannot be overlooked for the purposes of this essay.

1. Branching toward the Second Pillar

In view of the objective of police co-operation under the third pillar—a high level of safety in relation to (organized) crime—it has, since the entry into force of the Treaty of Maastricht, gone without saying that this form of co-operation could not remain limited to the domestic policy of the Member States but would sooner or later also have to be related to their foreign policy—thus the domain of the second pillar—even though there is on this point no explicit connection made between the two pillars in the provisions of Title VI of the TEU. The fact is that many variants of organized crime include illegal trade in persons, goods, services, and capital and are frequently committed at geographic levels that originate beyond the territorial borders of the European Union. Consider, for example, the intercontinental trade in humans, the trade in illicit drugs, and trade in illegal weapons. This international, not to mention worldwide, dimension of organized crime was of course also not unknown to the creators of the third pillar. This can be seen best in various provisions of the Europol Convention and in particular in its Article 18, which, subject to a number of conditions, offers room for exchange of information with third countries and third organizations.

Nevertheless, it was not until the Tampere Summit in 1999 that the Council expressly took a position with respect to the role of police and judicial co-operation in EU foreign policy. One of the conclusions at this Summit reads that 'clear priorities, policy objectives and measures for the

Union's external action in Justice and Home Affairs should be defined. Specific recommendations should be drawn up by the Council in close co-operation with the Commission on policy objectives and measures for the Union's external action in Justice and Home Affairs, including questions of working structure, prior to the European Council in June 2000'.[34] The question is what until now has come of this plan, particularly in the domain of police co-operation?

Until now, the Council has certainly developed a few starting points for the foreign dimension of the third pillar, but it has not yet developed a general policy plan according to which the objectives and main points of the policy are elaborated, how the deliberation regarding this policy is organized within the EU, in what way it is thought the objectives can be reached, and so on.[35] Thus the development of such a policy is still just in the initial stages, as the European Parliament recently observed.[36] There are doubtless various reasons why this policy remains in its infancy. It is certainly worth mentioning the great obstacles already present under the second pillar to pursuing a common foreign policy, the enormous diversity of subject matters on which police co-operation can focus, and the great variety of states with which the EU in one way or another has a relationship with a security dimension. This, however, is certainly not to say that nothing has occurred since Tampere. Since that summit, each Presidency of the EU, along with its predecessor and successor, has formulated a 'troika programme for external relations in the field of Justice and Home Affairs'. These programmes explain which policy is or will be pursued as much with respect to (combinations of) countries and international institutions as with respect to specific subject matters like migration and organized crime.

Where it involves the role police co-operation occupies in these programmes, it must be stated that this subject matter comes up for discussion unevenly in both sectors and not always in connection with the theme to which it is most relevant, namely organized crime.[37] Due to this it is only through meticulous analysis of policy papers in all possible fields that any insight can be gained into the role police co-operation plays in foreign policy. Even then the picture is still very fragmented. For example, in the policy

[34] C. Fijnaut, 'Het Politiebeleid van de Europese Unie', in G.J.M. Corstens and M.S. Groenhuijsen (eds), *Rede en Recht* (Deventer: Kluwer, 2000), at 249.

[35] European Council, *European Union Priorities and Policy Objectives for External Relations in the Field of Justice and Home Affairs*, Brussels, 6 June 2000, 7653/00, JAI 35.

[36] European Parliament, *Report on the Council Report on Justice and Home Affairs: EU Priorities and Policy Objectives for External Relations*, Brussels, 21 November 2001, A5-0414/2001 final.

[37] See, for example, European Council, *Multipresidency Programme for External Relations in the Field of Justice and Home Affairs (2001–2002)*, Brussels, 3 January 2002, 5004/02, JAI 1, and European Council, *Troika Programme for External Relations in the Field of Justice and Home Affairs*, Brussels, 5 July 2002, 10685/02, JAI 159.

regarding Russia, justice and home affairs co-operation plays an important role, but the relevant policy documents make no similar mention with respect to countries with whom such co-operation is just as important in certain respects.[38] The same can be said for the subject-matter centred policies. For example, even the action plan for the years 2000–2004 concerning the production, trafficking, and use of drugs scarcely mentions police co-operation with countries in Central Europe or South America.[39] This is almost inconceivable as police co-operation with these parts of the world in the field of drug trafficking is so important and needs to be very intensive.

The 'rest of the world' does not include the countries that will soon become members of the European Union. Police co-operation plays as important a role in the general policy that, as of 1997, was generally pursued towards accession, as in the particular policy that, in this same connection, was especially pursued with respect to the fight against organized crime. Accordingly, here one should consider co-operation not only as understood under Article 30 TEU, but also for reforming the police systems in the candidate countries such that they fulfil, as regards both organization and powers, the conditions imposed by the EU with a view to their accession.[40] It would be going too far here to enter into a discussion of how much of the so-called EU *acquis* in the field of police the future Member States have already incorporated into their legislation and their institutions.[41] What should be noted, however, is that it is exceptionally difficult to obtain a clear picture—not only because it is unclear what this *acquis* precisely consists of but also because it is scarcely possible to infer, from the official public reports concerning their accession, the points on which the candidate countries fulfil the requirements and the points on which they do not (yet).[42] However, it also appears from the literature that a number of these countries have made a great deal of effort, at least in the formal sense—via

[38] European Council, *Common Strategy of the European Union of 4 June 1999 on Russia*, OJ 1999 L157/1. Compare this policy plan with the plans that have been set out in agreements with South America or North Africa, for example, European Council, *Council Decision of 7 April 1998 Concerning the Conclusion of a Framework Agreement on Cooperation between the European Economic Community and the Cartagena Agreement and its Member Countries*, OJ 1998 L127/10.

[39] European Commission, *Communication on a European Union Action Plan to Combat Drugs*, Brussels, 26 May 1999, COM(99)239 final.

[40] European Commission, *Agenda 2000: for a Stronger and Wider Union*, Brussels, 15 July 1997, COM(97)2000 final, and European Council, *Pre-accession Pact on Organised Crime between the Member States of the European Union and the Applicant Countries of Central and Eastern Europe and Cyprus*, OJ 1998 C220/1.

[41] In a recent communication, the Commission also gave the candidate countries new guidelines in the domain of 'justice and home affairs' with a view to their integration into the EU. See European Commission, *Further Indicative Guidelines for the Candidate Countries*, Brussels, 12 March 2003, COM(2003)110 final, at 10–11.

[42] C. Fijnaut, 'De Uitbreiding van de Europese Unie en de Strafrechtsvergelijking', in E.H. Hondius (ed.), *De Meerwaarde van de Rechtsvergelijking; Opstellen Aangeboden aan prof. Mr. H. U.*

adjustment of the legislation and reorganization of services—to become acceptable to the EU on this point. Whether everything also works in practice as the EU would like is another matter.[43]

This also applies to police co-operation in a narrow sense, especially as regards Europol. In March 2000, the Council empowered the director of Europol, subject to conditions, particularly in matters concerning the protection of personal information, to enter negotiations with third countries—above all the future EU Member States—and with international organizations—in the first place Interpol—with a view to concluding co-operation agreements.[44] In the context of this authorization, Europol has drafted two kinds of agreements: agreements for strategic and technical co-operation and agreements for operational co-operation. Only the latter kind of agreement makes exchange of personal information possible.[45] It is fairly difficult to know with which countries and organizations co-operation agreements have in the meantime been concluded because they are not published in the Official Journal. Europol's annual reports, however, do indicate what progress has been made on this point. It appears from the 2001 annual report that agreements have been reached with Estonia, Hungary, Iceland, Norway, Poland, Slovenia, and the United States as well as with Interpol.[46] As to what in each case the agreements are about, it is or is almost impossible to say because their texts are generally not accessible to third parties. Nevertheless, in some cases one can get a better picture here on the basis of Council documents. One can, in this sense, consider both the agreement between Europol and Interpol and the—contentious—complementary (operational) agreement between the United States and Europol regarding the exchange of personal data.[47]

Jessurun d'Oliveira (Deventer: Kluwer, 1999), at 201. There are certainly exceptions to this rule, for example, the reports on training the police in candidate countries. See Association of European Police Colleges, *Ten Candidate Member States on Their Way to the EU* (2001).

[43] See, for example, R. Cholewinsky and E. Slavenas, 'Foreign Policy Implications of the EU Justice and Home Affairs Acquis: the Case of the Baltic States', in Anderson and Apap (eds), *supra* note 6, at 103; D. Polt, 'Transborder Operational Activities', and N. Dimitrova, 'Police and Judicial Cooperation in Combating Organized Crime', both in B. de Ruyver *et al.* (eds), *Strategies of the EU and the US in Combating Transnational Organized Crime* (Antwerp: Maklu, 2002), at 189–196, 245–250.

[44] Council Decision of 27 March 2000, OJ 2000 C106/1.

[45] C. Rijken, 'Legal and Technical Aspects of Co-operation between Europol, Third States and Interpol', in V. Kronenberger (ed.), *The European Union and the International Legal Order: Discord or Harmony?* (The Hague: T.M.C. Asser Press, 2001), at 577.

[46] European Council, *Europol Annual Report 2001*, Brussels, 30 April 2002, 8381/02, Europol at 25, 23.

[47] European Council, *Authorisation of the Director of Europol to Conclude a Co-operation Agreement between Europol and Interpol*, Brussels, 21 May 2001, 8803/01, Europol 43, and *Draft Supplemental Agreement between the United States of America and the European Police Office on the Exchange of Personal Data and Related Information*, Brussels, 4 November 2002, 13689/02, Europol 82.

Europol's annual plans do reveal some of the activities that, in the framework of these agreements, are developed with respect to the fight against (organized) crime. They certainly cover the exchange and analysis of information, but also the deployment of liaison officers at Europol, setting up multinational investigation teams and criminal investigations, training investigators with a view to the application of special investigation techniques, and so on.[48] What these plans do not reveal, of course, is how these forms of co-operation operate in practice and what effects they have on the nature, the scope, and the development of (organized) crime in Europe. However, this is also true for police co-operation that Member States organize with countries in Central and East Europe outside the framework of the European Union.

2. *Branching toward the First Pillar*

The first pillar includes everything that traditionally belonged to the European Community (EC). The Treaty of Rome (1957), on which the EC was founded (ECT), was revised on important points (including points as regards police co-operation between Member States of the EC/EU) as much through the Treaty of Maastricht as through the Treaty of Amsterdam. Of central concern here is Article 280, which deals with the fight against fraud against EC resources (EC fraud) and Title IV (Articles 61–69), which, since the Treaty of Amsterdam, have covered issues concerning asylum, immigration, and other aspects of the free movement of persons. Although the manner in which the Commission currently tracks down breaches in the sphere of competition law often seems to resemble closely the way in which criminal investigations are carried out, this quasi-criminal approach by the Commission will not be addressed here.[49]

The fight against EC fraud is an issue that has been the cause of many policy headaches in Brussels since the 1960s. Toward the end of the 1980s, special measures were only just beginning to be taken to tackle the fraud in question. Of particular relevance here was the establishment of the *Unité de la Coordination Anti-fraude* (UCLAF) within the framework of the Commission in 1988. This unit—then chiefly comprising representatives of the Commission and of the relevant regulatory agencies of the Member States—can be considered as the embryo from which, after the resignation of the Commission in 1999 as a result of a report from a committee of experts regarding the dishonest action of (at any rate) one of the members of the

[48] See, for example, European Council, *Europol Work Programme 2003*, Brussels, 30 April 2002, 8385/02, Europol 27.

[49] C. Harding, *European Community Investigations and Sanctions: the Supranational Control of Business Delinquency* (Leicester: Leicester UP, 1993). See also the Council Regulation 1/2003 of 16 December 2002 on the Implementation of the Rules on Competition Laid Down in Articles 81 and 82 of the Treaty, OJ 2003 L1/1.

Commission, the OLAF (*Office de la Lutte Anti-fraude*) was formed.[50] OLAF can be considered a genuine executive police department of the EC, but with the understanding that for the performance of its tasks it only has administrative powers and no judicial powers. In other words, formally OLAF is not a criminal investigation department in the true and strict sense of the word. This can in part be inferred from Article 280(4), in which the Council is given the power to take measures to fight fraud, but where it is expressly stated that these measures cannot affect the application of national criminal law or the national administration of justice. The limited competence of the new office also emerges very clearly from the regulations issued by the Council on 18 December 1995 and 11 November 1996 with a view to organizing the fight against fraud.[51] On the basis of these regulations, the members of UCLAF/OLAF only have the power to carry out inspections 'on the spot'. That the reports they draft regarding their investigations on the basis of Article 8(3) of the last-mentioned regulation may serve in certain circumstances as evidence in criminal cases does not alter the basically administrative character of the investigations. Yet this possibility also reveals that OLAF, in spite of its limited powers, can nevertheless operate under certain conditions—and in fact does so operate—as a supranational quasi-investigation department in criminal investigations into EC fraud.[52] The Commission's proposal to set up a European public prosecution department, again with a view to the protection of the financial interests of the EC, is in essence nothing more than an attempt to give shape to this (form of) supranationalization of criminal justice at the level of prosecution as well.[53]

It may seem anomalous that the EU Member States have indeed accepted an independent police department (OLAF) within the context of the first pillar while in the context of the third pillar they did not under any circumstances want to establish a similar force (Europol). This inconsistency may be to a

[50] J. Vervaele, *Fraud against the Community: the Need for European Fraud Legislation* (Deventer: Kluwer, 1992), and also his article, 'Towards an Independent European Agency to Fight Fraud and Corruption in the EU?', 7 *Eur. J Cr. Cr.L Cr.J* (1999) 3, at 331. See further S. White, *Protection of the Financial Interests of the European Communities: the Fight against Fraud and Corruption* (The Hague, Kluwer, 1998).

[51] OJ 1995 L312/1, and OJ 1996 L292/2.

[52] The annual reports of OLAF do not allow for any misunderstanding here. See European Commission, *Report of the European Anti Fraud Office: Activity Report for the Period 1 June 2000–31 May 2001*, OJ 2001 C365/31, and European Commission, *Report of the European Anti Fraud Office: Third Activity Report for the Year Ending June 2002*, OJ 2002 C128/1.

[53] European Commission, *Green Paper on Criminal-law Protection of the Financial Interests of the Community and the Establishment of a European Prosecutor*, Brussels, 11 December 2001, COM(2001)715 final. For a commentary on the history, the foundation, and the content of this proposal, see Fijnaut and Groenhuijsen, *supra* note 30. See also, for example, F. Bruner and H. Spitzer, 'Der Europäische Staatsanwalt; ein Instrument zur Verbesserung des Schutzes der EU-Finanzen oder een Beitrag zur Verwirklichung eines Europas der Freiheit, der Sicherheit und des Rechts', 22 *Neue Zeitschrift für Strafrecht* (2002) 8, at 393–398.

certain extent illusory, since *both* cases demonstrate that the Member States in the final analysis apparently do not want to relinquish any of their criminal jurisdiction. Yet it remains worthy of note that the one (supranational) service, without too many problems, has enjoyed administrative powers that it can apply independently in a quasi-criminal manner within the territories of the Member States, while the other (intergovernmental) service, even after many years of intense discussion, has scarcely assumed a supporting role when participating in criminal investigations in the Member States.

However this asymmetrical relationship between the two forces may in fact have originated, it creates problems in the relations between them that appear to be scarcely soluble. For years there have been fruitless discussions over a co-operation agreement between OLAF and Europol.[54] These difficulties are certainly a result of their different positions in the EU and the different institutional concerns that are at play under the first and third pillars. Yet they also stem from the fact that the two forces are competent to address an overlapping range of crime problems. The fight against fraud is not monopolized by OLAF since fraud is also one of the kinds of (organized) crime governed by Article 29 TEU and is thus also a matter that can, in the context of the third pillar, be the subject-matter of police co-operation. The Member States, however, have scarcely made use of this possibility until now. Indeed, in the agreement concluded in 1995 better to protect the financial interests of the EC against fraud, direct co-operation between their police departments did not play a role.[55] What then is the source of the friction between OLAF and Europol? It is because overlap is no mere theoretical possibility, as a (small) part of EC fraud is *in fact* committed in the context of organized crime. Both forces thus have good reason to demand a role in the co-ordination and support of criminal action of the Member States where such fraud is involved.[56] Europol cannot remain aloof in cases, for example, of worldwide cigarette smuggling, in which large crime syndicates from South America, Europe, and Asia also play active roles. In such cases the financial interests of the EC are not the only security issues at stake![57] With a view to a co-ordinated

[54] Recently—on 18 February 2003—after two years of negotiations, a framework agreement was concluded ('Administrative Agreement on Co-operation between the European Commission and the European Police Office') between the European Commission and Europol. The agreement covers, for instance, mutual exchange of information (not yet published).

[55] OJ 1995 C316/48.

[56] C. Fijnaut, 'De Connecties tussen EG-fraude en Georganiseerde Misdaad', in H. de Doelder (ed), *Bestrijding van EG-fraude* (Arnhem: Gouda Quint, 1990), at 87–96, and C. Fijnaut, 'De Strafrechtelijke Bescherming van de Financiële Belangen van de Gemeenschap tegen Fraude', 30 *Delikt en Delinkwent* (2000) 10, at 972–988.

[57] See, for example, the complaint of the European Community against, among others, R.J. Reynolds Tobacco Company before the United States District Court, Eastern District of New York. See also in this context L. Joossens, *Smuggling and Cross-border Shopping of Tobacco Products in the European Union* (Health Development Agency).

approach to such crime problems, it is thus desirable that this institutional conflict be settled. But how? This is difficult not only on account of the different structural positions of these two services in the EU but also because of long-term dilemmas concerning the regulation of their mutual relations. In the long run, does the EU want to distribute its police capacity over special services organized according to the problem or complex of problems, or does it prefer a concentration of this power in one or more general services?

This strategic question leads to the second common ground between the third and first pillars on the police domain: policing of the EU's external borders. Articles 61 and following of the ECT, inserted by the Treaty of Amsterdam, assign the Council the task of taking a number of measures, with a view to achieving an 'area of freedom, security and justice', in the sphere of free movement of persons and especially in the field of asylum and immigration. With these measures, the concern is, for instance, the prevention of and fight against crime in conformity with Article 31 (e) TEU, and police and judicial co-operation in criminal cases in conformity with Articles 30 and 31 of the same Treaty. That the pillars ultimately are parts of one and the same structure—the EU—in the field of police co-operation finds expression nowhere better than here. Before the TEU entered into force, the otherwise traditional connection between immigration policy and police policy was already clearly expressed in the 1990 Schengen Convention. While Title II of this Convention deals with the 'abolition of checks at internal borders and movement of persons', Title III, as already noted above, has to do with 'police and security'. As the section of this Convention that deals with the free movement of persons—Title II—was incorporated into the first pillar as a result of the Treaty of Amsterdam, and the other section—Title III—into the third pillar, it is certainly not surprising that, with a view to the elaboration of the above-mentioned provisions of the EC Treaty—and under pressure from the future integration of a number of Central and East European countries into the EU at a time when the issue of massive (illegal) immigration and those of organized crime and terrorism in the existing Member States are high on the political agenda—the Amsterdam drafters explicitly referred back to the relevant sections of the Schengen agreement. Indeed, it would be reasonable to say that Title IV EC, rather than replacing Schengen as such, has simply provided a new constitutional foundation for this part of the 1990 Schengen Convention.

In the context of the current revision of the 1990 Schengen Convention, the Council decided in May 2001 to identify 'best practices' as regards external border controls in order to create optimal standards for their execution. This research led to the establishment of a catalogue of recommendations—issued in February 2002.[58] This catalogue demonstrates manifestly

[58] European Council, *EU Schengen Catalogue: External Borders Control, Removal and Readmission*, Brussels, 28 February 2002.

that police co-operation such as that developed under the third pillar is becoming increasingly interrelated with police co-operation undertaken in the context of Title IV of the first pillar. In more than one place, indeed, it is contended that 'border checks and border surveillance, based on risk analysis' not only enhance the fight against illegal information, smuggling, and trade in humans but also the fight against cross-border (organized) crime in general. This document argues therefore in favour of forming 'specialised multidisciplinary units fighting border-related crime'.

In May 2002, following discussions on the way in which external border controls must be organized in the future, the Commission published a communication that set out not only challenges faced by the EU at its external borders with a view to its domestic safety but also how an 'integrated management of the external borders' might look. In the opinion of the Commission 'the effectiveness of the fight against illegal immigration, while respecting the principles of the right to asylum, trafficking in human beings and trafficking of all kinds connected with organised crime, including drugs' belongs squarely to the challenges facing the EU. With a view to the improvement of the effectiveness of this fight, the Commission prepared a large number of proposals for the short and medium terms among which were the exchange of liaison officers, the conclusion of bilateral border agreements, the adoption of risk analysis, and the forming of multidisciplinary units. It considered the formation of a European Corps of Border Guards desirable in the long term.[59] In December 2002, the European Parliament had itself placed its support behind most of these proposals.[60] On some points, it would like to go even further than the Commission. It would, for instance, like to see Europol responsible for drafting risk analyses, and co-operation between Europol and Schengen intensified. Should this indeed occur, then the *top down* and *bottom up* approaches to police co-operation in the EU will become increasingly intertwined.

The European Parliament earlier passed a resolution on 20 September 2001 in which, in a familiar refrain, it complained of the fact that the Council and the Commission did not involve it enough in the incorporation into the EU of key agreements such as the 1990 Schengen Convention, and also criticized the lack of transparency with regard to the manner in which police co-operation between the Member States is organized in the EU at present and the confusion that this deficiency instils in ordinary citizens.[61] This criticism can only be endorsed here. Police co-operation under and between

[59] European Commission, *Towards Integrated Management of the External Borders of the Member States of the European Union*, Brussels, 7 May 2002, COM(2002)233 final.

[60] European Parliament, *Report on the Communication from the Commission entitled 'Towards Integrated Management of the External Borders of the Member States of the European Union'*, Brussels, 10 December 2002, A5–0449/2002 final.

[61] OJ 2002 C77/141.

the three pillars has become even for specialists a non-transparent matter, and with respect to an issue that is so politically sensitive—immigration, (organized) crime, and terrorism in an enlarged EU—this is particularly undesirable. Inadequate organization of police co-operation is not only an obstacle to achieving the purposes of this co-operation, but may also promote, however unintentionally and inadvertently, public perceptions of immigration flows and immigrants that are entirely inappropriate and a danger to peace and tolerance in the EU.[62]

4. POLICE CO-OPERATION AND (ORGANIZED) CRIME

As stated in the introduction, we want to ask not only how police co-operation is evolving at the level of agreements between the Member States and the decisions of the Council but also whether this co-operation adds value through increased safety as regards cross-border (organized) crime in the EU. The first question is a matter of prescribed rules and institutional designs, and, through reference to a wide variety of documentary sources, is, all in all, relatively easy to answer. The great majority of the literature on police co-operation is engaged for good reason at this formal level. Conversely, the second question is empirical, and, due to the poverty of research and data, is more difficult to answer than the prescriptive question. Why is it more difficult? Or perhaps expressed better: why is this—certainly at the level of the EU in its entirety—in fact impossible? It is so for a combination of two reasons: as much for a lack of overview and insight into (organized) crime as for a lack of overview and insight as regards (a part of) the solution, namely police co-operation. These two questions are examined in turn below.

A. The Lack of Overview and Insight with respect to Organized Crime

The first reason is, as stated, shaped by the fact that, for all intents and purposes, it is impossible to have an overview of the nature, scope, and development of (organized) crime in the EU and its neighbouring countries. The only sources that provide a general picture of this is Europol's annual reports.[63] Certainly since they were recently adapted to a new model,

[62] See with respect to this the contributions of G. Wyn Rees and M. Webber ('The Governance of Crime and Insecurity across Europe'), J. Goodey ('Whose Insecurity? Organised Crime, its Victims and the EU'), and H. Albrecht ('Immigration, Crime and Unsafety') in A. Crawford (ed.), *Crime and Insecurity: the Governance of Safety in Europe* (Cullompton: Villan, 2002), at 77–101, 135, and 159.

[63] These reports can be found on the Europol website, http://www.europol.eu.int. The last report is the *2002 EU Organised Crime Report* (non-classified version), dated 31 October 2002. Europol also regularly issues informative reports on special problems in the sphere of

these reports have given in some respects a considerable impression of the picture that the police in a number of Member States have of organized crime, but they are nevertheless for all manner of methodological reasons of only limited use as an indicator of this crime in Europe. Anyone wanting to use these reports as such must complement them at least with the analyses prepared annually by the police services in various Member States, for example, by the *Bundeskriminalamt* in Germany, the National Criminal Intelligence Service in England and Wales, and the *Federale Politie* in Belgium. Moreover, the reader should consider them alongside the results of academic research on organized crime that has been done until now in the EU and, more broadly, in Europe. This research is, however, scarce. As yet, there have been no scholarly studies that attempt to chart organized crime in Europe or the EU. Why not? First of all, in most of the Member States there are simply too few researchers to carry out such studies, and, secondly, the Commission has not as yet been prepared to finance such studies. Why is there a lack of qualified researchers in many Member States? Several reasons can be given for this but the important ones are, in particular: lack of interest in organized crime in the research field and, where there is interest, often insufficient access to police and judicial sources to be able to conduct such studies on any scale.[64] And why is the Commission not interested in European studies with respect to organized crime? Because it does not consider that such studies have sufficient practical use.[65]

Nevertheless, scholarly research on organized crime is making progress. This is apparent from the publication of studies on the manner in which organized crime can be researched and the way in which the results may be analysed.[66] In addition, more studies on the nature, scope, and development of forms of organized crime are appearing in some more Member States. In this respect, one can first consider the broad research regarding the nature and

organized crime, in 2001, for example, a *European Union Situation Report on East European Organised Crime; Based on Information from 1996 to 2000.*

[64] C. Fijnaut, 'Empirical Criminological Research on Organised Crime; the State of Affairs in Europe', in *L'Evolution de la Criminalité Organisée: Actes du XVIIIe Cours International de Haute Spécialisation pour les Forces de Police, Paris 17–24 Septembre 1996* (Paris: La Documentation française,1996), at 47–60.

[65] This is based on the author's personal experiences with the Commission in obtaining financing for research as it is meant here. In collaboration with L. Paoli from the Max Planck Institute for Foreign and International Criminal Law in Freiburg, I set up a self-funded European project on which at least thirty researchers from all over Europe are working. The title of the project is 'Organized Crime in Europe: Conceptions, Patterns and Policies in the European Union and Beyond'. The results will be published as a book sometime in 2004.

[66] C. Besozzi, *Organisierte Kriminalität und Empirische Forschung* (Chur: Verlag Rüegger, 1997), and C. Black *et al., Reporting on Organized Crime: a Shift from Description to Explanation in the Belgian Annual Report on Organised Crime* (Antwerp: Maklu, 2001).

development of organized crime in the Netherlands[67] and also the recent in-depth studies on the Mafia in Italy,[68] collections of comparative articles on organized crime in Germany, Austria, Italy,[69] and also in accession countries such as Hungary and the Czech Republic,[70] and publications on organized crime in European regions like the Balkans and the region around the Baltic Sea.[71] Secondly, one can refer to research on specific forms of organized crime. This is often concerned with human trafficking, but research on the arms trade can also be cited.[72] However, the progress that has been made is insufficient, whether or not in combination with the reports from Europol and from national police services, to permit reliable statements about the nature, scope, and development of the problem of organized crime in Europe or the EU. This is only possible, within certain limits, for a few Member States. The only thing that can be argued is that the problem of organized crime in the EU indeed shows certain dominant characteristics—above all it has to do with the illegal trade in goods and humans on the one hand and the illegal supply of services on the other hand—but that the situation differs from country to country on important points. The situation in Denmark is simply completely different from that in Italy. While in one country organized crime in certain regions exerts illegal control over legitimate sectors of the economy, such a situation is not at all the case in other countries.[73]

[67] C. Fijnaut *et al., Organized Crime in the Netherlands* (The Hague: Kluwer, 1998), and E. Kleemans *et al., Georganiseerde Criminaliteit in Nederland* (The Hague: WODC, 2002).

[68] L. Paoli, *Fratelli di Mafia: Cosa Nostra e 'Ndrangheta* (Bologna: Il Mulino, 2000), and M. Jacquemet, *Credibility in Court: Communicative Practices in the Camorra Trials* (Cambridge: CUP, 1996).

[69] C. Mayerhofer and J-M. Jehle (eds), *Organisierte Kriminalität; Lagebilder und Erscheinungsformen: Bekämpfung und Rechtliche Bewältigung* (Heidelberg: Kriminalist Verlag, 1996), V. Militello *et al., Organisierte Kriminalität als Transnationales Phänomen* (Freiburg: Editions Iuscrim, 2000), and C. Reiners, *Erscheinungsformen und Ursachen Organisierter Kriminalität in Italien, den USA und der Bundesrepublik Deutschland* (Frankfurt am Main: Peter Lang, 1989).

[70] P.C. van Duyne *et al., Cross-border Crime in a Changing Europe* (Tilburg: Tilburg UP, 2000).

[71] N. Miletitch, *Trafics et Crimes dans les Balkans* (Paris: Presses Universitaires de France, 1998), and *Organized Crime in the Baltic Sea Area* (Toulouse: Erès, 1998).

[72] See with respect to smuggling humans, for example, F. Laczko and D. Thompson (eds), *Migrant Trafficking and Human Smuggling in Europe: a Review of the Evidence with Case Studies from Hungary, Poland and Ukraine* (Geneva: IOM, 2000) and D. Heine–Wiedenmann and L. Ackerman, *Umfeld und Ausmasz des Menschenhandels mit Ausländischen Mädchen und Frauen* (Stuttgart: Kohlhammer, 1992). As regards arms smuggling consult, for example, A. Spapens and M. Bruinsma, *Smokkel van Handvuurwapens vanuit Voormalige Oostbloklanden naar Nederland* (Tilburg: IVA Tilburg, 2002).

[73] C. Fijnaut, 'Georganiseerde Misdaad: Echt een Bedreiging voor de Europese Unie?', in B. Raaymaekers and A. van de Putte (eds), *Lessen voor de Eenentwintigste Eeuw XXI* (Leuven: Universitaire Pers Leuven,1998), at 165–185.

For this reason, therefore, it is at present impossible to state whether, through police co-operation—and disregarding all the other factors that play a role in the development of organized crime—safety in the EU as regards this problem has improved. There is simply a lack of sufficient understanding of organized crime itself to be able to determine this.

B. The Lack of Overview and Insight as regards Police Co-operation

The second reason why the added value of police co-operation in terms of increased safety and protection from organized crime cannot presently be determined, certainly indeed at the level of Europe or the EU, is that there is no, or hardly any, research being carried out on how this co-operation actually operates and what effects it has on the problem of crime. As already stated, most of the literature about this co-operation is normative, formal by nature, and completely disregards the practice of police co-operation or reflects only the personal impressions of the researchers on this point.[74]

Thus, in fact, almost nothing can be said about the way in which Europol functions in practice. The annual reports from this service do indicate that it was, in past years, involved in one way or another in hundreds of investigations in the Member States of the EU, but what this involvement represented in practice, what added value was gained from these investigations, what effects these investigations had on the problem of organized crime and so on are all questions which an outsider cannot in fact answer in the absence of scholarly research.[75] And the messages—both positive and negative—about the functioning of Europol that are circulating in the literature do not, of course, form an alternative to such research.[76] From the rare reports from members of Europol on the way in which co-operation with police services in the Member States in fact operates, particularly in cases of significant forms of organized crime like counterfeiting of the euro, smuggling humans, and drug trafficking, it can in fact be surmised that this co-operation varies a great deal from case to case. The gathering of the necessary information does not always proceed quickly enough and must regularly be stimulated in less bureaucratic and more direct ways, while the final preparation of analyses or the granting of technical assistance evidently normally

[74] P. Tak, 'Bottlenecks in International Police and Judicial Cooperation in the EU', 8 *Eur.J Cr.Crim.L Crim.J* (2000) 4, at 343–360.

[75] These annual reports have been published recently and can be accessed through the Europol website, http://www.europol.eu.int.

[76] For an example of the positive role of Europol see J. Mooney, *Gangster: the Inside Story of John Gilligan, His Drugs Empire and the Murder of Journalist Veronica Guerin* (Edinburgh: Cutting Edge Press, 2001), at 121–134. The sceptical attitude of Belgian police agents towards Europol a few years ago was expressed by J. Vanderborght, *Over de Grens: Internationale Politiesamenwerking Getoetst aan de Praktijk* (Brussels: Politeia, 1997), at 249–268.

operates reasonably smoothly. Why Europol cannot always immediately offer the added value in concrete cases that is expected of it, particularly in the sphere of policy circles, has as much to do with, for example, the rigidity of procedures that Europol must comply with as it does with the lack of collaboration that Europol receives from the police services in Member States.[77]

The direct co-operation between police services of the Member States at the national level in the fight against (organized) crime is just as difficult to assess as their mutual co-operation through Europol. Throughout the EU, there is, to the knowledge of the author, no research in which this form of co-operation is systematically examined. Whether it operates in most of the cases satisfactorily for all parties and thus delivers a significant contribution to the fight against (organized) crime or not is thus an open question. Unfortunately, this matter has not until now formed a part of the reciprocal evaluation of co-operation in criminal matters to which the Member States are bound. Because of this, there is also no general evaluation report of police co-operation available comparable to that prepared for judicial co-operation. In fact, that report belies the often very pessimistic voices on the manner in which judicial co-operation operates in the EU, its first general conclusion stating in any case that 'while mutual assistance does not have the level of perfection and reliability expected by many practitioners, it does not operate as badly as some claim'.[78] Thus, perhaps police co-operation, too, does not operate as badly as is sometimes certainly suggested.

Police co-operation in border regions is certainly being studied empirically. However, the problem with this research is that it usually cannot be determined to what extent the results of this research refer to problems of organized crime. Even in cases of cross-border surveillance there is not necessarily an issue of (organized) crime, as surveillance can be applied to all possible forms of (cross-border) crime.[79] The only study in which, based on a number of cases, police co-operation in a number of border regions in the domain of (organized) crime was researched, was carried out recently under the supervision of M. den Boer and A. Spapens.[80] This study revealed that trust and reciprocity between the two parties involved are of prime importance for co-operation to be successful. The willingness to co-operate increases through actual co-operation with each other; police co-operation

[77] See the case histories in *From Europol to Parlopol: Interparliamentary Conference on Democratic Control of Europol* (Amsterdam: Boom, 2002), at 44–124.

[78] I mean here the *Final Report on the First Evaluation Exercise—Mutual Legal Assistance in Criminal Matters*, OJ 2001 C216/14.

[79] S. Brammertz, 'Cross-border Operational Activities', in de Ruyver *et al.* (eds), *supra* note 43, at 133–154.

[80] M.G.W. den Boer and A.C. Spapens (eds), *Investigating Organised Crime in European Border Regions* (Tilburg: IVA Tilburg, 2002).

across borders is thus something that must first be *put into practice* if long-term results are to be hoped for. For some time, the available treaties have not always been fully implemented. They have tended to be invoked and utilized only to the extent necessary for the exchange of information. Yet information is what organized crime is chiefly about, and so remains the key to its challenge. Procedural issues, organizational problems, and cultural differences may certainly hinder cross-border co-operation, but precisely because of informal contacts between police agents, the negative effects of these difficulties on the progress of investigations can be reduced.

Thus direct police co-operation in the EU in practice operates perhaps more smoothly than is generally thought, just as judicial co-operation does. However, this does not alter the fact that it has also been demonstrated that there is not much that can be said at the moment about the precise value that direct and indirect police co-operation adds to the level of safety in the EU in relation to (organized) crime. There has simply been no systematic research into whether there is added value and in what this concretely consists.

C. Police Co-operation and Terrorism

The problem of terrorism has been intentionally put to one side up to this point. For the TEU, this issue is a part of the problem of (organized) crime, although this viewpoint is certainly not shared by everyone in Europe, given the difference—at least in theory—between the aims of each form of crime. Organized crime is generally associated with financial gain, while terrorism is considered to have political motives. However this may be, police co-operation in the EU with a view to the fight against terrorism cannot be disregarded here, all the more because—as was described earlier—it has seen a comparatively sharp increase since the attacks of 11 September 2001.

What applies to the problem of organized crime certainly applies to that of terrorism. Apart from a single exception, there are no comprehensive studies on the nature, scope, and development of this problem in the EU or Europe.[81] Anyone who wishes to gain a complete and profound picture must thus gather together a broad range of studies and press releases about terrorist movements (in the Basque Country, Northern Ireland, Corsica, and so on) or about certain kinds of terrorism (Islamic terrorism). Europol also prepares reports about the situation in the EU on this point, but in any case the open versions of these reports merely give a superficial picture of what is really going on.[82] In the absence of clear insight into this situation, it is thus

[81] See, for example, X. Crettiez and J. Ferret (eds), *Le Silence des Armes? L'Europe à l'Epreuve des Séparatismes Violents* (Paris: La Documentation française, 1999).

[82] European Council, *Non-confidential Report on the Terrorism Situation and Trends in Europe*, Brussels, 20 November 2002, 14280/02, ENFOPOL 140.

by definition all but impossible to say anything in general about the effectiveness of police co-operation in the EU on this point.

Yet it might still be possible to say something of substance about effectiveness if one at least had a good understanding of the practice of co-operation. However, this is also lacking here. What holds for police co-operation in general applies all the more to police co-operation as regards terrorism in the EU: the vast majority of what has been written about this co-operation deals with its formal organization and completely disregards its practical function.[83] Considering the small number of researchers in Europe who are interested in terrorism and considering the large barriers to access to police and judicial information on this issue, this is of course understandable, but the lack of understanding is no less serious for that. From Council documents—concerning the policy launched after the 11 September attacks—it can at least be inferred that there are plans to integrate the Counter-Terrorism Task Force at Europol in its standard organization and that attempts have been made to allow the Council's Working Group on Terrorism to work more coherently and more efficiently.[84] On other points, police co-operation as regards terrorism is still very much in the formative stage. Relations between the EU and the US remain a concern, as does the formation of joint teams specifically for investigating the financing of terrorist activities.[85]

5. VISIONS FOR THE FUTURE OF THE EUROPEAN CONVENTION AND THE EUROPEAN COMMISSION

The contemporary development of police co-operation in the EU has been considered in terms of a formal and material analysis in consecutive steps. This analysis has been made with a view to evaluating the plans for the future laid by the European Convention, including the contribution made by the Commission. To do this, it is obvious that their content must first be set out. However, before doing so, a brief summary of the principal results of the

[83] See, for example, N. Cettina, *Les Enjeux Organisationnels de la Lutte contre le Terrorisme* (Paris: L.G.D.J., 1994); P. Lejeune, *La Coopération Policière Européenne contre le Terrorisme* (Brussels: Bruylant, 1992), F. Thuiller, *L'Europe du Secret; Mythes et Realité du Renseignement Politique Interne* (Paris: La Documentation française, 2000), and R. Wehner, *Europäische Zusammenarbeit bei der Polizeilichen Terrorismusbekämpfung aus Rechtlicher Sicht; Aufgezeigt am Beispiel der Bundesrepublik Deutschland* (Baden-Baden: Nomos Verlagsgesellschaft, 1993).

[84] European Council, *Draft Recommendations of the Management Board to the Council on the Future of the Counter-terrorism Task Force*, Brussels, 8 November 2002, 13699/1/02, EUROPOL 86, and European Council, *Role and Future Working Methods of the Working Group on Terrorism*, Brussels, 31 July 2002, 11231/02, COTER 41.

[85] European Council, *European Union Action Plan to Cambat Terrorism—Update of the Roadmap*, Brussels, 14 November 2002, 13909/1/2, JAI 243, 6, 14, and 31.

foregoing analysis is provided. This will simplify somewhat the evaluation of the plans.

A. Summary of the Analysis of Present Development

The initial formal analysis brought to light the fact that in past years important *bottom up* as well as *top down* work was developed under the third pillar: starting from the TEU and the corresponding action plans, a comprehensive framework of significant possibilities for stimulating police co-operation between the Member States was created—as much through the 1990 Schengen Convention and the 1995 Europol Convention as through the 2000 EU Convention. This, however, does not alter the fact that it gradually became evident that sooner or later a solution to a number of resilient problems would have to be found. One should recall the procedural problem of a very complicated decision-making mechanism in which policy initiatives would be translated into concrete implementation measures often only after many years. A telling example of this is the delayed amendment of the Europol Convention to implement the letter of the Treaty of Amsterdam. However, one should also recall institutional issues, in particular, the tenacity of the distinction between the three pillars in the domain of police. The connection between these three fields of work of the EU has now become increasingly apparent, and the policy of the Council and the Commission has been stressing this coherence more strongly. There are also various matters of substance for which sooner or later solutions must be found. First, reference here can be made to the very problematic relationship between Europol and OLAF, with the question behind it being how the EU wants to organize its policing power in the long run—given that the pillar structure is set to be largely dismantled. Secondly, there is the question of the difficult prospects for a transparent and coherent EU foreign police policy being pursued across what will remain the somewhat diverse institutional landscape presently inhabited by the three pillars. Thirdly, on the horizon there is the problem of judicial authority over the actions of Europol and OLAF, as much in the form of the construction of a European public prosecution department as in the form of further involvement of the Court of Justice in Luxembourg.

The subsequent material analysis sought to demonstrate that it is in fact impossible to say what the actual effect is or was of the efforts that the EU has made over the last ten years in police co-operation in terms of safety levels in the face of (organized) crime in the 'area of freedom, security and justice'. No one is likely to dispute that the opportunities that have arisen to co-operate in various cases have certainly played a role in the successful completion of criminal investigations. Why should these opportunities otherwise have been taken? However, considered more generally—at the level of the nature, scope, and development of crime in the EU—not much, if anything, can be said about effectiveness. On the one hand, this is because there is insufficient research as regards (organized) crime in the EU, certainly in relation to the forms of this crime that are listed in the TEU. On the other hand, it is because very little or no research has been done on the practice of police co-operation in the sphere of (organized) crime, not to mention into the effects of this on safety in the EU. This is, of course, a rather unfortunate conclusion after so many years of co-operation and debate over co-operation, but it is a conclusion that forces itself on anyone who wants to recognize the facts. This means that the third pillar is still more of a political undertaking than a governmental operation. Political ideas still carry more weight than hard facts.

Before evaluating the plans of the European Convention and the independent contribution made by the Commission in light of the foregoing conclusions, these proposals must of course first be set out.

B. The Proposals of the European Convention

On 28 October 2002, the chairperson of the Convention revealed the rough draft of a Constitutional Treaty that in his opinion should form the future foundation for the EU. This Treaty would have to take the place of the two existing treaties, the TEU and the ECT. The Treaty would contain a section provisionally entitled 'Internal Security' that would no longer deal only with police and judicial *co-operation* but with 'policy on police matters and against crime'[86] more generally. The meaning of these nebulous words can to some extent be inferred from the final report of Working Group X on 'freedom, security and justice'.[87] This working group concluded that all the provisions in the new Treaty concerning the 'area of freedom, security and justice' must be placed under a single title and that, for their development, elements of the Community method—legislative measures decided by a (qualified) majority of votes, power of co-decision for the European Parliament, and so on—must be combined with strengthened co-ordination of operational co-operation at the level of the EU and simultaneous strengthening of the role of the national parliaments. The working group favoured such a sweeping change because most of the existing 'third pillar' conventions of the EU have still not been ratified by all the Member States—and even if ratified are then very difficult to change—and because the 'softer' alternatives such as decisions and resolutions do not have any direct effect at the national level. Other instruments are thus required.

[86] European Convention, *Preliminary Draft Constitutional Treaty*, 28 October 2002, CONV 369/02.

[87] European Convention, *Final Report of Working Group X 'Freedom, Security and Justice'*, 2 December 2002, CONV 426/02.

In July 2003, the analyses of the various Working Groups and of the many plenary deliberations of the Convention eventually bore fruit in a draft Constitutional Treaty. As far as the Area of Freedom, Security, and Justice was concerned, the draft Treaty largely confirmed the proposals of Working Group X, including the abolition of the Pillar structure.[88] In what follows, however, we will concentrate on the Working Group Report itself rather than the later draft Treaty, and this for three reasons. First, the Working Group Report (as is also the case with the Commission proposals), unlike the draft Treaty, is a reasoned document, and so provides some indication of the underlying philosophy behind reform. Secondly, as already noted, the draft Treaty largely follows and gives textual form to the conclusions of the working group. Thirdly, the draft Treaty is in any event not the final word. The fate of its text is in the hands, first, of the Intergovernmental Council which began its work at Rome in October 2003, and, secondly and ultimately, the Member States of the EU which will be required to ratify the conclusions of the Intergovernmental Council. It might be premature, therefore, to set too much store by the draft Treaty.

As regards police co-operation, the working group indicates that the general description of it under Article 30 TEU is 'broadly adequate'. By contrast, in its eyes the distribution of operational responsibilities between national services, Europol, OLAF, and in the future perhaps a European Border Guard lacks 'efficiency, transparency and accountability'. To correct these problems, the legislative tasks within the Council should be distinguished from the operational tasks and the latter should be assigned to a special organ.[89] It does not, however, argue for merging, for example, Europol and OLAF. The description of Europol's tasks should be replaced by a more general provision in the new Treaty to allow the legislator more play 'to develop Europol's tasks and powers'.[90] This room should be used not only to mark off Europol's central role in European police co-operation but also to indicate that Europol's powers may 'include powers relating to intelligence, co-ordination and carrying out of investigations, as well as participation in operational actions to be carried out jointly with Member States services or in joint teams'. Certainly if Europol were to develop into a similar executive investigation service to OLAF, democratic control over this service should come to reside in the European Parliament and the Council and judicial control in the European Court of Justice.[91] Other issues were more

[88] OJ 2003 C169/3. See in particular, Part III, Title II, Chapter IV on the 'Area of Freedom, Security and Justice' (Arts. III–158–178).

[89] See now Art. III–162, draft Constitutional Treaty

[90] See now Art. III–177, draft Constitutional Treaty

[91] There is considerable improvement in the degree of judicial oversight by the ECJ in the draft Constitutional Treaty, but the exclusion of jurisdiction 'to review the validity or proportionality of operations carried out by the police or other law-enforcement services of

contentious in the working group. Opinions were sharply divided both over the expansion of Eurojust to a European public prosecution department and over the formation of a public prosecution department to serve the sole purpose of protecting the financial interests of the EC.[92]

C. The Proposals of the European Commission

The Commission found two ways to reveal its opinions about the reforms to the foundations of the EU. First, on 4 December 2002, indirectly in answer to the proposal of the Convention, it issued a communication on the future institutional structure of the EU. Secondly, through its Presidency it published a rough draft of a constitution for the EU that had been prepared by a group of experts.[93] In both of these documents, the Commission concurred with the Convention's opinions that there must be a single constitutional treaty. Not a great deal of attention was devoted to what is now the third pillar. It is only noted that, with the pillar structure falling away, there is no longer any reason not to allow police and judicial co-operation in criminal matters to fall under the same general rules as those that are applicable to the policy of the EU in general. Part III, Section 3, of the rough draft deals with the 'reinforcement of the area of freedom, security and justice', and here 'criminal law and police co-operation' come up for discussion.

Article III–91 provides a more detailed description of the subjects that qualify as police co-operation in general: collection and so on of information, training and outfitting, and common operations by services of a number of Member States. Where Europol in particular is concerned is set out in paragraph 2 of Article III–92. Its task will be 'to organise the collection and processing of relevant information that the services of the Member States submit to it and to organise and co-ordinate specific investigation activities and operational activities carried out by the authorities of the Member States or by joint teams involving a number of such authorities'. Otherwise, Europol is designated as an 'agency of the Union' for which the structure and operation will be laid down in a separate law.

To get a complete picture of how, in the framework of the Commission, the future of police co-operation is assessed, one should examine its earlier

a Member State or the exercises of responsibilities . . . with regard to the maintenance of law and order and the safeguarding of internal security, where such action is a matter of national law' is continued. See Art. III–283, draft Constitutional Treaty.

[92] In the event, the draft Constitutional Treaty provides very general permission for the establishment of 'a European Public Prosecutor's Office from Eurojust' (Art. III–175).

[93] European Commission, *For the European Union Peace, Freedom, Solidarity; Communication of the Commission on the Institutional Architecture*, Brussels, 11 December 2002, COM(2002)728 final/2, and European Commission, *Constitution of the European Union; Contribution to a Preliminary Draft; Feasibility Study*, Brussels, 4 December 2002.

communications on the future of the EU.[94] In these communications, it views police and judicial co-operation in close association with border patrol and policy on foreign nationals: 'The removal of economic borders and freedom of movement go hand in hand with rights and guarantees and are difficult to reconcile with the maintenance of police and judicial borders which protect the perpetrators of illicit activities.' Furthermore, the foreign dimension of this complicated issue may also certainly not be disregarded 'for it will add to the close and privileged relations the Union intends to cultivate with its neighbours'. In terms of policy all this means that collective action is necessary in the sphere of 'control and surveillance of our external borders' and in the sphere of 'immigration and asylum'. In addition, to be able to take effective action against organized crime and terrorism it is necessary to develop a common framework 'for inter-country judicial and police cooperation in investigations and prosecutions'.

The Commission explains which precise task the EU must fulfil in this context when in the same communication it is stated that, in the field of police co-operation, most of the goals can be reached by co-operation between the police authorities of the Member States: '[t]he Union's potential action should be limited, within the Treaty, to defining conditions for introducing mechanisms whereby the national authorities can exchange information and co-operate effectively'. In its view, this does not alter the fact that Europol, in operational terms, must be placed at the same level as Eurojust 'in order to guarantee the effective running of police and judicial investigations at the European level'. It adds here that in the future the issue of the democratic and judicial control of Europol must also be resolved, although it offers no opinion on how to do so. The Commission, finally, does argue for the formation of a European public prosecution department with a view to the protection of the financial interests of the EC and, as an extension of this, asks for the 'adoption of rules on criminal proceedings in cases of cross-border fraud'. The Commission, however, completely disregards OLAF, let alone examines the relations between this 'first pillar' police service and Europol.

D. An Evaluation of the Proposals in the Light of the Analyses of Present Developments

In evaluation of these proposals for the future development of police co-operation in the light of the conclusions as regards the current development of it, the following remarks are offered.

[94] European Commission, *A Project for the European Union*, Brussels, 22 May 2002, COM(2002)247 final.

First, the proposal of both the Convention and the Commission, subsequently endorsed in the draft Constitutional Treaty, to abolish the pillar structure and create from the existing treaties a single constitutional treaty with a single institutional template can only be approved. The existing structure has in the past played a very important role in developing formal frameworks for operational co-operation in the field of police, but now it is largely an obstacle to further development. To be sure, considering the role of the police in upholding the sovereignty of the Member States and in the performance of their monopoly over force—there is a strong case for reserving for police co-operation its own distinctive place in the institutional and procedural structures of the EU as they are defined in the final Constitutional Treaty, but still to shape decision-making as regards this form of co-operation in broad accordance with the general Community method so as to shorten substantially the distance between policy initiatives and their practical implementation.

Yet, secondly, it must be noted that the Convention does not in fact associate any significant consequences with the abolition of the pillar structure, and thus in essence clearly has no consideration for the need to integrate the diversity of police policy that is presently managed under the three pillars. In its proposals, it limits itself—oddly enough—chiefly to observations on police co-operation as it has been organized up to the present in the framework of the third pillar. The Commission, by contrast, clearly indicates that an integrated police policy must be sought across the EU in its entirety. Yet it still does not grasp the core of what is necessary to launch such policy. As to what is necessary in this regard, one can certainly refer to one theme that is mentioned briefly by the Convention: the organization of the Council and, it may be added, the organization of the Commission. Are these institutions sufficiently able to develop a suitable police policy in consultation with the European Parliament and the national parliaments and to monitor adequately its implementation and exercise? In the current situation, definitely not.

Thirdly, it is obvious that both the Convention and the Commission overlook various important issues that relate to the organization of the police in the EU. In particular, neither of them says anything about the relationship between OLAF and Europol. Was this topic simply too hot to handle? Be that as it may, it cannot be ignored. With an eye to the disappearance of the pillar structure, the Convention cannot avoid tackling the question of how the EU police apparatus should be organized in the future. Another important point is that the Convention—as opposed to the Commission—is sensitive to a more executive Europol in the future but, strangely enough, it ignores the issue of judicial authority over this service. Of course, this omission, too, is not sustainable in the long term: the issue must be settled, and preferably sooner rather than later. Clearly, the difference in opinion over the future of

Eurojust and the European Public Prosecution department played a part in the irresolution of the Convention. The Commission rightfully indicated that this issue calls for a settlement, yet it in fact has no great plans for the future accountability of Europol. Finally, there is the point that the Commission does clearly state that in the new EU police co-operation between the Member States remains of the greatest importance, while the Convention in general pays no attention to the role of the Member States in this area. This is all the more unusual because, in May 2002, the Commission had already indicated the direction it wanted to take on this point: the introduction of 'mechanisms' to promote this co-operation. In addition, the question of which 'mechanisms' there may be in the future is thus certainly very relevant. Is it because the Convention, more than the Commission, was still blind to police co-operation between the Member States as it actually occurs every day?

Fourthly, in connection with this last observation, it is a remarkable fact that neither offering at any point raises the question of the effectiveness of police co-operation or the sufficiency of our present understanding of it. What has in fact been achieved under the third pillar appears to be of little account to either the Convention or the Commission when addressing the future. Evidently 'Brussels' has complete faith in the individual impressions of the factual situation and/or it allows itself to be completely led by the political salience of proposals. The question whether or not the proposals that are finally decided will add to the safety of the European Union has thus not been posed, and certainly not answered one way or another. That this is an unwarranted course of action speaks for itself. Safety, for many citizens in the EU, is justifiably a great concern and the damage to it by various forms of organized crime is a serious problem. For policy makers, it is therefore a matter of assessing the extent of this problem (or allowing it to be assessed) as accurately as possible and making proposals commensurate with its seriousness to deal with it.

6. CONCLUSION

The focal point of this essay was the hard core of police co-operation as governed by Articles 29–30 TEU: co-operation to control (organized) crime, including terrorism. That the accent was placed on the repressive element of the fight against such crime is not surprising. The preventive form, however important it also is, has still not properly emerged in the framework of the EU.[95] Police co-operation in the sphere of public order and assistance, due to

[95] See, for example, C. Fijnaut (ed.), *The Administrative Approach to (Organised) Crime in Amsterdam* (Amsterdam: City of Amsterdam, 2002).

a lack of space, was not considered at all,[96] although it is becoming ever more important for the EU Member States.[97]

In its 'Biannual update of the scoreboard to review progress on the creation of an area of "freedom, security and justice" in the European Union', the Commission gives a moderately positive opinion on the progress that was achieved in the sphere of police co-operation: '[t]he fight against crime, including terrorism, is a Union priority on which substantial progress was made both in operational cooperation and in the European-level legislative basis to promote and facilitate such cooperation'.[98] This evaluation, as far as legislation is concerned, matches the evaluation made in the present essay. A great deal has indeed been achieved where it comes to the creation of formal frameworks for police co-operation. As far as the operational aspect is concerned, however, the evaluation made in this essay is much more reserved. It is difficult to say whether there has in fact been so much progress in operational co-operation. Considering the various reports on Europol's operation there is reason to doubt the validity of this claim. From the lack of scholarly research into the actual circumstances of police co-operation as regards (organized) crime in the EU, it is difficult to establish who is correct.

Nevertheless, doubt about the level of recent real achievement is not the only reason to ask for more independent and impartial research concerning an issue that is so high on the European political agenda. The other reason is the need for a more open and more in-depth debate about the future of police co-operation in the EU. In this regard it was demonstrated that the proposals made by the Convention and the Commission give no or insufficient answers to important formal and material questions. Moreover, because they are in no way related to the actual problems of (organized) crime in the EU, they do not appear to be very innovative; indeed they appear even bureaucratic. Partly for this reason, following the example the Hubert Committee set in France a few years ago, a great deal can be said for developing or having developed scenarios in which, in the context of concrete problem formulations and given certain political and juridical frameworks, one examines the manner in which police co-operation between Member States can or should be developed.[99] Such a methodology not only stimulates the imagination but also generates a profound discussion about what is at stake.

[96] The Police Co-operation Working Party has, in the past, mapped out in which domains co-operation takes place or where it is at least possible. See European Council, *Police Cooperation Matrix*, Brussels, 27 May 2002, 9231/02, ENFOPOL 70.

[97] A good example of this is the co-operation at large football events. Compare O. Adang and C. Cuvelier, *Policing Euro 2000; International Police Co-operation, Information Management and Police Deployment* (Beek: Tandem-Felix, 2001).

[98] European Commission, Brussels, 30 May 2002, COM(2002) 261 final, 8.

[99] Commissariat Général du Plan, *Quels Avenirs pour l'Europe de la Justice et de la Police? Rapport du Groupe Presidé par Patrick Hubert* (Paris: La Documentation française, 1999).

Consider, for example, the Commission's standpoint that the Union must limit itself in the future to 'defining conditions for introducing mechanisms whereby the national authorities can exchange information and co-operate effectively'. This task formulation can be interpreted very narrowly: further refinement of the treaties that must make all this formal. However, it can also be interpreted very broadly and—following the example set by the Commission with respect to modernizing European law of trusts—mean that the Union must not only further refine the network of treaties but also must have the authority to generate standards to which the organization and the operation of police apparatuses in the Member States must comply with a view to EU policy priorities and their mutual co-operation in their accomplishment.[100] And not only must the EU have the authority to generate paper standards but it must also be allowed to determine whether these standards are being met in practice. It was with this kind of comprehensive monitoring and learning exercise in mind that the Hubert Committee prepared its problem-solving scenarios.

It must, in a sense, be regretted that the Convention that produced the new Constitutional Treaty and the subsequent IGC have operated at such a high tempo and without much by way of public dialogue with a wide variety of interested and concerned groups. Consolation may be found in the fact that with such a treaty the EU is certainly not complete. Over the coming years, there will be plenty of room for debate over its further design, certainly on the very sensitive issue of police co-operation. In addition, perhaps future constitutional debate will make policy makers more aware of the need for adequate scholarly research into (organized) crime and police co-operation. The conduct and evaluation of such a comprehensive research programme would, indeed, confront them with all sorts of new questions.

[100] European Commission, *White Paper on Modernisation of the Rules Implementing Articles 85 and 86 of the EC Treaty*, Brussels, 28 April 1999, Commission Programme 99/027. See in this context C. Fijnaut, 'De Strafrechtelijke Bescherming van de Financiële Belangen van de Gemeenschap tegen Fraude', 30 *Delikt en Delinkwent* 2000, at 972–988.

Index